The Competency Restoration Handbook

The Competency Restoration Handbook

A Guide and Resources for Clinicians

Edited by

LAURA M. GROSSI

OXFORD
UNIVERSITY PRESS

OXFORD
UNIVERSITY PRESS

Oxford University Press is a department of the University of Oxford. It furthers the University's objective of excellence in research, scholarship, and education by publishing worldwide. Oxford is a registered trademark of Oxford University Press in the UK and in certain other countries.

Published in the United States of America by Oxford University Press
198 Madison Avenue, New York, NY 10016, United States of America.

CIP data is on file at the Library of Congress

ISBN 9780197768044

DOI: 10.1093/9780197768075.001.0001

Printed by Marquis Book Printing, Canada

The manufacturer's authorized representative in the EU for product safety is Oxford University Press España S.A., Parque Empresarial San Fernando de Henares, Avenida de Castilla, 2 – 28830 Madrid (www.oup.es/en).

MIX
Paper | Supporting responsible forestry
FSC® C103567
FSC www.fsc.org

CONTENTS

LIST OF FIGURES

LIST OF TABLES

THE CLINICAL-FORENSIC CONTEXT

Increasingly, individuals with mental health problems are arrested and incarcerated in the U.S. Some have hypothesized that this is related to the dehospitalization ("deinstitutionalization") movement, which led to a number of inpatient psychiatric hospitals closing or being reduced in size over the past several decades (Fuller et al., 2016) and more individuals living without adequate mental health care or access to resources. Data indicate that individuals with mental illnesses and related disabilities are more likely to be arrested in the U.S. than their psychiatrically stable and neurotypical counterparts (Gottfried & Christopher, 2017), perhaps due to the functional impairments associated with their mental health condition(s). In lay terms, individuals experiencing major mental health symptoms, significant personality pathology, and/or cognitive deficits may not have the ability to avoid, remove themselves from, or advocate for themselves in the context of arrest as effectively as a more stable or savvy individual.

Persons who are arrested and who have a mental health condition are doubly vulnerable; there are some legal protections established to protect this population as they move through the legal system. At times defendants are identified as not competent to proceed with their pending legal case(s) due to limited knowledge of how the court system functions, impaired understanding of their legal situation, and/or deficits in their ability to meaningfully assist in their defense (Pirelli et al., 2011). This may or may not be related to current psychiatric or cognitive impairments. In order to maintain their right to due process, such defendants are typically court ordered to receive competency restoration services.

SYSTEMIC FACTORS

Historically, competency restoration has been conducted primarily on an inpatient basis, with mental health problems as a common reason that defendants are not competent to proceed. With an increase in evaluations of competence to proceed and findings of incompetence, state hospitals across the U.S. are increasingly admitting individuals court ordered for competency restoration rather than patients who need more traditional inpatient mental health treatment (Murrie et al., 2022). With limited bed space, inpatient hospitals are simply unable to keep up with the demand for competency restoration, and forensic patients across the U.S. are on wait lists to be admitted to hospitals for treatment. In many jurisdictions, competency restoration services are being offered on an outpatient basis, in jails and/or in the community. Although correctional facilities are well established as the largest providers of mental health services in the U.S. (Torrey et al., 2010), there is still minimal infrastructure for competency restoration in jails settings across the country (Murrie et al., 2022).

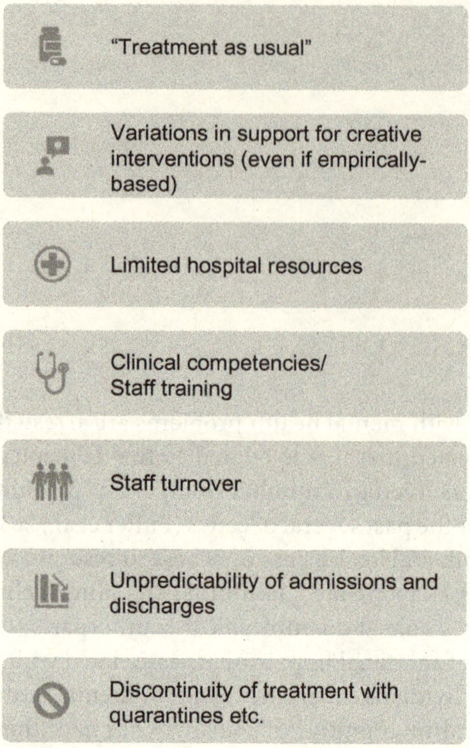

Figure F.1 Common Barriers to Intervention

Clinicians in inpatient psychiatric hospitals, jails, and the community are thus increasingly tasked with stabilizing and educating defendants to the extent that they can move forward with one or more pending legal case(s). Competency restoration providers must maximize the efficiency and effectiveness of their interventions in order to adhere to the spirit of court orders to restore individuals to competency. They are tasked with doing so while faced with burgeoning caseloads and various systemic pressures, including those related to a national competency crisis. Assorted materials exist for competency restoration providers (e.g., Kim, 2019; Substance Abuse and Mental Health Services Administration, 2023). However, there is no gold-standard protocol for competency restoration and no widely accepted collection of competency restoration materials already aggregated for use by competency restoration providers across the U.S. (Murrie et al., 2023).

Occasionally, a defendant is identified as someone who is not capable of being restored to competency in the foreseeable future (Zapf & Roesch, 2009). This may be the case, for example, when psychiatric medications do not effectively mitigate the person's mental health symptoms, and these remain the main barrier to competency. When the court makes a determination that a defendant is not restorable, the defendant's pending charges may be nolle prossed or dismissed, and civil commitment proceedings may be initiated. That can be perceived as an injustice for the identified victim(s) of the alleged crime(s), and at times raises concerns for the broader safety of the community (Karas & Treleaven, 2023). Given the potential long-term implications of an unrestorability finding, such determinations are relatively rare (Mossman, 2007). In deciding about restorability, the court must consider whether all efforts have been exhausted to restore the defendant to competency. This includes educational efforts, psychiatric interventions, and nonpharmacological therapeutic interventions.

The field of forensic mental health is just beginning to consider what can be done, beyond providing basic education and pharmacological interventions to restore individuals to competency (Murrie et al., 2023; Zapf & Roesch, 2011) (Figure F1). Recent publications and presentations at the American Psychology-Law Society (AP-LS) conference provide support for this shift; however, these research-focused forums may not be accessible to the clinicians who actually conduct competency restoration in practice. With this handbook, we hope to bridge that gap.

HUMAN FACTORS

In different states, facilities, and agencies, individuals with different backgrounds provide competency restoration services (Danzer et al., 2019). Often, competency restoration efforts are led by psychologists, psychiatrists, social workers, counselors, and other clinicians (e.g., music therapists) who have completed significant coursework and training within the scope of their fields. In the U.S. and beyond, such clinicians are typically trained as generalist practitioners first and can specialize in working with forensic populations later in their training (e.g., Norcross & Sayette, 2022). Often, mental health clinicians are the primary competency restoration providers, as they are uniquely qualified to conduct individualized competency restoration services; restoration takes the form of a legally focused "therapy." At times competency restoration providers function as a part of a larger interdisciplinary treatment team and otherwise may serve as consultants to other clinicians. Although competency restoration providers often have significant clinical training, their clinical skills are often underutilized due to the presumption that they are required to act more as legal tutors.

Naturally, some restoration providers are satisfied with this work, and others experience less job satisfaction. Anecdotally, one of the reasons clinicians have provided for lack of job satisfaction is that they are not using the clinical skills and training they developed through years of graduate school and practical experience when conducting competency restoration. This at times has led to career changes, including for clinicians who genuinely care about the population with whom they work(ed). Incorporating a restoration provider's clinical knowledge and skills into the competency restoration process is proposed as a means of better utilizing the education, training, and skills of competency restoration providers. Intentional and targeted use of clinical interventions in competency restoration may help add meaning to this kind of clinical-forensic work, enhancing job satisfaction, and improving retention of clinicians employed in these contexts. Additionally, this may lead to better short-term outcomes (e.g., facilitating successful resolution of their pending charges) and long-term outcomes (e.g., successful reintegration into the community) for defendants undergoing competency restoration.

Competency restoration is a forensic treatment program. However, there is significant variability in how competency restoration is conducted across the U.S. (Schneider, 2021), as individual competency restoration providers are often tasked with curating their own materials. This may involve creative efforts, a search of the internet, and/or consultation with colleagues for restoration materials. Materials shared across jurisdictions tend to be loosely based on the federal case law (Dusky v. United States [1960] and Drope v. Missouri [1975]) or may be designed for a specific state. This may require competency restoration providers to adapt materials from one state for use in another state as a secondary step. In short, competency restoration providers across the nation are independently developing and accumulating competency restoration resources, with time that they may not have. This is contributing to burnout for professionals, and burnout is in turn exacerbating the competency crisis.

SPECIFIC AIMS OF THIS HANDBOOK

This handbook is a collection of foundational materials for competency restoration providers who work with adult pretrial defendants in the U.S. We first describe the legal context related to adjudicative competence and provide an overview of foundational competency restoration practices. We expand upon these foundational resources by explaining how various clinical interventions can be adapted to help restore individuals to competency. We attempt to explain and model a holistic, multidisciplinary/interdisciplinary, and culturally conscious approach to restoration. Covering empirically informed, theoretical, and creative approaches that can be individualized for each specific defendant, we aim to encourage and facilitate best practices in competency restoration. The reader is encouraged to adopt the interventions illustrated, within the scope of their professional competencies, to address defendant-specific barriers to adjudicative competence. Unfortunately, there is still very little outcome research on the utility of incorporating these and other clinical approaches in competency restoration; we echo the call (Murrie et al., 2023; Zapf & Roesch, 2011) for future research in this area. Competency restoration providers are encouraged to consider adapting other treatment modalities not mentioned in this handbook (i.e., particularly those which are empirically supported, or newly developed, for clinical use) to facilitate competency restoration.

Our team of authors includes multiple licensed clinical psychologists, board-certified music therapists, forensic psychiatrists, and others with knowledge and practical experience with competency restoration services. We have practical experience with competency restoration and/or evaluations in Massachusetts, New York, Pennsylvania, Washington, DC, Virginia, Texas, and Oregon at minimum. We are practicing clinicians who are intimately familiar with barriers to competency and have personal experience with what has and has not worked in practice. We are also very aware of the need for a handbook such as this for restoration providers in hospitals, jails, and communities across the country who do not have the time or bandwidth to locate relevant resources or create their own competency restoration materials for their "toolbox." Several of our authors have already published in empirical journals on these and related subjects and/or written their (yet unpublished) master's thesis or doctoral dissertation on these subjects. Some have also presented their respective topics verbally at professional conferences. We have attempted to consolidate that academic knowledge and writing experience to create an accessible handbook for other practitioners and the defendants we serve.

ORGANIZATION AND GUIDING PRINCIPLES

At the start of this handbook, we provide information about the psycholegal context for competency restoration. Next, we provide an overview of foundational competency restoration practices. In each clinically oriented part of this handbook, we address a common barrier to competency and review specific treatment approaches that may be incorporated in the competency restoration process to help a defendant overcome that particular barrier. This is not to say that a specific intervention nested within one section may not be useful for addressing a different barrier to competency. Further, as humans, defendants are complicated. One defendant may have any combination of cognitive, situational, major mental health, personality-based, and motivational barriers to competency. Cultural/diversity factors (e.g., race, socioeconomic status) and interpersonal factors (e.g., family influence, group identification) may also color how a defendant perceives the psycholegal processes and moves through the criminal justice system. Competency restoration providers are encouraged to take a biopsychosocial approach to conceptualizing defendants who undergo competency restoration to best understand whether and to what extent particular interventions are merited.

In the appendices, we present a collection of competency restoration materials, including study guides, vocabulary-based games, and other hands-on activities that can be provided to, or used with, defendants undergoing competency restoration in the U.S. These were modeled after, or inspired by, materials already in use around the country, including Florida State Hospital's CompKit.[1] In addition, we include more treatment-oriented worksheets and activities that can be used when adapting the clinical interventions discussed in this book for competency restoration. Where complete sentences are used on these appendix materials (e.g., the "Legal Dictionary" and "Competency Restoration Study Guide"), active efforts have been made to keep the reading level low (i.e., seventh-grade Flesch Kincaid reading level or lower). This way, the materials can be used when working with individuals with lower educational attainment and/or those for whom English is a second language; such individuals tend to be overrepresented in the justice system. The font used in these materials was also selected to maximize accessibility, in accordance with the Americans with Disabilities Act (ADA). In short, the appendix materials are primarily designed for the defendants undergoing competency restoration rather than for a competency restoration provider's own knowledge alone.

INTENDED AUDIENCE

Unfortunately, clinicians are often tasked with conducting competency restoration without formal education or training in forensic work, although the task at hand is psycholegal. Too many times have we heard that a new competency restoration provider was told to "just go do restoration" without having the academic knowledge, on-the-job training, modeling, or experience to do so effectively. The population of defendants undergoing competency restoration in the U.S. is too vulnerable, and too large, for bumbling; the seriousness of their legal situations demands knowledgeable and intentional care.

As such, this handbook is primarily intended for those who are new to providing competency restoration services, including trainees. It also may be of relevance to experienced restoration providers looking to expand their repertoire and clinicians who are for the first time working with forensic patients. In addition, this handbook may be of relevance to various courtroom personnel. Specifically, the information in this handbook may help judges better understand what competency restoration entails. Further, it may inform defense attorneys and prosecutors who must formally argue in court about whether a particular defendant is restorable, question competency restoration providers about what

1. The 2011 version of the Florida State Hospital CompKit can be downloaded for free here: https://docplayer.net/1263202-Florida-state-hospital-compkit.html

interventions were attempted to restore a defendant to competency, and question competency evaluators as expert witnesses, by providing such personnel with knowledge of what resources/services are possible.

LIMITATIONS

This handbook should not be considered adequate as a stand-alone training tool for individuals who aim to become practitioners, supervisors, or experts otherwise in competency restoration. New restoration providers and trainees should not be tasked with reviewing this handbook as their sole training for providing competency restoration services. We merely aim to lay the groundwork on which further training and experience can be built. Further, this handbook is not exhaustive and is not intended to be a sole resource for competency restoration. For example, state-specific resources can and should be used in conjunction with the more general resources herein to address jurisdiction-specific laws, sentencing guidelines, penalties, procedures, etc. Facility/program-specific resources can and should be used to explain the specific competency restoration program in which a defendant is participating, including the expectations for that program. This handbook is intentionally general, so as to be helpful to a wide audience; using these resources in conjunction with more specific information may be necessary.

Additionally, with a focus on implementing competency-related interventions, we spend little time on observation of a defendant's competency-related knowledge and abilities outside of targeted restoration sessions. We also spend little time in discussing documentation, including parallel assessment documentation, although documentation is integral to the competency restoration and evaluation processes; without adequate documentation, a post-restoration competency evaluator may not be able to formulate and justify an opinion for the court. We strongly encourage the reader to review other writings (e.g., Stredny, et al., 2009) for more detail on what can, should, and should not be documented in the course of competency restoration.

While we have attempted to maximize accessibility with our appendix materials, additional supplemental resources may still be necessary for use with individuals with low educational attainment, learning disorders, etc. Handouts and worksheets may need to be significantly enlarged for individuals with mild to moderate vision impairments; poor vision may impede the competency restoration process, and defendants undergoing competency restoration may not have timely access to the eyewear or procedures necessary to correct their vision. Translated materials can and should be used with defendants for whom English is not their first/primary language. Use of such resources should of course be facilitated by qualified interpreters who are familiar with the legal system (e.g., certified court interpreters) whenever possible (Tribe, 2005).

Finally, this handbook is also not designed for use with children and adolescents, who may be undergoing similar pretrial processes with cases pending in the juvenile justice system. The juvenile justice system functions differently than the adult criminal court system, and often different terminology is used. That said, competency restoration providers working with emerging adults, juveniles with cases waived to the adult criminal court system, or intellectually/developmentally delayed/disabled individuals are encouraged to adapt competency restoration materials designed for adolescents in their competency restoration efforts. We will discuss some such adaptations later in this handbook.

References

Danzer, G. S., Wheeler, E. M. A., Alexander, A. A., & Wasser, T. D. (2019). Competency restoration for adult defendants in different treatment environments. *Journal of the American Academy of Psychiatry and the Law, 47*, published online. doi:10.29158/JAAPL.003819-19

Florida State Hospital. (2011). *CompKit: Competency to stand trial training resources.* https://docplayer.net/1263202-Florida-state-hospital-compkit.html

Fuller, D. A., Sinclair, E., Geller, J., Quanbeck, C., & Snook, J. (2016). *Going, going, gone: Trends and consequences of eliminating state psychiatric beds.* Treatment Advocacy Center. https://www.treatmentadvocacycenter.org/storage/documents/going-going-gone.pdf

Gottfried, E. D., & Christopher S. C. (2017, July). Mental disorders among criminal offenders: A review of the literature. *Journal of Correctional Health Care, 23*(3), 336–346. doi:10.1177/1078345817716180

Karas, B. & Treleaven, S. (2023). *Unrestorable* [Audio podcast]. iHeart. https://www.iheart.com/podcast/1119-unrestorable-124203513/

Kim, R. S. (2019). *Competency to stand trial: A manual for forensic providers.* Self-published.

Mossman, D. (2007). Predicting restorability of incompetent criminal defendants. *The Journal of the American Academy of Psychiatry and the Law, 35*, 34–43. http://www.jaapl.org/

Murrie, D. C., Gowensmith, W. N., & Boccaccini, M. T. (2023). *Competence evaluation and restoration services.* In E. Verona & B. Fox (Eds.), *The handbook of evidence-based criminal justice practices* (pp. 247–257). Routledge.

Murrie, D. C., Gowensmith, W. N., Kois, L., & Packer, L. (2022). Evaluations of competence to stand trial are evolving amid a national "competency crisis." *Behavioral Sciences & the Law, 41*(5), 310–325. doi:10.1002/bsl.2620

Norcross, J. C., & Sayette, M. A. (2022). *Insider's guide to graduate programs in clinical and counseling psychology* (2022/2023 ed.). Guilford Press.

Pirelli, G., Gottdiener, W. H., & Zapf, P. A. (2011). A meta-analytic review of competency to stand trial research. *Psychology, Public Policy, and Law, 17*, 1–53. doi:10.1037/a0021713

Substance Abuse and Mental Health Services Administration. (2023). *Foundation work for exploring incompetence to stand trial evaluations and competence restoration for people with serious mental illness/serious emotional disturbance* [HHS Publication No. PEP23-01-00-005]. https://store.samhsa.gov/sites/default/files/pep23-01-00-005.pdf

Schneider, M. S. (2021). *Competency restoration across the United States* [Doctoral dissertation]. Fairleigh Dickinson University, Teaneck, NJ.

Stredny, R. V., Torres, A. N., & Wolber, G. J. (2009). Parallel assessment of competence to stand trial. *American Journal of Forensic Psychology, 27*(1), 5–22. https://www.forensicpsychology.org/journal.htm

Torrey, E. F., Kennard, A. D., Eslinger, D., Lamb, R., & Pavle, J. (2010) *More mentally ill persons are in jails and prisons than hospitals: A survey of the States.* Treatment Advocacy Center. http://www.treatmentadvocacycenter.org/storage/documents/final_jails_v_hospitals_study.pdf

Tribe, R. (2005). Working with interpreters. In K. H. Barrett & W. H. George (Eds.), *Race, culture, psychology, and law* (pp. 163–176). Sage. doi:10.4135/9781452233536.n11

Zapf, P. A., & Roesch, R. (2009). *Evaluation of competence to stand trial.* Oxford University Press.

Zapf, P. A., & Roesch, R. (2011). Future directions in the restoration of competency to stand trial. *Current Directions in Psychological Science, 20*, 43–47. doi:10.1177/0963721410396798

Editor

Laura M. Grossi, PhD, ABSMIP

Dr. Laura M. Grossi is a licensed clinical psychologist in the Commonwealth of Virginia who is board certified in serious mental illness (SMI) psychology. She currently works as a forensic evaluator at Eastern State Hospital (Williamsburg, VA) and in private practice. She has conducted over 1,000 pretrial criminal forensic evaluations to date, with her work focusing primarily on evaluations of adjudicative competence and mental state at the time of the offense. She also serves as a direct supervisor for the postdoctoral fellow, as the psychology practicum training director, and as chair of the hospital's Research & Review Committee. She has experience working in state psychiatric hospitals in New York, New Jersey, and Virginia. Of relevance, she has practical experience conducting competency restoration in group and individualized formats in Virginia in an inpatient psychiatric setting. She has academic experience as an adjunct instructor at Fairleigh Dickinson University. Her research areas include psychodiagnostic assessment, malingering assessment, sexual/physical violence and victimization risk, and mental health policy. To date, she has authored/co-authored 14 empirical journal articles, three book chapters, and numerous conference presentations. She is a prior recipient of the American Psychological Foundation (APF) and American Psychological Association (APA)-Division 42's Steven O. Walfish Grant (2016), and the American Academy of Forensic Psychology's (AAFP'S) Dissertation Grant in Applied Law/Psychology (2017). She is an active member of the American Psychology-Law Society (APA Div 41) and Psychologists in Public Service (APA Div 18). She earned her PhD in clinical psychology with an emphasis in forensic psychology, MA in forensic psychology, and MA in general/theoretical psychology from Fairleigh Dickinson University. Her BA in psychology and BA in law/justice studies are from Rowan University. https://orcid.org/0000-0001-5873-5841

Chapter Authors/Co-Authors (alphabetically)

Alexandra Brereton, PhD

Dr. Alexandra Brereton is a licensed psychologist in the Commonwealth of Pennsylvania and State of New Jersey. She is also certified as a therapeutic game master. She works as an inpatient psychologist and assistant training director for the psychology internship program at a psychiatric hospital in Philadelphia, PA. She has previously conducted competency restoration groups in New York, as well as risk assessments with individuals found non-restorable to competency in Pennsylvania. She has also worked as an adjunct instructor at Fairleigh Dickinson University. Her research interests include violence risk assessment, fire-setting, non-restorability, and psychosis. To date, she has authored-co/authored eight journal articles, two book chapters, and numerous conference presentations. She earned her PhD in clinical psychology with an emphasis in forensic psychology and her MA in forensic psychology from Fairleigh Dickinson University. Her BA is in psychology from Rutgers University. https://orcid.org/0000-0002-6733-6532

Lyndsay Brooks, PsyD

Dr. Lyndsay Brooks is a psychologist licensed in Texas, California, and Illinois. Dr. Brooks is a forensic evaluator with experience conducting competency to stand trial evaluations and providing expert testimony in multiple jurisdictions. She has provided clinical and forensic services in various forensic hospitals and correctional settings throughout her career, including the California and Texas state hospital systems, as well as pretrial detention centers. Dr. Brooks has provided clinical and administrative supervision for psychology staff, as well as doctoral students in training. This includes training on competency restoration, competency to stand trial evaluations, violence risk assessments, and providing evidence-based treatment in forensic settings. In addition, Dr. Brooks has academic experience serving as an adjunct professor at Pepperdine University, teaching various master's-level courses. She has her master's in clinical psychology, with an emphasis in marriage and family therapy, from Pepperdine University. She also earned her doctorate in clinical psychology from Pepperdine University.

Meredith Cain Munson, PsyD

Dr. Meredith Cain Munson recently received her doctorate in clinical psychology from Regent University. She previously earned her MA in clinical psychology from Regent University, and her BA in general psychology from Marshall University. Dr. Cain Munson is currently employed as a forensic psychologist at Central State Hospital (Petersburg, VA). She has experience conducting competency restoration at two inpatient hospitals in Virginia (i.e., both minimum and maximum security), using individual and group formats. Her research interests include serious and persistent mental illness, trauma, diversity (particularly identity, race, and gender and sexual minorities), and spirituality. Her dissertation was entitled, "The Relationship Between Schizophrenia and Clinically Significant Religious Impairment." She has presented her research at the Diversity Challenge at Boston College, Regent University, the American Psychological Association's annual conference, and Eastern State Hospital.

Elizabeth "Betsy" Hunt, PhD, ABPP

Dr. Elizabeth "Betsy" Hunt is a licensed clinical psychologist and board certified in forensic psychology. She currently serves as the forensic evaluation manager for the Department of Behavioral Health and Developmental Services for Virginia, which involves oversight of all court-appointed pretrial forensic evaluations conducted in Virginia. The goal of the program is to continue to improve the overall quality of pretrial evaluations in Virginia through peer review, training, and supervision. Dr. Hunt also has oversees the newly established Central Office Forensic Evaluation Team, which conducts forensic evaluations across the Commonwealth of Virginia. She previously served as a contractor for the University of Massachusetts Medical School Center of Excellence for Specialty Courts, updating the site on research regarding mental health and other specialty courts. Dr. Hunt has experience conducting individual and group competency restoration in Virginia, largely in inpatient settings. She has taken an individualized approach when necessary, identifying individual needs and adapting evidence-based approaches to the restoration context. She has provided facility-level and statewide training on competency restoration services for Virginia.

She has authored or co-authored 16 peer-reviewed publications that span a variety of topics, including risk assessment, juvenile offenders, distress tolerance, and psychopathy. She also has authored five book chapters on topics related to forensic evaluation and mental health courts, and she has presented at national conferences as well. Dr. Hunt has interests in research involving mental health policy and related systemic issues, as well as pretrial evaluations. Dr. Hunt graduated from the University of Pittsburgh with a dual BS in psychology and anthropology, as well as a minor in administration of justice. She went on to pursue an MS in psychology from Drexel University. From there, she obtained her PhD in clinical psychology from the University of South Florida. Dr. Hunt completed postdoctoral training in forensic psychology through the University of Massachusetts Medical School. https://orcid.org/0009-0002-5145-7302

Kendall Joplin, MME, MT-BC

Kendall Joplin is a board-certified music therapist and a current doctoral student in the expressive arts therapy PhD program at Lesley University. She earned her master's in music education in music therapy at the University of Kansas and her bachelor's in music therapy at Sam Houston State University. She is currently employed as a creative arts therapist, internship director, and ethics and trauma-informed care committee member at St. Elizabeths Hospital (Washington, DC). Since 2016, she has practical experience facilitating group-based competency restoration in Washington, DC and at two state psychiatric hospitals in Virginia (i.e., both minimum and maximum security). She has also worked as an adjunct professor at Washington Adventist University and Molloy University. Additionally, she has guest lectured at the University of Kansas and West Virginia University. Her primary research interest currently involves using a post-critical lens to explore the musical decision-making processes of music therapists. Thus far, she has authored or co-authored two peer-reviewed journal articles, one book review, and several conference presentations to disseminate her research at local, regional, national, and international conferences. https://orcid.org/0009-0004-4182-760X

Mollimichelle McClendon (née Cabeldue), PhD

Dr. Mollimichelle McClendon is a licensed clinical psychologist in Texas, Louisiana, and Colorado. She currently works in private practice completing forensic evaluations, primarily competency to stand trial and mitigation evaluations. She also teaches as an adjunct instructor at the University of the Incarnate Word, where she created an undergraduate Introduction to Forensic Psychology class; previously she has also taught at Fairleigh Dickinson University. Dr. McClendon has practical experience conducting competency evaluations and competency restoration in group and individualized formats in various states including New York, Virginia, Louisiana, Colorado, and Texas. Her research primarily focuses on forensic psychology and improving the competency restoration process; her dissertation was entitled "Factors Related to Repeat Forensic Hospital Admissions for Restoration of Competency to Stand Trial." To date she has authored/co-authored nine empirical journal articles, one book chapter, and numerous conference presentations. Dr. McClendon earned a BA in psychology and criminal justice from the University of the Incarnate Word, an MA in clinical psychology from Sam Houston State University, and a PhD in clinical psychology with an emphasis in forensic psychology from Fairleigh Dickinson University. She completed postdoctoral training in forensic psychology through Tulane School of Medicine. https://orcid.org/0000-0003-0378-4325

Sidra Qadir, MD

Dr. Sidra Qadir is a psychiatrist currently serving as the assistant medical director at Central State Hospital (Petersburg, VA). She previously worked as a staff psychiatrist at Eastern State Hospital (Williamsburg, VA), primarily on a pretrial unit with a focus on competency restoration. She has completed formal training through the Institute of Law, Psychiatry, and Public Policy (ILPPP) on forensic evaluations with adult defendants and is on the approved list of competency and sanity evaluators in the Commonwealth of Virginia. She graduated from psychiatry residency at MedStar Georgetown University Hospital, in the global health track, after completing her intern year of training at Rutgers New Jersey Medical School. She completed medical school at Allama Iqbal Medical College (Lahore, Pakistan) and has extensive work experience in resource-impoverished settings (i.e., in the U.S. and Pakistan).

Shree Sarathy, MD

Dr. Shree N. Sarathy is a forensic psychiatrist who is board certified in both general and forensic psychiatry. Her academic journey began at Texas A&M University (College Station, TX), where she completed her undergraduate and medical education. Following this, she pursued psychiatry residency training and a fellowship in forensic psychiatry at Case Western Reserve University. She began her career working in state hospitals, including Saint Elizabeths Hospital (Washington, DC), and Patton State Hospital (Highland, CA). Her work in these settings included the treatment of defendants deemed incompetent to stand trial, those found not guilty by reason of insanity, and civilly committed individuals. She also conducted various forensic evaluations, including competency evaluations, sanity evaluations, and risk assessments. Following her time working in state hospitals, Dr. Sarathy transitioned into correctional psychiatry with the County of Riverside (Riverside, CA). There, she oversaw psychiatry services across all five of the county's jails as the associate medical director for forensics. While there, she built the county's first Felony Incompetent to Stand Trial Diversion program, an initiative aimed at addressing California's state hospitals waiting-list crisis. Dr. Sarathy's contributions to the County of Riverside also extended to medical education and training. She served in pivotal roles as associate program director and later program director for the county's inaugural psychiatry residency program. Under her leadership, the program achieved full accreditation from the Accreditation Council for Graduate Medical Education (ACGME). Dr. Sarathy has spent much of her career teaching and mentoring medical students and psychiatry residents through didactic lectures and clinical supervision. She has also shared her expertise widely through lectures on forensic psychiatry topics at local, regional, and national conferences. Currently, she is transitioning into private practice, bringing her wealth of experience and expertise to serve her patients in a new capacity.

Maddison Schiafo, PhD

Dr. Maddison Schiafo is a licensed clinical psychologist in the Commonwealth of Virginia. She currently works in private practice conducting court-ordered forensic evaluations (i.e., competency to stand trial and sanity at the time of the offense) as well as psychodiagnostic evaluations. She has been conducting competency to stand trial evaluations and providing competency restoration services since 2015 and 2019, respectively. Dr. Schiafo has experience providing individual and group-based competency restoration services in three state hospitals across the country (TX, OR, VA). She has also supervised doctoral-level students in the provision of competency restoration. Dr. Schiafo has co-authored two empirical journal articles and numerous conference presentations. She is the recipient of the Association for the Treatment of Sexual Abusers (ATSA) Predoctoral Research Grant, which funded her dissertation. Dr. Schiafo has academic experience teaching and providing guest lectures in doctoral-, master's-, and undergraduate-level courses including Assessment of Intelligence and Academic Achievement, Doctoral Practicum, Psychopathology, and Introduction to Psychology. Dr. Schiafo received her BA and MA in psychology from Marist College, and her MA in clinical psychology from Sam Houston State University. She received her PhD in clinical psychology from Sam Houston State University, where she was trained extensively with regard to the intersection of psychology and the law. https://orcid.org/0000-0002-4850-3331

Melanie Schneider, PhD

Dr. Melanie Schneider is an admissions unit psychologist at Kirby Forensic Psychiatric Center, a maximum security forensic psychiatric hospital (New York, NY). She has a wealth of experience conducting assessments with patients undergoing competency restoration and currently conducts group and individualized competency restoration on an inpatient basis. She has worked in various inpatient psychiatric and correctional settings across New York and New Jersey. She has academic experience as an adjunct instructor at Fairleigh Dickinson University. Her research interests include violence risk assessment, competency malingering, and competency restoration practices. Her dissertation was entitled, "Competency Restoration across the United States." To date she has authored/co-authored five empirical journal articles and numerous conference presentations to disseminate her research. She earned her PhD in clinical psychology with an emphasis in forensic psychology, and MA in general/theoretical psychology from Fairleigh Dickinson University. Her BA in psychology and BA in philosophy are from Rutgers University.

Kate Stanley, MMT, MT-BC

Kate Stanley is a board-certified music therapist, who currently works as a creative arts therapist at St. Elizabeths Hospital (Washington, DC). There she has been conducting Music and Competency groups as part of her clinical caseload since 2016. She also serves as an adjunct faculty member at Washington Adventist University, where she teaches clinical musicianship and supervises practicum students. In addition, she has guest lectured at West Virginia University and Temple University. She earned her bachelor's degree in music therapy from Montclair State University, and her master's in music therapy is from Temple University. Her master's thesis was entitled, "Music Therapy, Serious Mental Illness, and Adjudicative Competency Restoration." For that project, she created a treatment manual using music therapy interventions for competency restoration. She has published three journal articles and has presented at national conferences, as well as the Music Therapy World Congress. Her research areas include the use of music in competency restoration and in treating women with major mental illness, complex trauma histories, and substance use disorders.

Kevin Waymire, PhD

Dr. Kevin Waymire is a licensed clinical psychologist in the Commonwealth of Virginia. He is currently a full-time forensic evaluator for the Virginia Department of Behavioral Health and Developmental Services. He also works in private practice conducting forensic evaluations, as well as those psychodiagnostic and neuropsychological in nature. Dr.

Waymire has conducted competency to stand trial evaluations since 2015 and provided group and individual competency restoration services while working at Oregon State Hospital as a postdoctoral resident. During this time, he supervised a doctoral-level student in the provision of competency restoration services. Dr. Waymire previously served as a clinical assistant professor at Old Dominion University. During his time in academia, he taught graduate and undergraduate courses in psychology and supervised clinical internships and practica for undergraduate and doctoral students, respectively. Dr. Waymire received his MA in clinical psychology from Sam Houston State University, his MEd in counseling from the University of Houston, and his BA in psychology from the University of Texas at Austin. He earned his doctorate (PhD) from Sam Houston State University's program in clinical psychology, which provides generalist training, though with a forensic focus.

ACKNOWLEDGMENTS

The authors recognize that one of the primary reasons a broadly applicable competency restoration handbook like this does not already exist is that competency restoration providers and competency evaluators are incredibly busy and battling burnout. We would like to take this opportunity to thank competency restoration providers and evaluators across the country and beyond for the work that they do to ensure that all persons maintain their right to due process. To those of you who have created and shared your own competency restoration materials with us and others, thank you for supporting your colleagues and the defendants they serve(d).

As clinicians ourselves, the authorship team would also like to thank our former and current employers, supervisors, and colleagues for their support and encouragement as we put together this handbook. We thank those professors and supervisors who reminded us that we are first and foremost clinicians, with a mere secondary identification as "forensic." In the end, that frame set up this handbook and has benefited the defendants and inmates with whom we work.

Additional thanks to our non-clinical partners and friends who provided support and feedback throughout this process. Special thank you to Dr. Grossi's parents, who helped develop new answer keys to the word games when she failed to save the originals. Thank you to Jacqueline "Jackie" Smith, PhD and Stephanie Ellison, LPC for providing formal peer review and encouragement, and Alexandra "Allie" Brereton, PhD for stepping up to assist other authors on their respective chapters. Thank you to Lori Jones for creating a beautiful and neutral courtroom illustration. Thank you to Barry Wall, MD, and Eleanor Slater Hospital of the Rhode Island Department of Mental Health Retardation and Hospitals, for permission to partially reproduce Slater Method materials. Thank you also to Sarah Harrington (executive editor), Mary Funchion (project editor), and the rest of the editorial staff at the Oxford University Press involved in this publication.

Finally, we preemptively thank those of you reading this book who are considering, or just beginning, to join the clinical-forensic field in providing competency restoration services. We hope that this handbook helps you on that journey.

DISCLAIMERS

This book reflects the thoughts and suggestions of the authors, based on their training and clinical experiences. It does not reflect the views of the institutions with which we are or have been employed or otherwise affiliated.

PART I

The Psycholegal Context

Introduction to Adjudicative Competence

ELIZABETH HUNT, PHD ABPP (FORENSIC) AND LAURA M. GROSSI, PHD, ABSMIP

DEFINING ADJUDICATIVE COMPETENCE

The construct of adjudicative competence (also referred to as competence to stand trial, competence to proceed, fitness to stand trial, or fitness to proceed) has foundations in the protection of the defendant as well as the integrity of the legal system. References to this concept have been present since the 17th–18th centuries, when concerns arose in English courts regarding individuals who did not speak in court and whether this was by choice or due to some type of impairment. The underlying notion was that it was unfair to subject certain groups of individuals to trial and standard legal proceedings. Early American courts adopted this stance, and the construct of adjudicative competence reached constitutional status in American courts in the late 1800s.

The criminal court process in the U.S. operates under the notion that trial involves equally matched adversaries. Additionally, defendants have many rights, including the right to a fair trial, to be represented by effective counsel, and to confront their accuser. They must also be capable of participating in legal proceedings. Thus, holdings related to incompetent defendants have traditionally been rooted in both 6th and 14th Amendment rights. Protection of these fundamental rights and preserving the functioning of criminal proceedings are clear foundational elements of the competency doctrine.

While many states may define adjudicative competence in various ways, most standards have their basis in the findings from *Dusky v. United States* (1960), which defined competency as "whether [the defendant] has sufficient present ability to consult with his lawyer with a reasonable degree of rational understanding and whether he has a rational as well as factual understanding of the proceedings against him." Further examination of the definition highlights several important components of the construct (Kruh & Grisso, 2009; Melton et al., 2018). For example, it is noted that competence is a "present" ability, suggesting abilities may fluctuate or the assessment of these abilities may only represent functioning at a particular point in time. There is also an emphasis on one's "ability" or capacity for these areas of functioning, as opposed to one's willingness to engage in the process. For example, a defendant who is unwilling—simply chooses not to discuss their current legal case or courtroom proceedings—does not necessarily lack the capacity or have an impairment in their ability to do so. Thus, there is an important distinction between willingness and ability in defining this construct.

Elizabeth Hunt and Laura M. Grossi, *Introduction to Adjudicative Competence*. In: *The Competency Restoration Handbook*. Edited by: Laura M. Grossi, Oxford University Press. © Laura M. Grossi (2025). DOI: 10.1093/9780197768075.003.0001

The definition of adjudicative competence uses the phrase "reasonable degree," suggesting there is flexibility in terms of level or degree of abilities; the threshold may be determined by other contextual factors such as severity of charges or complexity of court proceedings. This definition also highlights two major "prongs" to competency: the capacity to understand the legal process and its application to their particular case, and the ability to function within the process. Furthermore, the emphasis on "rational and factual understanding" suggests consideration of cognitive functioning and that both elements must be present for one to be deemed competent to proceed. Although all states have incorporated *Dusky* either with the same or similar language, there are still elements of each statute that make them unique. Thus, it is important for forensic evaluators and competency restoration treatment providers to be familiar with the relevant statutes and definitions.

Defendants are generally presumed to be competent, unless the issue of competency is raised and there is reason to believe a defendant is unable to move forward with legal proceedings. The holding in *Pate v. Robinson* (1966) noted that any party may raise the issue of competency if there is a "bona fide" doubt in a defendant's competence to proceed. This was further noted in the case of *Drope v. Missouri* (1975), which indicated that the issue should be raised if there is "sufficient doubt" in a defendant's competency and that defense counsel does not have the sole burden of raising the issue. Furthermore, *Drope* highlighted that a court should be cognizant of any changes to the defendant's presentation over the course of proceedings that may suggest there is an issue with competency. Thus, the issue may be raised at any point in the criminal process, although a motion typically occurs prior to the beginning of trial, entering a plea, or sentencing. In addition, any party may raise the issue, though there has been debate about prosecution raising the issue (see *Pate v. Robinson* for further discussion), particularly in the absence of defense counsel or prior to defense counsel being appointed. The burden is typically on the party claiming the defendant is incompetent, such that they must prove that the defendant is incompetent, though this burden and the burden of proof may vary by state. Some guidance on this matter was provided in *Medina v. California* (1992), where the Supreme Court upheld the constitutionality of a presumption of competence, placing the burden on the party claiming incompetence and preponderance of the evidence as the burden of proof. Thus, while this finding highlights what is deemed constitutional, it is not required; although, it still offers some guidance to states in determining their own procedures and guidelines for adjudication of competence.

EVALUATION PROCESS AND PROCEDURES

Issues pertaining to adjudicative competence are generally of concern in about 10%–15% of adult criminal court cases, though a motion for an evaluation occurs in less than half these cases (Melton et al., 2018). A recent study exploring rates of competency evaluations estimated that 1.5% of arrests were associated with a competency evaluation (Kois et al., 2024). Evaluations of adjudicative competence are the most frequently ordered mental health evaluations in criminal courts (Melton et al., 2018). Historically, it was estimated that around 60,000 evaluations of competence to stand trial were ordered annually (Poythress et al., 2002), however more recent estimates indicate an increase to around 84,000–140,000 annually (Kois et al., 2020; Kois et al., 2024; Murrie et al., 2023). It is difficult to truly estimate the number of these evaluations occurring annually, as states operate and collect data differently (Kois et al., 2024), and there is naturally variation in changes in the rate of demand for competency evaluations across jurisdictions and states. For example, Gowensmith (2019) noted that evaluations in Wisconsin rose 32.5% over a five-year period whereas Los Angeles County reported a 273% increase over a similar time period. A recent national survey regarding incompetent defendants found that 82% of states indicated that referrals for evaluations of competence to stand trial were increasing (Warburton et al., 2020). When asked about factors associated with the increase, inadequate community mental health services, community inpatient beds, and assertive community treatment services were among the top reasons.

Once an evaluation is ordered, a qualified and trained forensic evaluator completes the evaluation. Most competency evaluations are conducted by state evaluators, or, alternatively, the evaluator is compensated through state or court funds (Gowensmith et al., 2015). As a result, many states have oversight processes that provide guidance and requirements for evaluators, and some states also have certification and training requirements for those performing competence to proceed evaluations. Qualifications (e.g., required experience or training) vary across states, though, at the very least, most states require licensure as a psychologist or psychiatrist. In the most recent survey and review of state procedures, Gowensmith and colleagues (2015) found that psychiatrists were eligible to act as competency evaluators in all states, while psychologists were eligible in every state except Rhode Island and Vermont. Furthermore, as of that publication approximately 15 states allowed other mental health professionals and 11 states allowed general physicians (with 10 of those states requiring the physicians to be qualified or possess specialized training in forensic evaluation) to conduct competency evaluations. Of the 38 states that responded to their survey, 19 reported that they had a mandatory certification process and typically included elements such as participation in initial training (89.5%), passing review of submitted materials (52.6%), completing a mentorship process (36.8%), or having previous clinical experience (21.1%). In addition, 78.9% of states with a mandatory certification program have additional requirements to maintain certification once obtained. In some states, evaluations by multiple evaluators are required per code. Per Gowensmith and colleagues (2015), 80.4% of states require only one evaluator, eight states always assign two or more evaluators, and Hawaii and Nevada assign multiple evaluators only for more serious cases. Some states assign a variable number of evaluators depending on certain factors, such as severity of the charge or where the defendant is placed. For states routinely assigning more than one evaluator, 82.4% allow them to communicate with each other regarding their findings and opinions.

State statutes vary on the timeline allotted for completion of a competency evaluation (i.e., after receipt of the court order), the location of the evaluation (i.e., inpatient or outpatient), as well as the contents or specific language required in the written report. In some states, there is no specified timeline in the legal statute, although the court may indicate a "due date" on the court order; this is typically when the next hearing is set, which is usually a review or status hearing, though some do represent an actual hearing on competency. Other states have timelines that range from 7 days to 90 days, with extensions possible (Substance Abuse and Mental Health Services Administration [SAMHSA], 2023) and may vary based on the location of the evaluation. A majority of initial evaluations of adjudicative competence occur in the jail or community (i.e., if the individual is out on bond; Gowensmith et al., 2015). However, evaluations also occur on an inpatient basis (i.e., at state psychiatric hospitals or other mental health facilities), and many states limit the length of time an individual may be committed for an inpatient evaluation. For example, in South Carolina, "The examination must be made within thirty days after the receipt of the court's order and may be conducted in any suitable place unless otherwise designated by the court"; but if the person is committed to an inpatient facility for "examination and observation," the commitment may not exceed 15 days (SC Code § 44-23-410, 2022). After completion of the evaluation and submission of a report to the court, a hearing on the issue may occur, though many states do not require a hearing.

Following the initial competency evaluation(s), legal proceedings resume (e.g., with trial or disposition of the case) for individuals found competent to proceed. On the other hand, proceedings are typically paused for an incompetent defendant, and the defendant may be ordered to competency restoration services. As with competency evaluations, competency restoration services may be provided on an inpatient basis (state psychiatric facilities or other mental health facilities), within a jail setting, or in the community. However, it should also be noted that there are various alternative outcomes for individuals found incompetent to proceed, which may depend on a statutory guidance related to type of charge(s) and diversion opportunities.

THE COMPETENCY CRISIS

As the rate of competency evaluations has increased over time, the number of individuals being opined and adjudicated incompetent has increased. Many states have reported significant increases in the number of defendants opined incompetent and ordered into competency restoration services. For example, it has been documented that Colorado saw an increase from 200 to 2,400 defendants opined as incompetent over a 12-year period, where other states have noted their numbers doubled in just five years (Murrie et al., 2023). Historically, the rate of incompetence (or proportion of individuals found incompetent) was thought to be around 20%, with one meta-analysis providing an estimate of 27.5% (Pirelli et al., 2011). More recent estimates suggest this number is on the rise. In reviewing estimates from states that track competency evaluations, Murrie and colleagues (2023) noted that the majority of estimates appeared to be over and exceeding the commonly cited rate of 27.5%. Those authors highlighted that several states reported rates of incompetency closer to 45%–60%, which is almost double the previously reported rate.

The increase in defendants adjudicated incompetent to proceed and in need of restoration services has led to what has been termed the "competency crisis." In short, the resources available for competency restoration have not expanded in a manner that corresponds with the ballooning of defendants in need of competency restoration services. While much competency restoration has historically been done on an inpatient basis, many states and state hospital facilities have recently struggled to quickly admit individuals deemed incompetent to stand trial; this may be due to lack of available hospital beds and staff to provide treatment and restoration services, among other barriers. As such, there are "wait lists" across the United States, as well as numerous lawsuits regarding unconstitutional delays in competency restoration treatment (Gowensmith et al., 2016; Heilbrun et al., 2019). Some of these lawsuits have resulted in federal oversight and/or states being required to admit patients to state hospitals within a specific period of time (e.g., a certain number of days after the hospital has received the court order or after a finding of incompetency).

Gowensmith (2019) offered several potential reasons for the recent influx in restoration orders and findings of incompetence. With the issue of competency being raised more often over time, the courts have become more knowledgeable and aware of mental health issues, increasing the likelihood that concerns surrounding competency-related issues may arise. Another contributing factor may be ineffective community mental health systems that lack adequate support services (e.g., services to coordinate employment, housing and substance use treatment), leading to an increased likelihood an individual may engage in behavior that leads to involvement with the criminal justice system. Additionally, it is possible that courts utilize the competency system to address broader mental health assessment and treatment needs, as a way to mandate treatment or provide treatment access for those not able to access appropriate treatment in the community. Of course, it is also possible that trends are explained in part by each of these and additional factors.

INCOMPETENT DEFENDANTS AND BARRIERS TO COMPETENCY

There are a range of reasons that may cause a defendant to be incompetent to proceed: lack of experience with the legal system and/or knowledge about court proceedings, mental illness, issues with learning, intellectual disability, and other cognitive limitations. Numerous studies have explored differences between competent and incompetent defendants, with several reviews highlighting trends among these groups and factors associated with incompetence. A meta-analytic review from 2011 (Pirelli et al., 2011) found that incompetent defendants were slightly older, mostly nonwhite, had higher unemployment rates, and were not married. However, the biggest difference between competent and incompetent defendants emerged in relation to psychiatric variables. Specifically, defendants with a psychotic disorder diagnosis and previous psychiatric hospitalization were more likely to be found incompetent. A similar finding was noted in a different review of the adjudicative competence literature, such that defendants diagnosed with a psychotic disorder demonstrated greater impairment and were more likely to be found incompetent (Fogel et al., 2013).

While there tends to be a general assumption that incompetence is tied to "mental disease or defect" or that this prerequisite must exist, this relationship is not always well-defined in state laws governing this process. In a cursory review of statutory language defining adjudicative competence procedures, about 60% of states appear to explicitly tie incompetence to a "mental disease or defect" (or similar language). For example, North Carolina states, "No person may be tried, convicted, sentenced, or punished for a crime when by reason of mental illness or defect he is unable to understand the nature and object of the proceedings against him, to comprehend his own situation in reference to the proceedings, or to assist in his defense in a rational or reasonable manner" (NC Gen Stat § 15A-1001 et seq., 2022). Other states have more vague language surrounding the nature of incompetency, such as language like "mentally competent" (Vermont, 13 V.S.A § 4814, 2023) or incompetent "as a result of a lack of mental capacity" (South Carolina, SC Code § 44-23-410, 2022), which seems to imply some connection to mental illness or intellectual disability. There are also states that do not appear to include a qualifying mental disorder as a prerequisite for incompetency. In such cases, mental health becomes a consideration more for the placement of restoration services and specific treatment interventions.

Recent attention has been given to individuals only charged with misdemeanors who come through the competency evaluation and restoration processes and whether they are disproportionately represented in those processes. A review of court-ordered adjudicative competence evaluations in Virginia showed that individuals facing only misdemeanor charges were 1.33 times more likely to be opined incompetent than those facing felony charges (Murrie et al., 2022). Furthermore, misdemeanor defendants were 1.62 times more likely to present with symptoms of psychosis during the evaluation and 2.17 times more likely to present with symptoms of psychosis that directly impaired competence-related abilities. In another study exploring misdemeanor defendants, 71% of the sample had diagnoses reflecting psychotic symptoms and 18.3% had diagnoses reflective of cognitive impairments, with 81.7% having a history of psychiatric treatment (Tansey et al., 2022). Additionally, 71.4% were opined incompetent to proceed, and those opined incompetent were 4.9 times more likely to have a psychotic disorder diagnosis compared to those opined competent. These findings suggest that those charged with only misdemeanor offenses or lower level offenses may be more psychiatrically impaired than other defendants. Perhaps for these reasons, the costs associated with restoration, and limited benefit for the state in securing a misdemeanor conviction, some states (e.g., New York and Florida) do not allocate competency restoration resources to defendants only facing misdemeanors. Other states (e.g., Virginia and Texas) are currently establishing pathways to divert misdemeanor defendants to more traditional treatment (Obikoya, 2021) as an alternative to competency restoration (i.e., which has a more narrow focus and can be more expensive).

ORDERS FOR COMPETENCY RESTORATION AND SYSTEMIC CONCERNS

All states appear to have provisions for competency restoration services, though as previously noted, there is variability regarding whether restoration occurs for all types of charges and where restoration takes place. A review of state statutes indicates that, for most states, there are minimal specifications for restoration services between misdemeanor and felony charges, and thus there is a presumption that restoration may be ordered for either type of charge. Several states (California, Florida, New York) seem to only have restoration for felony charges or limit restoration to charges in circuit court (Alabama). Other states appear to have more flexibility about whether restoration *must* be ordered for misdemeanor charges. For example, the relevant Minnesota statute notes, "If the court finds the defendant incompetent, and the charge is a misdemeanor, the charge must be dismissed. If the court finds the defendant incompetent, and the charge is a felony or gross misdemeanor, the proceedings must be suspended except as provided in Rule 20.01, subd. 8" (Minn R. Crim. P., Rule 20.01, Subd 6, 2023) whereas the Alaska statute indicates the court "shall" commit a defendant charged with a felony and "may" commit a defendant charged with any other crime (AK Stat § 12.47.070, 2023). Other states highlight opportunities for diversion for misdemeanor charges in particular, that is, out of the criminal justice system and into other forms of treatment. For example, Hawaii's statute says, "When the defendant is charged with a petty misdemeanor not involving violence or attempted violence, the defendant shall be diverted from the criminal justice system" (HI Rev Stat § 704-406, 2023). Language in Washington's statute instructs the court to first consider "all available and appropriate alternatives to inpatient competency restoration" for non-felony crimes and further specifies this includes diversion programs and dismissal of proceedings (WA Rev Code § 10.77.088, 2023).

Consideration of offense severity and diversion within the competency process highlights commentary in recent years on expanding diversion opportunities for those with mental illness that come into contact with the criminal justice system. For example, Pinals and Callahan (2020) applied the sequential intercept model to the competency process, noting key points for diversion and linkage to appropriate services and treatment.[1]

1. The sequential intercept model details how individuals with mental illness and substance use-related challenges come into contact with and move through the criminal justice system (SAMHSA, 2022). It can be used to identify gaps in services and areas for diversion out of the criminal justice system. As an alternative pathway, these individuals can be connected with more appropriate treatment and services.

The National Center for State Courts (NCSC) has published various resources for the court system to enhance the response to defendants with mental illness (2021, 2023). Recommendations have typically included diversion of mentally ill defendants from the criminal justice system as early in the process as possible, limiting competency evaluation referrals to certain cases or at least providing more of a continuum of responses that encourages more appropriate use of that system, and a presumption for outpatient restoration or less restrictive placements.

Inpatient Restoration

Historically, competency restoration services have largely occurred in state psychiatric hospitals or other inpatient settings, despite the availability of community- and jail-based restoration in some states and recommendations to consider these options as less restrictive alternatives. On an inpatient basis, defendants can be closely monitored, provided with frequent opportunities to attend competency restoration programming (e.g., scheduled group-based interventions), and there are typically pathways for medication over objection to facilitate the competency restoration process. Inpatient restoration[2] typically involves psychiatric medication, individualized treatment planning, and legal education in group and/or individual format. However, inpatient restoration may not be the most appropriate setting or approach for many found incompetent to proceed; historically there has been an overreliance on inpatient systems to provide restoration services, with this route being the "default" option. Several reviews highlight the increasing number of forensic patients in state psychiatric hospitals, with the highest proportion of that population being competency restoration patients (Callahan & Pinals, 2020; Gowensmith et al., 2016). Inpatient settings may be located far from where the defendant lives and any community supports and is also the most expensive option for restoration (Murrie et al., 2023). Furthermore, those found incompetent to proceed solely based on knowledge deficits or intellectual limitations are not in need of the intensive monitoring, medication, and crisis stabilization services typically found in inpatient settings.

Thus, it may be helpful for stakeholders (i.e., courts, forensic evaluators, and competency restoration providers) to actively consider where restoration should occur, and some states have statutory requirements for evaluators to make a recommendation for the most appropriate setting for restoration to occur. For example, the Virginia Code (VA Code §19.2-169.1, 2023) requires competency evaluation reports to include "whether inpatient or outpatient treatment (community-based or jail-based) is recommended" in cases in which the evaluator identifies a need for treatment in the event the defendant is found incompetent but restorable. During the process of competency restoration, competency restoration providers may be able to knowledgably speak as to whether restoration in the assigned setting is still appropriate and make alternative recommendations as necessary. For example, a defendant initially ordered for inpatient competency restoration (i.e., at a psychiatric hospital) may stabilize to the extent that they become able to benefit from restoration services in a less restrictive setting (i.e., at the jail or in the community if on bond) to address their ongoing deficits in legal knowledge. Alternatively, a defendant initially ordered for community- or jail-based restoration may develop a need for inpatient services due to the emergence or exacerbation of major mental health symptoms.

2. For the purpose of this chapter, *inpatient restoration* refers to competency restoration occurring at a state psychiatric hospital or other hospital-based treatment facility.

For states that allow restoration across various settings, some statutory language includes consideration of certain criteria, similar to civil commitment (e.g., danger to self or others) for inpatient commitment for restoration. For example, the Iowa Code states, "If the court finds by clear and convincing evidence that the defendant poses a danger to the public peace or safety, or that the defendant is otherwise not qualified for pretrial release, or the defendant refuses to cooperate with treatment, the court shall commit the defendant to an appropriate inpatient treatment facility" (IA Code § 812.6, 2022). Similarly, in Nevada, defendants may be committed "if the court finds the defendant incompetent, and dangerous to himself or herself or to society" (NV Rev Stat § 178.425, 2022). Thus, inpatient restoration should be reserved for those in need of the highest level of care.

Community-Based and Jail-Based Restoration

In a review of state adult competence to stand trial statutes (McCormick et al., 2024; Substance Abuse and Mental Health Services Administration, 2023), more than half the states allowed outpatient[3] or other forms of restoration treatment or had provisions for it as "the least restrictive alternative." For example, the Indiana Code states, "The division of mental health and addiction shall provide competency restoration services or enter into a contract for the provision of competency restoration services by a third party in the: 1) location where the defendant currently resides; or 2) least restrictive setting appropriate to the needs of the defendant and the safety of the defendant and others" (IN Code § 35-36-3-1, 2022). Some states further specify that restoration services may take place in community-based or other less restrictive settings if the person is not a danger to themself or others (or some variation of this language). For example, the Arkansas Code notes, "However, if the court is satisfied that the defendant may be released without danger to himself or herself or to the person or property of another, the court may order the defendant's release and the release shall continue at the discretion of the court on conditions the court determines necessary" (AR Code, § 5-2-310, 2020).

Outpatient restoration[4] is typically most appropriate when the main barrier to competence is related to cognitive or intellectual deficits and/or the person is psychiatrically stable. In some cases, defendants are first committed to a state hospital prior to entering an outpatient program, whereas in others defendants are directly admitted to the outpatient program (Gowensmith et al., 2016). In a survey of outpatient restoration programs across states, 16 states had formal outpatient competency restoration programs, 19 did not, and 15 utilized more informal formats (Gowensmith et al., 2016). In exploring characteristics of defendants in outpatient restoration, they tended to have misdemeanor charges or nonviolent felonies, lacked lengthy criminal histories, were not perceived as a high risk for violence, were psychiatrically stable, and were able to take medications voluntarily.

Across outpatient competency restoration programs, Gowensmith and colleagues (2016) reported a range of restorability rates (35%–95%) with an average rate of restoration of 70% and average rate of unrestorability of 20.3%. The average time to restoration was approximately 149 days. However, much like restoration rates reported in other settings, there

3. This was not explicitly defined in the article, but it presumably refers to options outside of the state psychiatric or other hospital-based setting, such as community- or jail-based restoration.

4. For the purpose of this chapter, *outpatient restoration* refers to community-based programs (e.g., with defendants on bond) and *jail-based* restoration refers to programs and services provided in a jail.

are a range of restorability estimates for outpatient restoration, which are impacted by various factors (e.g., population differences, how "restored" is operationalized, and the nature or intensity of restoration services). For example, Heilbrun et al. (2019) reported restoration rates ranging from 18% to 94%. Outpatient restoration tends to occur in community mental health settings and involves education, medication management, psychotherapy, group and family therapy, psychological assessment, and drug screenings (Gowensmith et al., 2016). However, there is variability in the involvement of state mental health agencies and private companies in terms of oversight and provision of services. All states included in the Gowensmith et al. (2016) survey reported that community-based restoration programs save money, particularly when compared to inpatient restoration, but that it also had longer times to restoration.

In addition to outpatient competency restoration, there are also jail-based competency restoration programs. In surveying restoration options outside of inpatient hospitalization, Gowensmith and colleagues (2016) found that nine states offered restoration in jails. Several states include this specific location for services in the statutory language. For example, the Virginia Code (VA Code § 19.2-169.2, 2023) states that "outpatient treatment may occur in a local correctional facility," and the Texas Code indicates that in some cases defendants can be committed to "a jail-based competency restoration program under Article 46B.073(e)" (TX Code Crim Pro art 46B.071, 2023).

Many of these programs emerged in response to the increasing demand on inpatient facilities to admit defendants for competency restoration services and lack of beds to meet this demand. Wik (2018) identified two types of jail-based competency restoration programs: full-scale and time-limited programs. Full-scale programs are those that provide complete restoration programming, such that most defendants remain in the program until competency is attained (or alternatively, they are found unrestorable). Time-limited programs are designed to offer some restoration services until admission for inpatient restoration, which can help reduce the number of defendants on a state's wait list for inpatient competency restoration. Services may be provided by independent contractors, state hospital staff, or government agencies (Gowensmith et al., 2016; Wik, 2018).

There are many advantages to jail-based programming, including quicker access to restoration services (and potentially mental health services), reducing prolonged incarceration for those waiting to be admitted for inpatient restoration, higher rates of restoration in shorter periods of time, cost savings, and receiving care in a less restrictive alternative (Jennings et al., 2021; Wik, 2018). Despite these advantages, there is controversy surrounding restoration services in jails, given the variability in who provides the services, that a jail is considered less therapeutic than other settings, and that jails are unlikely to match the level of services in an inpatient program or dedicated outpatient programs that tend to have more of a treatment focus. Additionally, administering medications over objection can be difficult and limited in this setting (Heilbrun et al., 2019).

Restoration Timeframes

A majority of state statutes indicate an initial period of competency restoration, with specifications for extensions or additional periods of restoration. Per a review of statutes, initial periods of restoration across states range from 30 days to 15 months (SAMHSA, 2023). In some states, the initial period of restoration is dependent on the type of charge that is pending or there may be specifications for certain charges. For instance, Nevada specifies a three-month initial restoration period for misdemeanors, but a six-month period for all other cases (NV Rev Stat § 178.450, 2022). Another example is Virginia, where restoration is limited to 45 days for specific misdemeanors, such as trespassing, disorderly conduct, and petty theft (VA Code § 19.2-169.3, 2023).

If a defendant attains competence before the end of the initial restoration period, an outcome or post-restoration competency evaluation is conducted, and a report is submitted to the court at that time. Some states require periodic status reports be submitted to the court during the restoration period. For example, Maine requires reports to the court at 30, 60, and 180 days (15 ME Rev Stat § 101-D, 2022), whereas Iowa specifies an initial status report within 30 days and progress reports 60 days thereafter (IA Code § 812.7, 2022). In other states, particular courts may expect verbal or written status updates describing progress in restoration at certain intervals, without those updates being required by law. Generally, an outcome evaluation is conducted at or near the expiration of the initial order for competency restoration at the latest, if only to provide a status update to the court.

If the defendant does not attain competence within this initial period, the court is typically informed of the status of restoration, and additional periods of restoration may be ordered depending on the state's statutory guidance and the maximum time allotted for restoration services. For example, New Jersey allows for an initial restoration period of three months, with review and renewal at six-month intervals until the defendant attains competence or the charges are dismissed (NJ Rev Stat § 2C:4-6, 2023). Additional restoration time frames may be dependent on the nature of the charge. For example, Alaska allows a 90-day initial period, with a 90-day extension possible, but allows a six-month extension if the defendant is charged with a crime involving force against a person, the court finds a substantial danger of physical injury to other persons, and there is a substantial probability that restoration will happen within a reasonable period of time (AK Stat § 12.47.070 et seq., 2023).

Post-Restoration Competency Evaluations

For states where periodic updates are not required by the court, there is variability in how restoration programs identify individuals who have attained competence or may be ready for a post-restoration/outcome evaluation. For example, both inpatient and outpatient programs may operate under a referral system, such that treatment teams or restoration providers submit a referral once they believe someone has attained competence or treatment has otherwise been maximized (e.g. for possibly unrestorable defendants). Referrals may be managed by an evaluation team, independent evaluators who contract with the program, or a program administrator who then assigns the cases to available evaluators. Noffsinger (2001) noted the use of written tests and mock trials by some programs as precursors to formal competency evaluations being completed; in other cases, referrals are made without such structured screening processes.

Programs may operate under other (i.e., not referral based) approaches as well. Alternatives include assigning evaluators or an evaluation team to conduct periodic assessments of an individual's progress in restoration at designated intervals specified time frames (e.g., 30 days, 60 days), which can be informed by general length of stay data, and assigning cases to an evaluator upon entry into the competency restoration program for periodic assessment over the course of treatment, among other systematic processes.

A post-restoration evaluation must be completed in a reasonable period of time, and in some cases, an informal ultimate opinion may be conveyed to relevant stakeholders ahead of a formal report. Feedback may be provided to the referral source (e.g., a specific restoration provider or treatment team) should the evaluator not be able to make a definitive opinion, or if they do not agree with the referring party's preliminary assessment. The evaluator's opinion and feedback should inform further competency restoration efforts by identifying current barriers to competency.

RESTORABILITY AND UNRESTORABLE DEFENDANTS

There is significant variability in initial restoration periods, how long each state allows for restoration, and whether this varies according to offense type or other factors (e.g., misdemeanor vs. felony). This variability can make it difficult to estimate an average time to restoration or what might constitute a "best practice standard" in this regard. In general, it is estimated that around 75%–80% of defendants across settings attain competence within a six-month period, with most attaining competence within one year (Pirelli & Zapf, 2020; Zapf & Roesch, 2011; Zapf, 2013). More specifically, Zapf (2013) reviewed 15 studies on timelines for restoration and noted a range of 64 to 219 days with an average of 153 days. One attempted meta-analysis of studies on competency restoration published between 1975 and 2013 noted a restoration rate of 81%, with length of restoration ranging from 43 days to 1,108 days (median of 147 days) and an average of 175 days once outliers were removed (Pirelli & Zapf, 2020). The authors noted their inability to actually conduct a meta-analysis because of limitations in the research base, namely the lack of controlled studies that include comparisons between restored (meaning those who have been adjudicated competent by a judge post-restoration) and not restored defendants.

Moreover, program location, program design, and time limits on restoration services impact restoration rates and how outcome data from these programs are interpreted. Across jail-based programs with outcome data (nine programs), successful restoration rates varied greatly, ranging from 50% to 90% (Jennings et al., 2021). Most programs reported restoration rates of 79%–90% within an average of 77–120 days. However, it was noted that restoration rates were lower for programs designed to restore defendants within a specified period of time (e.g., a certain number of days, such as 60–70 days), despite having an average time to restoration of 45–57 days.

Competency evaluators and restoration providers not only consider the typical components of competency in the context of evaluation and treatment (see Part III) but also the probability that an individual can be "restored" or "achieve a higher level of competence" during what might constitute a "reasonable" period of time of treatment (Melton et al., 2018). Several "predictors" of restorability or factors that may impact restorability have been identified in the literature. That is not to say that defendants with these diagnoses and characteristics (i.e., risk factors for unrestorability) cannot attain competence. Specifically, Zapf (2013) noted that individuals with developmental disabilities and long-standing psychotic disorders may take longer to attain competence and have a lower likelihood of being restored. Common characteristics of those who do not attain competence included older age, more extensive histories of mental illness, psychotic disorder diagnoses, comorbid intellectual disability and mental illness, and low-level charges. Several reviews of the literature generally support these findings, adding other factors such as lower global functioning, a psychotic disorder accompanied by lengthy hospitalization, poorer response to interventions (e.g., psychiatric medication, psychoeducation), poor premorbid social functioning, negative symptoms, age of onset, and insidious onset (Heilbrun et al., 2023; Pirelli & Zapf, 2020). Despite recognition of these factors, there are limitations in the literature, much like other studies on competency restoration, given the variability across study designs, inconsistent policy and practice at the state statute level, and differences within restoration guidelines.

Identification of defendants who will not attain competence can be a difficult task, but it is an important one. Heilbrun and colleagues (2023) identified several problems in the current processes: prediction of unrestorability without a strong research base; restoration time frames dictated by state law that may deter the use of "reasonable" time frames; typical restoration interventions are not effective for some; competency restoration resources are finite; and communication of attempts at restoration and the basis for conclusions regarding restorability. Thus, they proposed the *Demonstration Model* that seeks to provide structure in delivering standard interventions, identifying those who do not respond to these interventions, identifying and targeting ongoing deficits and barriers, and carefully documenting responses to additional interventions until the individual has been restored or there are no remaining alternatives. What is being "demonstrated" includes the interventions by the restoration provider(s) and the defendant's response to those interventions. This information can then be used to provide an informed conclusion (and subsequent opinion) about unrestorability.

The first component of the Demonstration Model involves understanding the individual's situation, with consideration of charges, plea options, relevant law in the jurisdiction, attorney characteristics, and setting of restoration. The next component is assessing clinical, intellectual, cognitive, and developmental characteristics and their relation to competence-related abilities, as these will be targeted in treatment. Consideration of response style is also included in this assessment. This may occur at the beginning of the process or after a sufficient period of treatment specified by law or long enough to observe response to treatment. The last component is integrating all this information and formulating a recommendation or opinion, which includes determining whether all reasonably available interventions have been exhausted or if additional interventions might be attempted; this handbook reviews such interventions. The Demonstration Model's authors note that use of this model in formulating an opinion on unrestorability is "likely to be more meaningful and credible" (p. 561), as it promotes careful observation, consideration, and documentation of data. However, they also note that it is resource intensive and may not be feasible in all settings.

What is considered a "reasonable" period of time for competency restoration may depend on the circumstances of the case (e.g., possible penalties a person can face if convicted) and to a degree is subjective. Limitations on competency restoration and how long an individual can be committed as an incompetent defendant stem from the U.S. Supreme Court decision in *Jackson v. Indiana* (1972). In *Jackson v. Indiana*, the Supreme Court held that "a person charged by a State with a criminal offense who is committed solely on account of his incapacity to proceed to trial cannot be held more than the reasonable period of time necessary to determine whether there is a substantial probability that he will attain that capacity in the foreseeable future. If it is determined that this is not the case, then the State must either institute the customary civil commitment proceeding that would be required to commit indefinitely any other citizen, or release the defendant" (Jackson v. Indiana, 1972; U.S. 738, p. 406).

In response, many states amended their statutes to be more consistent with the holding in this case. In general, the maximum commitment time frames range from less than a year to 10 years, (though not all states specify a maximum time frame), and most states include a maximum length of restoration or align the maximum length of restoration with the maximum sentence possible if the individual was convicted for the most serious offense charged (or some variation on this; for a list of all statutes, see SAMHSA, 2023). Many states also have special provisions depending on the type or nature of the charge(s). For example, Florida Rules of Criminal Procedure (Fla. R. Crim. P. 3.213, 2023) notes:

> *After a determination that a person is incompetent to stand trial or proceed with a probation or community control violation hearing, the charge(s): (1) shall be dismissed 1 year after a finding if the charge is a misdemeanor; (2) shall be dismissed no later than 2 years after a finding if incompetency is due to intellectual disability or autism; (3) may be dismissed 3 years after a finding, unless a charge is listed in section 916.145, Florida Statutes; or (4) shall be dismissed after a finding that the defendant has remained incompetent for 5 continuous and uninterrupted years.*

Minnesota also has specifications for misdemeanors versus felonies, and the code (Minn. R. Crim. P. 20.01, 2023) states:

> *(1) Felonies. Except when the defendant is charged with murder, the criminal charges must be dismissed three years after the date of finding the defendant incompetent to proceed unless the prosecutor, before the expiration of the three-year period, files a written notice of intent to prosecute when the defendant regains competency. (2) Gross Misdemeanors. The criminal charges must be dismissed 30 days after the date of finding the defendant incompetent to proceed unless before that date the prosecutor files a written notice of intent to prosecute when the defendant regains competency. If a notice has been filed, the charges must be dismissed when the defendant would be entitled under these rules to custody credit of at least one year if convicted.*

While *Jackson* provided the states some guidance, it did not necessarily define "reasonable period of time" or "substantial probability." Although most states have provisions for length of restoration in response to *Jackson*, there is still criticism that the limits seem to extend beyond what may be considered "reasonable." What is reasonable may be at the discretion of the evaluator and court, perhaps taking into consideration soft factors such as the political climate in addition to more concrete factors such as the statutory maximum sentence a defendant faces.

Further, it did not address disposition on charges, such as whether a case should undergo a dismissal, nolle prosequi, or some other option. In some states, a defendant identified as unrestorable in the context of certain charges may still be required to serve a legal punishment, even without a conviction (e.g., registration and notification as a sexually violent predator [SVP], for certain sex offenses). While some of these "criminal" defendants may be converted to a "civil" status through use of civil commitment statutes (regardless of disposition on the charges), they may still be subjected to lengthier commitments and have more difficulty with eventual release (Melton et al., 2018).

SUMMARY

Adjudicative competence for adults in the United States is a complex construct, which focuses on a defendant's psycholegal functioning as related to their ability to understand the court system, their personal legal situation, and to assist in their defense (*Dusky v. United States, 1960*; *Drope v. Missouri, 1975*). A defendant has rights, rooted in both the Constitution and case law, to fair legal proceedings. There is variation in competency evaluation and restoration processes across the U.S., but the general pathway is largely consistent (see "Competency Evaluation & Restoration Flow Chart" in Appendix C). To begin, there is a presumption that defendants are competent to proceed in the U.S. (*Medina v. California*, 1992). However, their competency can be called into question by various parties, triggering a motion for an initial evaluation of adjudicative competence. These evaluations typically speak to whether a defendant appears competent to proceed, perceived barriers to competency, a clinical conceptualization or diagnostic assessment, whether the defendant might attain competence, the anticipated time frame for competency restoration, what interventions might be attempted to restore the defendant to competency (i.e., the focus of this handbook), and where competency restoration might occur. An initial competency evaluation can be conducted in the community (outpatient basis), at a jail (considered inpatient or outpatient, depending on the jurisdiction), or at a psychiatric hospital (inpatient basis), with the location often determined by state law; the same is true of competency restoration services and post-restoration/outcome evaluations. The specific statutory requirements a forensic evaluator will use for assessing competency (i.e., across initial evaluations and post-restoration evaluations), as well as the specific standard a competency restoration provider might consider in referring a defendant for a post-restoration/outcome evaluation, varies by state. When outcome evaluations occur by referral, referrals should be made when competency restoration services appear maximized (see "Referral Guide for Post-Restoration Competency Evaluation" in Appendix D), such that the defendant appears competent to proceed or efforts to mitigate the identified barriers to competency have been exhausted (see "Competency Restoration Guide" in Appendix D). A working understanding of the competency evaluation and restoration literature may also inform referrals. Post-restoration evaluations must occur within a reasonable period of time and by any deadlines set forth by the state and/or the court overseeing the case in question. Evaluators might consider the specific task demands a defendant is expected to face (e.g., testimony during trial, evaluation of a plea bargain offer) in formulating an opinion on competency. With the final decision on competency up to the presiding judge, factors such as the severity of a defendant's legal situation, the phase of proceedings (i.e., which can affect the demands for assisting in one's defense), and judicial discretion could also affect a final determination about whether a defendant is competent to proceed and the duration of active competency restoration efforts. The length of time allowed for competency restoration may be dictated by state law but generally cannot exceed the statutory maximum sentence for the defendant's charge(s). Defendants who do not attain competency may be civilly committed for treatment at a psychiatric hospital, and, in some jurisdictions, they may still be held accountable for their alleged offenses without undergoing a formal trial or conviction (e.g., registration and notification as an SVP). With long-standing implications for a defendant's liberty, justice for victims, the safety of society, future precedents, etc., forensic evaluators assessing competency and competency restoration providers alike have key roles in ensuring that the criminal court system functions as intended.

REFERENCES

Alaska Code, AK Stat § 12.47.070 (2023). https://law.justia.com/codes/alaska/title-12/chapter-47/section-12-47-070/

Arkansas Code, AR Code § 5-2-310 (2020). https://law.justia.com/codes/arkansas/2020/title-5/subtitle-1/chapter-2/subchapter-3/section-5-2-310/

Callahan, L., & Pinals, D. A. (2020). Challenges to reforming the competence to stand trial and competence restoration system. *Psychiatric Services, 71*, 691–697. doi:10.1176/appi.ps.201900483

Drope v. Missouri, 420 U.S. 162 (1975).

Dusky v. United States, 362 U.S. 402 (1960).

Florida Rules of Criminal Procedure, Fla. R. Crim. P. 3.213 (2023). https://casetext.com/rule/florida-court-rules/florida-rules-of-criminal-procedure/pretrial-motions-and-defenses/rule-3213-continuing-incompetency-to-proceed-except-incompetency-to-proceed-with-sentencing-disposition

Fogel, M. H., Schiffman, W., Mumley, D., Tillbrook, C., & Grisso, T. (2013). Ten year research update (2001–2010): Evaluations for competence to stand trial (adjudicative competence). *Behavioral Sciences and the Law, 31*, 165–191. doi:10.1002/bsl.2051

Gowensmith, N. (2019). Resolution or resignation: The role of forensic mental health professionals amidst the competency services crisis. *Psychology, Public Policy and Law, 25*, 1–14. doi:10.1037/law0000190

Gowensmith, W. N., Frost, L. E., Speelman, D. W., & Therson, D. E. (2016). Lookin' for beds in all the wrong places: Outpatient competency restoration as a promising approach to modern challenges. *Psychology, Public Policy, and Law, 22*, 293–305. doi:10.1037/law0000088

Gowensmith, W. N., Pinals, D. A., & Karas, A. C. (2015). States' standards for training and certifying evaluators of competency to stand trial. *Journal of Forensic Psychology Practice, 15*, 295–317. doi:10.1080/15228932.2015.1046798

Hawaii Code, HI Rev Stat § 704-406. (2023). https://law.justia.com/codes/hawaii/title-37/chapter-704/section-704-406/

Heilbrun, K., Giallella, C., Wright, H. J., DeMatteo, D., Griffin, P. A., Gowensmith . . . Pietruszka, V. (2023). Appraising Jackson-based unrestorability to competence to stand trial: The demonstration model. *Psychological Services, 20*(3), 553–564. doi:10.1037/ser000578

Heilbrun, K., Giallella, C., Wright, H. J., DeMatteo, D., Griffin, P. A., Locklair, B., & Desai, A. (2019). Treatment for restoration of competence to stand trial: Critical analysis and policy recommendations. *Psychology, Public Policy, and Law, 25*, 266–283. doi:10.1037/law0000210

Indiana Code, IN Code, § 35-36-3-1 (2022). https://law.justia.com/codes/indiana/2022/title-35/article-36/chapter-3/section-35-36-3-1/

Iowa Code, IA Code § 812.3 et seq. (2022). https://law.justia.com/codes/iowa/2022/title-xvi/chapter-812/section-812-6/

Jackson v. Indiana, 406 U.S. 715 (1972).

Jennings, J. L., Rice, K., & Baglio, C. (2021). Jail-based competency treatment comes of age: Multisite outcomes and challenges to the implementation of an evidence-based forensic continuum. *Behavioral Sciences and the Law, 39*, 83–105. doi:10.1002/bsl.2501

Kois, L. E., Potts, H., Cappello, V., Cox, J., & Zapf, P. (2020, March). *Updating the "magic number:" Contemporary competence to proceed metrics reported by U.S. judiciaries* [Paper presentation]. Annual meeting of the American Psychology-Law Society, New Orleans, LA.

Kois, L. E., Potts, H., Cox, J., & Zapf, P. (2024). Court-reported competence to proceed data across the United States. *Law and Human Behavior*, *48*, 182–202. doi:10.1037/lhb0000565.

Kruh, I., & Grisso, T. (2009). *Evaluations of juveniles' competence to stand trial*. Oxford University Press.

Maine Code, 15 ME Rev Stat § 101-D (2022). https://law.justia.com/codes/maine/2022/title-15/part-1/chapter-5/section-101-d/

McCormick, B. F., Nance, K., & Salekin, K. (2024). A comprehensive update and evaluation of state and federal statutes on competency to stand trial: *Dusky*, *Jackson*, *Sell*, and *Olmstead* considerations. *Psychology, Public Policy, and Law*, *30*, 237–259. doi: 10.1037/law0000415

Melton, G. B., Petrila, J., Poythress, N. G., Slobogin, C., Otto, R. K., Mossman, D., & Condie, L. O. (2018). *Psychological evaluations for the courts: A handbook for mental health professionals and lawyers*. Guilford Press.

Medina v. California, 505 U.S. 437 (1992).

Minnesota Criminal Procedure, Minn R. Crim. P. 20.01. (2023). https://www.revisor.mn.gov/court_rules/cr/id/20/

Murrie, D. C., Gardner, B. O., & Torres, A. N. (2022). The impact of misdemeanor arrests on forensic mental health services: A state-wide review of Virginia competence to stand trial evaluations. *Psychology, Public Policy, and Law*, *28*, 53–66. doi:10.1037/law0000296

Murrie, D. C., Gowensmith, W. N., Kois, L. E., & Packer, I. K. (2023). Evaluations of competence to stand trial are evolving amid the national "competency crisis." *Behavioral Sciences & The Law*, *41*, 310–325. doi:10.1002/bsl.2620

National Center for State Courts. (2021). *Leading reform: Competence to stand trial systems*. https://www.ncsc.org/__data/assets/pdf_file/0019/66304/Leading_Reform-Competence_to_Stand_Trial.pdf

National Center for State Courts. (2023). *Judges guide to mental health diversion*. https://www.ncsc.org/__data/assets/pdf_file/0031/85189/Judges-Guide-to-Mental-Health-Diversion.pdf

Nevada Code, NV Rev Stat § 178.425 et seq. (2022). https://law.justia.com/codes/nevada/2022/chapter-178/statute-178-425/

New Jersey Code, NJ Rev Stat § 2C:4-6 (2023). https://law.justia.com/codes/new-jersey/title-2c/section-2c-4-6/

Noffsinger, S. G. (2001). Restoration to competency practice guidelines. *International Journal of Offender Therapy and Comparative Criminology*, *45*, 356–362. doi:10.1177/0306624X01453007

North Carolina Code, NC Gen Stat § 15A-1001 et seq. (2022). https://law.justia.com/codes/north-carolina/2022/chapter-15a/article-56/section-15a-1001

Obikoya, K. A. (2021). Jail diversion for misdemeanors can be a first step to improve the competency to stand trial process. *Journal of the American Academy of Psychiatry and the Law*, *49*(4), 473–477; doi:10.29158/JAAPL.210124-21

Pate v. Robinson, 383 U.S. 375 (1966).

Pinals, D. A., & Callahan, L. (2020). Evaluation and restoration of competence to stand trial: Intercepting the forensic system using the sequential intercept model. *Psychiatric Services*, *71*, 698–705. doi:10.1176/appi.ps.201900484

Pirelli, G., Gottdiener, W. H., & Zapf, P. A. (2011). A meta-analytic review of competency to stand trial research. *Psychology, Public Policy and Law*, *17*(1), 1–53. doi:10.1037/a0021713

Pirelli, G., & Zapf, P. A. (2020). An attempted meta-analysis of the competency restoration research: Important findings for future directions. *Journal of Forensic Psychology Research and Practice*, *20*, 134–162. doi:10.1080/24732850.2020.1714398

Poythress, N. G., Bonnie, R. J., Monahan, J., Otto, R. & Hoge, S. K. (2002). *Adjudicative competence: The MacArthur studies.* Kluwer Academic/Plenum Press. doi:10.1007/978-1-4419-8493-7

South Carolina Code § 44-23-410 (2022). https://law.justia.com/codes/south-carolina/2022/title-44/chapter-23/section-44-23-410/

Substance Abuse and Mental Health Services Administration. (2022). *The sequential intercept model.* https://www.samhsa.gov/criminal-juvenile-justice/sim-overview

Substance Abuse and Mental Health Services Administration. (2023). *Foundation work for exploring incompetence to stand trial evaluations and competence restoration for people with serious mental illness/serious emotional disturbance* [HHS Publication No. PEP23-01-00-005].

Tansey, A., Brown, K. P., & Wood, M. E. (2022). Characteristics and outcomes for defendants charged with misdemeanors referred for court-ordered competency evaluations. *Psychological Services, 19,* 252–260. doi:10.1037/ser0000535

Texas Code, TX Code Crim Pro art 46B.071 (2023). https://law.justia.com/codes/texas/code-of-criminal-procedure/title-1/chapter-46b/subchapter-d/article-46b-071/

Vermont Code, 13 V.S.A § 4814 (2023). https://law.justia.com/codes/vermont/title-13/chapter-157/section-4814/

Virginia Code, VA Code § 19.2-169.1 et seq. (2023). https://law.justia.com/codes/virginia/title-19-2/chapter-11/section-19-2-169-1/

Warburton, K., McDermott, B. E., Gale, A., & Stahl, S. M. (2020). A survey of national trends in psychiatric patients found IST: Reasons for the reinstitutionalization of people with SMI in the US. *CNS Spectrums, 25*(2), 245–251. doi:10.1017/s1092852919001585

Washington Code, WA Rev Code § 10.77.088 (2023). https://law.justia.com/codes/washington/title-10/chapter-10-77/section-10-77-088/

Wik, A. (2018). Alternatives to inpatient competency restoration programs: Jail-based competency restoration programs. https://www.nri-inc.org/media/1500/jbcr_website-format_oct2018.pdf

Zapf, P. A. (2013). *Standardizing protocols for treatment to restore competency to stand trial: Interventions and clinically appropriate time periods* [Document No. 13-01-1901]. Washington State Institute for Public Policy.

Zapf, P. A., & Roesch, R. (2011). Future directions in the restoration of competency to stand trial. *Current Directions in Psychological Science, 20*(1), 43–47. doi:10.1177/0963721410396798

PART II

Competency Restoration Treatment as Usual (TAU)

2

Fundamentals of Competency Restoration in Practice

LAURA M. GROSSI, PHD, ABSMIP, ALEXANDRA BRERETON, PHD, MOLLIMICHELLE MCCLENDON, PHD, AND MELANIE SCHNEIDER, PHD

INTRODUCTION TO COMPETENCY RESTORATION

Competency restoration is an umbrella term for the process by which pretrial defendants currently facing legal charges attain competence to proceed, in accordance with case law (e.g., *Dusky v. United States, 1960*; *Drope v. Missouri, 1975*). Competency restoration occurs following a determination that a defendant is incompetent to stand trial (see Part I) pursuant to a court order. Restoration can occur in an inpatient (hospital-based), jail-based, or community-based setting. The goal of competency restoration is to help defendants attain an adequate factual understanding of the court system and their personal legal situation, a rational understanding of their personal legal situation, and the ability to assist in their defense. Competency restoration typically culminates in a post-restoration competency evaluation, as a kind of post-test assessment or exit interview. Still, the goal of competency restoration is not to help a defendant "pass" their post-restoration evaluation. The goal is for the defendant to gain the knowledge, skills, stability, and abilities to move forward with their legal defense in an informed, reasonable, and productive manner (i.e., actually attain competency).

There is no gold-standard "protocol" for competency restoration to date, although various resources exist to guide competency restoration services; standard practice for competency restoration is continually evolving (Heilbrun et al., 2019; Mueller et al., 2004; Mueller & Wylie, 2007; Samuel & Michaels, 2011; Zapf, 2013; Zapf & Roesch, 2011). Competency restoration services typically include educational interventions (e.g., by a competency restoration provider, who functions as a kind of legal tutor), pharmaceutical interventions designed to optimize mental health functioning (i.e., psychotropic medications), and independent study (e.g., the review of printed materials, such as a restoration workbook). In institutional settings, environmental cues (e.g., restoration-focused slideshows on televisions, legal-themed posters) may also be incorporated as part of the competency restoration process. When mental health functioning is a barrier to a defendant's competence, various clinical interventions can be incorporated in the competency restoration process, as illustrated throughout this handbook. In this chapter, we focus on the foundational components of competency restoration, describing "treatment as usual" (TAU). We emphasize what we believe are best practices in competency restoration, with respect to non-pharmaceutical interventions; use of prescription medications is detailed in Chapter 3.

Laura M. Grossi et al., *Fundamentals of Competency Restoration in Practice*. In: *The Competency Restoration Handbook*. Edited by: Laura M. Grossi, Oxford University Press. © Laura M. Grossi (2025). DOI: 10.1093/9780197768075.003.0002

Competency restoration, being a multifaceted habilitation/rehabilitation program, has traditionally been provided on an inpatient basis by a multidisciplinary treatment team. Psychiatrists, psychiatric nurse practitioners, and others with prescriptive privileges primarily contribute to competency restoration by prescribing psychotropic medications and making adjustments as clinically indicated. They, along with nursing staff, facilitate medication adherence, assess for possible side effects, and monitor for changes in the defendant's clinical presentation. Medical doctors, generalist nurse practitioners, and others with focus on general health functioning may assess, monitor, and intervene when physical health conditions (e.g., urinary tract infections) interfere with competency. For the purpose of this chapter, other personnel involved in providing competency restoration services we term *competency restoration providers*. In some settings/jurisdictions, a single competency restoration provider may be a stand-alone professional working to provide competency restoration services.

Competency restoration providers (i.e., across settings) may be psychologists, mental health counselors, social workers, music therapists, recreation therapists, trainees (i.e., postdoctoral fellows, interns, externs/practicum students), and others who contribute to the competency restoration process through nonmedical intervention. At times these personnel have completed formal coursework, in psychology/law, or forensic mental health, and are approaching restoration from an academic lens. Sometimes competency restoration providers have completed formal trainings, workshops, webinars, and so forth to prepare for the work from a practice-focused lens. For example, the Institute of Law, Psychiatry, and Public Policy (ILPPP) has in recent years offered self-paced Forensic Literacy Trainings[1] designed to provide an introduction to forensic work and concepts for individuals who have not had formal education in this area. Often, individuals new to providing competency restoration have developed skills/experience in clinical intervention or teaching, and they learn how to conduct competency restoration through on-the-job training and practical experience. We strongly encourage those intending to act as competency restoration providers to develop a foundational understanding of adjudicative competence and competency restoration processes before attempting interventions.

Over a decade ago, Samuel and Michals (2011) surveyed 11 forensic state hospitals that provided competency restoration. The majority of hospitals surveyed provided no competency restoration training to their clinicians and reported having no set timeline for providing treatment. Across the 11 programs, "The clinicians who administered the competency restoration programming, with two exceptions, did not receive competency restoration training. The two programs that provided training to staff who led the restoration of competency classes did so through workshops and educational handouts. The remaining nine programs used word-of-mouth as the means of educating their staff. Nine of the 11 programs stated that the competency restoration staff's work was not videotaped, observed, or routinely supervised" (p. 89). In their study, hospital staff was unable to provide information regarding the average number of individual sessions attended prior to a defendant attaining competence, whether group or individual treatment was more efficacious, or what kinds of patients benefited from which treatment approaches. More recently, Schneider (2021) conducted a survey of clinical administrators and clinicians representing 40 competency restoration programs across 26 states. Although competency restoration programs across the U.S. were captured by that survey, there was little evidence suggesting that established treatment programs (i.e., those described in the research literature) are

1. Registration for this and other ILPPP trainings can be done through their website: https://www.ilppp.org

widely implemented, and only 15% of surveyed competency restoration programs reported the use of evidence-based treatment protocols. Thus, it appears that institutions, agencies, and clinicians providing competency restoration would greatly benefit from standardized training and treatment recommendations in these areas. We strongly encourage use of active training, modeling, and supervision of new competency restoration providers, as well as seasoned providers working in a new setting.

TREATMENT AS USUAL (TAU) FOR COMPETENCY RESTORATION

In part due to professional consultation among forensic mental health providers, there is some consistency in competency restoration practices across the U.S., which we attempt to capture in this chapter. However, the specific materials used as intervention tools vary considerably. As indicated in the beginning of this handbook, more widely used resources tend to be hospital/state specific and modified for use in other jurisdictions.

The prototypical example of a competency restoration manual that has been modified and adapted for use across the country was developed for inpatient competency restoration in Florida. The Florida State Hospital (FSH) CompKit[2] (Florida State Hospital Strategic Plan Workgroup for Trial Competency Education, 2011) was first compiled in 2003, formally introduced in 2007, and subsequently revised. The current 184-page manual includes extensive materials for both instructors and defendants. Specifically, the FSH CompKit includes a 13-module instructor's manual for teaching, a 19-lesson "Competency Classroom Workbook," a "fast facts brochure," a "Pocket Guide to Competency" workbook, study guides, mock trial activities, vocabulary games, rational decision-making vignettes, and quizzes to serve as learning checks. The FSH CompKit has been posted for free use online, and over the course of more than a decade it has been adapted by competency restoration providers across the U.S. to meet the needs of individual defendants. Versions of the FSH CompKit materials have been created in English, Haitian Creole, Spanish, and Somali, at minimum, to best meet the needs of local defendants.

Many sites have adapted aspects of the FSH CompKit to meet the needs of their particular population and the legal specifics of their jurisdiction. This reflects typical practice in the field, and we strongly encourage continued adaptation of established materials to meet the unique needs of defendants. An example of an outpatient workbook explicitly based on the FSH CompKit is *Colorado's Adult Workbook: Competency Restoration Education*.[3] The workbook was produced in 2021 by the Colorado Department of Human Services' Colorado Office of Behavioral Health for use in the jails and community, and it is also freely available to restoration providers on their website. CompKit-style workbooks tend to include informational handouts, study guides, legal dictionaries, quizzes, and activity sheets in a structured and integrated packet. In some contexts, workbooks are provided to defendants for self-study (passive competency restoration), and in other settings/jurisdictions they are incorporated into lesson plans (active competency restoration). In some states/localities, standardized competency restoration lesson plans are in use for active competency restoration, presumably also based (at least in part) on the FSH CompKit's competency restoration modules and classroom workbook. For example, the

2. The 2011 revised version of the FSH CompKit is currently available for download at https://silo.tips/download/florida-state-hospital-compkit

3. The current version of the Colorado manual is available for download at https://bha.colorado.gov/sites/bha/files/2021-03/adult_workbook_revision.pdf

Virginia Department of Behavioral Health and Developmental Services (DBHDS) Office of Forensic Services developed the *Adult Outpatient Competency Restoration Manual* for the community agencies conducting competency restoration in that state.[4] This, along with other materials (e.g., PowerPoint presentations), in English and Spanish, are available for download on their website. Although the DBHDS resources were developed for outpatient use, they are regularly used at the state psychiatric hospitals in Virginia as well (i.e., with modifications for the different setting). Competency restoration providers and programs are encouraged to continually adapt publicly shared resources to meet their needs and to ideally share any resources they develop with other providers.

PHASE 1: BASELINE ASSESSMENT

Competency restoration is typically ordered following at least one initial adjudicative competence evaluation in which a defendant is found incompetent to proceed and specific barriers to competence are identified. For example, a defendant may have demonstrated limited factual understanding of courtroom procedures, poor rational understanding of their case, and/or mental health symptoms that may impact their ability to work with their attorney. A forensic evaluator who completes an initial competency evaluation also may provide recommendations for competency restoration services, with respect to the setting where restoration might be conducted and what types of interventions might be necessary for restoring a particular defendant to competency. When competency restoration occurs immediately after an initial competency evaluation, the evaluation itself may be considered an acceptable baseline assessment of the defendant's competence to guide restoration interventions; the competency restoration provider should consider the identified deficits as initial targets for intervention. As some time is likely to have passed between the initial competency evaluation and the start of competency restoration, it is considered best practice for a competency restoration provider to still conduct their own individualized baseline assessment.

Exceptionally, competency restoration can be ordered by a judge in the absence of a formal competency evaluation or if one or more initial competency evaluation yields indeterminate results. A judge may also order competency restoration when the defendant is initially opined as competent to proceed if they have reason to disagree with the professional opinion of the initial competency evaluator(s). In such cases, competency restoration providers may have little knowledge of a defendant's knowledge and abilities upon first meeting with the defendant. As an evaluation of a defendant's *present ability* to move forward with their legal defense, an outdated competency evaluation may also provide little-to-no information about where to focus competency restoration efforts. The defendant's knowledge, understanding, and psychiatric stability may be very different by the time they begin to receive competency restoration services. Especially when there is a notable delay between the initial competency evaluation and the provision of restoration services, it is necessary to conduct a new baseline assessment of a defendant's competency-related abilities.

A baseline assessment does not have to be as intensive as a formal competency evaluation. Still, it should involve screening the defendant's competency-related abilities, current

4. The current version of Virginia resources are available for download at https://dbhds.virginia.gov/forensic-services/adult-outpatient-competency-restoration/

barriers to competency, ability to learn and remember specific information, and preferred method of learning. A competency restoration provider can conduct a baseline assessment of the defendant's current competency-related knowledge and abilities by conversationally asking questions using an interview format or by having the defendant complete a written pre-test assessment independently. The assessment should involve screening the defendant's understanding of foundational terms and concepts, including the roles of major courtroom personnel, their role as a defendant, their legal rights as a defendant, the charges against them, penalties they might face if convicted (e.g., their sentencing guidelines, alternatives to incarceration), available plea options and plea bargaining, and basic legal processes (e.g., trial, appeal). Competency restoration providers can use their professional judgment and consultation in identifying whether responses in each of those domains are acceptable and which content areas need to be strengthened in competency restoration. Education can be provided in the course of this assessment. In short, a direct baseline assessment should gather enough information to identify the primary content areas of focus for competency restoration.

Collateral data should also be sought, as records can provide additional information regarding the defendant's baseline functioning, symptom history and symptom validity. To begin, prior mental health treatment records can provide information about a defendant's historical constellation of symptoms and diagnoses provided; this may be imperative to informing treatment, particularly if the defendant is not a reliable historian. Additionally, prior mental health treatment records may speak to what specific psychotropic medications have already been trialed for a particular defendant, which medications were effective or ineffective, and which had adverse effects. Prior psychological assessments (e.g., psychoeducational, psychodiagnostic, and neuropsychological assessments) may speak to a defendant's specific cognitive abilities (e.g., working memory, processing speed, verbal comprehension) and can substantiate a defendant's history of cognitive deficits and/or psychiatric symptoms. Previous psychological assessments and mental health treatment records may also identify a history of feigning/malingering, leading current restoration providers to proceed with caution regarding the genuineness of the defendant's current presentation and efforts in restoration; a referral for new psychological testing may be indicated. Identified areas of cognitive strengths and weaknesses may inform what types of interventions are attempted during the course of restoration (e.g., use of repetition, visual aids). Educational records may speak to a defendant's academic achievement, literacy level, and adaptive functioning; this may guide what language is used in sessions. For defendants who had a formal individualized education plan (IEP), 504 plan, and so on, the academic accommodations they were provided in school, as well as the rationale for those accommodations, should be clearly documented. These can guide competency restoration providers on how to approach the defendant to maximize their learning and optimize their engagement. For example, defendants with atypically low literacy levels may benefit from interventions using pictures and verbal education and are not expected to learn the requisite information from independently studying printed restoration materials. A defendant who in childhood required seating at the front of a school classroom may benefit from seating toward the front of restoration groups. A defendant who was allowed to take breaks as needed in school (e.g., due to limited distress tolerance) may benefit from individualized restoration sessions that are designed to be brief. In other terms, collateral data may speak to the clinically indicated competency restoration processes that are most appropriate for a specific defendant.

PHASE 2: INTERVENTION

As psychiatric functioning can be closely related to competency, it is generally recommended that individuals undergoing competency restoration follow mental health treatment as prescribed in their respective treatment settings. For example, on an inpatient basis, mental health treatment as usual often includes general psychoeducation groups, creative arts therapies, individual therapy/educational interventions, and/or medication management. Competency restoration-specific interventions tend to focus on skills related to competency, such as general knowledge, communication abilities, and decision-making (Heilbrun et al., 2019). Defendants may participate in competency restoration groups (see "Group-Based Interventions") and targeted one-on-one interventions (see "Individualized Interventions") to further bolster skills. Those tasked with helping a defendant attain competency should be mindful that they are practicing within the scope of their skills and training. Consultation with other providers or treatment team members should be sought as necessary, and referrals for adjunct interventions and testing should be made as necessary.

As detailed above, various competency restoration manuals (i.e., with educational lessons about the court system broken into modules based on a certain topic) are in use around the U.S. The specific content and information presented in educational programs for competency restoration are often dependent on the program used (or as noted above, on resources the clinician has access to), but many of these programs include components such as training on aspects of the legal system and participation in mock trials (Heilbrun et al., 2019). Different competency restoration manuals break down information into modules in different ways but tend to cover the same subject areas we recommended reviewing in a baseline assessment.

Education and additional interventions can be introduced via independent study, group-based interventions, and individualized interventions. The benefits and drawbacks to each of these approaches to competency restoration are detailed next. Use of multiple intervention approaches when possible is encouraged, assuming that resources for doing so are available.

Independent Study

Regardless of setting, defendants undergoing competency restoration may be provided with printed materials about the court system for study in their own time. Use of independent study materials allows for autonomy in functioning, self-paced learning, and may be especially helpful for visual learners. This is a key intervention for individuals who are otherwise unwilling to meet with a competency restoration provider for one-on-one or group-based intervention. Use of independent study materials is also indicated when resources (including staff/personnel) are not available to provide individual or group-based interventions frequently enough for progress to be made or when defendants are on a waiting list for formal competency restoration.

Independent study materials can take a variety of forms, including informational handouts, study guides, legal dictionaries, and worksheets for use as "homework." These may be provided one by one as stand-alone materials (e.g., to address a single concept) or at once, as part of a packet of materials provided to the defendant (e.g., a restoration workbook). Defendants should be offered the opportunity to ask questions about the information in the independent study materials and encouraged to advocate for additional materials to fill perceived knowledge gaps. Completed homework activities should be brought up for discussion by a competency restoration provider when possible; this may guide the provision of additional materials.

An example of a stand-alone, personalized, informational handout is a printout describing a specific defendant's current legal situation. For example, the "My Legal Information" worksheet in Appendix C might be used as a template to provide a defendant with information about their pending charges, charge classifications, sentencing guidelines, court of jurisdiction, and relevant courtroom personnel. A defendant might be provided with a handout such as this, with the personalized information included, for independent study, and then tasked with filling out a blank version from memory to assess their recall for information at a later date. A restoration provider may also use a worksheet such as this as a visual aid with specific prompts for discussion (e.g., "You wrote down that your attorney's name is Allie Fisher. That's correct! Have you had a chance to speak with them yet?") during individualized interventions.

Competency restoration study guides are typically brief documents (one-to-two pages) that explain key legal vocabulary and concepts. These highlight the most fundamental information about the court system and relevant vocabulary, helping defendants build the foundational language and knowledge upon which more complex concepts can be built. Many include sentencing guidelines specific to a state/jurisdiction from which defendants can deduce the sentencing guidelines for their own charges (i.e., applying personalized case information knowledge to a general study guide) at a factual level. An additional benefit of these study guides is that they are more portable than a full workbook (i.e., can easily fit in a pocket if folded), such that a defendant can bring them along for unexpected study opportunities. Additionally, because they are not personalized, they can be duplicated for use with many different defendants. The "Competency Restoration Study Guide" in Appendix C is an example of a competency restoration study guide, adapted from various CompKit fast-facts brochures.

Legal dictionaries (see "Legal Dictionary" in Appendix C) are lengthier, more detailed documents, which may be perceived as more cumbersome to read. These are variants of standard dictionaries, with the vocabulary limited to competency-related terms. In addition to serving as study material, these may be used to teach a defendant to look up the meaning of terms as needed and identify synonyms, functioning as a kind of word bank. For example, if a defendant with word-finding problems (or tip-of-the-tongue phenomenon) thinks that the word they are looking for starts with a "p," a legal dictionary provides a finite set of viable options that can be narrowed down further.

Worksheets (e.g., see Appendix C under "Competency Restoration Quizzes") somewhat mirror learning checks/chapter quizzes that accompany academic textbooks. These can be used to ascertain a defendant's level of knowledge without assistance, although a competency restoration provider should remember that such worksheets completed unsupervised (i.e., for homework) are not necessarily done by the defendant alone. A defendant who has difficulty answering quiz questions for conceptual reasons (e.g., not literacy reasons) may independently come to the realization that they could use more information about the court system, increasing motivation to participate in individualized or group-based interventions. We encourage competency restoration providers, rather than "grading" quizzes like these in an evaluative manner, to use the responses provided as a starting point for discussion and further education during individualized or group-based interventions.

In other words, rather than identifying a response as "right" or "wrong," it can be helpful to provide praise for accurate aspects of responses and to take that opportunity to elaborate upon a response (e.g., providing additional factual information in a "Yes, and . . . " manner, or tying information about one concept to another, or to the defendant's personal experiences).

Cautions

Of prime consideration when providing independent study materials to defendants is that the materials are only as useful as they are to the defendant. If a defendant cannot see, read, or understand what is on printed materials provided to them, the paperwork will not be helpful to them regardless of how well intended the item is. For example, "large print" versions of printed materials may be necessary for individuals with poor vision or cataracts. A restoration provider may also help a defendant advocate for prescription eyeglasses or reading glasses, particularly if those will facilitate independent study and expedite the competency restoration process. For those with serious visual impairment, they may need information read to them. Similarly, hearing aids or amplification devices may be necessary for defendants being educated verbally, and for their participation in court, if their hearing is limited or impaired. The reader is encouraged to refer to the Americans with Disabilities Act (ADA) accessibility guidance[5] for formal recommendations on how to maximize the likelihood that printed and web-based materials in particular are accessible, among other reasonable accommodations.

Materials should, whenever possible, be provided in the defendant's preferred language. According to the U.S. Census Bureau, as of 2019, nearly one in five people in the U.S. (i.e., 7.8 million people) spoke a language other than English at home. Spanish or Spanish Creole, Chinese, Tagalog, Vietnamese, and Arabic were identified as the most commonly spoken languages at home across the country, with variability by locality (Dietrich & Hernandez, 2022); it goes without saying that many more languages are spoken as first/primary languages in the U.S. A competency restoration provider may take resources available in English only and request that a qualified interpreter translate those materials into the desired/requisite language. Consultation and discretion should be used when deciding if providing informally translated materials to a defendant is likely to be more helpful or harmful, given other contextual factors.

When printed materials are provided to a defendant, consideration should also be given to the defendant's educational attainment and literacy. Literacy levels in the U.S. are lately believed to be falling, and for various reasons, a defendant's literacy level may not be as high as their educational attainment would suggest (e.g., Shippen et al., 2010). Keeping the reading level below a seventh-grade level, while being mindful that the materials are for adults, is strongly encouraged.

When physical materials are provided to defendants undergoing competency restoration, safety and facility policy should also be key considerations. For example, some institutions do not allow pretrial defendants to make use of spiral-bound or hardcover reading materials. Other institutions prohibit use of paperclips and staples due to safety concerns (e.g., the potential for self-injury by scraping/cutting or swallowing small metal objects). It is strongly encouraged that pages are printed/copied for use double-sided when possible to keep relevant information together and reduce the number of papers that need

5. The U.S. Department of Justice maintains ADA guidance and resource materials at www.ADA.gov

to be stored/organized; this may be a requirement of certain institutions/agencies for environmental and/or financial reasons. As an alternative to keeping paperwork loose, it may be indicated to provide defendants with a paper folder to store their independent study materials or to collaboratively identify some other organizational method. The defendant's ability to keep printed materials organized, and access specific pages as needed, may in itself speak to their adaptive and executive functioning abilities.

It is worth noting that it is not uncommon for individuals undergoing restoration to lose or misplace paperwork provided to them. Some of the same symptomatology (e.g., psychotic disorganization) that serves as a barrier to competency may also impact their ability to keep self-study materials safe and contained. Further, individuals other than the defendant undergoing competency restoration (e.g., a peer at a hospital, a cellmate at jail, family members in the community) may be able to access whatever materials are provided to the defendant. This could be well intended (e.g., someone helping the defendant study), more intrusive (e.g., someone being nosy), or accidental (e.g., someone taking the defendant's paperwork thinking it is theirs). Such disclosure of information could be exceptionally problematic if a person's legal charge(s) become more broadly known (e.g., if pending sex offense charges become known to a hospital roommate, unit, etc., as this could significantly increase the defendant's risk for victimization) or if incriminating information becomes public (e.g., if a person's written description of the offense, or other possible evidence, falls into the hands of a cellmate or other inmate at jail, the risk of it being turned over to the prosecutor increases). Restoration providers should therefore be very intentional and considerate in identifying what paperwork is provided to the defendant for independent study versus re-collected and saved for use as a visual aid in a personalized restoration session; they should always weigh the clinical benefits versus the potential harms in providing independent study materials to a defendant.

Group-Based Interventions

Competency restoration in a group format allows for several defendants to benefit from education provided at once. Group facilitator-to-defendant ratios may vary, but for the purpose of this chapter, we operationalize groups as including at least one group facilitator and three or more defendants. It can be beneficial to have two restoration providers act as group facilitators for a single group, particularly if the class size is large, if staffing allows. For example, when a defendant asks a specific/nuanced question in group, it is more likely to be answered in a timely and accurate manner if there is more than one group facilitator in the session. Regardless, group leaders and other restoration providers are encouraged to provide "I don't know, but I will find out" style responses as necessary (i.e., and then provide accurate information in a subsequent session) rather than providing inaccurate/misleading information that may stick with the defendant.

Groups are often didactic in nature, with restoration providers verbally providing generally applicable competency-related information to defendants. Group leaders may have the resources to use a chalkboard, whiteboard, poster paper, etc. as a visual aid in group. Key terms, diagrams, etc. written on display boards/easels should of course be written or drawn large enough for all group members to see them clearly. Televisions and computers may also be available for use to display information in a less improvised manner. For example, vetted websites (e.g., court case information websites), established intervention tools (e.g., instructional videos), and popular media (e.g., legal-themed television shows or movie clips) may be displayed in groups on a television or computer. Popular media can sometimes provide a helpful point of reference for certain aspects of the courtroom (e.g., representations of the major players in the room with respect to physical positioning in the room). References to well-known media representations of competency-related concepts and dynamics, as well as use of video clips, can at times be appropriate and help facilitate defendant interest/engagement. Restoration providers who use videos, however, are strongly encouraged to take an active role in facilitating viewing. That is, group leaders should be alert to and listen for myths or beliefs that they may have to dispel in the moment (e.g., that attorneys actively yell at each other) and facilitate discussion about the accuracies and inaccuracies of what is represented in the video clip. In groups and otherwise, restoration providers are encouraged to be mindful that, for many defendants, their primary source of information regarding how courtrooms operate may come from popular culture and media (e.g., *Law and Order*, *My Cousin Vinny*, *Court TV*). These stories are often sensationalized for viewers that are not justice involved and are not designed as learning tools.

Beyond lecturing traditionally at group participants, providing visual aids, and facilitating discussion, competency restoration group leaders often make use of games and activities to make the opportunity for intervention more engaging. For example, legal-themed word searches and word scrambles are paper and pencil tasks that can be used to introduce and review legal vocabulary in a nondidactic format. Terms that are identified through games such as these should be used as prompts for further education and/or discussion. Board games can help teach additional vocabulary and concepts in a manner that is less reminiscent of schooling; this can be especially helpful when working with defendants who have negative associations with their prior educational experiences. Standardized or homemade flashcards[6] depicting legal terms/concepts can be utilized to mimic popular games (e.g., *Heads Up*, *20 Questions*). Competency-themed trivia (e.g., *Jeopardy*-style trivia) and BINGO games are also commonly in use as group-based activities, providing defendants an opportunity to demonstrate and share their knowledge in a manner that also promotes sustained attention and self-advocacy. Case vignettes describing hypothetical defendants and their legal situations can be helpful for facilitating group discussions about specific barriers to competency, legal decision-making, etc. with less emotional charge than discussing someone's personal legal case; at times, hearing a peer's perspective on a case similar to a defendant's own situation may be better received than hearing the same perspective from a restoration or treatment provider. Mock trials allow defendants to observe and participate in a structured role-play activity, which may be especially helpful for procedural/tactile learners. Resources such as these can be found or developed on various websites designed for schoolteachers, and we have included samples in Appendix A.

Regardless of the specific intervention approach used while leading a competency restoration group, it is essential that competency restoration providers provide education about relevant terms and concepts and facilitate in-group discussion. It is not adequate for restoration providers to simply play a video or provide group members with pages of activity books to work from in a supervised setting. In addition to clinical benefits, and facilitating progress toward competency, discussions allow restoration providers to track and document more accurately progress made by the various group members.

6. Free digital legal flashcards (English and Spanish versions) are available online, including though the Virginia DBHDS's Office of Forensic Services website: https://dbhds.virginia.gov/forensic-services/adult-outpatient-competency-restoration/

Cautions

In group settings, defendants should be empowered to share, or not share, information about their own legal situation as they see fit. As a defendant with the right to remain silent, they should also hold the power to discuss or not discuss their legal situation as a group member; this may be considered a parallel process. It is thus not appropriate for a group facilitator to use guilt, coercion, or other such strategies to get a defendant to discuss their case in a context that the defendant may not perceive to be safe or supportive. If the group facilitator prompts the group to share personal case information, and group participants do not take advantage of that opportunity, a hypothetical case example might be used as an alternative. If a defendant voluntarily chooses to bring up their own legal situation during group discussion, it may be indicated to remind the group as a whole to be respectful and maintain their peer's privacy when group is done (i.e., not sharing information about a case other than their own with persons outside the group). It is strongly encouraged that ground rules encouraging mutual respect and confidentiality are introduced at the start of a group and brought up as reminders with some regularity thereafter.

Individualized Interventions

Individualized, one-on-one, interventions are opportunities for a restoration provider to target a specific defendant's barriers to competency, as identified in the initial competency evaluation or more recent screenings of their competency-related knowledge and abilities. This typically means providing focused education about specific topics that a particular defendant does not yet understand rather than covering competency-related topics broadly (i.e., with a "blanket approach" more appropriate for groups). This may also mean incorporating a particular clinical approach or technique in restoration sessions, as illustrated in subsequent chapters of this handbook (resources in Appendix B). Certainly, this involves discussing the defendant's personal legal situation in confidential meetings. An individualized competency restoration treatment plan should take into consideration the defendant's self-reported and perceived learning style, in addition to content-based areas to be strengthened. The competency restoration treatment plan should also be considered by the restoration provider each session and revised as needed as the defendant's knowledge and clinical presentation changes.

In targeting general knowledge deficits one-on-one, a competency restoration provider can and should use language that is familiar and preferable to the specific defendant (e.g., prosecutor v. prosecuting attorney v. commonwealth attorney v. district attorney v. DA). The language a competency restoration provider uses should also be thoughtfully and respectfully individualized to meet the defendant at their literacy level. Defendants who are auditory learners may benefit the most from verbal explanations and discussions, including those that occur in groups. Defendants who are visual learners may benefit from the use of visual aids (see Appendix A), including courtroom illustrations, diagrams, and flashcards with pictures (e.g., depicting major courtroom personnel). Flashcards can also be used creatively, such as by placing them visually to demonstrate adversarial allegiance, as "people" for role plays, etc. Nontraditional uses may help defendants bridge their factual understanding of the court with their understanding of their personal legal situation.

Privately discussing a defendant's personal legal situation is arguably the most important function of one-on-one restoration sessions. Defendants who are uncomfortable discussing their case in groups, in common areas where peers may overhear, in treatment team

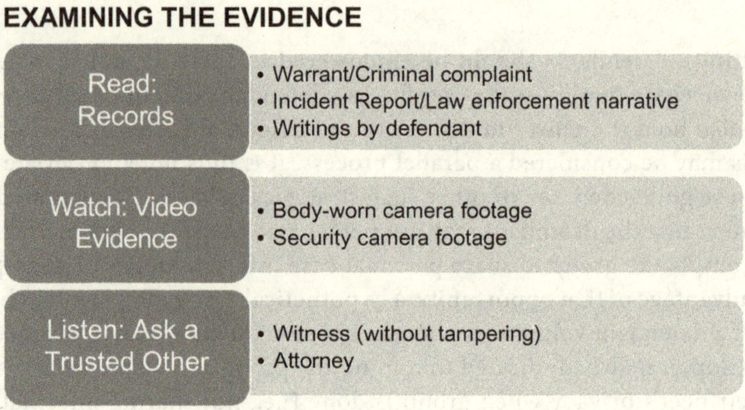

Figure 2.1 Use of Collateral Resources
Source: Author (Grossi)

meetings with multiple professionals at once, etc. may be comfortable discussing their case where confidentiality can be maintained. It may be more beneficial for some defendants to work on rationally understanding their case and contributing to their own defense in individual formats rather than discussing their concerns in a larger group format (e.g., Zapf & Roesch, 2011). Particularly for defendants not yet ready to discuss their case in-depth, discussion of hypothetical scenarios (described verbally or via handouts) can be used to assess and develop their decision-making processes and ability to apply general legal information to a specific case scenario.

Specifically, using physical or digital copies of warrants, incident/offense reports, law enforcement narratives, etc. may be key in educating a defendant about their charges, charge classifications, and the underlying allegations against them (see Figure 2.1). The content of these can be used to prompt focused discussion (i.e., enhancing rational understanding), including about what physical evidence might arise in their case, what witnesses might articulate to the court in testimony, and how such data might be received by the fact finder(s) in court. Integrating legal paperwork such as this in restoration can also be discussed on a process level, as reflective of their right to know the evidence against them, and to introduce certain legal terminology (e.g., *discovery*). In some localities, showing a defendant the status of their legal cases on an up-to-date and official court case information website, or a printout of that website, can be a useful intervention tool (if they mistakenly believe their charges have been dismissed, think they have already made a plea deal, etc.). Teaching the defendant how to use online legal resources can also foster their sense of agency and control over their legal situation, which ties into their ability to assist in their defense. What resources can be utilized as visual aids in individualized sessions may depend on jurisdiction or facility policy, as detailed above.

Individualized sessions may also be taken a step further, with restoration providers facilitating private phone or video calls between a defendant and their defense attorney. In some settings, a restoration provider may have to (e.g., per facility policy) stay with the defendant to monitor the call to ensure safety is maintained and technology is used appropriately (e.g., unapproved calls are not being made, phone cords are not being weaponized). In some contexts, at the request of the attorney or defendant, the restoration provider may also opt to stay with the defendant during the call to monitor the conversation. This can lead to good observational data, and at the same time, the restoration provider must attend to being brought within the bubble of attorney-client privilege. A restoration provider with decisional flexibility may also opt to leave the room during the call, out of respect for attorney-client privilege, assuming the defendant is perceived as stable enough to engage appropriately after they leave. The defendant's demonstrated ability to engage calmly and productively with defense counsel, rather than the specific content of the discussion, should be reflected in documentation of the call.

Defendants with pending legal charges do have a right to consult with their defense attorneys. However, defense attorneys—in particular public defenders and/or court-appointed attorneys—often abstain from talking to defendants they represent while the defendant is deemed incompetent and undergoing competency restoration. The attorneys may be focused on other (i.e., active) cases and, simultaneously, are not able to move forward with many requests or decisions a defendant may try to make while legally incompetent to assist in their own defense. That said, attorneys may be more willing to participate in a call mediated by a competency restoration provider. On the other side of the line, defendants are often hesitant to call defense attorneys out of mistrust of the legal system (e.g., due to adverse experiences with the current or previous attorney), frustrations with the system (e.g., not being able to get in touch with their attorney when they call), or concern for their privacy (e.g., calling on a recorded line at a jail, or in the milieu of a hospital where staff/peers might overhear the conversation). Facilitated phone calls can be excellent rapport-building and trust-repairing exercises for attorneys and clients.

Prior to an attorney phone/video call, it is indicated for a competency restoration provider to discuss and plan with the defendant about what they can and should (a) ask the defense attorney and (b) tell the defense attorney. If the defendant is concerned that they might not know what to say during a call while in the moment, practicing such interactions with role play may be helpful. It may also be indicated to have the defendant write down notes (e.g., key words or scripted questions) about what to say to the defense attorney that they can reference in the moment. This teaches ecologically valid skills, which a defendant might adopt should they find the strategies helpful.

After an attorney phone/video call, it is essential to process the interaction with the defendant. Discussion of what in particular went well, as well as what could have been better, can help a defendant come to an understanding of how to interpret a conversation that may have been emotionally charged. Processing general impressions (e.g., "vibes") can also be helpful, as a defendant's trust in their attorney and their judgment may affect how their case is handled moving forward. Both members of the attorney-client dyad might also be able and willing to convey and process with the current restoration provider how the current interaction differed from their prior interactions. Thus, it may also be indicated to speak with the defense attorney in consultation afterward. Defense attorney consultation can help a competency restoration provider track the attorney's perception of their ability to work with the defendant in their current state and identify current concerns that might be addressed in restoration moving forward. Defense attorneys may also be willing to provide contextual information (e.g., about the political climate in the court of jurisdiction, likely plea deals, the demands expected of a defendant moving forward) that they are not comfortable putting in writing or relaying with an incompetent defendant in the room.

Cautions

It is not uncommon for defendants to ask competency restoration providers for legal advice or for their thoughts about what will happen with their case when discussing their legal situation privately in session. It cannot be emphasized enough that competency restoration providers are not attorneys and should not provide legal guidance for defendants undergoing restoration, even if the defendant solicits that guidance. Should a defendant seek feedback about their case that the competency restoration provider is not competent to provide (e.g., how to plead, whether to take a plea deal, what the judge will decide in their case), it is indicated to deflect in a manner that maintains rapport, provides encouragement, and also re-establishes the distinct roles of relevant persons (e.g., "That is a really excellent question and definitely something that you should ask your attorney when you speak with them. They'll be able to give you the most accurate answer." Or, "Unfortunately I don't give legal advice, but I'm glad that you're asking questions like this because it shows me that you're able to ask your lawyer really good questions about your case").

PHASE 3: MAINTENANCE

Some jurisdictions are clear about when individuals should be referred for a formal post-restoration evaluation, or a post-restoration evaluation is scheduled to occur at a predetermined interval. For example, in Texas, individuals facing misdemeanor charges are hospitalized for a period of 60 days, and individuals facing felony charges are hospitalized for a period of 120 days, both with the possibility of one 60-day extension. At that point, regardless of restoration status, individuals are re-evaluated, and results are provided to the court. In some states, individuals can be referred for a post-restoration evaluation when they show signs of restored competency and improved psychiatric functioning. For example, some individuals may quickly stabilize on prescribed medications and be ready for an evaluation much more quickly than someone requiring multiple medication trials. Individuals who showcase improved clinical symptoms (e.g., lessened response to internal stimuli, improved mood stability, organized thought process) and an understanding of case-specific information and general legal knowledge may be referred for a post-restoration evaluation when the competency restoration provider(s) or team believes that they have attained competence.

Even after an individual is referred/scheduled for a post-restoration evaluation, and even after they are opined competent to stand trial, it is helpful for restoration services and clinical oversight to continue whenever possible. As resources are limited, particularly in inpatient and jail settings, it can be tempting to redirect services to more clearly incompetent individuals after someone is identified as probably competent. However, reallocation of resources may contribute to deterioration in competency-related knowledge and/or psychiatric relapse; individuals ordered for competency restoration should receive services for as long as possible to help ensure that their improved presentation is durable (see Figure 2.2).

Once an individual has been formally opined competent to proceed by a forensic evaluator, there may be some lag time prior to their discharge back to jail or release to the community, and additional lag time prior to their next court appearance. There are a number of factors that may interfere with psychiatric stability and maintenance of knowledge in that period. As such, competency restoration providers may have to take steps to ensure psychiatric stability and retention of competency-related knowledge for some time before a defendant's case is adjudicated. There are defendants who sometimes require multiple rounds of competency restoration, specifically due to destabilization or relapse prior to their case being adjudicated. Cabeldue and colleagues (2020) investigated factors that differentiated those defendants requiring a single hospitalization versus two or more inpatient admissions for restoration of competency. Slightly more than a quarter of their sample

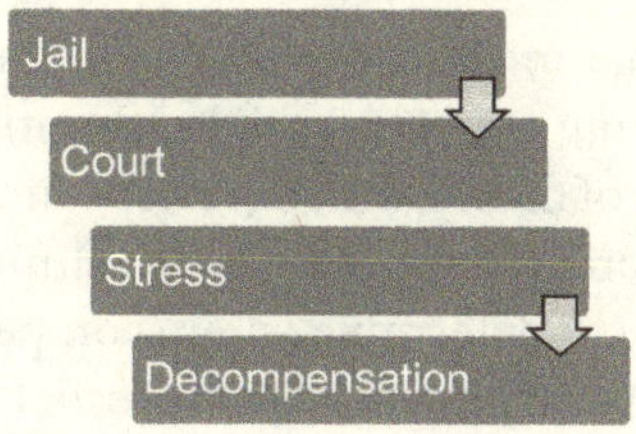

Figure 2.2 Contributors to Decompensation
Source: Author (Grossi)

underwent multiple admissions for competency restoration, and factors such as modality of medication, immigrant status, and effort/feigning-related concerns were all contributing factors. Interventions that can decrease readmissions should be emphasized.

Several of the chapters that follow identify treatment approaches that may be useful in promoting clinical stability throughout the duration of legal proceedings. Many of them include skills that focus on managing stress and utilizing coping skills, which can be useful as individuals wait for upcoming court dates. Additionally, many of these treatment approaches may assist in maintaining the durability of gains made during the competency restoration process. The next chapter (Chapter 3) addresses medication adherence, which is key for defendants with major mental illness in particular. Cabeldue and colleagues (2020) identified that the modality of medication that individuals were prescribed assisted in predicting who required multiple hospitalizations for restoration. Individuals who were prescribed injectable medication (either alone, or in conjunction with oral medications) were less likely to be readmitted for a subsequent hospitalization. Cabeldue and colleagues (2020) found that one in ten individuals within the sample was discharged on no psychiatric medications, and it was these individuals who had the highest odds of being admitted. As such, prescription of injectable medication (when clinically indicated) may assist in mitigating symptoms throughout the duration of legal proceedings.

SETTING-SPECIFIC MODIFICATIONS

Depending on the needs of the defendant, and the resources available in the jurisdiction, competency restoration may occur in a variety of different settings. The following sections describe several of the most common settings, as well as some factors and modifications that may be relevant in each setting.

Hospital-Based Restoration

The most traditional and common location for competency restoration is in a hospital-based setting, typically within a state hospital or a forensic psychiatric hospital; this is also considered the most restrictive setting. Generally speaking, hospitals provide a more traditionally therapeutic, rather than corrections-focused, setting for restoration. Hospitals are able to provide general psychiatric treatment and support services (e.g., therapeutic groups, medication management, milieu therapy) in addition to competency-related services. At the same time, there is infrastructure for the administration of medication over objection, intensive (i.e., 24/7) monitoring, use of physical restraint and seclusion, etc.

Kapoor (2011) hypothesized that most incompetent defendants would prefer undergoing restoration in a psychiatric setting over jail-based restoration, as inpatient settings are assumed to allow greater freedom of movement, have a specific intention to provide treatment instead of being punitive, and provide more access to clinical programming. As such, it is neither appropriate nor feasible to determine where competency restoration occurs based on a defendant's preference alone. Kapoor (2020) suggested that inpatient restoration might be most appropriate for defendants who are likely to require involuntary medication, have severe substance abuse concerns and are likely to relapse outside of a structured setting, are at a high risk for acting violently or attempting suicide, need constant observation to assess for malingering, are a high elopement risk, or have a high bond.

In at least 20 states, pretrial defendants are placed on lengthy wait lists for competency evaluations and/or admission to a hospital for restoration (e.g., Murrie et al., 2023; Wik et al., 2018) because there are only so many inpatient hospital beds available at any given time. These wait lists can significantly increase the time until a defendant undergoes an initial competency evaluation or between an initial finding of incompetence and the beginning of restoration services. In recent years, these wait lists have been growing (e.g., Clendenin et al., 2021; Murrie et al., 2023), with average wait times ranging from 7 to 252 days (Wik et al., 2018). The result is potentially unconstitutional delays (e.g., in hospital admission for restoration treatment) that have resulted in class action lawsuits in a number of states (Heilbrun et al., 2019).

Further, hospitalization can be costly and is often restricted in terms of patient rights (e.g., limits on personal items allowed, restrictions regarding community interaction and contact, limits on technology usage and availability, and potential medication overrides/treatment over objection). Due to the restrictions that accompany psychiatric commitment and hospitalization (e.g., materials on the unit, such as pencils and pens, may be limited; staffing concerns impacting the facilitation of groups), Miller (2003) recommended the development of outpatient or community-based restoration treatment programs.

Jail-Based Restoration

Outpatient and jail-based restoration programs potentially serve as a more affordable option to restore competency, with less wait time for hospital admission and a faster return to the legal system (Kapoor, 2011; Kapoor, 2020; Valerio & Becker, 2016). While inpatient restoration may still be recommended for individuals in certain circumstances (e.g., refusing to take medication with limited recourse from the jail for treatment over objection; severe symptomatology that cannot be safely managed in a jail setting), offering competency restoration services in jails to some portion of defendants can help reduce the strain on hospital systems and help make treatment more readily accessible to defendants (Felthous & Bloom, 2018; Wik, 2018).

Data have demonstrated that jail-based programs are less costly than inpatient programs (Wik, 2018). For example, jail-based restoration in Arizona was estimated to save almost four million dollars in one county in one year, based on calculations that determined it to be one-fifth the cost of inpatient restoration (Kapoor, 2011). Though savings have been reported by many states with jail-based restoration, meaningful comparisons can be challenging; variability in budgeting and available resources lead to differences in the way costs are calculated and reported by state (Wik, 2018).

Similar to hospital-based settings, there are safety and resource-based considerations that may impact how treatment, including competency restoration services, are provided in jail settings. Jails often have greater restrictions with respect to contraband compared to hospitals. Restoration providers may therefore face challenges related to limits to their ability to make use of technology aids (e.g., use of instructional videos where laptops/cell phones may be disallowed), limits on pens/pencils/paper, and limits to medication administration. Additionally, Kapoor (2011) indicated that mental healthcare in jails is often decentralized, such that contact with competency restoration providers, forensic evaluators, and other specialists is often dependent on the availability of correctional staff to transport defendants. Staffing in jail facilities may also vary within the span of a day based on shift changes, meals/programming schedules, and "count" time or other scheduled lockdown times. Increased access to technology in jail facilities over time, seemingly accelerated by the COVID-19 pandemic, may help mitigate some of these logistical barriers to restoration/evaluation in jail settings. Jail-based restoration providers should be prepared to adapt treatment to meet the needs and restrictions of their particular jail facility.

Wik (2018) published a brief description of jail-based restoration programs in various stages of development and implementation across 12 states. Almost universally, such programs were unable to accommodate those who were noncompliant with psychiatric treatment. Where data were available, most states described outpatient-style care, where incompetent defendants resided in the general population or specialized housing units and were either visited individually by clinical staff or gathered for group treatment. Restoration rates (i.e., over varying or unstated time frames) were reported when possible and ranged from 9.0% to 86.7%. Defendants who did not attain competency with jail-based restoration were either diverted out of the legal system or admitted to regional inpatient restoration programs.

In some parts of the U.S., competency restoration units are established or in development; these are specialized housing units, similar to a mental health pod, designed to minimize barriers to competency restoration in a correctional setting. One published study described the development of a competency restoration unit within the Fulton County Jail in Atlanta, Georgia. Ash and colleagues (2020) collected data during routine program operations over a seven-year period, beginning with the development of the unit in 2011. Jail-based restoration in that context was not presented as an alternative to other settings but as programming within a continuum of services. This systems-oriented perspective stressed the flexibility of matching defendants' restoration needs to an appropriate treatment setting, with the possibility of reassessment and reassignment as needed. In other terms, jail-based restoration can escalate to inpatient restoration in the context of psychiatric decompensation or medication nonadherence and can deescalate to community-based restoration if defendants are granted bond and demonstrate the ability and willingness to follow through on those services.

Community-Based Restoration

Community-based restoration might take place in-home (e.g., at a nursing home, rehab facility, or personal residence), at court clinics or treatment centers designed for providing outpatient services, remotely via phone/video, or through some alternative means; the location options for community-based restoration vary greatly by locality. Community-based restoration addresses issues of competency in the least restrictive setting available and theoretically best protects incompetent defendants' civil rights.

Miller (2003) asserted that outpatient/community-based restoration services ought to be utilized for any individual whose confinement to an inpatient psychiatric program is not clinically necessary. Kapoor (2020) suggested that this would include defendants who are independently cooperative with their prescription medication or do not require medication; need fewer or less frequent appointments, treatment, and/or education; have stable housing and reliable access/transportation to outpatient appointments; have no substance use concerns or are at low risk of relapse; and have paid/prepaid bond or are able to pay bond. In other terms, those defendants identified as the best fit for community-based competency restoration are likely perceived as stable in their mental health, able to follow through on the logistics of outpatient appointments, financially stable or well-supported in the community, and unlikely to flee. However, there may be ethical issues related to systematically finding indigent, disabled, or other persons (e.g., those not approved for bond due to their criminal history, immigration status, or some other static variable) inappropriate for participation in community-based competency restoration treatment programs.

In that vein, various bureaucratic, political, and economic barriers exist in the creation of such programs, which call attention to the fact that some individuals accused of crimes are out in the community. Prejudice and fear exist, and proposals for the creation of community-based restoration programs face public pushback. Limited funding and infrastructure for such programs means that there may not be adequate resources for those who are found eligible for community-based restoration. In more sparsely populated or rural areas, possible community-based locations for in-person competency restoration services may present an issue, as there are barriers to the provision of healthcare services generally. The location of community-based restoration programs may not be adequately accessible to sufficient numbers of incompetent defendants, or clinical staff, without substantive financial investments (Miller, 2003). Although increased availability of technology may help some defendants and competency restoration providers in more rural settings, the availability of consistent internet access in much of the U.S. remains very limited.

Outpatient competency restoration can take an extended period of time, and there may be fewer limits to the duration of community-based competency restoration specifically because the defendant is not confined. Over the course of extended community-based restoration, the circumstances of defendants can change. For example, a person may lose their stable housing or means of transportation, develop a chronic or serious physical illness, or decline in their mental health functioning. Community-based restoration providers might reconsider and alter their initial plan for the location and mode of services within the community based on the changing context (e.g., shifting from in-person to virtual services if that is allowable in their jurisdiction). Should it become clear that a defendant is not able to participate in community-based restoration services as expected, the overarching location of restoration services should be reconsidered. If a defendant on bond is not attending scheduled competency restoration appointments for an unknown reason or by choice, legal intervention (e.g., revoking bond, issuing a capias/warrant for their arrest) may unfortunately be the most appropriate step; ceasing to attend competency restoration as ordered by the court is at times taken as seriously as failing to appear at court, violating probation, or contempt generally. In such cases (e.g., with bond revoked), restoration services might begin or resume in the jail setting. If a defendant in the community becomes unable to attend, participate, or meaningfully engage in community-based competency restoration services because of a decline in their mental health (e.g., in the context of medication nonadherence), inpatient psychiatric hospitalization may be appropriate. Because of the dramatic difference in cost between hospital- and jail-based restoration, the need to provide finite inpatient mental health resources to those who are most in need, restrictions on the rights of defendants not as of yet committed of a crime, etc., community-based restoration providers are encouraged to be considerate of both personal and systemic factors in recommending an alternative placement for competency restoration to the court when multiple options are available.

USE OF TECHNOLOGY

Use of technology has proven to be helpful in the competency restoration process in numerous ways. Even prior to the COVID-19 pandemic, research suggested that forensic evaluations, specifically adjudicative competence evaluations, could be performed via videoconferencing technology and that patients viewed telemedicine as a viable alternative to live in-person interviews (Manguno-Mire et al., 2007). This was particularly useful in rural areas where forensic evaluators may have been limited. In the context of the COVID-19 pandemic, concerns about use of telemedicine were largely overridden by the need to provide services to defendants, so as to not violate the right to speedy proceedings. In recent years, aspects of the technology (e.g., HIPAA compliance and related security protections), as well as formal ethical guidance from professional organizations on use of technology (e.g., Batastini et al., 2023), have rapidly developed based on need and demand (Batastini et al., 2021; Kois et al., 2021). In the context of the pandemic, policies related to social distancing, quarantining, and limited visitation policies in correctional and mental health facilities impacted the availability of in-person competency restoration and evaluations, such that practical use of videoconferencing in competency restoration interventions and evaluations has increased substantially (e.g., Bernhard et al., 2021). Similarly, court policies at times demanded remote attendance, particularly at the peak of the pandemic. While at first allowances for remote participation in restoration, evaluations, and competency hearings were temporary solutions, changes to institutional and court policies on remote attendance at times became permanent.

The use of videoconferencing evaluations has been seen as a possible avenue for combatting the national competency crisis. Completing evaluations by video conferencing may increase access to defendants in rural areas who would otherwise face longer wait times for a competency evaluation. Trupp and colleagues 2021 surveyed forensic psychologists to examine opinions about using videoconferencing technology for competency to stand trial evaluations in the aftermath of the COVID-19 pandemic and found that 83.8% agreed it could reduce evaluation time for defendants. Further, 77.2% agreed that videoconferencing had the potential to increase efficiency for evaluators, with increased flexibility and reduced travel times.

An important consideration for use of technology in competency to stand trial related treatment is that many individuals with serious mental illness experience paranoia, and some may have paranoia specifically surrounding use of technology. Defendants who have been institutionalized (i.e., housed in hospitals and/or correctional facilities for much of their life) or are from an area with low technology access (e.g., rural areas, underdeveloped countries) may also have reality-based aversions to technology based on limited exposure/experience. In some cases, it may be contraindicated to use technology as part of treatment, with technology being an unnecessary hurdle. In other cases, interventions making use of technology may help a defendant to become more comfortable using technology as treatment progresses. This may be indicated for defendants likely to have to attend court or consult with defense counsel via a video platform. Having already had the opportunity to practice using video conferencing during restoration, treatment may contribute to ecological validity.

CULTURAL CONSIDERATIONS

Competency restoration providers are strongly encouraged to view defendants who participate in competency restoration through an intersectional lens, given the vast individual differences of defendants involved in the legal system. Age, socioeconomic status/financial autonomy, race/ethnicity, immigration status/level of acculturation, spirituality/religion, language, and (dis)ability are among layers that may affect how competency restoration is approached and what resources might be utilized in treatment.

Of particular relevance, individuals who have lived in other countries may require education about the U.S. legal system, especially if the court system of their country of origin is quite different from that of the United States. Cabeldue and colleagues (2020) found that individuals born in another country, regardless of how much time they had spent in the United States (i.e., an indicator of acculturation), were more likely to have multiple admissions for competency restoration. A number of factors may be underlying this finding, including communication barriers, different cultural views of mental illness, superficial understanding of the U.S. legal system, and diagnostic challenges. Even courts within the U.S. may function slightly differently, have different courtroom layouts, or use different terminology. Professional judgment, and trial and error if necessary, should be utilized in determining whether it is helpful to explain differences between one system/jurisdiction and another or attempt to explain the relevant system using a clean slate.

Defendants going through the legal process may also require adaptations based on individual differences. As emphasized above, it is helpful during the restoration process to be curious about a client's preferred language and to employ a client-centered approach when using legal terminology. Given the various languages spoken by individuals in the U.S., many defendants will require the use of an interpreter during the competency restoration process. Finding a qualified and available interpreter, and making use of interpretation services, can be an added challenge. Working with interpreters who have the appropriate training for a mental health and legal setting is vital, and it may be necessary to provide education to an interpreter about the restoration provider's specific needs for a session. For example, interpreters may require education about the importance of conveying exactly what a competency restoration provider asks, so as to not provide additional education or context clues when current knowledge is being assessed. While direct translation may not be feasible, having such a discussion may help align the interpreter's efforts and the goal of the session for the restoration provider. Consultation between the interpreter and competency restoration provider may be necessary to clarify whether and to what extent a defendant's speech is organized, tangential, vague, or otherwise atypical in structure.

Case Example

Mr. G is a 34-year-old defendant. He is a German, Protestant, White, queer, cisgender man who moved to New York City from Germany three years ago. When his lawyer met with him in jail, the lawyer had difficulty understanding Mr. G. His lawyer sought a German interpreter, but Mr. G appeared distrustful, made sidelong glances at the interpreter, and refused to speak with the interpreter present. This conflict persisted, with Mr. G unable to communicate clearly in English and refusing to utilize interpretation services. He was subsequently referred for a competency evaluation. The evaluation was conducted by two clinicians (i.e., as is standard practice in New York) in the presence of Mr. G's attorney. A different interpreter was present for this evaluation. Mr. G presented as suspicious and guarded, although he was more willing to utilize interpretation services. He frequently switched between English and German; however, his speech was disorganized regardless of language used. He was unable to discuss his charges or the allegations against him, denied past or present symptoms of mental illness, and suggested that his attorney and interpreter were gathering information to use against him. He appeared internally preoccupied and was observed mumbling to himself on multiple occasions. No collateral sources of information were available. His evaluators diagnosed him with unspecified schizophrenia or other psychotic disorder and found him incompetent to proceed. He was subsequently admitted to a forensic inpatient psychiatric facility for the restoration of competency.

The structure of treatment as usual in this facility included regular and as-needed patient meetings with an interdisciplinary treatment team, as well as daily group therapy that included psycholegal, psychoeducational, and recreation topics. The treatment team is comprised of psychiatry, psychology, social work, nursing, and rehabilitation disciplines. This facility also employs a number of interpreters that are onsite Monday through Friday from 9 a.m. to 3 p.m.; because of Mr. G's admission, at least one German language interpreter was consistently available during clinical hours. At other times, portable tablets are used that have an interpretation phone service application to facilitate communication.

Mr. G appeared confused and agitated during admission procedures. He refused to utilize interpretation services and was unable or unwilling to listen to the instructions provided through the interpreter. In the initial weeks of Mr. G's hospitalization, he continued to present as frequently and easily agitated. This was conceptualized as resulting from a combination of thought disorder, confusion regarding others' expectations of him, and his difficulty in communicating his needs. He appeared frustrated by staff's difficulty initially understanding him and the brief delay in connecting to video interpretation services. He was also distrustful of the intentions of each interpreter. Mr. G was prescribed a regimen of antipsychotic medication to address paranoia, thought disorder, and auditory hallucinations. The on-staff interpreter was utilized to explain the purpose of these medications to him. Despite initial confusion regarding the hospital medication line procedures, he was compliant with prescribed medication and procedures after a few days, at which point he was more familiar with the hospital routine. He also began attending groups after a few days but refused to sit next to his assigned interpreter. He made attempts to participate in group discussion, but his contributions were disorganized, and when decipherable, involved paranoid statements about treatment providers and legal personnel gathering information to use against him.

With continued medication adherence, Mr. G began demonstrating increasing psychiatric stabilization and improved ability to engage with restoration services. Mr. G's interpreter attended group and individual sessions alongside Mr. G in order to facilitate communication. Mr. G gradually appeared less suspicious of his interpreter and began more consistently using interpretation services. During a meeting with the team later that week, Mr. G was speaking largely in German with some English words mixed in. When his psychologist asked him a question, the interpreter repeated the question in German. Mr. G responded in German and the interpreter spoke again in German. Mr. G responded in German, and this repeated three more times before the interpreter provided an English response to the team. After this meeting, the team requested to speak with the interpreter, who explained that he was trying to clarify Mr. G's response so that it made more sense. Psychoeducation was provided to the interpreter that the nature and structure of Mr. G's responses were clinically informative and was asked to strictly interpret what is said by either party. The interpreter was informed that if a question needed to be rephrased or information needed to be clarified, the treating clinicians would do that themselves in a clinically indicated manner.

In this hospital, there is no standardized restoration curriculum. A number of binders and files are shared among restoration providers with handouts, lessons, and activities. These materials have already been translated into a number of languages, but not German. Mr. G's treating clinicians sought out Mr. G's interpreter for help in translating some materials from English to German. A legal study guide was translated and given to Mr. G for independent study. The group facilitators prepared lessons ahead of schedule and made sure to have a German translated handout for Mr. G whenever necessary. Lessons were chosen that involved image-based handouts when possible. German subtitles were selected for any videos presented in group settings. Most importantly, group facilitators and other clinicians paused their speech frequently so that the interpreter had time to interpret the verbally presented information in real time. Despite these measures, Mr. G struggled to keep up with and participate in discussions. Faster paced activities designed to improve defendants' procedural and conceptual understanding of the courtroom, such as mock trials and role plays, were ineffective and confusing for Mr. G.

Although in this facility individualized restoration sessions are not provided to every defendant, Mr. G was identified as a patient that would benefit from individual sessions. Within these sessions, with the support of his interpreter, time was spent verbally quizzing Mr. G on the roles of courtroom personnel and basic legal concepts as well as verbal exploration of his legal circumstances and options. Mr. G was provided a translated "My Legal Information" handout to complete independently between sessions, as well as a set of translated legal flashcards to facilitate independent study.

With continued medication compliance, Mr. G became increasingly organized in his speech and thought. He eventually no longer appeared internally preoccupied. He was able to explain that he previously experienced loud, intrusive auditory hallucinations and reported that they had decreased in both frequency and volume. He spoke English more often and expressed interest in exclusively communicating in English. On the unit and with peers, he was able to make his needs known and have basic conversations. He was able to learn and recite the roles of court personnel and other basic legal concepts in English. When asked to discuss his case and his legal strategy options, his responses were concrete. He was unable to discuss hypothetical legal outcomes or explain his thinking when weighing his legal options. When he was encouraged to utilize interpretation services, Mr. G was able to effectively speak about abstract concepts and discuss hypothetical outcomes. Although he was conversationally fluent in English, his ability was insufficient for legal purposes. Psychoeducation was provided, and although he remained suspicious of his interpreter, he better understood the utility of interpretation services and agreed to utilize them for further competency restoration, future evaluations, and in the resolution of his legal case.

During an individual session, Mr. G explained that his belief that his attorney was gathering information to use against him was based on his observation that the defense attorney appeared friendly with the district attorney outside the courtroom. Mr. G's restoration provider pivoted by asking him if he enjoyed sports, and Mr. G began excitedly speaking about his favorite Bundesliga football team (the German premier football league). The clinician suggested that two players on different teams might have a lot to discuss with each other and appear friendly while conversing off the field. However, when on the field it is their job to be adversaries. Similarly, the defense attorney and district attorney are fulfilling an adversarial job requirement in the courtroom, despite appearing friendly elsewhere. In a subsequent session, the clinician again brought up Mr. G's attorney and inquired if there were any questions Mr. G might want to ask him. A list of questions about Mr. G's legal circumstance and legal options were generated. With Mr. G's permission, the restoration provider scheduled a video call between Mr. G and his defense attorney. Mr. G requested the clinician be present for this call, and the restoration provider obliged. The clinician participated very little, only chiming in to remind Mr. G of a question on the list that he had forgotten to ask. Afterward, Mr. G and the restoration provider were able to discuss the content of the call, and the clinician corrected Mr. G's understanding of one or two points on which he was mistaken. Mr. G's attorney had stated his expectation that a specific plea bargain was likely to be presented once Mr. G was identified as competent. The pros and cons of accepting this plea bargain were discussed. Mr. G's interpreter wrote out this list in German for Mr. G to review and add to independently. The following week, Mr. G demonstrated improved motivation to attain fitness and continue on with his legal case. He expressed gratitude for his lawyer's work and legal advice, indicating willingness to trust and work with his attorney moving forward.

At this point in his treatment, Mr. G had demonstrated sufficient understanding of the roles of legal personnel and basic legal concepts, consistent knowledge of his charges and the allegations against him, the ability to logically consider his alternatives and make informed decisions, and a willingness to work with his attorney. He further denied ongoing auditory hallucinations, denounced previously held paranoid delusional beliefs, and communicated to staff and peers in an organized manner. The treatment team believed him to be restored to competency, and he was referred for a post-restoration competency evaluation. While awaiting this evaluation and after passing it, individual sessions were held at a decreased frequency (i.e., for the maintenance of competency) until his eventual discharge to Department of Corrections custody.

REFERENCES

Ash, P., Roberts, V. C., Egan, G., Coffman, K., Schwenke, T., & Bailey, K. (2020). A jail-based competency restoration unit as a component of a continuum of restoration services. *Journal of the American Academy of Psychiatry and the Law, 48*, 43–51. doi:10.29158/JAAPL.003893-20

Batastini, A. B., Guyton, M. R., Bernhard, P. A., Folk, J. B., Knuth, S. B., Kohutis . . . Tussey, C. M. (2023). Recommendations for the use of telepsychology in psychology-law practice and research: A statement by American Psychology-Law Society (APA Division 41). *Psychology, Public Policy, and Law, 29*(3), 255–271. doi:10.1037/law0000394

Batastini, A. B., Paprzycki, P., Jones, A. C. T., & MacLean, N. (2021). Are videoconferenced mental and behavioral health services just as good as in-person? A meta-analysis of a fast-growing practice. *Clinical Psychology Review, 83*, Article 101944. doi:10.1016/j.cpr.2020.101944

Bernhard, P. A., McDowell, L., & Vincent, G. M. (2021). Forensic practitioners' use and perceptions of telepsychology before and during COVID-19. *Law and Human Behavior, 45*(5), 468–480. doi:10.1037/lhb0000464

Cabeldue, M., Green, D., McGrath, R. E., & Belfi, B. (2020). Factors related to repeat forensic hospital admissions for restoration of competency to stand trial. *Journal of Forensic Psychology Research and Practice, 21*, 91–117. doi:10.1080/24732850.2020.1834834

Clendenin, S., Edens, C., & Warburton, K. (2021, August). DSH overview: Felony incompetent to stand trial challenges, data, and efforts [Presentation]. IST Solutions Workgroup, Sacramento, CA. https://www.chhs.ca.gov/wp-content/uploads/2021/08/DSH_IST_Overview.pdf

Dietrich, S., & Hernandez, E. (2022). Language use in the United States: 2019. American Community Survey Reports. https://www.census.gov/library/publications/2022/acs/acs-50.html

Drope v. Missouri, 420 U.S. 162 (1975).

Dusky v. United States, 362 U.S. 402 (1960).

Felthous, A. R., & Bloom, J. D. (2018). Jail-based competency restoration. *Journal of the American Academy of Psychiatry and the Law, 46*, 364–372. doi:10.29158/JAAPL.003772-18

Florida State Hospital Strategic Plan Workgroup for Trial Competency Education. (2011, August). *Florida State Hospital CompKit: Competency to stand trial training resources: A comprehensive approach to competency restoration training for criminal defendants*. Florida State Hospital.

Heilbrun, K., Giallella, C., Wright, H. J., DeMatteo, D., Griffin, P. A., Locklair, B., & Desai, A. (2019). Treatment for restoration of competence to stand trial: Critical analysis and policy recommendations. *Psychology, Public Policy, and Law, 25*(4), 266–283. doi:10.1037/law0000210

Kapoor, R. (2011). Commentary: Jail-based competency restoration. *Journal of the American Academy of Psychiatry and the Law, 39*, 311–315. https://jaapl.org/content/39/3/311.long

Kapoor, R. (2020). A continuum of competency restoration services need not include jail. *Journal of the American Academy of Psychiatry and the Law, 48*, 52–55. doi:10.29158/JAAPL.003926-20

Kois, L. E., Cox, J., & Peck, A. T. (2021). Forensic e-mental health: Review, research priorities, and policy directions. *Psychology, Public Policy, and Law, 27*(1), 1–16. doi:10.1037/law0000293

Manguno-Mire, G. M., Thompson, J. W., Shore, J. H., Croy, C. D., Artecona, J. F., & Pickering, J. W. (2007). The use of telemedicine to evaluate competency to stand trial: A preliminary randomized controlled study. *Journal of the American Academy of Psychiatry and the Law Online, 35*, 481–489. https://jaapl.org/content/35/4/481.long

Miller, R. D. (2003). Hospitalization of criminal defendants for evaluation of competence to stand trial or for restoration of competence: Clinical and legal issues. *Behavioral Sciences & the Law, 21*, 369–391. doi:10.1002/bsl.546

Mueller, C., Kennedy, R., Santee, J., & Lam, A. (2004, August). *Psycholegal competency restoration: Current trends and future directions* [Paper presentation]. 102nd Annual Convention of the American Psychological Association, Honolulu, HI.

Mueller, C., & Wylie, A. M. (2007). Examining the effectiveness of an intervention designed for the restoration of competency to stand trial. *Behavioral Sciences & the Law, 25*, 891–900. doi:10.1002/bsl.775

Murrie, D. C., Gowensmith, N., & Boccaccini, M. T. (2023). Competence to stand trial: Evaluation and restoration services. In E. Verona & B. Fox (Eds.), *Handbook of evidence-based criminal justice practices* (pp. 247–257). Routledge.

Samuel, S. E., & Michals, T. J. (2011). Competency restoration. In E. Y. Drogin, F. M. Dattilio, R. I. Sadoff, & T. G. Gutheil (Eds.), *Handbook of forensic assessment: Psycholegal and psychiatric perspectives* (pp. 79–96). John Wiley & Sons.

Schneider, M. A. (2021). *Competency restoration across the United States* [Doctoral dissertation, Fairleigh Dickinson University]. ProQuest Dissertations Publishing.

Shippen, M. E., Houchins, D. E., Crites, S. A., Derzis, N. C., & Patterson, D. (2010). An examination of the basic reading skills of incarcerated males. *Adult Learning, 21*(3–4), 4–12.

Trupp, G. F., Ricardo, M. M., Boccaccini, M. T., & Murrie, D. C. (2021). Forensic evaluators' opinions on the use of videoconferencing technology for competency to stand trial evaluations after the onset of COVID-19. *Psychology, Public Policy, and Law, 27*, 537–549. doi:10.1037/law0000322

Valerio, C., & Becker, J. V. (2016). Jail-based restoration to competency: An investigation of program recidivism and contested competency cases. *Journal of Forensic Psychology Practice, 16*, 61–73. https://www.tandfonline.com/journals/wfpp20

Wik, A. (2018). *Alternatives to inpatient competency restoration programs: Jail-based competency restoration programs.* NRI Analytics Improving Mental Health.

Zapf, P. (2013). *Standardizing protocols for treatment to restore competency to stand trial: Interventions and clinically appropriate time periods.* Washington State Institute for Public Policy.

Zapf, P. A., & Roesch, R. (2011). Future directions in the restoration of competency to stand trial. *Current Directions in Psychological Science, 20*, 43–47. doi:10.1177/0963721410396798

3

Psychotropic Medications and Competency Restoration

SIDRA QADIR, MD AND SHREE SARATHY, MD

This chapter focuses on the prescription of psychotropic medications for defendants lacking the competency to proceed with trial. Restoration efforts in defendants deemed incompetent to proceed integrate various areas of medicolegal practice and require an interdisciplinary approach to be effective. All efforts should be made to maintain the therapeutic alliance with patients while achieving maximum symptom relief with the goal of adjudicative competence.

As psychiatric interventions are often the primary treatment intervention for inpatient (i.e., hospital-based) competency restoration, this particular chapter is largely framed from an inpatient treatment perspective. Unfortunately, a majority of this patient population makes its first contact with mental health services in a correctional setting. There is growing evidence in favor of utilizing trauma-informed care and policies to mitigate adverse outcomes in this setting (Thordarson & Rector, 2020). A compassionate and holistic approach to understanding psychopathology and building rapport can go a long way in breaking the cycle of recidivism.

PRESCRIPTIVE AUTHORITY AND PRIVILEGE

The ability of healthcare providers to prescribe medications, including psychotropic medications, is termed *prescriptive authority*. Those with doctor of medicine (MD) and doctor of osteopathic medicine (DO) degrees have the highest prescriptive authority. They can prescribe controlled substances with a valid Drug Enforcement Administration (DEA) license. Physician assistants (PAs) and nurse practitioners (NPs) also have varying degrees of prescriptive authority based on state-specific laws. To some extent, a varying level of physician supervision is required for PAs universally, while NPs can have prescriptive authority independent of supervision depending on state specific laws and guidelines (Zhang & Patel, 2023).

EVALUATION OF CAPACITY TO MAKE MEDICAL DECISIONS

Assessment of the defendant's capacity to make medical decisions (i.e., a civil forensic mental health assessment), which is distinct from adjudicative competence (i.e., a criminal forensic mental health assessment), is the essential first step before initiation of treatment. Assessment of the capacity to make medical decisions must be made by a treating provider

Sidra Qadir and Shree Sarathy, *Psychotropic Medications and Competency Restoration*. In: *The Competency Restoration Handbook*. Edited by: Laura M. Grossi, Oxford University Press. © Laura M. Grossi (2025). DOI: 10.1093/9780197768075.003.0003 before the prescription of scheduled medications (Grisso & Appelbaum, 1998; Roth et al., 1977). This includes a formal evaluation of a defendant's capacity to make a decision regarding accepting and refusing medications, as well as other nuances of treatment being offered by the treating professional.

The capacity to make healthcare decisions generally has four dimensions: (a) understanding, (b) appreciation, (c) reasoning, and (d) expression of a choice. *Understanding* is the patient's ability to comprehend the treatment's nature, risks, benefits, and alternatives to proposed treatment. Being able to fully understand the offered treatment also includes the risks and outcomes of not receiving treatment. *Appreciation* refers to the patient's ability to personalize their understanding of the offered treatment and apply it to their own unique condition. *Reasoning* refers to the ability to rationalize the decision, and *expression of choice* is the unambiguous and consistent expression of a choice—verbal, written, or otherwise (Palmer & Harmell, 2016). A capacity evaluation is a clinical assessment, and although many instruments are available, no standardized instrument is considered the gold standard (Roth et al., 1977).

Once the patient is determined to have medical decision-making capacity, treatment can proceed in collaboration with the patient. See "My Medication Information" worksheet (Appendix B) for a tool that may be useful in discussions with such patients. On the other hand, if it is determined that the patient lacks the capacity to consent to treatment and requires a surrogate decision-maker, state laws determine the subsequent steps. These typically include an evaluation by a non-treating provider, a court hearing, or both. In certain contexts, it may be allowable to prescribe medications for use on an emergency basis only, before a surrogate decision-maker is formally established. See "Medication Over Objection" (Appendix B) for a worksheet that may be utilized when educating a defendant about the potential for surrogate medical decision-making.

Treatment Over Objection

Involuntary hospitalization does not automatically mean that treating professionals can medicate patients against their will. If treatment over a patient's objection is deemed necessary, rules and regulations established by state laws come into effect. Most states have adopted one of the two models of treatment over objection, as defined by two landmark cases: the "treatment-driven professional judgment approach" based on *Rennie v. Klein* (1983) and the "rights-driven approach" based on *Rogers v. Commissioner of Department of Mental Health* (1983).

The professional judgment model (*Rennie v. Klein*, 1983) allows the medical expert to override the patient's objections to treatment. After it is determined that a patient lacks the capacity to make medical decisions and is refusing treatment deemed necessary, the medical professional assesses the risks associated with nontreatment. This assessment includes elevated risk of violence and potential worsening of symptoms. Either the treating or non-treating provider, or both, or a committee of medical experts, can decide to override the patient's objection to medications based on state-specific procedures.

On the other hand, states that have adopted a rights-driven or substitutive judgment approach follow the *Rogers v. Commissioner of Department of Mental Health* (1983) model. This case established that only a judge, after a judicial hearing, can determine that a person with a mental illness can be treated with psychotropic medication over objection. The treating medical professional cannot treat a patient over objection without adjudication from a judge or magistrate. Of relevance, the court deciding upon proposed treatment over objection (i.e., a civil matter) may not be the same court that ordered competency restoration nor the same court deciding the defendant's criminal cases (i.e., criminal court matters).

Nearly all states follow one process or the other, or a combination of the two, in defining their state-specific procedures for forced medications (Appelbaum & Gutheil, 2007). The state of Utah is unique in being the only state where the court has to find that the patient lacks the capacity to make medical decisions as a prerequisite for civil commitment. None of these models preclude treatment over objection during psychiatric emergencies.

At times, defendants who are incompetent to proceed with their legal case(s) but possess medical decision-making capacity are not willing to accept psychotropic medications as part of the competency restoration process. Even if they are otherwise not presenting an acute danger to self or others, these defendants can still be treated with psychotropic medication over objection. Treatment over objection in this situation, however, requires that the following criteria be met, as defined by *Sell v. U.S.* (2003):

> *(1) the government must present an essential state interest that outweighs the individual's interest in remaining free from medication; (2) the government must prove that there is no less intrusive way of fulfilling its essential interest; and (3) the government must prove by clear and convincing evidence that the medication is medically appropriate.*

Medication is perceived as medically appropriate if:

> *(1) it is likely to render the patient competent, (2) the likelihood and gravity of side effects do not overwhelm its benefits, and (3) it is in the best medical interest of the patient.*

Regarding the state's interest in prosecuting the defendant, factors such as the duration of time defendant has already been confined, seriousness of charges, and the risk associated with release into the community that could be mitigated by treatment at a psychiatric facility are some that are identified. Hence, defendants with nonviolent but serious charges who are found incompetent to proceed with trial can be medicated over their objection solely for the purpose of competency restoration (Fitch, 2007). The treatment must be medically indicated and have a reasonable likelihood of restoring the defendant to competency. It must also be in the best medical interest of the defendant, and side effects should not outweigh the inherent benefits associated with using the medication. The procedure to request a *Sell* hearing varies by jurisdiction but is typically initiated by the treating providers, requiring their review and expert testimony in a court of law.

COMMON PRESENTING PROBLEMS IN RESTORATION

The following discussion focuses on the psychiatric illnesses most commonly encountered in incompetent defendants needing psychiatric care in inpatient, community-based, and jail-based settings. It is important to note that the presentation of mental illness is typically complex, especially in patients with serious mental illness. It is essential to remain cognizant of the co-occurring combination of thought and mood disorders with anxiety disorders, substance use disorders, and personality traits/disorders, and physical health conditions with effects on mental health functioning. Treating professionals must consider various factors in determining the choice of psychotropic medication, including prior history and response to treatment, side-effect profile, and tolerability. Those who consult with prescribers may consult up-to-date references designed for interdisciplinary work, such as the *Quick Reference to Psychiatric Medications* (Preston & Moore, 2021), to best address questions/concerns.

Schizophrenia Spectrum and Other Psychotic Disorders

Schizophrenia and schizoaffective disorder are among the most common diagnoses in this patient population. Treating professionals must consider various factors in determining the choice of psychotropic medication, including prior history and response to treatment, side-effect profile, and tolerability. Prescribers are encouraged to utilize *The American Psychiatric Association Practice Guideline for the Treatment of Patients with Schizophrenia*, 3rd ed. (Keepers et al., 2020) in identifying a treatment plan.

Interventions

A long-standing history of primarily untreated or partially treated mental illness due to nonadherence or limited resources, or both, is prevalent among this patient population. Obtaining a history of treatment to ascertain the efficacy of psychotropic agents is important before the initiation of treatment. Long-acting injectable antipsychotics may be essential in ensuring long-term adherence moving forward, particularly if there is an existing history of poor follow through with prescribed treatment. Medication adherence can be monitored by ensuring precautions at daily medication distribution rounds in inpatient settings, utilizing liquid and dissolvable formulations, and monitoring therapeutic drug levels.

Typical, or first-generation, antipsychotics are dopamine receptor antagonists and have more pronounced extrapyramidal side effects (EPS), anticholinergic side effects, and tardive dyskinesia; these categories of side effects are detailed below. Atypical, or second-generation, antipsychotics have both dopaminergic and serotonergic antagonism and are more effective in treating both positive and negative symptoms of psychosis. Glutamate receptor modulation is yet another evolving avenue of treatment of psychosis. Olanzapine is being hypothesized to have modulatory effects on glutamate receptors along with development of newer treatment options (Egerton et al., 2017).

Starting treatment with second-generation antipsychotics (SGA) and optimizing the dose while monitoring serum levels is generally recommended as the next step. Monitoring drug levels helps determine adherence versus treatment refractoriness if the expected treatment response is lacking. An optimal trial of a different SGA at a therapeutic dose, before switching to a trial of clozapine, is indicated. Clozapine is an underutilized but highly effective treatment option, especially for treatment-resistant psychosis. It has supportive evidence to address both positive and negative symptoms of psychosis, as well as reducing the risk of aggression and suicide, and it can be used to treat tardive dyskinesia. If symptoms continue to persist with optimal dosing and a therapeutic serum level of clozapine, guidelines recommend augmentation of clozapine with a second antipsychotic, preferably aripiprazole (de Bartolomeis et al., 2022). The use of two or more antipsychotics simultaneously ("polypharmacy") is still a controversial approach, although prevalent in clinical practice. This includes using combinations of antipsychotics with different receptor affinities and mechanisms of action. These combinations can work synergistically to target the different theorized pathways of psychosis (Galling, et al., 2017).

It is essential to note the rapidly growing evidence in support of obtaining plasma levels for antipsychotic therapy, especially in treatment-resistant cases. Low antipsychotic levels generally point toward nonadherence, for which adherence monitoring with possible long-acting injectables should be considered. In ultra-rapid metabolizers, not taking enzyme inhibitors or inducers, genetic testing remains an option. However, if a patient develops EPS or akathisia, a medication trial is considered concluded. Some patients do not develop neurologic side effects despite taking high doses of antipsychotics, which speaks to the importance of drug-level monitoring. It is also important to familiarize oneself with response and tolerability thresholds for various antipsychotics, especially for treatment-resistant psychosis, according to emerging evidence. Obtaining through plasma levels is generally recommended (Schatzberg & Charles, 2018).

Electroconvulsive therapy (ECT) remains the treatment of last resort in highly refractory patients. Despite being a long-debated and controversial option, ECT maintains favor in addressing refractory affective disorders and schizophrenia, according to emerging research. Varied molecular and neurobiological mechanisms are hypothesized in the multimodal response to ECT, especially in schizophrenia with catatonic features (Rojas et al., 2022).

Psychotic agitation and impulsivity raise concerns about patient and staff safety and management of the milieu. To address this, mood stabilizers, such as divalproex, are commonly utilized in conjunction with antipsychotics, although the evidence for this remains limited. Improved frustration tolerance can enhance comportment for adjudicative competency. Short-term use of benzodiazepines is also effective in reducing aggression by promoting sedation while antipsychotics take effect, but they can cause paradoxical agitation. Hence, caution is warranted (Paton, 2002).

Side Effects

Common side effects of antipsychotics include, but are not limited to, anticholinergic side effects, EPS, tardive dyskinesia, neuroleptic malignant syndrome (severe but rare), metabolic syndrome (more pronounced with certain antipsychotics such as olanzapine), prolonged QTc interval and other heart rhythm abnormalities, lowering of seizure threshold, and somnolence, among others. All antipsychotics have a black box warning for increased risk of mortality in elderly patients with dementia, so caution should always be used in this patient population.

Anticholinergic side effects are characterized by dry mouth, constipation, blurring of vision, increased heart rate, confusion, and alteration of attention and concentration. EPS include dystonia, akathisia, drug-induced parkinsonism, and tardive dyskinesia. Dystonia is the acute and involuntary muscle contractions associated with recent exposure to antipsychotics. Various muscle groups can be affected including neck, jaw, eyes, abdomen, and torso. Assessment for air-way patency is imperative as breathing and swallowing can be impaired. Akathisia is the subjective feeling of restlessness, and drug-induced parkinsonism presents with rigidity, tremors, and bradykinesia. Tardive dyskinesia is manifested by the painless but debilitating involuntary choreoathetoid movements, mostly impacting facial and tongue muscles, that can be permanent (Lieberman, 2004).

Recent advances in treatment options for anticholinergic side effects include VMAT-2 inhibitors, valbenazine, and deutetrabenazine. However, their use is currently limited due to access and affordability (Solmi et al., 2018). Use of the Abnormal Involuntary Movement Scale (AIMS), lipid panel, comprehensive metabolic panel, and EKG monitoring per schedule can reduce risk. Clozapine has specific monitoring guidelines set forth by the U.S. Food and Drug Administration (FDA) due to the associated risk for agranulocytosis. It also carries other severe but unusual side effects, such as myocarditis.

Psychotropic Formulations

There have been recent advances in the development of new formulations of psychotropics, including liquid, orally dispersible, and short- and long-acting injectable formulations. In correctional settings, liquid formulations can help monitor adherence and reduce the diversion risk. There is evidence in support of liquid antipsychotics having a faster onset of action than the solid oral formulation, which can be efficacious in addressing acute emergencies. Liquid formulations can prevent the need to alter solid oral formulations for dose adjustment, which can result in errors. Liquid oral formulation can also provide an added benefit in patients with swallowing difficulties, such as the elderly (Papazisis & Siafis, 2019).

Olanzapine, risperidone, aripiprazole, and clozapine are some of the antipsychotics available in orodispersible tablets (ODT). Some patients prefer the use of ODT due to its ease of swallowing. Adherence monitoring and surveillance with orodispersible and liquid formulations are more reliable and eliminate the need to alter the solid oral formulations, such as crushing and dissolving the tablets.

Short-acting injectables are used for emergencies and involuntary medication administration over objections in patients lacking the capacity to make medical decisions with the consent of a surrogate decision-maker or court order. Long-acting injectable formulations are essential in reducing medication nonadherence, re-admissions, and relapses and in preventing any risk of diversion associated with correctional settings.

Bipolar Disorders

A significant proportion of defendants deemed incompetent to proceed have a diagnosis of bipolar disorder, with or without psychotic features. The ability of a defendant to proceed with trial is dependent on comportment, among other factors (see Chapter 1). This will determine if they are able to attend court proceedings without causing disruption and sustain attention and concentration in assisting their counsel. Stability of mood enhances a defendant's ability to do so successfully.

Interventions and Side Effects

Mood stabilizers address symptoms of mania and are often anticonvulsants as well. Mood stabilizers are typically available in liquid and sprinkle formulations to maximize adherence and have the added benefit of serum-level monitoring to ensure adherence. The two most commonly utilized mood stabilizers in this population are divalproex and lithium. The mechanism of action of divalproex includes the modulation of gamma-aminobutyric acid (GABA) receptors. It has some efficacy in managing aggression and impulsivity associated with psychosis as well, although the evidence is limited. The specific mechanism of action of lithium is elusive, but the medication can be extremely effective in addressing acute mania, aggression, impulsivity, and suicidality. It has also been posited to be neuroprotective at a cellular level, via neurotrophic effects (Manji et al., 2000). Monitoring guidelines for mood stabilizers are essential to ensure adherence and mitigate side effects.

Lithium, divalproex, lithium, and carbamazepine are approved for acute mania as monotherapy or combined with an SGA. Asenapine, olanzapine, quetiapine, risperidone, and chlorpromazine are also FDA approved for the management of acute mania (Christian et al., 2012, Appendix A). For bipolar depression, the FDA has approved quetiapine, a combination of olanzapine and fluoxetine, and lurasidone (as an adjunct to lithium or divalproex). Familiarity with the usual dosage range, serum therapeutic levels, and drug interactions is critical when using mood stabilizers.

For divalproex, the usual dose is 15–60 mg/kg/day, and a serum level of 15–125 mcg/mL is considered therapeutic. A level of more than 175 mcg/mL is concerning for toxicity and should warrant further assessment for adverse effects (Rahman et al., 2024). Signs of toxicity, which include central nervous system depression, confusion, drowsiness, ataxia, diplopia, tremors, and coma, should warrant an assessment for metabolic acidosis, hypernatremia, hyperammonemia, and hepatotoxicity. Hematological, neurological, and gastrointestinal side effects are commonly seen with divalproex use. Liver function tests should be obtained at baseline and then monitored at regular intervals, especially within six months of starting treatment. A complete blood count, coagulation tests, and ammonia levels should be tested at baseline and periodically, especially before surgical procedures and during pregnancy (Ghodke-Puranik et al., 2013).

Lithium should be avoided in renal impairment with more than 30 mL/min creatinine clearance. Before initiation of treatment, kidney and thyroid function tests must be obtained. At the age of 50 and beyond, a baseline EKG is essential due to the cardiac conduction effects of lithium. Trough levels of lithium should be obtained 8 to 12 hours after the most recent dose, and the recommended therapeutic range is 0.8 to 1.2 mEq/L. During initial titrations of lithium, levels should be obtained frequently. After a maintenance dose is achieved, follow-up levels every two to three months for six months are recommended. Dehydration, infection, and diarrhea can result in patients developing lithium toxicity, which is considered a medical emergency and identified at a level of 2mEq/mL. Interstitial nephritis, sick sinus syndrome, hypotension, seizures, and arrhythmia can occur as a result of lithium toxicity. Hydration and discontinuation of therapy remain the mainstay of treatment for lithium toxicity, though severe cases may require renal dialysis (Chokhawala et al., 2024).

Similarly, therapeutic monitoring for carbamazepine, lamotrigine, and other anticonvulsants is warranted. Specific attention should be paid to monitoring for neutropenia with carbamazepine and Stevens-Johnson syndrome with lamotrigine.

Depressive Disorders

In general, depressive symptoms in patients have a lesser degree of correlation with being found incompetent to proceed. This is because patients with depressive disorders, who lack associated psychotic symptoms, typically retain the reality testing, appreciation, understanding, and reasoning needed to participate in court proceedings. Psychotic symptoms in severe depression, however, can present with the challenge of emotional withdrawal, pessimism, and persecutory beliefs and delusions. Still, depressive disorders are rarely the reason for being found unrestorable. Defendants with the diagnosis of depressive disorders are generally able to achieve adjudicative competence fairly quickly with treatment.

Interventions and Side Effects

Selective serotonin reuptake inhibitors (SSRIs), serotonin and norepinephrine reuptake inhibitors (SNRIs), and antidepressants such as bupropion and mirtazapine are all considered first lines of treatment. Firstline treatment can be augmented with FDA-approved antipsychotics (aripiprazole, brexpiprazole, and quetiapine), while monitoring for tolerability and side effects. Lithium and triiodothyronine (T3), tricyclic antidepressants (TCAs), and monoamine oxidase inhibitors (MAOIs), as well as ECT for patients at acute risk of suicide, are also to be considered. Certain barriers such as duration of court order for restoration to competency, complexities pertaining to administration of ECT over objection, and the need for multiple ECT sessions are some that are commonly encountered in this patient population.

Neurocognitive Disorders

Amnestic disorders resulting in an inability to recall and retain information can impact a defendant's adjudicative competence, especially if the amnesia is surrounding the crime. The diagnosis of amnesia alone, however, does not render a defendant incompetent to proceed, as outlined in *Wilson v. United States* (1968). Various other factors are to be considered, including the ability to assist counsel and testify, the reconstruction of facts by other means, and the government's assistance in rebuilding facts. It was also ruled that a post-trial review should be conducted to determine if the defendant could perform the functions "which are essential to the fairness and accuracy of a criminal proceeding" before conviction. Given this ruling, it is unlikely that a defendant with amnesia but no concurrent mental illness would be deemed incompetent to proceed.

Major neurocognitive disorder, on the other hand, is a more common finding in elderly defendants deemed incompetent to proceed. The underlying causes of dementia include cerebrovascular disease, traumatic brain injury, substance use (particularly chronic alcohol use disorder), chronic malnourishment, autoimmune illnesses, infectious diseases, and brain tumors, among others (Arvanitakis et al., 2019). The extent of cognitive recovery in dementia is generally variable but primarily modest. Neuropsychological assessment can help determine the extent and nature of deficits. A referral for neurological evaluation and radiological/functional imaging is typically warranted. Collateral information from treating providers in the community and family/caregivers can delineate current baseline abilities for an informed clinical opinion.

Treatment options for cognitive recovery are limited to cholinesterase inhibitors (donepezil, rivastigmine, and galantamine) and memantine, which is an N-methyl-D-aspartate (NMDA) antagonist. It is a progressive illness with very modest recovery even with treatment. Defendants with more advanced dementia are often found unrestorable and may require commitment (see Part III).

Personality Disorders

Personality disorders are generally not considered a primary barrier to competency to proceed with trial (see Chapter 10). When personality disorders do interfere with competency, however, it is usually related to a defendant's ability to cooperate with and assist their attorney with their defense. Certain personality disorders (e.g., paranoid personality disorder) present with paranoia, which can impair a defendant's ability to work with their attorney. One court case, *U.S. v. Veatch* (1993), specifically outlined such a scenario, which rendered the defendant suffering from a personality disorder unrestorable. Personality disorders diagnosed in defendants found incompetent to proceed tend to be concurrent with a major mental illness that is impacting their competency. Trials of antipsychotics and mood stabilizers have some evidence of addressing impulsivity and agitation as well as brief psychotic breaks in borderline personality disorder. Schizotypal and schizoid personality disorders can also present with altered perception of reality, and treatment is tailored to individual presentation with antipsychotics used commonly in clinical practice.

Substance Use Disorders

Substance-induced psychotic or mood disorder can render a defendant incompetent to proceed with trial. The basic tenets of treatment are the same as with primary thought and mood disorders. According to the *DSM-5-TR* (American Psychiatric Association, 2022), obtaining evidence for symptoms of a mood or psychotic disorder preceding the use of a substance is essential for diagnostic clarity. The persistence of symptoms beyond an extended period (a month) also indicates a primary psychopathology after acute intoxication or withdrawal from substance use.

Initial competency evaluators suspecting substance withdrawal or intoxication at the time of evaluation are recommended to coordinate with the care providers (e.g., at the jail). It may be indicated for a second evaluation interview to occur when intoxication/withdrawal has resolved, as otherwise a true estimate of a defendant's competency-related abilities (i.e., when sober) cannot be estimated. Competency restoration providers who suspect that a defendant with whom they are working is under the influence of, or withdrawing from, substances of any kind are encouraged to consult with medical staff/providers about protocols for safely facilitating sobriety. Intoxication/withdrawal symptoms can be treated in the community or the jail and may necessitate a delay or pause in competency restoration services; acute intoxication or withdrawal symptoms do not necessitate inpatient competency restoration services.

Some substances, such as benzodiazepine and alcohol, can cause life-threatening withdrawal symptoms that require immediate medical attention. Delirium tremens, a severe condition most commonly caused by abrupt withdrawal from alcohol, has a predicted mortality rate of 37% if untreated (Rahman & Paul, 2023). Symptomatic management of detoxification of substances is tailored to the psychoactive and systemic effects of the used substance. Medication-assisted treatment (MAT) is the evidence-based treatment for opioid and alcohol use disorders but remains underutilized in correctional settings. There is evidence to support that MAT reduces recidivism and the risk of re-arrest for those re-entering communities from correctional settings, in addition to clinical benefits. MAT is typically offered to patients withdrawing from opiates, pregnant women with opioid use disorder, and as maintenance therapy in these settings. Some of the medications used for MAT are methadone, buprenorphine, and naltrexone (Friedmann et al., 2012).

Intellectual and Developmental Disorders

According to the DSM-5-TR, an intellectual developmental disorder is identified as a disorder with onset during the developmental period. Restorative efforts for competency for this patient population present a specific challenge as these deficits are both cognitive and adaptative by definition. Limitations on reasoning, problem-solving, planning, abstract thinking, judgment, and academic learning are all concerns that highlight difficulties during the restoration process. Collateral information from community resources can help determine the level of functioning in conceptual, social, and practical domains. Due to the concrete and largely immutable nature of deficits, the rates of being unrestorably incompetent are high in this patient population (Wall & Christopher, 2012).

Severe intellectual deficits are also commonly associated with impulsivity, aggression, and self-injurious behaviors. Antipsychotics, mood stabilizers, antidepressants, and anxiolytics are used for behavioral dysregulation and concurrent anxiety and impulsivity, with variable efficacy and response depending on individual outcomes. Comorbidities also include attention deficit/hyperactivity disorder and various neurological conditions (e.g., including seizure disorders), which can complicate the psychotropic management due to side effects such as worsening or anxiety and lowering of seizure threshold. Aripiprazole and risperidone are the only FDA-approved antipsychotics for behavioral dysregulation in autism spectrum disorder, which can co-occur with other neurodevelopmental disorders. Comorbidities also include attention deficit/hyperactivity disorder and various neurological conditions (e.g., seizure disorders), which can complicate the psychotropic management due to side-effects such as worsening or anxiety and lowering of seizure threshold.

POSSIBLE COMPLICATING FACTORS

There are naturally a number of factors that may complicate prescribing psychotropic medications. For example, various medical conditions may affect a person's mental health functioning and ability to tolerate medications. Screening for such conditions is necessary at the start of the therapeutic relationship (i.e., intake), so that an appropriate mental health diagnosis can be established and symptoms can be effectively treated. When a complicating medical condition is identified, a referral to a primary care physician or relevant specialist may be indicated so that appropriate intervention can occur (e.g., vitamins/thiamine for chronic alcohol use, antibiotics for urinary tract infections [UTIs], etc.). When psychological testing appears indicated, a referral to a clinical psychologist or neuropsychologist may be similarly indicated. The following factors we believe are particularly relevant, given higher prevalence rates; however, these do not comprise a comprehensive list of possible complicating factors.

Diversion and Misuse of Prescription Medications

Prescribing in correctional settings is not without its challenges and complexities. The decisions made by healthcare professionals are informed by local policies, safety standards, cost-effectiveness, and clinical effectiveness, as well as the potential risk of diversion. The diversion, sale, and distribution of prescription medications is a commonly encountered phenomenon in this patient population, often occurring under duress. Quetiapine, bupropion, mirtazapine, buspirone, and benzodiazepine are some of the commonly misused medications. Misuse can take various forms, including sharing, forcefully obtaining, or purchasing from other patients, as well as hoarding to consume prescribed medication in doses higher than prescribed or to conceal nonadherence. These medications are sometimes snorted for psychoactive effects. "Crush and float" orders are primarily ineffective at reducing this risk, due to the settling of solid particles that are retained for snorting.

Individual surveillance for each medication pass can be time-consuming and presents staffing challenges. The potential impact of the misuse of medications on the correctional system is significant, underscoring the urgency and responsibility of implementing safe prescribing measures, such as limiting or eliminating the use of commonly misused medications; monitoring serum levels of medications; and using ODT, liquid, and long-acting injectable formulations to reduce the risk of diversion. Crushing and mixing solid tablets in pudding or applesauce is commonly used to improve adherence and reduce the risk of snorting or hoarding. Regular room checks and monitoring for alteration of mentation in patients (e.g., somnolence, agitation, irritability, and development of side effects not expected with prescribed medications or dosages) should prompt the healthcare providers to address possible diversion and misuse.

Pregnancy

There are multiple ethical issues inherent to treating pregnant individuals with mental illness due to the associated risks to the fetus in particular (Desai & Chandra, 2009). Antipsychotics, other than risperidone and paliperidone, are generally considered safe during pregnancy (Betcher & Wisner, 2020). Quetiapine and olanzapine, while safe to use during pregnancy, can increase the risk of gestational diabetes. Dosage adjustment is recommended due to altered pharmacokinetics during pregnancy. Lithium carries a significant risk of cardiac malformation and spontaneous abortion, mainly if exposure occurs in the first trimester and at higher doses (Fornaro et al., 2020). Divalproex is associated with the potential risk of neural tube defects in the fetus, estimated to be 10 times higher than the general population. Antipsychotics, other than risperidone and paliperidone, are generally considered safe during pregnancy. Quetiapine and olanzapine, while safe to use during pregnancy, can increase the risk of gestational diabetes. Dosage adjustment is recommended due to altered pharmacokinetics during pregnancy. There is recent evidence surrounding the use of SSRIs indicating a slight increase in the risk for adverse neonatal outcomes (Lebin & Novick, 2022). These include, but are not limited to, preterm delivery and neonatal ICU admissions. Although there is no current evidence for neurodevelopmental disorders associated with SSRI use during pregnancy, inconclusive evidence persists for some adverse cognitive and affective outcomes for the newborn.

Malingering

Malingering refers to the feigning and/or exaggerating symptoms for secondary gain. This is a commonly encountered scenario in pretrial settings, with an estimated prevalence ranging from 5% to 45% in North America. Various testing measures, including the Test of Memory Malingering (TOMM), the Rey 15-Item Test (FIT), the Miller Forensic Assessment of Symptoms Test (M-FAST), the Structured Interview of Reported Symptoms, 2nd ed. (SIRS-2), and the Minnesota Multiphasic Personality Inventory-3 (MMPI-3), are utilized in formal malingering assessment (Myers et al., 2013). However, clinical interviews, observation, and collateral information are often the most valuable in ruling out malingering. Testing alone is not confirmatory of malingering and must have clinical correlation. Thorough assessment at times requires clinical evaluation observation over a period of time in an inpatient setting, regardless of testing outcomes. If symptom presentation and historical information about disease progression is atypical, inconsistent, or appears exaggerated, further assessment to rule out malingering is warranted. Open-ended questions are encouraged to assess for inconsistencies and reduce suggestibility (Resnick, 1999).

It is also important to note that malingering does not mean absence of genuine symptoms. Exaggeration and misrepresentation of present symptoms for secondary gain is also commonly observed in clinical settings. Patients who need treatment for ongoing symptoms of mental illness must be provided the necessary treatment even if it is determined that they may be exaggerating some symptoms for secondary gain. If the patient reports or continues to present with worsening symptoms with treatment, or no treatment intervention seems to make any difference in presentation, there is reason to suspect malingering. It always helps to have multiple data points of observation (i.e., by nursing staff and/or mental health technicians, when interacting with family during visitations, etc.), which can ascertain a pattern of discrepancy of report versus observation of symptoms, as well as cognitive abilities and acuity.

LOCATION OF MEDICATION-FOCUSED INTERVENTIONS

Inpatient Settings

On an inpatient basis, medication adherence can be monitored by ensuring precautions at scheduled medication distribution rounds in inpatient settings, utilizing liquid and dissolvable formulations, and monitoring therapeutic drug levels. An inpatient setting also lends itself well to making medication changes, dosage adjustments, and monitoring therapeutic levels of drug effectively. It should be emphasized, however, that inpatient settings are not the only settings where interventions with psychotropic medications can occur. Given the burden on inpatient pretrial services, medication management for further remission of symptoms and medication maintenance can continue in the jail or community outpatient settings. Thus, patients should be discharged from the inpatient level of care as soon as they are deemed competent to proceed, regardless of remaining residual symptoms, which can be addressed in a lower level care setting.

Jail Settings

Prescribers working in correctional settings are encouraged to consult the "American Academy of Psychiatry and the Law Practice Resource for Prescribing in Corrections" (Tamburello et al., 2018). Certain barriers can preclude effective medication management for jail-based treatment. They include, but are not limited to, suboptimal access to prescribers for medication management and follow-up and complicated infrastructure to establish or enforce medication over objection for patients lacking decision-making capacity. In some jurisdictions, medication over objection is legally allowed, but pretrial detention facilities have no mechanism for actually providing defendants with medications involuntarily.

Limited formulary, constrained resources and audits, diversion, and polypharmacy are some of the other challenges for providers in jail settings. Understaffing and rapid staff turnover can also disrupt the continuation of care, hamper staff training and education efforts, and result in suboptimal patient outcomes.

Community Settings

Defendants on pretrial release must be offered treatment in the community, assuming that mental health treatment is indicated. Given adequate resources, if pretrial release has been denied or the defendant does not meet conditions for pretrial release, treatment may be initiated in the jail. Otherwise, treatment resumes in a mental health facility (Appelbaum & Gutheil, 2007).

The transfer of care between inpatient and jail services can be challenging, particularly in ensuring consistent access to care and medications, such as long-acting injectables, to prevent relapse. Successful treatment of opioid use disorder in jail settings with MAT and the subsequent transition to the community offer hope by potentially preventing relapse and overdose.

TREATMENT OF PSYCHIATRIC EMERGENCIES

Defendants who are bonded out and receiving community-based restoration are typically perceived as posing a low risk of harm to themselves or others in the community. Those who pose a greater risk of harm or recidivism tend to be denied bond, such that restoration interventions occur in an inpatient or jail setting. In inpatient and jail-based settings, mental health staff may be available around the clock; this is important, as timely psychiatric intervention may aid in the management of psychiatric emergencies. Aggression and agitation and posing a danger to self and others represent a psychiatric emergency requiring immediate intervention. Self-report and historical risk factors must be assessed for risk of aggression during psychiatric evaluation. It is essential to individualize care and mitigate factors that can contribute to aggression to avoid further stigmatizing and isolating patients with serious mental illnesses.

Psychopharmacological and behavioral interventions to address the imminent danger are paramount in ensuring the safety of the patient and the staff. Once a psychiatric emergency has been recognized, the first step is to assess the severity of the situation and the patient's symptoms to determine the best next course of action. As noted, self-report and historical risk factors must be considered during psychiatric evaluation. The physician must choose the least restrictive means of addressing the emergency (e.g., voluntary relocation away from a stressor). There are times when isolative seclusion may be less restrictive than the administration of emergency psychotropic medication, especially if the emergency is unrelated to symptom exacerbation. If it is determined that emergency medication is required, the physician must choose whether oral medication would be adequate to address the emergency or if intramuscular medicines are needed. According to the American Association for Emergency Psychiatry's consensus statement (Wilson et al., 2012) concerning oral medications, olanzapine and risperidone are considered first-line agents for intervention. Haloperidol, in combination with a benzodiazepine, would be regarded as a second-line recommendation for patients with a known psychiatric disorder. Regarding intramuscular medications, these are to be considered if the patient declines oral medications or clinical urgency necessitates intramuscular intervention. Olanzapine and ziprasidone are again considered first-line agents, while haloperidol, with a benzodiazepine, is a second-line agent for addressing psychiatric emergencies. Diphenhydramine is routinely used in conjunction with haloperidol to offset possible EPS symptoms and promote sedation. It should be avoided in delirium and can have anticholinergic side effects and paradoxical worsening of agitation.

In a psychiatric emergency, the goal of treatment should always be to utilize the least restrictive method to manage and mitigate imminent risk. Verbal de-escalation, offering a quiet alternative environment, and pharmacological interventions are preferred over physical restraint (Knox & Holloman, 2012). If needed, physical restraint should only be used for the minimum amount of time required to de-escalate the situation while considering other less restrictive means. Continuous assessment and monitoring during the episode should focus on whether the imminent danger has resolved to reduce the time a patient is restrained (Hoffmann et al., 2021).

Assessing vital signs, monitoring for side effects, and considering alternative and behavioral interventions are crucial aspects of managing psychiatric emergencies. Medical issues such as untreated UTIs resulting in alteration of mental status should be considered for intervention following the resolution of the psychiatric emergency, especially if there is a change from baseline when managing agitation. This may involve consultation or collaboration between the psychiatric prescriber and general medical provider.

CULTURAL CONSIDERATIONS AND TECHNOLOGY

Education and awareness about linguistic and cultural diversity is becoming increasingly relevant as the patient population shifts in correctional settings. Age, race, gender, religion, and ethnicity, along with the complicated "prison culture," impact patient outcomes (Kapoor et al., 2013). Limited access to interpretation services is generally considered to be the biggest barrier to providing culturally informed care and video/audio conferencing can help provide access to quality care to the patients including education regarding competency restoration.

When medical care or treatment contradicts the patient's religion, an advanced directive is typically required for the patients lacking the capacity to make clinical decisions. Both the medication and inert additives such as gelatin can be the reason the patient refuses to take medications for religious reasons. Alternatives and available formulations should be discussed and offered for the best outcome. In certain situations, the necessity of a potential court review becomes crucial in delineating the next steps.

REFERENCES

American Psychiatric Association (2022). *Diagnostic and statistical manual of mental disorders* (5th ed., text revision).

Appelbaum, P. S., & Gutheil, T. G. (2007). *Clinical handbook of psychiatry & the law* (4th ed.). Lippincott Williams & Wilkins.

Arvanitakis, Z., Shah, R. C., & Bennett, D. A. (2019). Diagnosis and management of dementia: Review. *JAMA: The Journal of the American Medical Association, 322*(16), 1589–1599. doi:10.1001/jama.2019.4782

Betcher, H. K., & Wisner, K. L. (2020). Psychotropic treatment during pregnancy: Research synthesis and clinical care principles. *Journal of Women's Health, 29*(3), 310–318. doi:10.1089/jwh.2019.7781

Chokhawala, K., Lee, S., & Saadabadi, A. (2024, January). *Lithium*. StatPearls Publishing. https://www.ncbi.nlm.nih.gov/books/NBK519062/

Christian, R., Saavedra, L., Gaynes, B. N., Sheitman, B., Wines, R. C. M., Jonas, D. E., . . . Carey, T. S. (2012, Feb.). *Future research needs for first- and second-generation antipsychotics for children and young adults*. Agency for Healthcare Research and Quality. https://www.ncbi.nlm.nih.gov/books/NBK84656/

De Bartolomeis, A., Ciccarelli, M., Vellucci, L., Fornaro, M., Iasevoli, F., & Barone, A. (2022). Update on novel antipsychotics and pharmacological strategies for treatment-resistant schizophrenia. *Expert Opinion on Pharmacotherapy, 23*(18), 2035–2052. doi:10.1080/14656566.2022.2145884

Desai, G., & Chandra, P. S. (2009). Ethical issues in treating pregnant women with severe mental illness. *Indian Journal of Medical Ethics, 6*(2), 75–77. doi:10.20529/ijme.2009.025

Egerton, A., Bhachu, A., Merritt, K., McQueen, G., Szulc, A., & McGuire, P. (2017). Effects of antipsychotic administration on brain glutamate in schizophrenia: A systematic review of longitudinal 1H-MRS studies. *Frontiers in Psychiatry, 8*(66), published online. doi:10.3389/fpsyt.2017.00066

Fitch, W. L. (2007). AAPL practice guideline for the forensic psychiatric evaluation of competence to stand trial: An American legal perspective. *The Journal of the American Academy of Psychiatry and the Law, 35*(4), 509–513. https://jaapl.org/content/35/4/509.long

Fornaro, M., Maritan, E., Ferranti, R., Zaninotto, L., Miola, A., Anastasia, A., . . . Solmi, M. (2020). Lithium exposure during pregnancy and the postpartum period: A systematic review and meta-analysis of safety and efficacy outcomes. *The American Journal of Psychiatry, 177*(1), 76–92. doi:10.1176/appi.ajp.2019.19030228

Friedmann, P. D., Hoskinson, R., Gordon, M., Schwartz, R., Kinlock, T., Knight, K., . . . Frisman, L. K. (2012). Medication-assisted treatment in criminal justice agencies affiliated with the criminal justice-drug abuse treatment studies (CJ-DATS): availability, barriers, and intentions. *Substance Abuse: Official Publication of the Association for Medical Education and Research in Substance Abuse, 33*(1), 9–18. doi:10.1080/08897077.2011.611460

Galling, B., Roldán, A., Hagi, K., Rietschel, L., Walyzada, F., Zheng W., . . . Correll, C. U. (2017, February). Antipsychotic augmentation vs. monotherapy in schizophrenia: Systematic review, meta-analysis and meta-regression analysis. *World Psychiatry, 16*(1), 77–89. doi:10.1002/wps.20387

Ghodke-Puranik, Y., Thorn, C. F., Lambda, J. K., Leeder, J. S., Song, W., Birnbaum, A. K., . . . Klein, T. E. (2013, April). Valproic acid pathway: Pharmacokinetics and pharmacodynamics. *Pharmacogenetics and Genomics, 23*(4), 236–241. doi:10.1097/FPC.0b013e32835ea0b2

Grisso, T., & Appelbaum, P. S. (1998). *Assessing competence to consent to treatment: A guide for physicians and other health professionals*. Oxford University Press.

Hoffmann, J. A., Pergjika, A., Konicek, C. E., & Reynolds, S. L. (2021). Pharmacologic management of acute agitation in youth in the emergency department. *Pediatric Emergency Care, 37*(8), 417–422. doi:10.1097/PEC.0000000000002510

Keepers, G. A., Fochtmann, L. J., Anzia, J. M., Benjamin, S., Lyness, J. M., Mojtabai, . . . Hong, S. H. (2020). *The American Psychiatric Association practice guideline for the treatment of patients with schizophrenia* (3rd ed.). doi:10.1176/appi.books.9780890424841

Kapoor, R., Dike, C., Burns, C., Carvalho, V., & Griffith, E. E. H. (2013). Cultural competence in correctional mental health. *International Journal of Law and Psychiatry, 36*(3–4), 273–280. doi:10.1016/j.ijlp.2013.04.016

Knox, D. K., & Holloman, G. H. (2012). Use and avoidance of seclusion and restraint: Consensus statement of the American Association for Emergency Psychiatry project beta seclusion and restraint workgroup. *The Western Journal of Emergency Medicine, 13*(1), 35–40. doi:10.5811/westjem.2011.9.6867

Lebin, L. G., & Novick, A. M. (2022). Selective serotonin reuptake inhibitors (SSRIs) in pregnancy: An updated review on risks to mother, fetus, and child. *Current Psychiatry Reports, 24*(11), 687–695. doi:10.1007/s11920-022-01372-x

Lieberman, J. A. (2004). Managing anticholinergic side effects. *Primary Care Companion to the Journal of Clinical Psychiatry, 6*(2), 20–23. https://www.ncbi.nlm.nih.gov/pubmed/16001097

Manji, H. K., Moore, G. J., & Chen, G. (2000). Clinical and preclinical evidence for the neurotrophic effects of mood stabilizers: Implications for the pathophysiology and treatment of manic-depressive illness. *Biological Psychiatry, 48*(8), 740–754. doi:10.1016/s0006-3223(00)00979-3

Myers, W. C., Hall, R. C. W., & Tolou-Shams, M. (2013). Prevalence and assessment of malingering in homicide defendants using the Mini-Mental State Examination and the Rey 15-Item Memory Test. *Homicide Studies, 17*(3), 314–328. doi:10.1177/1088767912465609

Palmer, B. W., & Harmell, A. L. (2016). Assessment of healthcare decision-making capacity. *Archives of Clinical Neuropsychology: The Official Journal of the National Academy of Neuropsychologists, 31*(6), 530–540. doi:10.1093/arclin/acw051

Papazisis, G., & Siafis, S. (2019). The added value of liquid antipsychotics: The case of quetiapine. *Current Clinical Pharmacology, 14*(2), 101–107. doi:10.2174/1574884713666181102145236

Paton, C. (2002). Benzodiazepines and disinhibition: A review. *Psychiatric Bulletin, 26*(12), 460–462. doi:10.1192/pb.26.12.460

Preston, J. & Moore, B. A. (2021). *Quick reference to psychiatric medications.* https://www.apadivisions.org/division-55/councils/research/quick-reference.pdf

Rahman, M., Awosika, A. O., & Nguyen, H. (2024). *Valproic acid.* StatPearls Publishing. https://www.ncbi.nlm.nih.gov/books/NBK559112/

Rahman, A., & Paul, M. (2023, August). *Delirium tremens.* StatPearls Publishing. https://www.ncbi.nlm.nih.gov/books/NBK482134/

Rennie v. Klein, 720 F. 2d 266 (1983).

Resnick, P. J. (1999). The detection of malingered psychosis. *The Psychiatric Clinics of North America, 22*(1), 159–172. doi:10.1016/s0193-953x(05)70066-6

Rogers v. Commissioner of Department of Mental Health, 390 Mass. 489 (1983) (Rodgers IV).

Rojas, M., Ariza, D., Ortega, Á., Riaño-Garzón, M. E., Chávez-Castillo, M., Pérez, J. L., . . . Bermúdez, V. (2022). Electroconvulsive therapy in psychiatric disorders: A narrative review exploring neuroendocrine-immune therapeutic mechanisms and clinical implications. *International Journal of Molecular Sciences, 23*(13), 6918. doi:10.3390/ijms23136918

Roth, L. H., Meisel, A., & Lidz, C. W. (1977). Tests of competency to consent to treatment. *The American Journal of Psychiatry, 134*(3), 279–284. doi:10.1176/ajp.134.3.279

Schatzberg, A. F., & Charles, D. (2018). The black book of psychotropic dosing and monitoring. *Psychopharmacology Bulletin, 48*(1), 64–153. Retrieved from https://www.ncbi.nlm.nih.gov/pubmed/29382960

Sell v. U.S., 539 U.S. 166 (2003).

Solmi, M., Pigato, G., Kane, J. M., & Correll, C. U. (2018). Treatment of tardive dyskinesia with VMAT-2 inhibitors: A systematic review and meta-analysis of randomized controlled trials. *Drug Design, Development and Therapy, 12*, 1215–1238. doi:10.2147/DDDT.S133205

Tamburello, A., Metzner, J., Fergusen, E., Champion, M., Ford, E., Gancy, G., . . . Ourada, J. (2018). The American Academy of Psychiatry and the Law Practice Resource for Prescribing in Corrections. *Journal of the American Academy of Psychiatry and the Law*, *46*(2), 242–243. doi:10.29158/JAAPL.003762-18

Thordarson, H., & Rector, T. (2020). From trauma-blind to trauma-informed: Re-thinking criminalization and the role of trauma in persons with serious mental illness. *CNS Spectrums*, *25*(5), 577–583. doi:10.1017/S1092852920001169

U.S. v. Veatch, 842 F. Supp. 480 (W.D. Okla. 1993).

Wall, B. W., & Christopher, P. P. (2012). A training program for defendants with intellectual disabilities who are found incompetent to proceed. *Journal of the American Academy of Psychiatry and the Law*, *40*(3), 366–373. https://jaapl.org/content/40/3/366

Wilson v. United States, 391 F.2d 460 (D.C. Cir. 1968).

Wilson, M. P., Pepper, D., Currier, G. W., Holloman, G. H., Jr, & Feifel, D. (2012). The psychopharmacology of agitation: Consensus statement of the American Association for Emergency Psychiatry project beta psychopharmacology workgroup. *The Western Journal of Emergency Medicine*, *13*(1), 26–34. doi:10.5811/westjem.2011.9.6866

Zhang, P., & Patel, P. (2023, November). *Practitioners and prescriptive authority*. StatPearls Publishing. https://www.ncbi.nlm.nih.gov/books/NBK574557/

PART III

Cognitive Abilities as a Barrier to Competency

4

Competency Restoration for Defendants With Intellectual and Developmental Disabilities (the Slater Method)

MADDISON SCHIAFO, PHD AND KEVIN WAYMIRE, PHD

INTELLECTUAL AND DEVELOPMENTAL DISABILITIES

In this chapter, we discuss how intellectual and developmental disabilities (ID/DD or IDD) may serve as barriers to adjudicative competence. We provide an overview of the *Slater Method*, a structured program for restoration for individuals with ID/DD and discuss the practical utility of this approach across restoration settings.

Developmental disabilities (DD) are characterized by deficits in physical, cognitive, or behavioral areas of functioning, which tend to manifest during the developmental period and persist throughout the lifetime. Examples may include autism spectrum disorder (ASD), Down syndrome, and intellectual disabilities. Intellectual disabilities (ID) are a subtype of developmental disability typified by cognitive limitations, such as learning/memory and executive functioning (e.g., planning, organizing, reasoning) deficits. ID deficits are chronic in nature and are accompanied by affective deficits in addition to cognitive deficits. Additionally, IDs are characterized by difficulties in the development of adaptive behaviors (i.e., age-appropriate skills beginning in childhood), which ultimately lead to diminished success relative to typical adult functioning (American Psychological Association, 2023). Impairment may range from mild to profound based on an individual's adaptive deficits (i.e., without ongoing support) in one or more functional domains of daily life (e.g., communication, social participation, and independent living). Severity is also graded based on functioning across multiple environments, such as school, home, or work (American Psychiatric Association, 2022).

A majority of individuals (i.e., around 85%) with ID present with mild impairment (Patel et al., 2020). Mild ID tends to have less clear etiology than more severe ID, and it is often influenced by environmental or external risk factors such as low socioeconomic status (Harris, 2006). Severe intellectual disabilities tend to have underlying genetic (e.g., Prader-Willi syndrome, Down syndrome, fragile X syndrome), biological (e.g., phenylketonuria), or neurological (e.g., neurodegenerative diseases or infections) contributions that can be in identified in more than two-thirds of cases (Patel et al., 2020). Given that a majority of individuals with ID tend to present with mild impairment, and may not have accompanying developmental disabilities, this chapter will focus primarily on restoration with individuals whose primary difficulties are attributable to ID.

Maddison Schiafo and Kevin Waymire, *Competency Restoration for Defendants With Intellectual and Developmental Disabilities (the Slater Method)*. In: *The Competency Restoration Handbook*. Edited by: Laura M. Grossi, Oxford University Press.
 DOI: 10.1093/9780197768075.003.0004

As outlined above, individuals with ID evidence a variety of cognitive and executive functioning limitations, such as expressive and receptive language, reading and writing, abstract thinking, and planning, which can adversely impact their ability to learn and retain information. Importantly, this does not reflect an inability to do so but rather a variability in abilities and associated educational needs. This suggests a unique and tailored approach to education to promote retention may be necessary for ID individuals, compared to those with neurotypical cognitive functioning (Hauser et al., 2014). Educational research suggests that individuals with intellectual impairments may learn best when offered specialized teaching models (Ault et al., 1989; Forness & Kavale, 1993).

Indeed, the individualized educational needs of people with IDD is so supported that it has been progressively integrated into the U.S. judicial system over recent decades, eventually becoming enshrined into law under the Individuals with Disabilities Education Act (IDEA). The IDEA indicates that students with disabilities have a right to an education that is tailored to their needs. Prior to the IDEA, the U.S. legal system saw increasing attention to the needs of children with disabilities over the 1970s and 1980s through the All Handicapped Children Act, which afforded caregivers additional input on educational plans for children with disabilities. Around 1990, the All Handicapped Children Act transitioned to the IDEA, which expanded the definition for qualifying disabilities and ultimately provided more comprehensive resources for students in order to maximize their education by tailoring education to their needs.

Case law relative to individuals with ID has also shaped several key associated issues with regards to legal proceedings. In terms of adjudicative competence issues, individuals meeting criteria for ID may represent rather unique challenges in terms of the competency standard, as described in *Dusky v. United States* (1960). Specifically, *Godinez v. Moran* (1993) addressed potential difficulties individuals experiencing ID may face in terms of understanding the gravity of certain waivers related to competency—namely pleading guilty and proceeding without legal counsel. The Supreme Court determined that defendants seeking to waive their right to trial and right to counsel must be held to the same standard as defendants competent to proceed generally. Additionally, the Court decided a competency-related matter relative to execution (i.e., as opposed to trial competency); *Atkins v. Virginia* (2002) prohibited the execution of individuals meeting criteria for ID in the context of the Eighth Amendment's ban on cruel and unusual punishment (Pifer, 2016). Case law resulting from *Hall v. Florida* (2014) went a step further, mandating that additional evidence beyond a rigid intelligence quotient (IQ) score of 70—such as adaptive functioning—be taken into consideration when determining if an individual meets criteria for ID (Cooke et al., 2015). In the same vein, competency restoration providers would be doing themselves and their patients a disservice by considering IQ only relative to service provision without a more nuanced understanding of their patient's adaptive functioning capabilities.

ID AS A BARRIER TO COMPETENCY

At the outset, it is important to mention that individuals meeting criteria for ID are overrepresented in the criminal justice system, both as victims and perpetrators of crime (Stancliffe & Frantz, 2024). The current section will focus only on individuals alleged to have committed offenses as opposed to survivors of criminal contact.

Although several studies have attempted to estimate the precise number of incarcerated individuals with ID, numbers vary widely. Spreat (2020) pointed out that accepting a midpoint in varying estimates translates to roughly 7% of individuals incarcerated in the U.S. meeting criteria for ID. In other words, the proportion of incarcerated individuals with ID may be seven times that of the general U.S. population. Furthermore, individuals in correctional settings tend to present with mild ID as opposed to more severe presentations (Wall et al., 2003a). Individuals with ID may encounter the justice system in a variety of ways, some of which may be a product of a lack of community resources to support these individuals. For instance, individuals with ID may lack appreciation for aspects of their behavior that violate laws (e.g., taking snacks from a convenience store because they are hungry without appreciation that this is illegal), resulting in arrests. Alternatively, they may have difficulty navigating public transit to attend required necessary appointments, resulting in violations of probation (e.g., for failure to comply with court requirements) or increased likelihood to utilize illegal methods as a simpler solution (e.g., taking a bicycle without permission).

Those with more severe intellectual and adaptive functioning impairments are more likely to be identified as eligible for, and provided with, more frequent care and supervision, which reduces the opportunity to engage in acts for which they might be arrested. For instance, individuals with impairment requiring significant support may have legal guardians or reside in group homes due to an inability to effectively care for themselves. The oversight inherent to these situations likely decreases an individual's opportunity and/or need to engage in acts that violate the law. Those with milder levels of impairment, however, may be less likely to receive services (e.g., they may not qualify for services due to the level of impairment not being severe enough) and may have more opportunities to encounter law enforcement (i.e., with more autonomy, and less structure/supervision). Individuals with mild ID are also less likely to be identified as having a disability due to their outward presentation appearing more consistent with nondisabled individuals. This makes them more vulnerable both in the community where they reside (e.g., being taken advantage of by criminogenic peers) and in a correctional setting. Salekin and colleagues (2010) also highlight that, often times, those with mild or borderline ID are not easily distinguishable, given that IQ occurs on a continuum.

Accordingly, it is likely competency restoration providers are *more likely* to encounter patients struggling with intellectual deficits than they might otherwise via community-based treatment. It is estimated that up to 36% of individuals with ID/DD who are evaluated for adjudicative competence are determined to be incompetent to stand trial. In this context, it is paramount that competency restoration providers understand the difficulties and limitations potentially faced by these individuals relative to understanding the proceedings against them in a factual and rational manner, as well as in terms of effectively communicating with their legal counsel.

Appelbaum and Appelbaum (1994) describe impairments across cognition, conation, and communication that can interact and result in impairment across adjudicative competence. As with individuals with serious mental illness, presentations and barriers among individuals with ID are multifaceted in nature. Individuals with ID may demonstrate impairment in their ability to understand factual information related to the legal proceedings. Indeed, these individuals are more likely to demonstrate deficits in factual knowledge as a primary barrier to competency compared to those incompetent as a result of psychiatric impairment who tend to present with deficits across rational appreciation and the ability to consult with their attorneys (Anderson & Hewitt, 2002). For example, they may demonstrate impairment in rote memorization and require repetitive exposure to the same information to facilitate recall. Alternatively, some individuals may demonstrate significant skill relative to rote memorization; however, they may struggle with truly understanding and applying relevant concepts, particularly if abstract thinking is required. Further, their cognitive deficits may impede decision-making abilities as well as a defendant's ability to serve as an active participant in their proceedings against them. Cognitive deficits can include deficits in executive functioning with regard to organization, planning, and logical reasoning, for example. Furthermore, some individuals with ID/DD demonstrate a tendency to conform and agree to please others. Such individuals may be more likely to blindly defer to their attorney without a genuine appreciation for the identified strategy and its associated risks and benefits. An individual opined as incompetent may have been thought to lack competence as a result of one or many of these deficits.

COMPETENCY-RELATED ASSESSMENT WITH ID INDIVIDUALS

Testing as a component of adjudicative competence evaluations and competency restoration is not necessarily common practice, though it can have utility. Murrie and colleagues (2020) found that intelligence tests were the most commonly used kinds of tests (35.9%) among a sample of practitioners that employed psychological testing in competence to stand trial evaluations. Of research that has addressed the restoration of individuals with ID, most can agree that restoration with these individuals requires careful assessment of one's cognitive abilities in order to tailor interventions to the appropriate level of functioning. To this end, cognitive and/or intelligence testing can be useful to identify a client's strengths and weaknesses, particularly in the context of limited historical records (e.g., pertaining to educational history). For instance, testing may be useful at times to understand a client's verbal knowledge, comprehension abilities, and/or working memory in order to craft one's approach in sessions. Someone with higher verbal abilities but more limited working memory abilities may require less tailoring of language but shorter and more repetitive sessions. Conversely, if an individual has significant impairments in verbal knowledge and abstract reasoning, they may likely require simplified language in addition to extensive practice applying knowledge to situations.

With regard to forensic assessment instruments, the Competence Assessment for Standing Trial for Defendants with Mental Retardation (CAST-MR) is one of the only measures validated for individuals with ID (Melton, 2017) and assesses three primary areas: *basic legal concepts, skills to assist defense, and understanding case events*. The measure combines multiple choice questions with open-ended questions about the individual's case. The CAST-MR has also been used to assist in determining pre- and post-intervention competency knowledge (Anderson & Hewitt, 2002). Notable criticisms of the CAST-MR focus on the lack of real-world generalizability of the measure. For example, the multiple-choice format does not translate to the real-world demands of a trial process (Grisso, 2002).

As with psychiatric barriers to competency, providers should always consider the genuineness of a client's presenting cognitive deficits. Research on the feigning of intellectual deficits has had little attention, and so there are few effective methods at distinguishing genuine intellectual deficits in comparison to those feigning said intellectual and adaptive deficits (Salekin et al., 2010). As ID is a lifelong disorder with onset prior to age 18, providers should pay close attention to any historical information that can help distinguish between those who have had difficulties throughout their life in comparison to those who may suddenly be presenting with cognitive difficulties. Importantly, cognitive deficits that first appear in adulthood do not necessarily indicate a feigned presentation. Rather, these may be suggestive of an acquired deficit, such as a traumatic brain injury or neurodegenerative process (e.g., dementia).

RESTORATION WITH INDIVIDUALS WITH ID

Although defendants, including a majority of individuals with ID, are presumed to be competent by the court, it is posited that many individuals with ID may likely never have been competent to begin with. That is, many individuals with ID may never have possessed the knowledge and abilities necessary for competency because of their cognitive deficits. In fact, the competency restoration process has oft been described as the *attainment* of such knowledge as opposed to the *restoration* of such knowledge (Anderson & Hewitt, 2002). Only approximately one-third to one-half of defendants with an ID are estimated to attain competency if initially opined as not competent (The Arc's National Center on Criminal Justice & Disability [NCCJD], 2017). This is likely, in part, not only due to the chronic deficits inherent to ID, but also a lack of interventions tailored to those deficits. As suggested above, there is need for a thorough assessment of domains of impairment for individuals with ID so that restoration can be tailored to address the specific deficits. However, there is also a distinct lack of appropriate restoration programs for these individuals given that a majority of restoration has been developed for psychiatric barriers to competency. Indeed, across most states and jurisdictions, individuals are often admitted to psychiatric institutions for competency restoration—this includes individuals with ID/DD—despite psychiatric institutions not necessarily being the most appropriate setting for someone with these disabilities.

Whereas restoration for individuals with psychiatric impairment may rely heavily on the use of antipsychotic medication (see Chapter 3) and thus are appropriate for inpatient restoration, said treatment is not generally adequate nor appropriate for those with intellectual disabilities. Indeed, Wood and colleagues (2019) note that treatment via pharmacotherapy would likely not only be ineffective or inadequate for individuals found incompetent to proceed but that pharmacotherapy in such cases could also be unethical. More traditional methods of competency restoration may be less effective for individuals with ID, as varying cognitive weaknesses (e.g., relative to working and long-term memory) are likely to pose barriers, which can otherwise be diminished in others found incompetent to stand trial (e.g., with memory problems caused by major mood or psychotic symptoms).

Some jurisdictions have alternatives to inpatient hospitalization for restoration of those with ID/DD such as habilitation or training centers for those with intellectual disabilities and community or outpatient restoration. Nevertheless, a majority of evaluators still recommend inpatient hospitalizations for restoration (Murrie et al., 2020). This may stem from a lack of available resources in the community (e.g., most, if not all, of the training centers in Virginia have closed, thereby removing this as a viable option for incompetent ID/DD defendants), a lack of knowledge of available resources, or the combination of intellectual deficits and serious mental illness.

Furthermore, group-based restoration (a common approach to traditional competency restoration) may not offer education presented in a sufficient manner to meet the intellectual needs of these individuals. That is, group approaches to restoration may use language that is more advanced than the defendant's capabilities, and/or they may be tailored to meet the needs of the majority. Further, groups may assume very basic knowledge that individuals with ID may not possess. It is also important to remember that group-based treatment for defendants with ID may also prove difficult, as the environment may be distracting, which can tax already poor working memory. Further, the materials may be presented too quickly in group for comprehension by individuals with slower processing speed, verbal comprehension, etc. Additionally, deficits in social functioning may also prove detrimental in such settings. This is not to say, however, that group format will not benefit individuals with ID. Restoration providers should take special care when relying on said format to promote progression toward adjudicative competence.

COMPETENCY RESTORATION PROGRAMS

Restoration with defendants with ID relies heavily on building basic knowledge of the legal system to develop a foundation from which they can learn to extend to their legal situation. As with restoration research in general, there are currently limited empirically supported approaches for restoration with individuals with ID/DD presentations. Regardless, common techniques for restoration interventions with ID defendants include altering and simplifying language, providing abbreviated and more frequent education, utilizing visuals/imagery and tangible examples when appropriate, and checking frequently for comprehension by having them put the information in their own words (Wall et al., 2003b; Siegel & Elwork, 1990).

The Slater Method

The Slater Method is a well-supported and increasingly common practice in the U.S. for providing competency restoration to individuals with low intellectual abilities, developmental disabilities, and/or learning disorders.[1] This method integrates legal education, psychological treatment, and individualized interventions in order to promote adjudicative competence. As we noted earlier, understanding the types of deficits these individuals present with is crucial to shaping our approach to restoration. Wall and colleagues (2003b) developed the Slater Method through Eleanor Slater Hospital for inpatient competency restoration with defendants in Rhode Island. They include in the instruction manual an overview of types of impairment that individuals with intellectual disabilities may demonstrate. Table 4.1 summarizes potential deficits adapted from the original manual, which may be targeted in restoration using the Slater Method.

The manual also discusses tips on how to interview someone with ID to make the interview more effective. These tips (aggregated in Table 4.2) may be of utility to restoration providers attempting to screen a defendant's current legal knowledge to guide further intervention efforts. It is crucial that providers review and understand the deficits as well as the corresponding tips for working with these individuals to ensure effective restoration.

As noted earlier, there is not much by the way of empirical research with regard to the Slater Method, as with most specific approaches to competency restoration. However, the extant literature is promising—at least in comparison to treatment as usual for defendants

1. Of note, the original Slater Method instruction manual was published in 2003 and uses the term "mentally retarded person," which was the appropriate terminology at the inception of the manual. More than two decades later, this term is outdated and discriminatory; as such, the current chapter will supplement with "individuals with intellectual disabilities" or "ID."

Table 4.1 ID/DD Deficits as Barriers to Competency

Cognitive	Communication	Emotional/Behavioral
Attention	Poor articulation	Passivity/withdrawal
Memory	Limited vocabulary	Emotion dysregulation
Logic/reasoning	Impaired syntax	
Problem-solving	Difficulty answering questions	
Learning from mistakes	Inability to read/write effectively, mimicking responses	

Source: Adapted from Wall, Krupp, & Guilmette (2003b).

Table 4.2 Slater Recommendations for Interviewing ID/DD Individuals

Do	Don't
1. Use simple language	1. Avoid leading questions
2. Speak slowly, clearly, and calmly	2. Avoid questions about specific timelines
3. Use concrete terms and ideas	3. Avoid complex sequences
4. Ask open-ended questions	4. Avoid showing frustration
5. Repeat questions from different perspectives	5. Avoid distractions
6. Proceed slowly	6. Avoid nonverbal cues, such as nodding your head "yes" or "no" (unless providing direct feedback on correct or incorrect responses)
7. Give praise and encouragement	
8. Point out and repeat important information	
9. Provide direct, explicit feedback	
10. Take short breaks	

Source: Adapted from Wall, Krupp, & Guilmette (2003b).

with ID/DD. For instance, in their original article, Wall and colleagues (2003a) found that one-third of individuals attained competency. In an additional study, Wall and Christopher (2012) found that individuals who participated in the Slater Method were more likely to be opined competent post-restoration in comparison to those who received the standard care at Eleanor Slater Hospital.

The Slater Method: Training Content and Structure

The Slater Method manual divides instruction into five modules and two phases, which in combination are designed to cover core aspects of competency.

The modules are as follows: (1) *purpose of training; review of charges, pleas, and potential consequences*; (2) *courtroom personnel*; (3) *courtroom proceedings, trial, and plea bargain*; (4) *communicating with attorney, giving testimony, and assisting in defense*; and (5) *tolerating stress of proceedings*. Each module includes a series of questions, written in bold font, and adequate answers to each question, which are written in parentheses. The restoration provider uses these questions with the defendant to assess their current knowledge and to provide appropriate education where needed. Importantly, the manual is not intended to be a rigid, structured approach. Rather, clinicians are encouraged to alter the wording of questions and ask new questions that fit within the general concept of the module (using one's own professional judgment). Rephrasing questions over the course of intervention is particularly important with this population because some individuals with ID may be inclined to simply parrot the information back to the provider without a genuine understanding of material. By finding new ways to rephrase and ask questions, the provider can reduce this likelihood and promote comprehension. Additionally, the provider must be mindful to alter questions to be consistent with legal terminology in their jurisdiction(s), which may differ from the wording utilized in the original manual. For instance, Oregon utilizes a "guilty except for insanity" plea as opposed to a "not guilty by reason of insanity" plea, which is found in many other states. With this, the clinician would simply alter the questions and determine appropriate answers based on the provider's knowledge of the statutory requirements in their jurisdiction. In this regard, the manual is more in line with a semi-structured, sequential approach.

The Slater Method training program breaks up teaching into two separate phases of education (see Table 4.3): the Knowledge Phase (Phase I) and the Understanding Phase (Phase II). The Knowledge Phase (Phase I) includes the instruction of concrete, factual material relevant to the legal system such as people likely to be involved in legal proceedings, possible plea options, and appropriate behavior in the courtroom. The goal of Phase I is merely rote memorization of foundational knowledge. The Understanding Phase (Phase II) is geared toward the rational aspects of adjudicative competence, and it aims to improve the comprehension and application of material. For instance, this phase asks, "Why"- and "How come?"-style questions. This aspect of training is crucial for all defendants but particularly those with ID/DD, as these individuals may rely more heavily on cued recall and rote memorization without genuine comprehension, as noted above. By providing restoration in two phases, clinicians can focus on building a foundation of knowledge that the individual may not have had prior and from which they can then learn to apply their knowledge and gain an appreciation for their legal situation.

The Slater Method manual includes a workbook that supplies the provider with the Knowledge-Based Questions in Column A and the associated Understanding-Based Questions in Column B; a modified version of this workbook is available in Appendix B. Because individuals with ID may learn best with multifaceted approaches to education, the training program also uses pictures of courtrooms and personnel, in addition to suggested interactive activities such role playing and mock trial[2] in order to engage the client and improve retention and comprehension. The authors of the Slater Method note that this program is provided on an individual basis, as opposed to a group setting, because people with ID tend to learn best with more individualized approaches. Additionally, the original training program did not utilize handouts or written materials, given the high rates of illiteracy in the population. Use of interactive interventions, pictures, videos, etc. are encouraged as alternative visual aids to facilitate learning.

Also included in the manual is an answer sheet, which the provider is encouraged to use to document both the client's response and the *quality* of their response; the modified workbook in Appendix B includes an embedded column for scoring responses. The intention is to provide close monitoring and clear documentation regarding the client's progress

2. The reader is encouraged to review Appendix A, as well as the Florida State CompKit, for sample mock trial activities.

Table 4.3 Slater Method Guide

Impairment Domain	Phase I: Knowledge-Based Training	Phase II: Understanding-Based Training
Cognition	The client must learn • the purpose of training sessions • the charges (1) • possible pleas (1) • potential consequences (1) • the role of courtroom personnel (2) • the purpose of going to court (3) • the purpose of going to trial (3)	The client must understand that • this is an adversarial proceeding, and he/she is the accused (1, 3) • he/she cannot be punished just because he/she is accused (1, 3) • a plea is different from a finding (1, 3) • the case may go to trial, but it probably won't (1, 3, 4) • a plea bargain means giving up some rights (1, 3)
Communication	The client must learn • the importance of speaking with his/her attorney (4) • the importance of listening in court (4) • the importance of not saying "yes" if he/she doesn't understand something (4) • how to testify appropriately (4)	The client must be able to • understand that the opposing counsel may try to trip him/her up • tell his/her story without self-incrimination • tell all details of his/her story to the attorney • resist leading questions and appreciate and be able to stick to a defense strategy
Emotions and Behavior	The client must learn • to display appropriate behavior (5) • not to display inappropriate behavior (5)	• Role-playing sessions to assess ability to tolerate the stress of courtroom proceedings (1–5)

Note: Numbers in parentheses denote the main Slater Method module number(s) where this information is reviewed.
Source: Table adapted from Wall, Krupp, and Guilmette (2003b).

over the course of sessions. Responses are scored as Poor, Fair, or Good. The creators of the Slater Method provide the following guidelines for ratings: A rating of Poor is assigned if "the defendant does not answer questions, erroneously articulates a concept, or says 'I don't know' or 'I don't remember,' in response to questions." A rating of Fair is assigned to responses that provide a limited description of a concept or include some confused information and is somewhat understandable. A rating of Good is assigned if the client provides a generally complete and understandable answer.

The Training Process

The restoration provider starts by obtaining a baseline assessment of the client's knowledge and understanding by asking all questions from Phase I and Phase II of all five modules. The modules are then administered in sequential order of Phase I, and once complete, Phase II. That is, after a baseline is obtained, the provider starts by reviewing Module 1—Phase I (i.e., Column A) questions only. It is recommended that the provider reviews Phase I questions within each module a minimum of three times before moving on to the next module. The provider utilizes the answer sheet to record the client's responses and supplies a rating score for each pass through the modules. After the client provides responses rated to be Fair or Good, or after the module has been reviewed three times, the clinician can move on to the next module. After completing Phase I, the provider and the client then incorporate Phase II (i.e., Column B) questions. Because this training method is only semi-structured and is adapted to fit the needs of the client, the length of sessions and number of repetitions will vary per client and per module. After the client completes both phases in their entirety, they are intended to be referred for a mock trial to afford them an opportunity for role playing and to gauge their ability to tolerate the stress of the proceedings.

At its inception, the Slater Method was designed to be administered one to five days per week, with sessions lasting between a few minutes up to one hour. It is important to note here that given the variable needs of each client, there is not necessarily a clearly delineated length of time that the Slater Method should be administered to determine its efficacy, or lack thereof, with a client. Wall and colleagues (2003a) note that based on their limited experience implementing the tool, some clients may show improvement in which they are restored within "a few months," whereas others may not demonstrate improvement in the time allotted by the court (e.g., two-thirds the maximum sentence). Indeed, the appropriate length of treatment will likely depend on a number of factors. First, the frequency with which sessions are held and the duration of the sessions. For instance, intervention in which sessions occur three times per week for 20 minutes may result in observable improvement more quickly in comparison to sessions held only once weekly. Second, the individual client's motivation and engagement will also need to be assessed and accurately addressed. That is, a client's motivation may wax and wane throughout restoration, which may require additional factors to be addressed and/or lead to a disruption in progress. Third, and no less important, is the statutory requirements of each jurisdiction with regard to length of competency restoration services. For instance, some jurisdictions dictate a set length of time an individual can spend in inpatient restoration, whereas others may differ depending on the maximum sentence associated with the individual's charge. Furthermore, some states have different rules regarding the length of time allotted for inpatient restoration versus outpatient restoration. Lastly, jurisdictions can differ with regard to expectations and thresholds for findings of unrestorability, which can shape the length of treatment required by the court.

Importantly, the manual highlights that individuals may be opined competent subsequent to successful restoration using the Slater Method yet later encounter novel situations as court proceedings unfold, which would result in difficulty with decision-making in the moment. Wall and colleagues (2003a, p. 193) offer that the restoration provider can be "available to be physically present in the courtroom to help determine whether the defendant is making decisions consistent with the training tool as the process unfolds, as well as whether the defendant understands the decisions he or she appears to be making." That is, the authors suggest that there is utility in allowing the Slater Method provider to be present during or prior to court proceedings once an individual is opined competent to facilitate both their understanding of courtroom proceedings and to assist the attorney in understanding and communicating with their client effectively.

This notion of supported decision-making/in vivo supports is not novel or unique to the Slater Method. Indeed, the Arc's NCCJD (2017) also discuss the utility of additional supports for ID/DD defendants (e.g., in the form of explaining complex terms, checking for comprehension, and helping the attorney understand or communicate with the defendant) particularly in the context of reasonable accommodations under the Americans with Disabilities Act (ADA; 1990). There is legal precedent for the provision of reasonable accommodations for court; Wood and colleagues (2019) highlight two such examples from case law. In the first, the Supreme Court of Washington ruled that "courts may also accommodate the needs of a particular defendant by modifying trial schedules and day-to-day courtroom procedures to make the proceedings more accessible to a party. Such accommodations, when appropriate, are permissible exercises of judicial discretion—but are distinct from the legal analysis of competency to stand trial" (*State v. Ortiz-Abrego*, 2017). In the second example, which took place in Vermont, the court ultimately ruled that finding a defendant with cognitive deficits competent to proceed "contingent upon the assistance of a 'cognitive facilitator'" was appropriate. The court went on to say, "There is nothing to prevent a court from qualifying its competency finding and suggesting accommodations that will enable the defendant to better capitalize on his capacity to understand and participate effectively in the proceedings" (*State v. Cleary*, 2003). In sum, individuals with ID/DD should be afforded reasonable accommodations throughout various stages of the legal process to ensure adequate opportunity to meaningfully engage in proceedings.

Using the Slater Method in an Inpatient Setting

One benefit of the Slater Method is that it was created to be used with an inpatient population. Implementation in an inpatient or structured facility allows for more frequent interactions and sessions. With individuals who are hospitalized or detained, there tends to be more ease of access to clients than with those residing in the community, where sessions may rely on their ability (or caregiver's ability) to take them to sessions.

The individualized nature of the Slater Method holds both positive and negative implications for the inpatient provider. On the positive side, the individualistic approach allows for alterations in questions, session length, and content to match the client's needs. This contrasts with group-based interventions common in inpatient settings, wherein the content is utilitarian. A downside to this, however, is that an individualized approach is more resource intensive in nature. For instance, this approach may require multiple sessions per week, which may not be feasible for providers. As we know, low staffing and skyrocketing rates of inpatient admissions for competency restoration amid a national competency crisis can make the administration of such a tool challenging. Similar critiques are true for jail-based implementation of the program. It is possible that providers may not always be able to implement the training program multiple times per week. To this end, it is useful to remember that some education utilizing a tailored and clinically indicated approach is likely better than no individualized education. If multiple sessions per week are not feasible, the provider may wish to aim for once per week and try to enlist the help of unit staff or others to review certain topics in between sessions.

Visuals/Handouts

One consideration suggested when utilizing the Slater Method is to incorporate a variety of pictures (see for example the "Courtroom Illustration" in Appendix A) and even videos when possible. Although the original manual includes some court-related pictures for use in session, the provider may find that utilizing pictures from juvenile competency restoration and court-related workbooks for youth can be effective for some individuals. This can include using images to help portray a witness testifying, a jury, a judge, attorneys in a courtroom, etc. to guide discussion of terms. For instance, the Virginia Department of Corrections' *Going to Court Activity Book for Children* is a useful resource for simple pictures, with little text, related to the courtroom that can be used in session;[3] other activity books have been produced for use in different states. In addition to using pictures to help teach court-related terminology, court pictures such as these also afford the opportunity to incorporate mindful coloring to the restoration sessions. If a client enjoys coloring, they can be given crayons to color a picture of the judge while discussing the judge's role and/or they may be rewarded with a coloring sheet of the judge after reviewing the module.

Another useful adaptation is to include simplified handouts. Although the original manual steered away from utilizing handouts due to the high rate of illiteracy, simple handouts can be useful tools when appropriate. If a defendant is able to read and/or write, simple word banks (see for example "Legal Word Bank" in Appendix B) and labels on pictures can be of use to help the client when reviewing information between restoration sessions.

Positive Reinforcement

As with many incompetent defendants, low motivation may impede progress when using the Slater Method. Indeed, individuals with intellectual disabilities may present with a sense of learned helplessness stemming from a history of difficulty learning information, whether in academic settings or in general. In other words, individuals may be aware of their prior difficulty with learning, which can contribute to their own sense of an inability to learn. With the belief that they are not able to learn, motivation to engage in learning activities may decrease. This can potentially lead providers to perceive the client as unable to learn the material and falsely attribute their perceived inability to severe learning deficits. In reality, we know that many individuals with ID can learn but may need different approaches to education. It is crucial that restoration providers accurately assess the role of motivation and potential learned helplessness in contributing to learning difficulties and retaining material and address this accordingly.

Another consideration is that individuals with ID/DD may have historically been more heavily cared for by family members than counterparts without ID/DD. This can be beneficial for overall mental health, although it may also lead to reduced autonomy, including while navigating the legal system. For instance, individuals may have previously relied on

3. This activity book by the Virginia Department of Criminal Justice Services by the U.S. Department of Health and Human Services is available for download on their website: https://www.dcjs.virginia.gov/sites/dcjs.virginia.gov/files/publications/victims/going-court-activity-book-children_0.pdf

parents or caregivers to make decisions for them, but in the context of their current legal situation, they will need to develop more autonomous decision-making skills. As such, some individuals with ID may demonstrate decreased motivation in the context of others having historically provided for them.

One recommendation for restoration providers is to incorporate a token economy or positive reinforcement system, when feasible, to encourage treatment participation and active engagement. Positive reinforcement systems are useful tools for shaping behavior. In general, positive reinforcement is anything that tends to increase a behavior, which can include adding something (e.g., something tangible or an experience/activity) that the client wants, in order to increase a positive behavior. These principles are how people train animals, how parents effectively reduce tantrums and increase positive behaviors in children, and how we learn to interact with others. Reinforcers are not *inherently* universal; what might be reinforcing to one client might not be reinforcing to the next person. Reinforcers can include a smile, verbal praise, playing a game, having a conversation, or any other activity or item that is rewarding to the patient (as permitted by the institution). Reinforcements should be provided immediately following a tangible/observable behavior for maximum effect. They also should be provided in a genuine manner. For example, when praising someone, this should sound authentic and not be exaggerated or disingenuous, as this can be sensed by the client. Some of the most common, or easiest-to-provide, reinforcers in restrictive settings can be praise and social interaction (e.g., spending time with a preferred staff member).

Importantly, some hospital settings may already incorporate positive reinforcement programs/token economies. For instance, some inpatient settings offer a system in which a patient earns points for participation in varying aspects of treatment that they can later redeem for certain rewards or privileges. When this is the case, it can be fairly easy to apply this program to participation in restoration sessions using the Slater Method for (see "Case Example 2: The Slater Method Using a Token Economy"). However, with a bit of creativity, positive reinforcement systems can be provided for participation even in the absence of formal token economies. The book Don't Shoot the Dog authored by Karen Pryor (2019) is an excellent resource for learning the ins and outs of positive reinforcement.

Managing Distress

A potential challenge that can arise from lengthy sessions and/or repeated exposures to material is the resulting frustration from the client. Even if not making use of the Slater Method specifically, utilizing brief sessions (e.g., 15–20 minutes) multiple times per week (e.g., three sessions per week) whenever feasible with this population can be beneficial in comparison to long (e.g., 50 minute) sessions when working with defendants with ID/DD. Having brief, recurrent sessions not only allows time for encoding material and assessing retrieval of information but can also reduce the likelihood of client frustration interfering with progress. Although repetition is inherent to the Slater Method training program, for some, the degree of repetition on certain topics can be particularly challenging and elicit many negative emotions. As such it may be useful to switch between modules and or skip over particularly triggering questions, based on one's judgment, depending on the client's presentation.

As individuals with intellectual disabilities may have lower thresholds for frustration tolerance and perhaps fewer coping skills, this step may be crucial to incorporate into training. To this end, part of the session and/or an entire session may need to be spent teaching and rehearsing coping skills in order to help the client manage distress associated with the training process. This strategy is modeled in "Case Example 1: Using the Slater Method." It is useful to have tools to assist the client in managing their frustration. We recommend utilizing clinical tools such as those found throughout cognitive behavioral therapy (CBT), acceptance and commitment therapy (ACT), and dialectical behavior therapy (DBT), which are discussed in Chapters 6 and 10 respectively. Additionally, Julie Brown's (2015) The Emotion Regulation Skills System for Cognitively Challenged Clients: A DBT-Informed Approach is a useful resource for adapting distress tolerance skills for individuals with cognitive disabilities.

Using the Slater Method in Outpatient Settings

Importantly, the Slater Method is not only applicable to inpatient settings. If a client is able to be safely and effectively managed in an outpatient setting, the Slater Method can also be a valuable restoration tool for clients with ID in the jail or community. Across the US, outpatient settings may look quite different due to different resources and legal statutes varying by state and jurisdiction. As suggested above, community settings may include group homes or adult assisted-living facilities that offer additional support to individuals while promoting generally independent functioning in the community. Community settings may also include individuals living entirely independently and attending restoration sessions through community providers.

Community settings may or may not be less stress inducing than inpatient settings, given increased autonomy and lack of structure in outpatient environments. On the one hand, this increase in freedoms may allow for more flexibility and empowerment of the individual. On the other hand, the lack of structure and support for those residing independently could contribute to increased stress in navigating needs. As the Slater Method works best with repeated, brief administration throughout the week, the client will need to be able to present to the setting of sessions multiple times per week. This can increase the likelihood of missed sessions, either due to logistical difficulty (e.g., obtaining transportation to appointments) or intentional choices (e.g., choosing to not attend an outpatient appointment). Of course, this would then lead to a disruption in progress.

Jail-based implementation of the Slater Method poses similar benefits and challenges as those outlined above. First, as with inpatient restoration, individuals who are detained in jail are accessible 24-hours a day. That is, providers have easier access to their clients, which allows more predictability in being able to provide/offer sessions. However, unsurprisingly, the stress associated with jail—particularly for vulnerable individuals including those with ID/DD—can certainly pose barriers to the individual's ability to focus and engage in sessions. Furthermore, jails often have numerous extraneous stimuli (e.g., yelling, banging, etc.) that may serve as major distractions to clients and impair their ability to give full attention. Additionally, given the punitive nature inherent to jail settings, modifications such as token economies are unlikely to be approved or offered. As such, extrinsic motivators to engage in restoration sessions may be difficult to obtain and implement.

Technology

It is possible that restoration sessions using the Slater Method could be conducted remotely via video-based platforms in order to increase accessibility to community-based clients or those in institutions who are not able to engage in in-person sessions (e.g., those in isolation at jail due to impulsive behaviors). Video platforms are encouraged above audio-only sessions, as video sessions allow for the provider to adequately assess the client's attention and engagement in session. The provider may also want to utilize the screen-sharing feature of video platforms in order to present pictures to the client. In some circumstances, the provider may be able to send the pictures to the client via email or an available platform for the client to keep. If this is done, the pictures should be clearly labeled and numbered for ease of reference (e.g., "Let's look at Picture 1").

However, providers are reminded that the needs of those with ID are unique and the clients may need further support to gain meaningful knowledge through video-based platforms. For instance, the provider will have less control with regards to situational distractions and audio/visual quality for the clients. To this end, setting clear expectations for sessions using simplified language is encouraged. For instance, providers may want to detail the expected length of session (e.g., "We will be meeting until 1:30"), the plan for the session, (e.g., "I will show you some pictures on the screen as we are talking"), and rules (e.g., "I will need you to focus on the computer and don't click on anything else"). Often, individuals with ID undergoing community-based competency restoration may be residing in a group home and/or with a caregiver. When this is true, the provider may seek to review the basic necessities of the sessions with the caregiver to improve likelihood of attendance as well as to increase the likelihood that the client has access to a quiet space with minimal distractions and access to a computer. Additionally, the provider may wish to seek support from the caregiver in downloading and making the pictures available for the client.

Cultural Considerations

At times, clients may have immigrated from other countries that have fundamentally different justice systems. The United States has an adversarial justice system from which the Slater Method questions are shaped. In essence, this adversarial justice system involves a neutral trier of fact who ensures proceedings are fair and laws are followed adequately. The prosecution and defense present evidence in an adversarial process in order to discover the truth. Other countries, such as Honduras, have differing approaches to justice systems such as an inquisitorial justice system; these differ with regard to the investigation procedures and judicial process. An inquisitorial system involves a more active, or hands on, role of the judge with regards to collecting and reviewing evidence, questioning witnesses, and investigation. This system promotes more initial investigation to avoid bringing an innocent person to trial. As such, these countries also differ with regard not only to the investigatory and trial process but also to treatment of individuals accused of committing crimes. If a client is only familiar with an inquisitorial system, for instance, discussion of the adversarial system may be confusing. An individual with ID may have increased difficulty grasping the differences in systems as an adversarial system might differ fundamentally from their pre-established knowledge, requiring not only the acquisition of new material but also increased flexibility in applying that material. As such, there may be additional education needed, which may require the provider to educate themselves on the judicial processes of the client's country of origin in order to more effectively explain the difference to the client. The investigative role of police, presentation of evidence by attorneys, the neutral role of the judge, etc. may need to be reviewed more thoroughly with the client. To this end, it can be helpful to have the client explain their understanding of their own judicial system. By gaining awareness of the client's preexisting knowledge, the provider may be better able to explain fundamental differences in legal systems and identify the root of confusion. Furthermore, validating the client's confusion and acknowledging the complexity of the U.S. adversarial system can be beneficial to mitigate frustration and maintain motivation.

Relatedly, language barriers may be misperceived as cognitive deficits by attorneys, courtroom personnel, or treatment team members, due to difficulty with effective communication and comprehension. This can lead to referrals for competency evaluations and inappropriate orders for competency restoration. Alternatively, cognitive deficits may also be masked by or falsely attributed to language barriers. In these situations, it is particularly important to adequately assess the client's cognitive functioning, to the extent possible, using available resources such as collateral information from family (e.g., education level, history of special education or accommodations supports in the community, ability to take care of him/her/themselves, etc.). Furthermore, interpreters should be utilized for any initial clinical/intake interviewing and while implementing the Slater Method. In working with interpreters, providers should take into consideration the additional time needed when using the interpreter (i.e., as sessions are typically recommended to be brief). Additionally, as it is crucial to alter wording of questions to assure genuine comprehension rather than parroting of information, providers should take extra care in working with interpreters to clarify interpretations using the provider's wording to the extent possible.

Case Example 1: Using the Slater Method

Mr. E is a 34-year-old self-identified Black, cisgender man admitted to the state hospital for competency restoration. He is currently charged with three counts of burglary (felony). It is suspected he has an intellectual disability in addition to a diagnosis of schizophrenia, which is currently well managed with antipsychotic medication. Although Mr. E's psychotic symptoms have generally remitted with adherence to medication, he has been struggling to learn basic information related to the legal system. He has not been retaining information from group restoration classes and becomes easily overwhelmed by the amount of information presented in classes. Given these difficulties, the provider decided to utilize the Slater Method on an individual basis with Mr. E. Below is an outline of the sessions and progress.

Week 1
Session 1 (40 minutes): The goal of the first session is to gain a baseline understanding of the client's knowledge.

Modules administered: All
Summary: The provider administered all questions from Columns A and B from all modules to gain a baseline of Mr. E's knowledge. Mr. E became quite frustrated around 20 minutes into the session, and he demonstrated difficulty maintaining focus as the session progressed.
Ratings: Mr. E's responses were generally scored as Poor with only some that are determined to be Fair or Good.

Session 2 (20 minutes): The provider decided to conduct shorter sessions based on Mr. E's presentation in the first session.

Modules administered: Phase 1, Module 1
Summary: The provider asked questions from Column A, Module 1 twice through and provided corrective feedback to Mr. E. The provider knew that Mr. E has an eighth-grade education and reading level and supplied Mr. E a handout with the four plea options in large font for him to review. Mr. E was encouraged to ask

staff for assistance reviewing the four plea options in between sessions. Validation was provided when Mr. E expresses frustration.

Ratings: Mr. E's responses were generally scored as Fair, with a few answers scored as Poor.

Session 3 (15 minutes): The provider continued with shorter sessions.

Modules administered: Phase 1, Modules 1 & 2

Summary: The provider asked questions from Module 1 another time. Although Mr. E still had one or two questions that his answers were determined to be Poor, the provider moved on to Module 2 in order to reduce the likelihood of frustration from repeated administrations of Module 1. The provider incorporated the use of pictures from a juvenile competency workbook to assist with discussion of a judge, an attorney, a jury, and a witness.

Ratings: Mr. E's responses were generally scored as Fair, with a few answers scored as Poor.

Week 2

Sessions 4 & 5 (15 minutes each): The provider continued with shorter sessions.

Modules administered: Phase 1, Modules 1 & 2

Summary: The provider reviewed the material from both modules; she altered the wording of the sample questions and added new questions in order to facilitate learning. For instance, in discussing the roles of courtroom personnel, the provider asked Mr. E: "Who is in charge of the courtroom?" "What can the judge decide?" "Who can decide if you are guilty or innocent?" "What does a witness talk about?"

Ratings: Mr. E's answers to the first two modules were all scored as Fair or Good during these two sessions.

Week 3

Sessions 6 & 7 (15 minutes each): The provider continued with shorter sessions.

Modules administered: Phase 1, Module 3

Summary: The provider noticed that Mr. E was becoming frustrated and/or anxious with the repetition and feedback of sessions. Validation and praise were not as effective as before. Mr. E often replied, "I can't learn this!" and "We've already been through this!" Further, the provider noticed Mr. E became irritable when he was provided corrective feedback as he appeared to be aware that he was struggling, stating, "I'll never be able to learn it," and "It's pointless." Given his level of distress, the provider decided to incorporate a coping skill at the beginning of the next session because of his frustration. The provider spent session 7 going over diaphragmatic breathing.

Ratings: Mr. E's answers were scored as Poor or Fair.

Week 4

Sessions 8 & 9 (15–20 minutes each): The provider tailored sessions to incorporate coping skills in addition to Slater Method modules.

Modules administered: Phase 1, Module 3

Summary: Mr. E was engaged in a breathing exercise for three to four minutes at the beginning of each session. Then the provider asked the remainder of Module 3's questions.

Ratings: Mr. E's answers were scored Poor to Good.

Weeks 5–8

Sessions 10–17 (15–20 minutes each): The provider continued to administer Phase I, as outlined in the workbook, and utilized brief sessions multiple times per week.

Modules administered: Phase 1, Modules 3, 4, & 5

Summary: The provider asked the questions in Module 3 a total of five times until all answers were scored as Fair or Good. Questions were reworded and added to ensure comprehension. The provider administered Modules 4 and 5 a minimum of three times.

Ratings: Mr. E's answers were scored Fair to Good.

Weeks 9–14

Sessions 18–22 (15–20 minutes each): The provider continued to utilize brief sessions when transitioning to Phase II.

Modules administered: Phase II, Modules 1–4

Summary: After going through all of Phase I, the provider then moved on to Phase II. This involved administering all Phase I questions as well as the Phase II understanding questions. The provider changed the wording of questions to help Mr. E develop a genuine understanding of material. For instance, in Module 1, the provider asked, "If you say you didn't do it, will the judge definitely believe you?"

Ratings: Mr. E's scores were initially rated as Poor to Fair; over time, his scores were rated as Fair to Good, with a few items still rated as Poor.

Week 15

Sessions 23 & 24 (15–20 minutes each): The provider provided feedback regarding Mr. E's presentation in session.

Modules administered: Phase II, Module 5

Summary: The provider addressed Mr. E's tendency to roll his eyes and interject when discussing his case. The provider told Mr. E, "I notice when we discuss your case, you seem pretty upset. It sounds like you have a lot of important information to say, and you want to be sure I know about this stuff. Let's practice talking about it in a calm way." The provider also worked with Mr. E to reduce interrupting: "Remember, we can't interrupt the judge or lawyers when they are talking. Let's practice talking only when we're called on by the judge." The provider also incorporated coping skills learned earlier in restoration to assist Mr. E in using them when he is in court: "Let's practice using deep breathing when talking about your charges, so it is a little easier for you in court."

Ratings: Mr. E's scores ranged from Fair to Good.

Case Example 2: The Slater Method Using a Token Economy

Mr. M is a 65-year-old self-identified Asian American cisgender man admitted to the hospital for competency restoration. He is currently charged with murder (felony). His current barriers to competency are cognitive deficits including difficulty with retention, comprehension, and motivation. He has been meeting with a provider for restoration sessions utilizing the Slater Method. However, he has not been engaged, typically replies "I don't know," and ends sessions early. The provider decides to incorporate the hospital's token economy into his sessions in order to improve motivation. The hospital awards points for participating in treatment activities such as treatment team meetings, group attendance, and unit meetings. Patients can trade in points for items or activities at the end of each week. Mr. M is generally uninvolved in treatment activities, so this allows him to earn points/rewards in another manner.

After talking with Mr. M to establish rapport, the provider learned that he has a particular interest in a specific band. Collaboratively with Mr. M and his treatment team, the provider develops a plan for Mr. M to earn points based on his attendance and involvement in restoration sessions. At the outset of sessions, Mr. M is able to earn 2 points for simply attending sessions and providing some effort to answer questions. Mr. M can exchange 6 points for a video of a live performance from his favorite band. This means that if Mr. M participates in three sessions per week, he can earn one video per week. The provider utilizes the Slater Method in sessions and awards Mr. M points following each session. Mr. M's motivation increases. The reward system is gradually adjusted so that Mr. M earns 2 points *only* if he provides answers to a majority of questions rather than stating "I don't know." Mr. M is allowed to earn partial credit (i.e., 1 point) for attending a session if some effort is exhibited (e.g., he states, "I don't know" to some questions and scores Poor or Fair on others). After a few weeks of this reinforcement schedule, the reinforcement schedule is adjusted again. In this final version, Mr. M earns 2 points only if he provides answers that are scored Fair or Good to a majority of questions in each module. He is still able to redeem 6 points in exchange for viewing one video.

Alternatively, if resources were limited or setting restrictions prevented the restoration provider from utilizing tangible rewards, using resources that are already available would have been indicated. For instance, activities such as playing a game with a staff member of choice, spending extra time getting fresh air, playing a game of basketball, or providing the client with printed coloring could all be potential rewards.

REFERENCES

American Psychological Association (2023, November 15). *Developmental disability.* APA Dictionary of Psychology. https://dictionary.apa.org/intellectual-disability

American Psychiatric Association (2022). Neurodevelopmental disorders. In *Diagnostic and statistical manual of mental disorders* (5th ed., text rev.).

Anderson S. D. & Hewitt J. (2002). The effect of competency restoration training on defendants with mental retardation found not competent to proceed. *Law & Human Behavior, 26*(3), 343–351. doi:10.1023/a:1015328505884

Appelbaum, K. L., & Appelbaum, P. S. (1994). Criminal-justice-related competencies in defendants with mental retardation. *Journal of Psychiatry & Law, 22*, 483–503. https://journals.sagepub.com/home/plxa

The Arc's National Center on Criminal Justice & Disability. (2017). *Competency of individuals with intellectual and developmental disabilities in the criminal justice system: A call to action for the criminal justice community.* https://thearc.org/wp-content/uploads/2019/07/16-089-NCCJD-Competency-White-Paper-v5.pdf

Atkins v. Virginia, 536 U.S. 304 (2002).

Ault, M. J., Wolery, M., Doyle, P. M., & Gast, D. L. (1989). Review of comparative studies in the instruction of students with moderate and severe handicaps. *Exceptional Children, 55*, 346–356. doi:10.1177/001440298905500410

Brown, J. F. (2015) *The emotion regulation skills system for cognitively challenged clients: A DBT-informed approach.* Guilford Press.

Cooke, B. K., Delalot, D., & Werner, T. L. (2015). Hall v. Florida: Capital punishment, IQ, and persons with intellectual disabilities. *Journal of the American Academy of Psychiatry and the Law Online, 43*(2), 230–234. https://jaapl.org/

Dusky v. United States, 362 U.S. 402 (1960).

Forness, S. R., & Kavale, K. A. (1993). Strategies to improve basic learning and memory deficits in mental retardation: A meta-analysis of experimental studies. *Education and Training in Mental Retardation, 28*, 99–110. https://www.jstor.org/stable/23878846

Godinez v. Moran, 509 U.S. 389 (1993).

Grisso, T. (2002). *Evaluating competencies: Forensic assessments and instruments* (2nd ed.). Kluwer Academic/Plenum.

Hall v. Florida, 572 U.S. 701 (2014)

Harris, J. C. (2006). *Intellectual disability: Understanding its development, causes, classification, evaluation, and treatment.* Oxford University Press.

Hauser, M. J., Olson, E., & Drogin, E. Y. (2014). Psychiatric disorders in people with intellectual disability (intellectual developmental disorder): Forensic aspects. *Current Opinion in Psychiatry, 27*(2), 117–121. doi:10.1097/YCO.0000000000000036

Melton, G. B., Petrila, J., Poythress, N. G., Slobogin, C., Otto, R. K., Mossman, D., & Condie, L. O. (2017). *Psychological evaluations for the courts: A handbook for mental health professionals and lawyers.* Guilford Press.

Murrie, D. C., Gardner, B. O., & Torres, A. N. (2020). Competency to stand trial evaluations: A state-wide review of court-ordered reports. *Behavioral Sciences & the Law, 38*(1), 32–50. https://doi.org/10.1002/bsl.2436

Patel, D. R., Cabral, M. D., Ho, A., Merrick, J. (2020). A clinical primer on intellectual disability. *Translational Pediatrics, 9*(Suppl 1), S23–S35. doi:10.21037/tp.2020.02.02

Pifer, N. A. (2016). The scientific and the social in implementing Atkins v. Virginia. *Law & Social Inquiry, 41*(4), 1036–1060. doi:10.1111/lsi.12156

Pryor, K. (2019). *Don't shoot the dog: The art of teaching and training.* Simon & Schuster.

Salekin, K. L., Olley, J. G., & Hedge, K. A. (2010). Offenders with intellectual disability: Characteristics, prevalence, and issues in forensic assessment. *Journal of Mental Health Research in Intellectual Disabilities, 3*(2), 97–116. doi:10.1080/19315861003695769

Siegel, A. M., & Elwork, E. (1990). Treating incompetence to stand trial. *Law & Human Behavior, 14*, 57–65. doi:10.1007/BF01055789

Spreat, S. (2020). Persons with intellectual disability in prison. *Journal of Intellectual Disabilities and Offending Behaviour, 11*(4), 233–237. doi:10.1108/JIDOB-03-2020-0006

Stancliffe, R. J., & Frantz, B. L. (2024). Criminal justice and people with intellectual and developmental disabilities. *Intellectual and Developmental Disabilities, 62*(3), 211–224. doi:10.1352/1934-9556-62.3.211

State v. Cleary, 824 A.2d 509 (Vt. 2003).

State v. Ortiz-Abrego, 387 P.3d 638 (Wash. 2017).

Wall, B., & Christopher, P. (2012). A training program for defendants with intellectual disabilities who are found incompetent to stand trial. *The Journal of the American Academy of Psychiatry and the Law, 40*, 366–373. https://jaapl.org/content/40/3/366

Wall, B., Krupp, B., & Guilmette, T. (2003a). Restoration of competency to stand trial: A training program for persons with mental retardation. *The Journal of the American Academy of Psychiatry and the Law, 31*, 189–201. https://jaapl.org/content/31/2/189.long

Wall, B., Krupp, B., & Guilmette, T. (2003b). *Returning your client to court: The Slater Method: An educational tool to restore competence to stand trial in mentally retarded defendants.* Department of Mental Health, Retardation and Hospitals, Eleanor Slater Hospital.

Wood, M. E., Lawson, K. M., Anderson, J. L., Kinney, D. I., Nitch, S., & Glassmire, D. M. (2019). Reasonable accommodations for meeting the unique needs of defendants with intellectual disability. *The Journal of the American Academy of Psychiatry and the Law, 47*(3), 310–320. doi:10.29158/JAAPL.003855-19

5

Cognitive Remediation (CogRem) and Competency Restoration

ALEXANDRA BRERETON, PHD AND LAURA M. GROSSI, PHD, ABSMIP

Previous research suggests that the strengthening of cognitive functioning that occurs with *cognitive remediation* (CogRem) may aid in the competency-restoration process and help improve specific competency-related abilities (e.g., Schwalbe & Medalia, 2007). In their article on future directions for competency restoration, Zapf and Roesch (2011) describe the argument for incorporating CogRem in competency restoration as sound and rational. More than a decade later, the process for implementing CogRem in competency restoration has not been well established. In this chapter, we aim to explain and demonstrate how CogRem can be used as an adjunct to competency restoration. A fictionalized case example is included at the end of this chapter to illustrate relevant processes and techniques.

COGNITIVE FUNCTIONING OVER TIME

An individual's baseline level of cognitive functioning (i.e., their cognitive skills and abilities when unhindered by substances, temporary medical problems, significant stress, or acute mental health symptoms) typically does not improve over time, regardless of medications, supplements, or behavioral practices. Although a person may be able to maximize their cognitive functioning through practice (e.g., brain training) and circumstance (e.g., enough sleep), one's inherent cognitive abilities typically do not grow over time.

Rather, a mild degree of cognitive decline is considered normative as individuals age. It is well-known that cognitive decline can be elicited or exacerbated by injuries (e.g., traumatic brain injuries), substance use (e.g., long-term alcohol use), and chronic medical problems (e.g., Hepatitis C). Living with serious mental illness (SMI) can also contribute to a more substantial decline in a person's baseline cognitive functioning over time (Maxmen et al., 2009). This is particularly true for individuals who do not consistently take psychotropic medications as prescribed over their lifespan and/or chronically use substances that exacerbate cognitive deficits. Persistent SMI is associated with difficulties with memory, processing speed, attention, and problem-solving (Medalia et al., 2018). Such deficits may be evident in the presence, or absence, of a co-occurring neurocognitive disorder.

Impaired cognition is often associated with poor functional outcomes, such as difficulties with employment, education, and living independently. Cognitive deficits can also increase the risk of psychiatric decompensation, due in part to stress caused by difficulties related to cognitive deficits and limited skills for coping with those stressors. Approaching treatment from both sides—addressing both psychiatric symptoms and cognitive deficits—is thus good practice for maximizing an individual's stability and functioning.

Alexandra Brereton and Laura M. Grossi, *Cognitive Remediation (CogRem) and Competency Restoration*.
In: *The Competency Restoration Handbook*. Edited by: Laura M. Grossi, Oxford University Press. © Laura M. Grossi (2025).
DOI: 10.1093/9780197768075.003.0005

OVERVIEW OF COGNITIVE REMEDIATION

CogRem is an empirically supported intervention approach specifically designed to help improve cognitive deficits and functional outcomes, to a degree reversing cognitive decline associated with SMI. The target patient population for CogRem is adults with SMI symptoms/diagnoses. The Cognitive Remediation Experts Working Group (2010, as cited in Bowie et al., 2020, p. 50) defined CogRem as "a behavioral training intervention targeting cognitive deficits (attention, memory, executive function, social cognition, or metacognition), using scientific principles of learning, with the ultimate goal of improving functional outcomes." In other words, CogRem involves a set of interventions that aim to strengthen specific cognitive abilities and help individuals to develop skills that will ultimately improve their daily functioning. Like physical therapy after an injury, the intervention does not dramatically improve cognitive abilities beyond premorbid functioning.

Efficacy research has led to a general acceptance of CogRem in the field of mental health at an international level (Vita et al., 2022). Generally, extant research has demonstrated that CogRem is effective in improving cognitive abilities and functional outcomes in individuals with psychotic disorders such as schizophrenia (Bowie et al., 2020; van Duin et al., 2019), following a period of decline in abilities. With consistency, improvements in global cognitive functioning, executive functioning, orientation, attention/processing speed, calculation, planning, verbal learning, verbal memory, and working memory have been identified as specific outcomes of CogRem through meta-analysis (e.g., Kurtz et al., 2001; Samamé et al, 2023; Thérond et al., 2021). Results regarding improvements in spatial/visuospatial memory have been more mixed (Thérond et al., 2021; Chen et al. 2022). In brief, CogRem has been shown to optimize cognitive performance generally, and when provided in addition to traditional psychiatric rehabilitation, improves functional outcomes (e.g., psychosocial functioning) in individuals with psychosis (McGurk et al., 2007).

To date, differential effects have been observed among individuals with different presenting problems who undergo CogRem interventions. The extant research suggests that individuals with greater cognitive impairments benefit more from CogRem than individuals with less impairment (e.g., DeTore et al., 2019; Revell et al., 2015). Among forensic and mental health patients with schizophrenia, CogRem has been shown to reduce negative symptoms of psychosis (Cella et al., 2017). In addition, CogRem has helped to reduce behavioral difficulties including agitation, verbal aggression, and physical aggression in this population (Ahmed et al., 2015). With early psychosis, CogRem has been shown to improve neurocognition generally, and also social cognition, and potentially reduce the risk of long-term functional impairment (Vidarsdottir et al., 2019). Beyond psychotic disorders, support has recently been found for use of CogRem to improve the cognitive and/or adaptive functioning of adults experiencing symptoms of depression (Legemaat et al., 2021; Thérond et al., 2021; Rhee et al., 2024), Bipolar disorder (Samamé et al., 2023), mild cognitive impairment (Kim et al., 2011; Tulliani et al., 2022), HIV-associated neurocognitive disorders (e.g., Zondo et al., 2023), and vascular dementia (e.g., Chen et al., 2022), among other presenting problems. Unfortunately, Samamé and colleagues (2023) found that for patients with bipolar disorder, statistical improvements did not translate to practically meaningful improvements in functioning for their sample. In conducting a retrospective study examining characteristics of individuals who showed improvement when engaging in a CogRem program, Medalia and Richardson (2005) found that among those who demonstrated the most improvement, prior to training, clinicians tended to rate those individuals as having higher baseline social skills, greater cooperativeness, better work habits, higher quality of work, and better personal presentation. Interestingly, attendance was found to be unrelated to better work habits.

There are some caveats to the findings related to CogRem treatment gains. For one, it should be emphasized that CogRem does not improve a person's cognitive functioning above and beyond what they are capable of at their baseline. Additionally, those with more intractable SMI (i.e., those with over two years of inpatient hospitalization) may require more sessions to demonstrate improvement when compared to less impaired individuals (Medalia & Richardson, 2005). Further, some research (Tulliani et al., 2022) suggests that the benefits of CogRem on independent living skills may be short-lived. This speaks to the need for ongoing interventions and/or maintenance sessions for treatment gains to be maintained. Given the findings of Medalia and Richardson (2005), such sessions may not need to be frequent.

Researchers have not yet examined the interaction between cognition-enhancing medication[1] and CogRem, although it is possible that such a combination could prove useful; it has been hypothesized that individuals utilizing both might show greater improvements than either alone (e.g., Michalopoulou et al., 2013). Meta-analyses have clarified that functional gains in the context of CogRem are moderated by the presence or absence of co-occurring rehabilitation programs (e.g., those that promote adaptive living skills; Bowie et al., 2020; Wykes et al., 2011). However, research to date has not yet explored whether competency restoration programming (i.e., a rehabilitation aimed at improving psycholegal knowledge, skills, and abilities; see Chapter 2) has this kind of mediating effect. Future research should examine the possibility, given the focus on strategic learning in both competency restoration and CogRem.

COGNITIVE REMEDIATION CORE COMPONENTS

In their white paper on the key techniques of CogRem, Bowie and colleagues (2020) emphasize that CogRem has evolved over time, such that a variety of specific behavioral intervention techniques fall under the CogRem umbrella. These varied interventions share core principles and are implemented with consideration of the theory underpinning CogRem. Bowie and colleagues (2020) identified 13 key concepts for clinicians who are implementing CogRem: a trained therapist, introduction/orientation, pre-intervention assessment, collaborative goal setting (short and long term), the practice of cognitive exercises, repetition, frequency, homework, progress tracking, self-monitoring, feedback, attention to the development of cognitive strategies, and procedures to facilitate the transfer of cognitive gains to everyday functioning. Their workgroup identified "a trained therapist, the practice of cognitive exercises, attention to the development of cognitive strategies, and procedures to facilitate the transfer of cognitive gains to everyday functioning" (p. 50) as the core components of CogRem.

1. The term *cognition-enhancing medication* is used to refer to psychotropic medications designed for memory, cognition, and dementia-related behaviors. In this context, we refer to medications approved by the Food and Drug Administration (FDA) as an intervention to slow cognitive decline (e.g., cholinesterase inhibitors and glutamate regulators). For more information, see: https://www.alz.org/alzheimers-dementia/treatments/medications-for-memory

A Trained Therapist

It is worth observing that the trained therapist is listed first by Bowie and colleagues (2020) in their list of essential elements. Medalia and Richardson (2005) similarly noted that CogRem participants tend to have greater gains when groups are facilitated by clinicians with greater formal training in mental health (i.e., doctoral-level staff). It is necessary to ensure that competency restoration providers who seek to use these techniques have the clinical skills and training necessary to implement the interventions efficaciously (e.g., with knowledge of cognitive processes, how impairments in cognitive abilities can impact everyday life; Bowie, 2020). Many graduate mental health programs only require introductory courses to cognition without instruction on CogRem as an intervention. As such, it may be up to individual trainees and clinicians to seek out instructional workshops and clinical-training opportunities (e.g., neuropsychology clinics, inpatient psychiatric facilities) where they can gain competence and experience in facilitating CogRem.

The Practice of Cognitive Exercises

CogRem can be conducted in an individual (one-on-one) or group setting. While there is no explicit rule regarding group size for CogRem groups, facilitators should use their clinical judgment and ensure that they are able to effectively manage and work with the number of individuals they accept into the group. There may be practical constraints on group size (e.g., number of computers or tablets available, size of the room, number of chairs) that affect decision-making in this regard.

Leading up to the start of CogRem, abilities to be strengthened, and specific and achievable goals should be collaboratively established between the participant and facilitator. Regardless of whether CogRem is conducted in an individual or group format, in each session treatment participants work independently on their own assigned tasks based on their treatment needs and goals. When CogRem is conducted in a group setting, all the individuals in a group may be working on completely different tasks. Typically, each participant moves on from one task to the next when their first task is completed rather than at the start of the next session. Tasks that are not completed within a CogRem session may be resumed in the next session. Unrushed task completion allows for the development of confidence and a sense of mastery.

In CogRem, repetition and frequent practice is key for participants to make gains; generally individual or group sessions should occur at least twice a week (Bowie et al., 2020; Medalia & Richardson, 2005). According to Bowie and colleagues (2020, p. 51), repetition and frequent doses of the intervention are core features of successful CogRem.

CogRem can occur in an analogue (i.e., pen and paper) format or through computer-based programs (e.g., HappyNeuron, Lumosity). Research has demonstrated that both format types have similar overall efficacy and contribute to general cognitive improvements in schizophrenia (Zhu et al., 2022). Analogue activities are most easily adapted to the psycholegal context of competency restoration, although other aspects of CogRem (e.g., bridging sessions, described later in this chapter) allow either format to be a part of the competency restoration process.

Analogue Treatment Programs

Analogue format CogRem programs typically involve completing pen and paper tasks, such as solving mazes, matching symbols to numbers, completing puzzles, and using other worksheets (e.g., math problems, word searches). Members of the same group will generally be working on different tasks based on their individual needs and treatment goals. However, depending on the treatment setting, the facilitator may adapt more traditional cognitive remediation and opt to pick a "theme" for the day and have members work together on the same tasks to facilitate prosocial interactions among group members; this may be the preferred method in inpatient hospital settings. With this in mind, analogue intervention tools could be easily modified or supplemented for competency restoration by adding legal themes to the tasks (see "Legal Math Worksheet" in Appendix B). For instance, a jigsaw puzzle of a courtroom scene could be introduced in addition to, or instead of, a puzzle of a nonlegal subject. Worksheets such as legally themed word searches and word scrambles (see Appendix A) are already in use across the U.S. as part of competency restoration toolkits.

An example of an analogue CogRem treatment program is the Frontal/Executive Program (FEP; Delahunty & Morice, 1993), which was developed in Australia. In the FEP, a therapist conducts hour-long, one-on-one sessions. The sessions involve pencil and paper tasks, as well as tasks that utilize hand movements and physical manipulation (e.g., sorting tokens, manipulating blocks). There are three primary modules: *cognitive flexibility* (enhance flexibility in attention and cognition); *working memory* (mentally manipulating sets of information); and *planning* (make a plan for a task and perform that task according to the plan).

Computer-Based Treatment Programs

With computer-based CogRem treatment programs, individual participants complete exercises on a computer or tablet, such as memory games or solving puzzles. As with the analogue programs, members of the same group may be working on different tasks based on their individual needs and treatment goals. Depending on the treatment setting, CogRem may involve readily accessible games (e.g., I Spy, Carmen SanDiego, Zoombinis) that involve various cognitive processes to play (e.g., attention, memory, executive functioning), without a formal protocol. There are also more formalized programs that develop individualized protocols and assign exercises based on an initial diagnostic test. Of course, from the available options, the CogRem facilitator can and should select exercises based on the goals and needs of each participant.

The Neuropsychological Educational Approach to Remediation (NEAR; Medalia et al., 2018) computerized CogRem protocol is an example of a structured protocol. NEAR was developed by Alice Medalia, PhD and colleagues for use with psychiatric patients. This protocol is typically conducted in small groups of six to eight participants using computer programs. Each participant completes tasks tailored to their individual needs and work at their own pace. The therapist provides feedback and encouragement and helps bridge tasks to daily functioning. At the end of the group, the group participants come together to further discuss how the skills they worked on today could be applied to everyday life. Typically, within the NEAR protocol, the group has two sessions per week, with each session lasting 60 to 90 minutes.

Attention to the Development of Cognitive Strategies

During each session, the CogRem facilitator introduces and encourages use of strategies for approaching tasks and increasing the participant's confidence in their ability to complete their assigned task. Regardless of the modality used, clinicians facilitating the group should focus on helping participants identify cognitive strategies used to complete various tasks. This may involve explicitly identifying various strategies someone is using (e.g., systematically searching through rows of a word search, crossing out incorrect options when using trial and error to solve a task), or asking what skills they are using while completing specific tasks (e.g., planning and spatial reasoning when trying to manipulate blocks to match a sample).

During CogRem, participants may be encouraged to take notes of skills and strategies for later reference or study; in general, note-taking is a good strategy for individuals with cognitive impairment to practice. Depending on motor ability and literacy, assistance in such note-taking may be necessary. If necessary, CogRem facilitators may also provide some assistance in session with manipulatives (e.g., pens, computer mouses) necessary to complete tasks. However, the facilitators are not completing the tasks for the participants or giving them the answers to the problems they aim to solve.

Sometimes, group members may help each other complete tasks, in a mentor-mentee role, allowing participants to share strategies that work for them. However, as each group member is likely enrolled in the group because they may benefit from CogRem interventions, participants may also be redirected to focus on their own lessons.

Procedures to Facilitate the Transfer of Cognitive Gains to Everyday Functioning

At the end of each CogRem session, once tasks are completed for the day, the participant(s) and group facilitator come together for a bridging discussion. The key piece of CogRem (i.e., even beyond drawing attention to cognitive strategies in the moment), regardless of format, is this bridging discussion (Bowie et al., 2020). This bridging discussion involves CogRem participants discussing the tasks they completed and skills they worked on during that day's session and how those tasks and skills may apply to everyday life. An effective bridging discussion helps facilitate generalization to "real-world" scenarios outside of the treatment room. In incorporating CogRem with competency restoration, the facilitator may bring into the bridging discussion how the strategies etc. they practiced could be used within the psycholegal context (see "What Can Help Me Reach My Goals" in Appendix B for a relevant strategies and accommodations worksheet).

At the end of a CogRem session, CogRem facilitators may assign homework, challenging each treatment participant to try to use various strategies in their daily life between sessions. Homework activities allow participants to continue to practice and utilize skills outside of session, which allows for greater generalization of skills learned in session. The participant(s) may then discuss their difficulties and successes in utilizing the skills during the next bridging discussion. Homework may be informal (e.g., asking participants to notice when they use a skill) or more structured (e.g., asking participants to log when they use a skill in their notebook). Some CogRem clinicians may wish to assign practice exercises or worksheets to be completed between sessions.

THE CASE FOR USING COGNITIVE REMEDIATION AS AN ADJUNCT TO COMPETENCY RESTORATION

In considering that navigating one's legal defense is a requirement of everyday functioning for pretrial defendants, and that CogRem is designed to improve the daily functioning of treatment participants, the clinical rationale for incorporating CogRem strategies into competency restoration becomes clear.

As noted above, a general goal of CogRem is to improve a person's adaptive functional abilities (Bowie et al., 2020). As such, CogRem and related interventions are often used to strengthen a person's ability to function as a human at a basic level. While skills for maintaining one's activities of daily living (ADLs) may not, at first glance, be directly relevant to competency, a defendant is expected to be bathed and appropriately dressed for court, navigate whatever transportation is needed to attend court as scheduled, plan to feed themselves and use the bathroom around the court's schedule, adhere to expectations for courtroom behavior, and advocate for themselves as needed. For individuals with significant mental or physical health problems, filling prescriptions, organizing their medications, and taking them as prescribed may be necessary for maintaining their level of adaptive functioning. Adaptive functioning, including the management of health problems (e.g., mental health symptoms), is essential for defendants who need to be able to actively assist in their defense and maintain decorum in court.

Individuals with pending legal charges are also regularly tasked with meeting court-related demands. At a foundational level, the ability to assist in one's defense requires several specific functional and neurocognitive abilities. Defendants are required to remember and attend scheduled court dates (global cognitive functioning, orientation, planning), comport themselves appropriately in a courtroom (emotion regulation, impulse control), track court proceedings (attention, processing speed), ask questions and advocate for themselves as needed (communication), engage in problem-solving (executive functioning, calculation), learn new information about the legal system and their case (verbal learning, verbal memory), and apply knowledge of the court system to their personal situation (working memory). While other functions are also in use for pretrial defendants, we call attention to these because with consistency, improvements in global cognitive functioning, executive functioning, orientation, attention/processing speed, calculation, planning, verbal learning, verbal memory, and working memory have been identified as specific outcomes of CogRem through meta-analysis (e.g., Kurtz et al., 2001; Samamé et al., 2023; Thérond et al., 2021).

Metacognition, one area that can be strengthened with CogRem, refers to the ability to think about and consider one's own thoughts. This is essential for defendants who may need to testify as to what occurred in the time leading up to their arrest or convey to a forensic evaluator what transpired for the purpose of a sanity evaluation. *Social cognition*, another complex process that can develop with CogRem (Vidarsdottir et al., 2019), involves processing, remembering, and applying information about other people and group dynamics; this may be especially relevant to competency, as a defendant considers how a judge or jury might perceive their case in a trial, for example. Social cognition and related interpersonal skills (psychosocial functioning) are also necessary for a defendant who needs to interact productively with their defense attorney.

CogRem's ability to fortify a person's neurocognitive abilities generally—and help them feel a sense of mastery in their ability to navigate complex situations—is also relevant to defendants. Although the bulk of the research on the efficacy of CogRem focuses on improvements in executive functioning among individuals with schizophrenia and related psychotic disorders (e.g., Bowie et al., 2020; Cella et al., 2017; Vidarsdottir et al., 2019), individuals without a formal psychotic disorder may also benefit from relevant interventions and theory. For example, the problem-solving strategies taught through CogRem may help improve the psycholegal functioning of pretrial defendants undergoing competency restoration without SMI or neurocognitive problems, for whom reasoned decision-making is essential, by boosting their confidence in their ability to assist in their defense. Individuals with word-finding problems may benefit from CogRem-inspired memory aids (see, e.g., "Legal Word Bank" in Appendix B). Visuospatial memory and verbal fluency, which have not been consistently shown to improve with CogRem, are arguably less essential to competency, although they can be capitalized on with competency restoration interventions (e.g., using legal flash cards and courtroom diagrams).

These authors are aware of only one program that is designed to formally incorporate cognitive skills building and competency restoration using CogRem principles. The Functional Rehabilitation and Education Experience (FREE) program is a 12-week blended (computerized/analogue hybrid) program with curricula for both English-speaking and monolingual Spanish-speaking defendants. An early effectiveness study (Aguilar & King, 2024) yielded promising results regarding the acceptability of the program and attendance rates as well. These data suggest that the adult (mean age 43.79, *SD* = 12.95; range 20–70) felony defendants with psychotic disorders who participated in this program found the training engaging and also beneficial. Trial competency progress was perceived as significantly improved over the course of 12 weeks, for both English-speaking and Spanish-speaking defendants. That program is still in development, and protocols are not yet available to clinicians outside of the California state hospital system.

COGNITIVE REMEDIATION AND COMPETENCY RESTORATION IN PRACTICE

At the start of CogRem, the facilitator should introduce themselves and orient the participant(s) to CogRem as a modality. If CogRem is to be conducted in a group setting, an introduction to the group rules and group members is also indicated. Additionally, it is as necessary to orient the defendant to the available technology as to the treatment itself. This is particularly true when using computers/tablets and working with older adults (i.e., who are most likely to be experiencing cognitive decline associated with serious mental illness and/or neurocognitive decline) and others who have not spent the majority of their lives without access to modern technology (e.g., those who were imprisoned or hospitalized for much of their lives). When CogRem is introduced as part of competency restoration, the facilitator should educate the new participant about the role CogRem has in competency restoration early on. Participants should be made aware that their statements and behaviors during group may be documented in progress notes or otherwise relayed to other treatment providers, as is the case in other clinical interventions. Protections and limitations to confidentiality should be reviewed.

During this introductory meeting or in a subsequent meeting, a pre-intervention assessment should be conducted. A participant may have already completed a cognitive-screening measure or intellectual assessment leading up to the referral for CogRem. However, a pre-intervention assessment typically involves administration of several broadband neurocognitive measures (e.g., Wechsler Adult Intelligence Scale-IV [WAIS-IV]; Repeatable Battery for the Assessment of Neuropsychological Status [RBANS] Update) that can provide both baseline measurements for the individual's current cognitive functioning and identify key areas of weakness that can be targeted during interventions. The results of this assessment may inform goal setting and treatment planning within CogRem. That is, the clinician and participant will collaboratively identify the participant's specific cognitive problems and establish achievable long- and short-term goals. When CogRem is used in the context of competency restoration, the primary long-term goal of treatment is naturally for the participant to attain competency. However, this may be broken down into smaller, more manageable sub-goals that are specific to the treatment participant and their identified deficits (see "My CogRem Goals" worksheet in Appendix B). While motivation to resolve one's legal situation may be enough to motivate some participants for treatment, other defendants may benefit from identifying more personal (i.e., nonlegal) goals. The participant's personal goals can be added or adjusted over the course of treatment. The overarching psycholegal goal (competency attainment) may be removed if the person's psycholegal situation changes (e.g., if their charges are dropped).

As indicated above, CogRem can be introduced in an individual or group-based setting. This means that CogRem can be introduced as a general clinical group parallel to other competency restoration interventions, in a legally themed group, by a trained therapist who is not also a competency restoration provider, or as part of one-on-one competency restoration services. CogRem facilitators may opt to use a formal analogue or computerized protocol for interventions or use less structured CogRem interventions if that is what is available at their facility. With more formalized protocols, it may be necessary to make adjustments in implementation based on the setting (see "The Treatment Context" later in this chapter).

The bulk of individual CogRem sessions is typically spent on practicing cognitive exercises relevant to participant goals. Repetition (i.e., practicing select tasks more than once) and frequency (i.e., holding sessions at least twice weekly) are imperative. This emphasis on repetition and frequent doses is similar to the Slater Method (a protocol for competency restoration with defendants who have intellectual disabilities; see Chapter 4). The practice of cognitive exercises and attention to the development of cognitive strategies can be supplemented with homework. For example, a defendant participating in CogRem as part of competency restoration may be encouraged to complete worksheets involving legal-themed word puzzles between sessions, using the skills they recently learned or practiced.

During CogRem sessions and CogRem-informed restoration sessions, the clinician should frequently provide in vivo feedback. This may contrast sharply with the format of a formal competency evaluation, wherein feedback on how a participant is doing (i.e., whether specific responses are adequate, and whether they "pass" or "fail" the evaluation) tends to be minimal; that may need to be processed. It is generally agreed that feedback in CogRem should focus more on praise for trying different strategies and staying on task rather than on actual task performance or completion (Bowie et al., 2020). This helps promote intrinsic motivation and reduces the risk of participants making negative attributions associated with performance on the tasks themselves.

Throughout this intervention phase, defendants participating in CogRem should be encouraged to self-monitor and track their own progress, as the clinician does the same. The clinician should help the participant(s) develop methods of self-monitoring their use of different techniques and strategies they find useful, so that they can be shared with the clinician or other participants in session (Bowie et al., 2020). It is necessary to ensure there is a way to track progress made during treatment, both so gains are perceived and so that new goals can be set if needed. It may also be helpful to ask participants to keep track of competency-related interactions (e.g., restoration groups, conversations with their attorney) to see if they notice a difference in competency-related abilities over the course of treatment.

As noted earlier in this chapter, bridging discussions to help promote generalization of skills to real-world activities is critical in maintaining the gains made during the treatment (Bowie et al., 2020). The workgroup with Bowie and colleagues (2020) noted that use of staged tasks may also help maximize the ecological validity of the CogRem interventions. In the case of CogRem as a component of competency restoration, use of simulated tasks and role-play activities may help the defendant practice the skills they are learning in a way that translates directly to their real-world situation. A defendant may benefit, for example, from a simulated conversation with the clinician acting as their defense attorney (e.g., with the participant engaged in a targeted discussion about the allegations against them or legal strategies that might be pursued) or from participating in a mock trial (see "Mock Court" in Appendix A). The clinician may pause such experiences to remind the participant to use specific cognitive strategies and coping skills and/or to provide education in the moment. The experience can be discussed afterward in a debriefing; this may inform the defendant's short-term goals moving forward. Actively going through the motions of such tasks, with varying levels of support, may help the defendant gain a sense of mastery over their new cognitive skills and increase their comfort in the simulated psycholegal situation. Further, such activities can be implemented in the maintenance phase of competency restoration to forestall a deterioration of hard-earned gains in functioning.

CULTURAL CONSIDERATIONS AND RULE OUTS

Depending on modality and protocol, there are various factors that clinicians may want to consider when deciding if CogRem would be appropriate and beneficial for a particular individual. Medalia and colleagues (2018) recommended the following screening criteria for the computerized NEAR protocol: sufficient psychiatric stability to sit for sessions, age between 13 and 65 years old, premorbid intelligence level estimated at borderline range or higher (IQ > 70), reading level greater than or equal to the fourth grade, no traumatic brain injury (TBI) within the past two years, and no active substance or alcohol dependency such that CogRem begins at least one month after detoxification. Still, many individuals undergoing competency restoration that are engaged in CogRem may not meet these criteria. Protocols can to an extent be adapted to best match the functioning and needs of the defendants.

One of the primary prerequisites for CogRem is that an individual needs to be able to tolerate engaging in the remediation activities for 45-minutes to an hour. Thus, individuals often need to have some degree of psychiatric stability before engaging in CogRem. Individuals who are not behaviorally stable enough to make appropriate use of manipulatives (e.g., pencils, paper, puzzles) or who are at elevated risk of damaging resources (e.g., computers) may not be appropriate for participation in CogRem. Safety and risk management are paramount.

It is worth drawing attention to the fact that older adults (age 65+) are identified as those to be excluded from this computer-based protocol. It is unclear if the rationale is related to concerns about natural cognitive decline or assumptions about fluency in use of modern technology. If the latter, individuals of any age raised with low or no access to computers, tablets, etc. might also be excluded from computer-based CogRem programming. Analogue CogRem programming may be an appropriate alternative, so as to not deprive such individuals of clinically indicated services; screening out individuals based on lack of lifetime access to technology has the potential to lead to discriminatory practices against folks raised with lower socioeconomic status, Indigenous persons, the Amish, etc. As our population ages and modern technology becomes more commonplace, and the new generation of older adults has more and more experience with technology, age-based exclusionary criteria might be revisited. Youth under the age of 13 are also identified as inappropriate for the NEAR protocol; other CogRem programs (e.g., Favre et al., 2018) are being used with younger children, however. In this chapter, we focus on CogRem as part of the competency restoration process for adults.

With respect to baseline intelligence and no recent TBI as inclusion criteria, extant research generally demonstrates that there is lower CogRem engagement among individuals with lower neurocognitive functioning (Altman et al., 2023). Additionally, factors related to premature dropout of CogRem interventions include "higher negative symptomatology and baseline self-efficacy, and lower baseline cognitive functioning and intrinsic motivation" (Altman et al., 2023, p. 139).

THE TREATMENT CONTEXT

Generally speaking, access (or lack of access) to technology has a great impact on the availability of CogRem programming (Altman et al., 2023) as well as treatment fidelity. Across contexts, low budgets for mental health services may limit access to technology to facilitate computer-based sessions. Clinicians set on introducing CogRem into competency restoration may need to adapt treatment to account for the lower availability of technology (e.g., smaller groups if there are only a few computers available; more pencil and paper tasks). Analogue CogRem may be pursued if appropriate technology is entirely unavailable (e.g., in jail or inpatient hospital settings).

Across contexts, there may be disruptions in CogRem services due to issues such as low staffing and quarantines that demand a suspension of services as an infection control precaution. Because CogRem interventions are individualized, and each participant works on tasks at their own pace, missed sessions (i.e., due to decompensation or otherwise) may not derail progress. If a significant amount of time lapses between sessions, it may be necessary to begin the CogRem processes over (i.e., starting with the pre-intervention assessment).

Considerations for Inpatient Hospital-Based Interventions

As noted in other chapters, hospital-competency restoration is often more expensive than restoration conducted in other settings (Kapoor, 2011), and there are a limited number of hospital beds available for individuals to undergo competency restoration. Despite the additional expenses, hospitals may be better equipped for CogRem than jails or other outpatient settings, with appropriate funding to manage a computer lab or other technological resources (e.g., tablets) to facilitate computer-based competency restoration services. In addition, hospitals typically have mechanisms to ensure that participants in treatment are simultaneously receiving and taking medications as prescribed, maximizing the likelihood of stability.

As emphasized above, individuals who participate in CogRem must be able to tolerate a full intervention session. In hospital settings, patients are also screened to ensure that they are safe enough behaviorally to participate in treatment programming on a given day. Often treatment interventions for inpatient defendants, including CogRem, occur in a treatment room off unit, and so elopement risk and related behavioral concerns must be cleared before they are allowed to attend treatment services in a less secure area than their unit. In hospital settings, computer-based CogRem protocols are likely to be limited to patients who are unlikely to act out in a room with expensive equipment. There also may be institutional concerns about what programs, applications, and websites can be accessed by patients using select computers; consultation with colleagues in the instructional technology (IT) department may be necessary. When using analogue CogRem protocols, pens and related manipulatives could present as a tool that increases risk of harm to the defendant or others. Psychiatric administration typically restricts what items are allowed in the hospital buildings or sections of buildings (the treatment mall or unit in particular), and clinicians may need to be prepared to adapt CogRem protocols to match those restrictions.

Given that each defendant's psychiatric and behavioral stability varies over time, a group participant initially deemed appropriate for CogRem interventions may become an inappropriate candidate thereafter. Efforts should be made to maintain rapport and encourage skills for coping when a defendant is suspended or otherwise deemed ineligible for CogRem interventions; at times, acting-out behaviors can result when a patient is restricted from programming that they want to attend. Such behavior could affect the patient's ability to attend treatment programming more broadly, beyond CogRem.

If CogRem interventions are taking place on an inpatient unit (versus a treatment mall), there may be additional environmental concerns. For one, there may be interruptions to treatment at regular intervals, due to staff performing patient observations as required by the facility in particular. In addition, there may be interruptions from peers who are intrigued by the interventions (i.e., which typically do look like games), wander into the treatment intervention area (e.g., to socialize), or otherwise pose a disruption in the milieu (e.g., responding to hallucinations without awareness that a treatment intervention is occurring nearby). Beyond concerns for the treatment participant being able to make responsible use of therapeutic tools, clinicians need to be conscious of the potential that peers in the shared space may get hold of manipulatives, etc.

Considerations for Jail-Based Interventions

The considerations for health and safety identified for inpatient CogRem generally apply in jail settings, as do some unique factors. As in other contexts, quarantines may disrupt CogRem interventions in jails, with communicable diseases able to spread rapidly in correctional facilities. Building infrastructure and limited space for treatment programming may also pose as barriers to treatment. In addition, lockdowns in correctional settings can restrict movement within the jail and limit access to mental health services generally (e.g., Felthous & Bloom, 2018; Kapoor, 2011).

Jails are also typically more restrictive than hospitals, with respect to safety and contraband policies. Thus, incarcerated pretrial defendants may have less access to technology and other CogRem resources than defendants in other settings. Clinicians may have to make more adaptations to protocols to make CogRem work in the jail setting. With more limited intervention options and less clinical staff, clinicians may opt to have treatment participants work on the same exercise in a group setting, rather than personalizing exercises for each individual participant, maximizing access to treatment. With more emphasis on detainment and less on treatment, pretrial inmates may have fewer opportunities to practice skills learned in CogRem outside of the treatment interventions (i.e., compared with defendants receiving services in other contexts).

Considerations for Community-Based Interventions

Community-based interventions often occur in settings that are less controlled than hospitals and jails. CogRem services may be administered via competency restoration at an outpatient mental health clinic, for example, with greater flexibility than in other settings. Skills can be practiced at home for individuals with access to personal technology (e.g., computer, smartphone, tablet) or analogue resources (e.g., I Spy books, puzzles), or they can be practiced at a local library.

Conversely, outpatient treatments put the burden of attendance on the defendant and their caregivers. Transit to the intervention setting for a scheduled appointment demands adaptive functioning, including skills related to scheduling, identifying how to travel to treatment, and actually executing those plans. For individuals who are good candidates for CogRem (i.e., those with cognitive problems because of chronic SMI), navigating public transit and related multistep tasks may be extremely difficult. Consideration of whether a defendant is functionally capable of attending treatment as scheduled may be part of the screening process. In addition, defendants out on bond who are participating in outpatient competency restoration/CogRem treatment also have greater access to illicit substances (Danzer et al., 2019), and they are most able to discontinue psychiatric medication against medical advice; both of these are barriers that can impact treatment engagement and treatment outcomes. A recent meta-analysis identified multiple factors, including "exacerbation of symptoms, change in residence, lack of interest, lack of perceived relevance, travel burden, and time constraints," related to outpatient treatment dropout (Altman et al., 2023, p. 145); all of these factors can also impact the success of outpatient CogRem and competency restoration.

With respect to intrinsic factors, individuals in the community who are undergoing competency restoration may be less motivated regarding treatment (e.g., only attending because of a court mandate). In a review of the literature, Medalia and Saperstein (2011) found that, in an outpatient sample (where voluntary attendance can be assumed to be a measure of motivation for treatment), there was a higher rate of motivation in individuals who responded positively to CogRem interventions. Conversely, individuals with lower rates of motivation responded more negatively to CogRem interventions.

Case Example

Brett is a 60-year-old cisgender Japanese American man who is currently hospitalized in the forensic unit of a state psychiatric hospital for competency restoration. He was found incompetent to stand trial on a lead charge of aggravated assault due to inadequate factual and rational understanding of the court and his legal situation. During his most recent competency evaluation, he had trouble recalling who the key players in the courtroom are as well as factual details related to his case and charges. He also had trouble considering his options and thinking through potential outcomes of his case. It is unclear if he is experiencing cognitive decline because of a dementia-related condition or secondary to living long-term with schizophrenia. His psychiatric provider already prescribed cognition-enhancing medication to slow further possible decline; however, that medication is not expected to restore any of his cognitive functioning.

With respect to medical diagnoses, Brett is diagnosed with hypertension, and there is a family history of hypertension and stroke. He was first psychiatrically hospitalized at age 20 for symptoms of psychosis and has been in and out of hospitals every few years. This current legal case is his first involvement with the legal system. In between hospitalizations, he worked with various construction companies, with his longest consecutive period of employment being five years. He was never married and has no children. He has limited family contact; his older sister (age 65) would like to be more involved in his treatment, but she does not currently have the means to do so, as she lives in another state.

A psychologist, Dr. Johnson, conducts CogRem groups for the various units within the hospital. Dr. Johnson is a doctoral-level clinician who has taken classes in neuropsychology, and has some experience conducting cognitive/neuropsychological assessments, but is not a neuropsychologist. She has also attended several training sessions on the practice and implementation of CogRem, and she is familiar with the competency restoration work that occurs within the forensic unit.

Brett's treatment team refers him to Dr. Johnson's group. Dr. Johnson initially meets with him individually to orient him to the group. She describes the group structure (the group meets twice a week for an hour: 45 minutes of computer exercises, 15 minutes of bridging discussion) and works with him to identify personalized goals for treatment. Brett identifies memory and problem-solving as areas he would like to work on. Dr. Johnson walks Brett through a few sample exercises in the computer program to help him orient to the technology and the program itself. Dr. Johnson also conducts a brief assessment of his current neurocognitive abilities and identifies any other weaknesses that could be worked on during the group. Given her personal competencies and available resources at the hospital, she administers the Wechsler Abbreviated Scale of Intelligence, 2nd ed. (WASI-II) to get a general sense of Brett's intellectual functioning across domains. She also administers the RBANS Update, which can be administered in pre-test/post-test fashion, at the start and end of the CogRem group to assess for change in his cognitive functioning over time.

The assessment suggests that Brett has weaknesses in the domains of processing speed and memory and that verbal abilities are an area of strength. Dr. Johnson provides feedback to Brett about the testing results, and he agrees with the findings based on his experiences. The two work together to formulate specific and feasible goals for Brett's CogRem treatment (e.g., strengthen memory abilities so he can remember more specific details about his court case and the roles of key players in court). Dr. Johnson makes sure that there are some verbal tasks built into Brett's training program to help bolster his strengths while he works on his weaknesses.

The following week, Dr. Johnson brings Brett into the larger group for the first time. There are currently five other members who have been participating in the CogRem program for varying periods of time thus far. Dr. Johnson facilitates introductions then has the group begin working on their individual training plans on the computers. Dr. Johnson and another group facilitator are present to answer any questions, provide feedback on effort, and encourage use of different strategies to complete the exercises. One of the group members indicates she is having trouble with a task that involves solving a world puzzle, and another group member shares a strategy that worked for him when trying to complete a similar task. After 45 minutes, Dr. Johnson brings the group together to have a bridging discussion. That day's discussion focuses on memory, particularly on different strategies to remember information (e.g., mnemonics, making a list as a compensatory strategy). During this bridging discussion, Dr. Johnson prompts group participants to consider the ways in which memory affects a person's ability to assist in their defense, and she encourages consideration of how to apply the discussed strategies for remembering information in a legal context. As the group is ending, Dr. Johnson asks the group to try out the different memory strategies during the next few days (before the next group) and be prepared to share with the group how the strategies worked for them or what difficulties they ran into. Dr. Johnson provides the group with a self-monitoring form so they can track when they used different strategies and how well they worked. Dr. Johnson also shares a progress report from the computer program with Brett and explains that he will see these forms at the end of every group; these will allow him to keep an eye on his progress.

At the next group, Brett starts his CogRem exercises. He tells Dr. Johnson that the exercises seem harder. Dr. Johnson explains that the program is adapting to his skills and abilities, and she works with him to help develop different strategies to complete his more difficult exercises. At the end of the group, the group continues their discussion on memory from last time. The group members share how they used different strategies during the week and provide feedback to each other on their efforts. They continue to discuss how to apply those strategies to real-world situations, including specific legal situations. Brett provides the example that he could bring notes with him on the witness stand, if he chooses to testify about what happened leading up to his arrest, to help him remember the details he needs to convey. The group suggests that Brett's lawyer may be able to help him create those notes.

The group continues much the same way over the next several weeks. The group shifts from working on memory to discussing various problem-solving strategies. Some of the bridging discussions include ways that problem-solving strategies may be relevant to their case (e.g., if they are in the courtroom, how can they appropriately address disagreements with what is being said about them? How might they go about considering different plea options available to them?). After 10 weeks in the group, Brett has another competency evaluation. The evaluator notes that his factual understanding has greatly improved, as has his ability to consider different options available to him in his case, and he is found competent to proceed.

REFERENCES

Aguilar, C., & King, L. C. (2024, June). *Improving accessibility and relevance of cognitive remediation in a forensic state hospital for English and monolingual Spanish speaking individuals* [Symposium]. 26th Annual Cognitive Remediation in Psychiatry Conference, New York, NY.

Ahmed, A. O., Hunter, K. M., Goodrum, N. M., Batten, N. J., Birgenheir, D., Hardison, E., . . . Buckley, P. F. (2015). A randomized study of cognitive remediation for forensic and mental health patients with schizophrenia. *Journal of Psychiatric Research*, *68*, 8–18. doi:10.1016/j.jpsychires.2015.05.013

Altman, R. A. E., Tan, E. J., & Rossell, S. L. (2023). Factors impacting access and engagement of cognitive remediation therapy for people with schizophrenia: A systematic review. *The Canadian Journal of Psychiatry*, *68*(3), 139–151. doi:10.1177/07067437221129073

Bowie, C. R., Bell, M. D., Fiszdon, J. M., Johannesen, J. K., Lindenmayer, J. P., McGurk, S. R., . . . Wykes, T. (2020). Cognitive remediation for schizophrenia: An expert working group white paper on core techniques. *Schizophrenia Research*, *215*, 49–53. doi:10.1016/j.schres.2019.10.047

Cella, M., Preti, A., Edwards, C., Dow, T., & Wykes, T. (2017). Cognitive remediation for negative symptoms of schizophrenia: A network meta-analysis. *Clinical Psychology Review*, *52*, 43–51. doi:10.1016/j.cpr.2016.11.009

Chen, H-Y., Li, M-C., Liao, D., Li, C., Ji, Q-M., Guo, . . . Zhai, W-H. (2022). The effect of computer-assisted cognitive remediation therapy on cognitive function, social function, and quality of life in patients with vascular dementia. *Journal of Multidisciplinary Healthcare*, *15*, 2473–2479. doi:10.2147/jmdh.s378079

Danzer, G. S., Wheeler, E. M. A., Alexander, A. A., & Wasser, T. D. (2019). Competency restoration for adult defendants in different treatment environments. *Journal of the American Academy of Psychiatry and the Law*, *47*(1), 68–81. https://jaapl.org/

Delahunty, A., & Morice, R. (1993). *A manual for neurocognitive rehabilitation for patients with chronic schizophrenia: Frontal Executive Program.* Albury New South Wales, Department of Health.

DeTore, N. R., Mueser, K. T., Byrd, J. A., & McGurk, S. R. (2019). Cognitive functioning as a predictor of response to comprehensive cognitive remediation. *Journal of Psychiatric Research*, *113*, 117–124. doi:10.1016/j.jpsychires.2019.03.012

Favre, E., Peyroux, E., Babinet, M-N., Poisson, A., & Demily, C. (2018). Computer-based cognitive remediation program from the treatment of behavioral problems in children with intellectual disability: the "Cognitus & MOI" study protocol for a randomized control trial. *BMC Psychiatry*, *18*, 235. doi:10.1186/s12888-018-1810-z

Felthous, A. R., & Bloom, J. D. (2018). Jail-based competency restoration. *Journal of the American Academy of Psychiatry and the Law*, *46*, 364–372. doi:10.29158/JAAPL.003772-18

Kapoor, R. (2011). Commentary: Jail-based competency restoration. *Journal of the American Academy of Psychiatry and the Law*, *39*, 311–315. https://jaapl.org/content/39/3/311

Kim, W. Y., Han, C. H., Heo, E. J., Kang, H. W., & Jeon, W. K. (2011). A review of non-pharmacological intervention efficacy in patients with mild cognitive impairment. *Journal of Oriental Neuropsychiatry*, *22*(3), 1–11. doi:10.7231/JON.2011.22.3.001

Kurtz, M. M., Moberg, P. J., Gur, R. C., & Gur, R. E. (2001). Approaches to cognitive remediation of neuropsychological deficits in schizophrenia: A review and meta-analysis. *Neuropsychology Review*, *11*(4), 197–210. doi:1040-7308/01/1200-0197/0

Legemaat, A. M., Semkovska, M., Brouwer, M., Geurtsen, G. J., Burger, H., Denys, D., & Bockting, C. L. (2022). Effectiveness of cognitive remediation in depression: A meta-analysis. *Psychological Medicine*, *52*(16), 4146–4161. doi:10.1017/S0033291721001100

Maxmen, J. S., Ward, N. G., & Kilgus, M. (2009). *Essential psychopathology and its treatment* (3rd ed.). W. W. Norton.

McGurk, S. R., Twamley, E. W., Sitzer, D. I., McHugo, G. J., & Mueser, K. T. (2007). A meta-analysis of cognitive remediation in schizophrenia. *American Journal of Psychiatry*, *164*(12), 1791–1802. doi:10.1176/appi.ajp.2007.07060906

Medalia, A., Herlands, T., Saperstein, A., & Revheim, N. (2018). *Cognitive remediation for psychological disorders: Therapist guide.* Oxford University Press.

Medalia, A., & Richardson, R. (2005). What predicts a good response to cognitive remediation interventions? *Schizophrenia Bulletin, 31*(4), 942–953. doi:10.1093/schbul/sbi045

Medalia, A., & Saperstein, A. M. (2011). The role of motivation for treatment success. *Schizophrenia Bulletin, 37*(2), S122–S128. doi:10.1093/schbul/sbr063

Michalopoulou, P. G., Lewis, S. W., Wykes, T., Jaeger, J., & Kapur, S. (2013). Treating impaired cognition in schizophrenia: The case for combining cognitive-enhancing drugs with cognitive remediation. *European Neuropsychopharmacology, 23*(8), 790–798. doi:10.1016/j.euroneuro.2013.03.012

Revell, E. R., Neill, J. C., Harte, M., Zhan, Z., & Drake, R. J. (2015). A systematic review and meta-analysis of cognitive remediation in early schizophrenia. *Schizophrenia Research, 168*, 213–222. doi:10.1016/j.schres.2015.08.017

Rhee, T. G., Shim, S. R., Manning, K. J., Tennen, H. A., Kaster, T. S., d'Andrea, . . . Steffens, D. C. (2024). Neuropsychological assessments of cognitive impairment in major depressive disorder: A systematic review and meta-analysis with meta-regression. *Psychotherapy and Psychosomatics, 93*(1), 1–16. doi:10.1159/000535665

Samamé, C., Durante, P., Cattaneo, B., Aprahamian, I., & Strejilevich, S. (2023). Efficacy of cognitive remediation in bipolar disorder: Systematic review and meta-analysis of randomized controlled trials. *Psychological Medicine, 53*(12), 5361–5373. doi:10.1017/S0033291723001897

Schwalbe, E., & Medalia, A. (2007). Cognitive dysfunction and competency restoration: Using cognitive remediation to help restore the unrestorable. *Journal of the American Academy of Psychiatry and Law, 35*, 518–525. http://jaapl.org/content/35/4/518/tab-article-info

Thérond, A., Pezzoli, P., Abbas, M., Howard, A., Bowie, C. R., & Guimond, S. (2021). The efficacy of cognitive remediation in depression: A systematic literature review and meta-analysis. *Journal of Affective Disorders, 284*, 238–246. doi:10.1016/j.jad.2021.02.009

Tulliani, N., Bissett, M., Fahey, P., Bye, R., & Liu, K. P. Y. (2022). Efficacy of cognitive remediation on activities of daily living in individuals with mild cognitive impairment or early-stage dementia: A systematic review and meta-analysis. *Systematic Reviews, 11*, 156. doi:10.1186/s13643-022-02032-0

Van Duin, D., de Winter, L., Oud, M., Kroon, H., Veling, W., & van Weeghel, J. (2019). The effect of rehabilitation combined with cognitive remediation on functioning in persons with severe mental illness: Systematic review and meta-analysis. *Psychological Medicine, 49*, 1414–1425. doi:10.1017/S003329171800418

Vidarsdottir, O. G., Roberts, D. L., Twamley, E. W., Gudmundsdottir, B., Sigurdsson, E., & Magnusdottir, B. B. (2019). Integrative cognitive remediation for early psychosis: Results from a randomized control trial. *Psychiatry Research, 273*, 690–698. doi:10.1016/j.psychres.2019.02.007

Vita, A., Barlati, S., Ceraso, A., Deste, G., Nibbio, G., & Wykes, T. (2022). Acceptability of cognitive remediation for schizophrenia: A systematic review and meta-analysis of randomized controlled trials. *Psychological Medicine, 53*(8), 3661–3671. doi:10.1017/S0033291722000319

Wykes, T., Huddy, V., Cellard, C., McGurk, S. R., & Czobor, P. (2011). A meta-analysis of cognitive remediation for schizophrenia: Methodology and effect sizes. *American Journal of Psychiatry, 168*(5), 472–485. doi:10.1176/appi.ajp.2010.10060855

Zapf, P. A., & Roesch, R. (2011). Future directions in the restoration of competency to stand trial. *Current Directions in Psychological Science, 20*, 43–47. doi:10.1177/0963721410396798

Zhu, X., Fan, H., Zou, Y., Tan, Y., Yang, F., Wang, Z., . . . Wykes, T. (2022). Computerized or manual? Long term effects of cognitive remediation on schizophrenia. *Schizophrenia Research, 239*, 47–54. doi:10.1016/j.schres.2021.11.019

Zondo, S. (2023). The cognitive remediation of attention in HIV-associated neurocognitive disorders (HAND): A meta-analysis and systematic review [version 1]. *F1000Research, 12*, 1133. doi:10.12688/f1000research.132166.1

PART IV

Situational Distress as a Barrier to Competency

6

Cognitive Behavioral Therapy (CBT) and Acceptance and Commitment Therapy (ACT) and Competency Restoration

KEVIN WAYMIRE, PHD AND MADDISON SCHIAFO, PHD

DISTRESS AS A BARRIER TO COMPETENCY

Symptoms of psychological distress are known to negatively affect an individual's ability to function to their fullest potential. For instance, both anxious and mood disorders are frequently associated with significantly poorer concentration. As such, diminished attentional functioning is a potential qualifying symptom common to both categories of psychological/emotional dysfunction (American Psychiatric Association, 2022). With respect to anxiety specifically, research findings have often demonstrated its manifestations tend to impair cognitive performance, particularly when individuals are taxed with complex and attentionally demanding tasks (Derakshan & Eysenck, 2009). Moreover, anxiety in general has been found to negatively impact verbal episodic memory (i.e., the ability to remember verbally presented information; Gifford et al., 2015) and executive functioning (Airaksinen et al., 2005), which consists of higher order cognitive processes such as planning, decision-making, and problem-solving (American Psychological Association [APA], 2023b).

With respect to mood symptoms, particularly those consistent with unipolar depression, associated disruptions of cognitive processes have also been well documented. For instance, depressed mood has been associated with mnemonic and executive deficits (Austin et al., 2001), as well as decrements in episodic memory and mental flexibility (Airaksinen et al., 2004). In cases of more severe depression—particularly with older adults—individuals may even appear to be experiencing symptoms consistent with dementia, though without associated neurodegenerative etiology (i.e., pseudodementia; Mouta et al., 2023). Moreover, some research findings suggest that when individuals are experiencing comorbid depression and anxiety, marked cognitive dysfunction may result, which is greater than that present when symptoms of either predominate (DeLuca et al., 2005; Basso et. al, 2007; Kizilbash et al., 2002).

Within forensic populations in particular, there are numerous potential stressors that may contribute to negative emotionality and which likely begin early in the legal process (i.e., contact with law enforcement). For instance, arrest itself may lead to the development of future-oriented stressors, insofar as obscuring certainty about the immediate and more distal future (Pearlin & Bierman, 2013). That is, individuals entering the criminal justice

Kevin Waymire and Maddison Schiafo, Cognitive Behavioral Therapy (CBT) and Acceptance and Commitment Therapy (ACT) and Competency Restoration. In: *The Competency Restoration Handbook*. Edited by: Laura M. Grossi, Oxford University Press. © Laura M. Grossi (2025). DOI: 10.1093/9780197768075.003.0006 system, whether for the first time or as someone who has experienced multiple contacts with the legal system, experience uncertainty relative to numerous issues, including possible trial, conviction, punishments (e.g., confinement/associated duration), and factors related to continued communications with family (Kohler-Hausmann, 2013).

Sugie and Turney (2017) also identified secondary stressors related to contact with the criminal justice system, such as the availability of online mugshots, which may then lead to difficulties with housing and occupational attainment post-arrest, conviction, and/or incarceration. Moreover, individuals entering the criminal justice system commonly experience more acute stressors in terms of their immediate situation and environment, including transition into and out of incarceration, loss of autonomy, personal safety/conflicts with others, etc. (Massoglia & Remster, 2019). Overall, the transition from community living to incarceration has been linked with depression and anxiety (Schnittker & John, 2007; Cloyes et al., 2006), as well as symptoms of post-traumatic stress (Wolff, 2009).

In the context of the aforementioned, psychological distress related to situational factors may present a substantial barrier to competency, as well as associated restoration processes. Accordingly, the use of psychological interventions to treat such distress (e.g., depression and anxiety) may be efficacious in deconstructing at least some obstructions along an individual's path to trial competence.

COGNITIVE BEHAVIORAL THERAPY FOR ANXIETY AND DEPRESSION

Cognitive behavioral therapy (CBT) is a well-established and empirically supported treatment modality for symptoms of anxiety, depression, and several other psychological disorders (Hofmann et al., 2012). The foundation of CBT rests on cognitive theory, which posits that psychological difficulties arise—in part—from maladaptive thinking patterns (Beck, A.T., 1970). The cognitive model proposed by Aaron Beck asserts that these maladaptive thinking patterns (e.g., unhelpful/irrational beliefs and cognitive distortions, such as all-or-nothing thinking, catastrophizing) act as a lens through which individuals perceive situations, leading to distressing emotions and problematic behaviors (Beck, A.T., 1963; Beck et al., 1979). Many of these thoughts/interpretations are said to be automatic in nature and partially based on attitudes and assumptions derived from past experiences (i.e., schemas; Beck et al., 1979). Overall, this repeated manner of thinking and perceiving situations leads to rather entrenched and negative beliefs about oneself, the world, and the future. As a result of these beliefs, varied psychiatric symptoms arise (Beck, A.T. 1979; Beck & Fleming, 2021). Ergo, if one can change these unhelpful thinking patterns, healthier emotions and behaviors will prevail (Beck, A.T. 1979). As the name suggests, CBT also incorporates techniques derived from behavioral theory (e.g., classical and operant conditioning) and which are based on the notion that problematic behaviors are learned/reinforced through environmental interactions. Thus, it is the extinction of these maladaptive behaviors, or the development of those more adaptive in nature, by which individuals may improve their overall functioning (Skinner, 1971).

In sum, CBT incorporates theory and interventions from both cognitive and behavioral approaches to address problematic elements relative to the interplay among thoughts, behaviors, and emotions (Knapp & Beck, 2008). In this chapter, we will discuss three primary CBT interventions for the use of reducing anxious and depressive symptoms consistent with situational distress, which may be a barrier to competency and/or impede competence restoration.

RELEVANT CBT INTERVENTIONS

The first, and perhaps most well-known, CBT intervention we will cover is *cognitive restructuring. Behavioral activation* and the development of *relaxation skills* in concert with the implementation of *exposure techniques* are also likely to be of significant utility relative to diminishing symptoms of depression and anxiety related to situational distress.

Cognitive Restructuring

In short, cognitive restructuring (CR) aims to aid clients in identifying, refuting, and modifying cognitive distortions in such a manner that more rational and adaptive thinking results, which in turn may serve to diminish psychological distress (APA, 2023a). It is of note that CR is not one intervention; rather, it is a suite of methods used to induce schematic change (Newman, 2016). As outlined by Clark (2013), there are three main components vital to the success of CR, and the first is *collaborative empiricism.* Collaborative empiricism highlights the notion that a working relationship between patient and provider is necessary for effective change, as is the continual re-evaluation of patients' entrenched beliefs/attitudes through an investigative lens. This component of change also emphasizes learning (e.g., to recognize cognitive distortions) and the experimental evaluation of one's beliefs (Kuyken et al., 2009). One method frequently employed by providers, which may serve to both establish a working relationship and gain insight into the validity/veracity of patients' cognitions/beliefs, is Socratic questioning (Clark, 2013), which we will briefly discuss later in this section.

The second component of CR detailed by Clark (2013) is the use of *verbal interventions.* These interventions are perhaps the most recognized component of CR; they are employed to appraise, refute, and modify maladaptive schemas (see Beck et al., 1979).[1] Although there are several verbal interventions, some of the most common consist of steps taken while completing thought logs/variations of ABC(DE) worksheets (see Appendix B for examples). For instance, a patient might be tasked with identifying an *activating* situation (i.e., one associated with psychological distress), their *belief* about said situation, and the (emotional/behavioral) *consequences* of their belief, followed by efforts to *dispute* said beliefs and to employ more *effective* manners of thinking. If completed successfully, this intervention should theoretically result in altered/improved emotional outcomes due to greater psychological flexibility, which undermines the negative emotionality and maladaptive behaviors associated with rigid (and perhaps irrational) thinking patterns (Reddy, et al., 2020).

The third component of CR (Clark, 2013) consists of *empirical hypothesis testing,* which is implemented after the identification of cognitive distortions associated with psychological distress and maladaptive behaviors. Empirical hypothesis testing tasks individuals with the formulation of hypotheses relative to distressing thoughts (e.g., "My legal case will never be over"), which frequently take the form of predictions about the future (Beck, J.S., 2011). Subsequently, clients are charged with gathering evidence for and against their hypotheses to test their associated likelihood of being true (Leahy, 2003). For instance, in order to test their hypothesis, an individual who believes their legal case may never end might ask their attorney if they have ever represented a client who has experienced such a situation.

1. Schemas represent entrenched/enduring beliefs individuals hold about themselves, others, and the world, whether or not they align with objective reality (APA, 2018).

Additionally, behavioral experiments may be performed to assess whether hypotheses come to fruition in real time. For example, if a defendant is declining to attend restoration groups due to fear of negative evaluation from others or concern relative to distress at the mention of legal materials, they may be tasked with in vivo attendance to test whether their hypotheses were correct or if they were perhaps skewed in the context of distorted thinking. Subsequently, the reevaluating of hypotheses may occur, and unhelpful beliefs may be modified with those more accurate and flexible in nature.

Behavioral Activation

Behavioral activation (BA) is an intervention designed to enhance a person's involvement in meaningful life activities by using guided goal setting to improve their thoughts, mood, and overall quality of life (APA, 2018). BA has strong research support relative to the treatment of depression, and it focuses on the interrelation of emotions and behaviors (Mazzucchelli et al., 2009). The primary aim of BA is to promote behaviors that increase individuals' exposure to environmental reinforcers while simultaneously diminishing behaviors (e.g., oversleeping, avoiding social contact) that are likely to keep said individuals from experiencing positive reinforcement (Quigley & Dobson, 2017).

Like other CBT techniques, specific steps in BA may be varied but do consist of several common elements, including psychoeducation relative to the development and maintenance of depression, monitoring daily activities, identifying personal goals and values, scheduling activities geared toward personal enjoyment/importance, and contingency planning regarding situations that represent obstacles toward progress (Kanter et al., 2010).

Relaxation Techniques

Relaxation techniques are primarily aimed at helping defendants better control symptoms of autonomic arousal (e.g., racing heart, uncontrolled breathing, trembling) consistent with symptoms of acute anxiety/panic. These symptoms tend to occur when an individual's body goes into "fight or flight" mode in response to a (real or imagined) threat. For most individuals, the use of relaxation techniques (e.g., diaphragmatic or paced breathing) is beneficial in terms of habituation to discomfort in anxiety-provoking situations. Of note, when autonomic dysregulation is successfully addressed via relaxation techniques, cognitive symptoms of anxiety/panic, such as racing thoughts, are also often reduced. Accordingly, psychoeducation and the practice of said techniques is strongly recommended *before* exposure techniques are implemented.

Exposure Techniques

Exposure techniques are also quite commonly employed in the context of CBT (Kaczkurkin & Foa, 2015). In short, exposure is typically used as a mechanism to help patients break a cycle of avoidance of feared stimuli; avoidance lends itself to short-term relief but ultimately reinforces said fear, which in turn leads to greater efforts to avoid the feared stimuli. Exposure is often implemented in a graded fashion, beginning with discussion of feared stimuli and creation of a fear/avoidance hierarchy, followed by imaginal, and eventually, in vivo (i.e., direct) exposure to the feared stimuli/situation (APA, 2017).

APPLICATIONS OF CBT INTERVENTIONS IN COMPETENCE RESTORATION

Please note that the use of the following techniques should be limited to professionals with adequate education, training, and supervision in implementing CBT. In short, inappropriate or inaccurate integration of any treatment modality may result in a host of poor outcomes, ranging from little to no patient response to actual psychological harm. In this context, we again stress the importance of clinical education, training, supervision, and continuing education.

The Therapeutic Relationship

As suggested above, therapeutic change via the use of CBT techniques requires a working collaboration between the provider and defendant. In this context, it is worth stating that the relationship between a mental health professional and defendant in the context of competency restoration is different than that developed between a provider and a patient in the community seeking mental health services on their own accord. The first difference, and perhaps the most obvious, is that treatment in the former context is often provided secondary to a court order and within a facility with restricted freedoms. Second, restoration services are geared toward dismantling barriers to competence—in some cases by diminishing psychological distress—which may be related to stressors stemming from the defendant's legal situation/immediate environment. The aim of most non-forensic mental health providers, however, is to decrease psychological distress in order to promote a greater sense of overall well-being and a higher degree of functioning. Although the result of using therapeutic techniques during the provision of competency restoration services may result in such an outcome, it is important to remember that the summative goal for restoration-focused providers is legally/forensically contextualized. That is, the efforts of the restoration provider may have a net positive effect on the defendant, although these efforts are primarily aimed at competency restoration.

Given the aforementioned, we must also note that a defendant's trust in treatment providers may be strained in forensic contexts, as said providers are likely to be employees of the very facility restricting the defendant's freedom. Building rapport, while outlining professional roles and goals, is likely to be the first step in successfully employing any psychological intervention. Clarification of specific goals in an open and honest manner may prove quite powerful in aiding the development of trust and, in turn, defendant buy-in. It may also provide the defendant with a better understanding of how they can help themselves begin the process, which will ultimately lead to a resolution in their case. As such, providers may benefit by using many of the rapport-building skills foundational to their education and training while clearly delineating their role relative to competence restoration.

A plethora of CBT resources are designed for outpatient use and may be appropriate for use in community-based competency restoration. As such, we emphasize possible adaptations for jail-based and hospital-based competency restoration in this section (i.e., more restrictive environments).

Cognitive Restructuring

As with the use of CBT interventions in other contexts, the provision of psychoeducation regarding theoretical underpinnings of CBT is likely a primary step in treatment. Given the situational stressors defendants are likely facing during the restoration process, a much simplified form of psychoeducation may prove more palatable. Very basic education may also be better suited to restrictive and distracting environments, as well as situations in which sessions may be abbreviated. Relatedly, and given that multiple pathways of data input/rehearsal (i.e., verbal and visual) tend to result in the best retention of information (Mayer & Moreno, 2003), it may be helpful to also provide defendants with simplified handouts (see Appendix B), which explain the interactions among thoughts, emotions, and behaviors inherent to CBT's underlying theory; these may incorporate pictorial depictions, charts, etc. In the same vein, psychoeducation specifically regarding cognitive distortions (i.e., what they are, how they come about, how they maintain negative emotionality, etc.) using lay terms is indicated. Using examples of common distortions (e.g., dichotomous thinking) is likely to promote ease of learning.

Moreover, and as with the use of cognitive restructuring in standard implementation of CBT, it is paramount in forensic contexts that the defendant and treatment provider understand the specific thoughts underpinning emotional distress and problematic behaviors. This might be accomplished in several ways, depending on the characteristics of the defendant and their environment. For instance, is a defendant allowed to possess a writing utensil? If so, and in consideration of their literacy skills, they might be instructed to keep a journal or log of situations in which they experience notable distress (e.g., anxiety, depression). In turn, this may be used in session to identify patterns in thinking, potential cognitive distortions, etc. Along with the simplified handouts, step-by-step instructions provided to defendants on how exactly to complete journal assignments/thought logs should not only be covered in session but also provided in written format. In some cases (e.g., working with defendants with significant visual impairment), it may be indicated to provide instructions via audio recording. If a defendant is unable or unwilling to complete worksheets in writing, the clinician may record written responses on their behalf.

It is not uncommon for individuals to lack motivation or to avoid tasks when experiencing psychological distress. Accordingly, having defendants review materials or complete assignments between sessions may be particularly challenging. In such cases, it may be useful to take advantage of a token economy or other means to promote participation.[2] Depending on the provider's specific role and organizational constraints, they may or may not be able to develop and implement such an economy on their own. In the case of the latter, a psychologist or other professional, who does have the ability to develop such a system, may need to be consulted. In all cases, professionals comprising the defendant's treatment team should be informed and their consultation sought. Consultation may help provide a more nuanced appreciation of the defendant (e.g., their likes, dislikes, history of compliance), which is important when tailoring and implementing a tool such as a token economy. As a secondary benefit, peer consultation may contribute to collegiality among professionals. Of note, all staff who interact with the defendant should be briefed on the stipulations of the token economy, as consistent reinforcement of desired behaviors will likely be paramount to its success.

During individual sessions, and with the use of defendant input from between sessions (if available), the provider should initially work with the defendant to identify problematic cognitions (i.e., associated with specific, identified situations or thoughts),

2. Token economies are programs that function via the reinforcement of desired behavior by way of providing the participant with tokens (e.g., gold stars, holes in a punch card), which can be exchanged for special privileges, goods, and other rewards (APA, 2018b).

underlying distressing emotions, and maladaptive behaviors. This may be done via *Socratic questioning*—a technique in which the provider asks calculated questions aimed at illuminating the defendant's cognitive distortions in the context of their interpretation of events (APA, 2023c). In this process it is important to remember that individuals entering the justice system may have jaded views of the system itself, which may reflect lived experience, as opposed to (or in addition to) overly negativistic distortions. In this context, attempting to adjust such views of events leading to defendants' loss of freedom may create reactance. Rather, focusing on potential thought distortions in a present- and future-oriented manner may serve to undercut perseveration on past events. In line with this notion, asking questions, such as the following, may prove useful:

- *I saw in your chart that you got upset today. That doesn't seem like you—I wonder what led to that situation?*
- *A lot of people who skip restoration groups feel relieved in some way by doing so—In what ways do you feel better when you don't go to groups?*
- *It's natural for people to feel nervous about their court cases—What might happen in yours that causes you to feel nervous?*

A logical next step would be for the provider to assist the defendant in connecting the underlying cognitions to each event/prediction, as well as its associated emotional/behavioral outcome. Of note, and as with many non-forensically involved individuals, defendants may not have a deep understanding of their own emotions or be able to readily identify them. Accordingly, use of simplified visual tools, such as an "emotions wheel"[3] or emotions word bank, may be beneficial. Such therapy aids can be particularly helpful when working with defendants who do not have the language to describe their emotional experience or resist prompts to do so (e.g., related to stigma associated with emotionality among those who have spent time in prison or those who are from certain cultures).

Finally, it will be important that the provider work with the defendant to develop alternative hypotheses in order to challenge cognitive distortions, which may then lead to more adaptive emotional and behavioral outcomes. Because defendants have legal involvement, it is possible that some alternative hypotheses may indeed be gloomy (e.g., in the case of depression/anxiety related to the possibility of a long prison sentence). In such circumstances, some validation of their unpleasant emotional experience may be indicated. The idea in such cases is not to have the defendant view their situation through rose-colored lenses. Rather, the intention is to encourage a higher degree of flexibility in thinking (e.g., to perhaps consider the best- and worst-case scenarios, as well as the most likely outcome of their legal situation). For instance, if an individual is facing a prolonged sentence for a serious crime, and this is increasing their distress, this may be a good opportunity to introduce information about reduced sentences via plea bargaining, sentence mitigation, or judicial discretion in sentencing if alternatives do not seem viable.

3. An emotions wheel is a visual aid that can be used to help an individual identify what emotions they are experiencing, or not experiencing, at a given point in time. These are typically circular diagrams, with some general emotions toward the inside of the wheel, and more numerous specific emotions toward the outside of the wheel. Various versions of this therapeutic tool are available for free online; for example: https://thinkcbt.com/images/Downloads/Other_CBT_Resources/THINK_CBT_EXERCISE_39_-_WHEEL_OF_EMOTIONS_V10.pdf

Importantly, false information may still be of concern relative to a defendant's beliefs about the nature and course of their personal legal situation, even for individuals well acquainted with the criminal justice system. Actively challenging false information (in a nonconfrontational manner) is likely to be of great utility. For example, if a defendant falsely believes they may receive life imprisonment for a relatively minor alleged offense (e.g., trespassing), it would be important to actively challenge this belief. In such a case, providing the defendant with a printout of the actual statute addressing the alleged offense, which lays out potential associated sentences, may offer them a foundation from which they may more realistically understand their legal situation. From there, processing the original belief (i.e., regarding the extended sentence) through the restructuring of cognitive distortions, and the development of alternative hypotheses in real time, may prove especially beneficial. In such cases, more positive emotional/behavioral outcomes may be pronounced.

Of note, some defendants may experience specific negative beliefs regarding participation in group settings (e.g., concerns about being ridiculed or the potential to be singled out). These may stem from early learning experiences, such as challenges in school classrooms. A clinician working with a defendant undergoing competency restoration may be key in challenging said cognitions. For example, helping the defendant understand that everyone attending a competency restoration group is doing so because they need assistance in understanding court proceedings and consulting with counsel may relieve some feelings of apprehension. Additionally, it may be helpful to discuss and process the discomfort that defendants may have with groups in the context of lived experience and to delineate the way in which restoration and other groups may be different from those previously attended. For defendants who are affected by beliefs that they have no control over their psycholegal circumstance, explaining the importance of group attendance and engagement, relative to their progression toward case resolution, may also prove useful.

Forensic environments (i.e., jails and hospitals) lend themselves to enhanced restrictions, such as reduced access to the internet or the telephone, which can be key tools when challenging potentially faulty assumptions. Although the implementation of empirical hypothesis testing and behavioral experiments is therefore likely to be limited in forensic institutions, defendants do have methods of gathering evidence for and against hypotheses derived from distorted thinking. For example, a prominent source of data is the restoration provider themselves. By nature of their position, the restoration provider should be familiar with much of the information (e.g., factual knowledge regarding court processes, legal personnel, potential outcomes, etc.) the defendant will need to know in order to attain competency and can provide information in that regard. In some settings additional interdisciplinary team members may be able to assist the defendant in pursuing evidence for hypothesis testing. As an example, a social worker may be able to provide information about post-release programs and/or help the defendant contact their family should they have related distressing thoughts (e.g., "I'll never talk to my daughter again," in the context of family member assault charges). Of course, restoration providers should ensure appropriate caution is taken in such cases via consultation and record review. For instance, we would not suggest the defendant try to contact a family member who has an active restraining order against the defendant; this may mean providing education about the restraining order, in explaining why such a call is contraindicated and/or alternative methods of challenging a belief are more appropriate. Finally, in all contexts where competency restoration occurs, defendants should have access to methods of communication to speak with their attorneys regarding their pending cases.

Behavioral Activation

Behavioral activation (BA) is an intervention designed to enhance a person's involvement in meaningful life activities by using guided goal setting to improve their thoughts, mood, and overall quality of life (APA, 2018a). Implementation of BA in a restrictive setting is likely to be a challenge; however, BA may still be an effective strategy in reducing symptoms of anxiety and depression associated with situational distress. For example, given that fatigue is a symptom common to mood, anxiety, and trauma/stressor-related difficulties, it is quite possible that defendants may feel as though their time is best spent resting/sleeping. Ergo, psychoeducation relative to this issue—specifically the notion that inactivity helps maintain undesirable psychological symptoms (e.g., via experiential avoidance in anxiety)—may be an initial step to intervention.

With BA generally, a discussion of client values, goals, likes, and dislikes commonly occurs early on in treatment; these help determine what might motivate a client and reinforce activity. This approach in competency restoration may prove fruitful in determining meaningful activities the defendant may engage in, in a general sense. However, it is important that the clinician work with defendants to tailor realistic activities that fit the immediate environmental context. Thus, having a detailed understanding of the defendant's schedule, restrictions, privileges, etc. is of great importance. In institutional settings, interdisciplinary team consultation, and perhaps consultation with administrative officials, may prove useful in this process.

When a defendant is undergoing community-based restoration, mobility, transportation, pretrial probation requirements, and other factors may still require consideration. Still, defendants undergoing outpatient competency restoration are more likely to be able to engage in their preferred activities. Defendants in jails/hospitals may be more limited in their ability to engage in activities once enjoyed in the community, and so providers would do well to assess elements of the identified activities that can realistically be implemented. For example, if a defendant formerly enjoyed walking through their neighborhood park, they may perhaps be amenable to the idea of taking advantage of outdoor time, especially if there are trees, birds, etc. visible from the recreation space. In such a case, helping the defendant understand that simply going outside and reframing the situation (i.e., that they are indeed able to enjoy pieces of formerly enjoyed activities) may help to promote buy-in/participation.

Of note, BA can be useful as a graded intervention. For instance, if a defendant previously took pride in their appearance, perhaps simply scheduling time for them to shower or otherwise groom themselves may be a good starting point. Such small steps may also function as a method of instilling a sense of autonomy (e.g., relative to self-care). Successively larger steps may then be implemented, such as pacing up and down a unit halfway a specified number of times (i.e., for exercise), perhaps followed by eating with others or joining others to watch television.

Of course, the end goal is to have defendants experience a reduction in distressing psychological symptoms, so that an erosion of competency barriers may take place. However, it may be the case that direct competency restoration-related activities do not represent palatable, initial steps to BA for defendant. More specifically, if a defendant is experiencing situational distress as the direct result of their legal situation, activities that aim to explicitly address said situation may initially increase depressive/anxious symptoms and, in turn, decrease a defendant's willingness to participate in further activities. Therefore, it is recommended that providers do their best to deftly make the transition from encouraging general activities to those including competency restoration services. In the example of the defendant who previously enjoyed walking through a neighborhood park, the provider might benefit from seeking to have individual sessions held outdoors when appropriate, as to combine an enjoyable activity with one necessary to the restoration process. Likewise, a provider might join a defendant while they walk the hallway and simultaneously quiz them on factual information relative to court proceedings.

Finally, it is important that clinicians in institutional settings continually troubleshoot potential difficulties with BA. For example, developing contingency plans for inclement weather, unit disruptions, lockdowns, changes to organizational/facility operations, etc., will be important as to not disrupt the defendant's progress, which could result in regression. This will of course be dictated or heavily influenced by their specific institution and restrictions that may require some creativity in developing a contingency plan. Clinicians are encouraged to work with the defendant's treatment team and other staff to develop feasible modifications. For instance, in the case in which defendants are restricted to their unit due to medical or safety restrictions, groups off-unit and time outside may not be accessible. Instead, the provider may be able to organize an on-unit group with the assistance of unit staff. This group could incorporate music, stretching, etc. to increase body movement.

As referenced in the context of cognitive restructuring, a lack of motivation may also contribute to a defendant's desire to not participate in BA activities. Accordingly, prior suggestions associated with reinforcement via token economies, etc. should be considered. Employing such strategies may be particularly useful for participation in competency restoration groups. For example, a defendant who attends a predetermined number of competency restoration groups may earn a reward of some kind; the requisite number of groups may also be increased over time. Likewise, group participation may be framed as a potentially enjoyable activity for individuals who previously enjoyed a high degree of sociability. For those who are not especially sociable, setting the frame that mere attendance (i.e., without participation) is initially acceptable may lead to enhanced comfort in group settings and perhaps future active participation. This notion may be more digestible to defendants if the restoration provider is leading said groups, such that the group leader is guaranteed to share that understanding. In some contexts, a restoration provider may also escort or accompany a defendant to groups, wherein another professional is leading instruction (i.e., providing in vivo support or a warm handoff).

Relaxation and Exposure Techniques

Relaxation techniques are frequently taught as a means to combat symptoms of panic, generalized anxiety, and other forms of anxiety. Associated skills function as a means to demonstrate to defendants that they do have varying degrees of control over autonomic functions, which impact experienced emotions, as well as physiological manifestations of distress (Newman et al., 2020). Relaxation techniques are also employed *prior* to the implementation of exposure to feared stimuli/situations as a means to aid clients in their habituation to said contexts. Although there are myriad relaxation techniques, some of the more prominent include paced diaphragmatic breathing, meditation, and progressive muscle relaxation. Although detailed discussion of each of these techniques is beyond the scope of this text, step-by-step explanations and methods of implementation can be found in most peer-reviewed manuals for treatment of generalized and social anxiety, as well as panic disorder (e.g. Barlow & Craske, 2006; Craske & Barlow, 2007). For purposes of defendant comfort, such skills are likely best taught at the individual level, though some defendants may benefit from group instruction (e.g., when resources do not allow for individualized intervention). Defendants may benefit from reminders to use their coping skills (e.g., relaxation techniques) before and/or during exposure exercises and from discussing how to use and apply those skills in future situations (e.g., in court).

In terms of exposure, construction of a fear/avoidance hierarchy may be beneficial in not only tailoring an individualized exposure plan but also in helping defendants understand their own reactions to situations, including their tendencies toward experiential avoidance. A fear/avoidance hierarchy is the structural basis for identifying feared stimuli/situations and for planning varied levels of exposure through which the defendant will progress based on the associated level of anxiety each elicits (Abramowitz et al., 2019). At this point, it is important to keep in mind that although it is tempting to cover an array of anxiety-producing content, providers should focus on those reflecting barriers to competency. For example, a defendant with social (performance) anxiety may identify fears related to competency (from least stressful to most stressful) as (1) the potential for performing poorly when working one-on-one with their usual restoration provider, (2) the potential for performing poorly in front of a small group of peers, (3) the potential for performing poorly in front of their lawyer, (4) the potential for performing poorly in front of the judge, (5) the potential for performing poorly in front of a large group of peers, (6) the potential for performing poorly with a competency evaluator, and (7) the potential for performing poorly in front of a full courtroom.

Once relaxation techniques are appropriately introduced and practiced, and a fear/avoidance hierarchy is generated, exposure may begin. As exposure is graded, the least feared situation should be faced first (e.g., reviewing competency restoration materials one-on-one), followed by successive contexts/stimuli that generate higher degrees of distress. Of note, imaginal exposure of said feared situations and stimuli is likely to be of utility *before* in vivo exposure; however, a defendant's wishes and environmental factors may facilitate some changes to this progression. For instance, if a defendant is confident that they can face their least feared scenario in real life using their learned skills, attempting to force imaginal exposure may create reactance. Additionally, defendants should not be pushed to face real or imaginal fear-inducing situations (e.g., engaging in a mock competency interview) before they are ready to do so, as such is likely to actually harm progress.

It is not uncommon for defendants to experience difficulties during exposure exercises, and so cognitive restructuring and more general processing of said experiences is likely to be of great utility. Emphasis on the notion that setbacks are a component of treatment may provide more confidence in the process. Some defendants participating in exposure exercises may experience physiological/cognitive symptoms that represent panic attacks. In such cases, psychoeducation relative to panic attacks (e.g., that they are not heart attacks, they are generally not physically harmful, the parasympathetic nervous system will not allow them to last forever, etc.) may prove beneficial. Accordingly, it may be incumbent on providers to discuss the mechanisms of change by which exposure works, including the notion that for some, it is a slower process than for others. In some situations, treatment teams, administrators, organizations etc. may have expectations in terms of length of stay, discharge, etc.; they also may require education about the pace of this graduated process in the context of competency restoration.

ACCEPTANCE AND COMMITMENT THERAPY FOR DEPRESSION AND ANXIETY

Another empirically supported approach for treating symptoms of depression and anxiety is *acceptance and commitment therapy* (ACT). Rather than attempting to have individuals modify cognitions, as in CBT, ACT is geared toward acceptance of one's thoughts and emotions, as well as empowerment through life changes germane to an individual's personal goals and values (Hayes et al. 1999). The theoretical underpinnings of ACT rest upon *relational frame theory* (Hayes & Brownstein, 1985), which aims to explain how individuals learn and implement language to relate to stimuli. Relational frame theory posits that language and cognitions interact to form perceptions of reality in a way that is context sensitive. In healthy individuals, the ability to adapt/to cope with a range of situations in a genuine and healthy manner results; however, this is thought to not be the case when individuals become deeply entrenched in their personal, verbal construals of reality. As a result, distressing and maladaptive cognitions, emotions, and behaviors may occur (Hayes et al., 2001).

As a treatment modality, ACT is implemented to promote psychological flexibility—a person's aptitude relative to being present in the moment and behaving in accordance with personal values (i.e., both during times of relative normality and in times of difficulty or distress; Hayes et al., 2012).

ACT Interventions

There are several interwoven intervention strategies comprising ACT that aid in the diminishment of power held by unhelpful/distressing thoughts, and which also equip individuals to engage in adaptive, values-driven behaviors. Core interventions of ACT include: *acceptance, cognitive defusion, being present, self as context, values*, and *committed action* (Hayes et al., 2006).

Acceptance

The core principle of ACT is the learned skill of accepting thoughts and emotions. That is, treatment aims to help individuals to experience their cognitions and feelings in a manner that excludes active attempts to avoid or change them, as doing so may stifle personal growth and lead to untoward distress (Hayes et al., 2012). Through acceptance, individuals learn to allow room for painful thoughts and feelings in the moment, all while viewing them in a nonjudgmental, objective manner (Li et al., 2022). In the context of competency restoration, this skill may be especially impactful in terms of helping defendants come to terms with their situation (e.g., the seriousness of their legal situation) and, in doing so, being able to take actionable steps toward resolutions (e.g., competency).

Cognitive Defusion

Cognitive defusion employs methods to help individuals disentangle their personhood from their thoughts. In essence, cognitive fusion takes place when an individual becomes so attached to and encumbered by specific ways of thinking that they have difficulty being present in the moment. Cognitive defusion techniques function to help individuals view their thoughts as temporary and contextually bound mental events, as opposed to absolute, stable truths. As such, individuals can learn to distance their sense of self from distressing thoughts, thereby "defusing" from them (Hayes et al., 2006).

Several techniques may be employed in cognitive defusion, including *mindfulness* exercises (see also Chapter 10), which promote observation of thoughts without judgment of or attachment to said thoughts (Hayes et al., 1999). The use of *metaphors* may also be helpful in terms of assisting defendants understand that thoughts, like physical objects, can be observed and then released (Hayes & Smith, 2005). For example, the cars of a train passing by and out of vision as a locomotive moves forward. Use of metaphors may be familiar to defendants undergoing competency restoration, as metaphors/similes related to the adversarial legal system are often used as teaching tools (e.g., "there are two teams at court, like in football," "the judge is like a referee"). *Verbal repetition* is the process by which a person repeatedly states a distressing thought until semantic satiation occurs and said thought loses its meaning as a kind of exposure exercise (Masuda et al., 2010). *Labeling thoughts* may also prove useful, as this defusion approach is straightforward and consists of literally labeling thoughts as such, as opposed to accepting them as reality (Hayes et al., 2006). The idea behind thought labeling is that statements, such as "I'll never learn this competency material," are a fusion of the self and the cognition. Conversely, the statement "I think I'm having a tough time learning this material today" separates the self from the thought and, accordingly, gives it less power to incite distress.

Being Present

In short, the aim of being present is to be in contact with the world in a direct manner. In doing so, individuals are more likely to engage in flexible thinking and values-driven behavior. Mindfulness, introduced earlier in this chapter, can help individuals better access the here and now. The core purpose of mindfulness is to unburden the self from preoccupation regarding the past or future, by being present in the moment, without judgment or avoidance (Harris, 2019). There are many and varied mindfulness techniques, including the five senses exercise, mindful eating, leaves on a stream, and mindful breathing (Harris, 2009). As such, there is great potential relative to finding an exercise suitable for most defendants. To promote presentness, defendants are also encouraged to actively use language to identify thoughts and feelings, which may serve to decrease the negative effects of associated judgments and predictions (Hayes et al., 2006).

Self as Context

Self as context is perhaps most easily conceptualized as an extension of mindfulness that aids an individual in maintaining a persistent sense of self that is capable of adapting to different circumstances in a healthy fashion. This component of ACT, which if employed effectively, may aid defendants in understanding they are observers of their thoughts/feelings and not defined/controlled by their presence. The goal of associated techniques is to promote psychological flexibility and resilience (Hayes et al., 2012).

Values

The elucidation of, as well as commitment to, personal values is also central to ACT. This allows individuals to engage in behaviors they find personally meaningful, which may result in a greater sense of purpose (Wilson & DuFrene, 2009). As such, values-based activities help defendants define personal values—a necessary step to engaging in purposeful and positive change. Similar to mindfulness exercises, values exercises are varied, and include (but are not limited to) the following: "Personal Values Card Sort" (Hayes et al., 2012), "Life Compass" (Harris, 2009), and "Imagine Your 80th Birthday" (Dahl et al., 2009).

Committed Action

Committed action focuses on individuals making formulated steps toward values-driven behavior, even when doing so may cause discomfort (Hayes et al., 1999). In essence, committed action is the mechanism by which tangible change is fostered (Chase et al., 2013). Of note, the ability to engage in committed action is developed through various behavior-based processes (e.g., skill building) over time (Hayes et al., 2006; Viskovich et al., 2021).

Applications of ACT Interventions in Competency Restoration

The notion of accepting thoughts and emotions may be more palatable to some defendants in forensic contexts than others. For example, some individuals may react negatively to the idea that their thoughts are filtered through distortions (i.e., as in CBT). Accordingly, such individuals may take more easily to working toward acknowledging their thoughts/emotions while simultaneously understanding they are not defined by them. In forensic contexts, distressing thoughts and emotions are not uncommon. To an extent, working toward acceptance may also prove to normalize the defendant's experiences.

As with the implementation of CBT relative to competency restoration, the theoretical basis for ACT should be explained in a simplistic manner. For instance, a provider might offer the following:

> We're going to be using exercises that might help you feel less stressed. The idea behind them is that sometimes people become so focused on, and used to, the way that they think, that they mistake their thoughts for facts. When this happens, people begin to feel controlled by their thoughts and get stuck worrying about the past or the future. In reality, people are not their thoughts—thoughts are temporary. In fact, we can choose to make room for our thoughts and emotions while observing them, like a person might observe a movie or a TV show. When we do this, we can live in the moment and start to identify and work toward our personal goals and values. For instance, we might be able to start getting you ready for court since leaving the hospital is high on the list of the things you've said are important to you. The exercises we'll be doing seem to work well for a lot of people, and I think they might work well for you too.

Of note, the current discussion of ACT and its use in competence restoration is somewhat less regimented than that previously detailing CBT, as many of the key elements of ACT are inextricably interwoven (i.e., consist of similar concepts/practices). These authors found that presenting these elements in a more fluid manner made for a more intuitive discussion.

In the context of *cognitive defusion*, the use of metaphors may be especially useful for forensic patients, as they require little to no physical resources, can be made easy to understand, and can easily be delivered in both individual and group formats. Providing lists of metaphors (e.g., leaves on a stream) may also help facilitate individual learning, as well as group discussion (e.g., What do each of you think this means? Can you think of a similar comparison?). Moreover, personally relevant metaphors may be developed that conform to the defendant's life and situation. Going back to our prior example of the defendant who previously enjoyed walking in the neighborhood park, a provider might help them come to understand how difficult/distressing thoughts related to their case are transient events, much like in the sighting of a migrating flock of geese overhead.

Likewise, the *labeling of thoughts* is another skill that lends itself to individual and group learning/discussion. It also represents an easy/straightforward skill for defendants to practice between sessions. This intervention may be especially powerful in the context of frustrations related to learning material or the slow pace of the legal system. For example, a defendant may state, "I'm trapped here forever," which may be reframed as something to the effect of, "I think I'm feeling trapped today because it's taking a long time for me to get out of the hospital."

Verbal repetition may also prove effective in decreasing distress relative to defendants' unease surrounding thoughts related to their legal situation. Specifically, such context-dependent thoughts resulting in situational distress may be constantly prompted by the defendant's immediate environment. In this context, any degree of power reduction relative to these cognitions is likely to prove helpful. For example, a defendant may find the notion of a guilty plea quite distressing. By repeating the word "guilty" over and over until semantic satiation occurs, the defendant may be able to move beyond the word and focus on the actual concept. Verbal repetition may also help promote levity in group settings (when comfort among attendees is established), which in turn may help reduce depression/anxiety stemming from associated thoughts.

Mindfulness may be especially helpful to guide defendants through mindfulness exercises at the outset and conclusion of restoration sessions. Regarding the former, defendants may engage in sessions with clearer minds and, as a result, be better equipped to attend to/retain information presented, as well as to take part in meaningful discussion. Regarding the latter, mindfulness may help alleviate tension and distress occurring from the restoration session itself (e.g., relative to discussing legal matters). Accordingly, it may decrease the likelihood of the defendant making an association between such sessions and resulting negative emotionality after the fact. Mindfulness works well in both individual and group settings and can also incorporate elements that promote participation. Additionally, incorporating mindfulness exercises that can extend and generalize outside the context of restoration sessions is particularly useful. To this end, engagement in deep breathing or grounding exercises may represent practical applications of mindfulness, which can be rehearsed in session and implemented by the defendant while in court.

Teaching this skill may also promote an individual's ability to focus their attention in important situations, such as when they are listening to their legal counsel or sitting in court. Many individuals also already have a frame of reference for some elements inherent to mindfulness, such as meditation or spiritual prayer (see Chapter 7). Thus, personal experiences from the defendant's life may be referenced to promote understanding of the process, as well as buy-in. Of importance, mindfulness is a generally difficult practice to master. Accordingly, ample encouragement and information should be provided. For example, clinicians should impress upon defendants that their mind will drift away from the present, but they need not be upset about this, as it is a natural aspect of the process—particularly toward the beginning.

Finally, assessing defendant *values* is critical in helping defendants clarify their goals, principles, etc. It is also a necessary step on their journey to engage in committed change. In this context, providers should tailor exercises and discussion regarding values in such a manner that they logically link back to aspects of restoration and, in doing so, lead to committed actions, which may promote competency. For example, if a defendant's highest value/goal is being present for their family, the provider might explain how engaging in competency restoration groups, adherence to medication management, etc., may assist them in resolving their legal case, and eventually returning to loved ones.

CULTURAL CONSIDERATIONS AND BEYOND

The use of CBT and ACT in competency restoration, as in other contexts, should be carried out with sensitivity and attention to cultural considerations. Both CBT and ACT place great emphasis on the individual, whether it be in terms of a person's ability to change their cognitions/behaviors or in terms of finding importance in individual goals and values to enact meaningful change. Although these elements may align well with Western (i.e., individualistic) cultural norms, they may be less relevant—and perhaps even off-putting—to individuals from non-Western cultures. For example, many collectivist cultures view distress and related mental health difficulties through complex interactions among community, family, and religious/spiritual elements (D. S. Fernando & S. Fernando, 2004). Incongruence between a defendant's cultural values and treatment interventions is unlikely to foster positive results.

Cultural elements regarding communication may also play a role in the effectiveness of both CBT and ACT. Specifically, both modalities rely on rather direct communications regarding thoughts, feelings, and behaviors. Such communication styles may not be valued or well practiced in individuals from non-Western cultures. For instance, CBT relies on actual confrontation of cognitions via the use of language, which may be a difficult practice for some—especially for those coming from a culture in which this style of communication, and confrontation in general, is viewed as inappropriate (Sue & Sue, 2016).

Additionally, both CBT and ACT use terms that may not lend themselves to ease of translation. When providing services to non-native English speakers, providers may benefit from adjusting language in a manner consistent with culturally appropriate norms. For example, adaptations may be made when employing the use of metaphors (Karekla et al., 2019) in order to make the metaphors more relevant and digestible for defendants (Fledderus et al., 2010).

Additionally, there may be stigma among inmates regarding acknowledging mental health needs and seeking treatment (Iwamoto et al., 2012), which serves as a barrier to competency restoration. Justice-involved individuals may be less willing to acknowledge their symptoms or to participate in treatment (i.e., including participating in competency restoration), as they may have been conditioned against doing so. In this context, the use of alternative language may also be helpful. For instance, the terms "nerves" or "worry" may be substituted for "anxiety" or "stress," while the phrase "feeling blue" or "feeling down" may be suitable to describe a depressed mood. It is also important to note that in forensic/correctional populations, behaviors/actions related to, or resulting from, mental health symptoms may lead defendants to inadvertently violate institutional/organizational rules (e.g., refusing to leave a bunk during a major depressive episode, particularly if they have not sought mental health treatment). In turn, these individuals may face punitive consequences, such as solitary confinement or a restriction in privileges (NAMI, 2024).

Finally, and beyond cultural considerations, there may be personal considerations that impact the use of CBT and ACT relative to competency restoration. Specifically, both approaches use a considerable number of varied terms and definitions, as well as concepts, which may be relatively inaccessible to individuals of lower cognitive functioning. As aforementioned, interventions are likely best delivered in a simplified manner in forensic contexts. Given that individuals experiencing lower levels of intellectual functioning are overrepresented in the justice system (Stancliffe & Frantz, 2024), special care should be taken when attempting to use more cognitively challenging treatment modalities, such as CBT and ACT. That being said, research findings suggest that proper adjustments to treatment delivery can still yield beneficial results (Willner, 2009).

Case Example

Mr. Smith is a 35-year-old African American man who was recently admitted to the state hospital for competency restoration. Restoration was ordered in the context of a class 1 misdemeanor, which carries a maximum possible jail sentence of 12 months in his state. During his hospitalization, Mr. Smith was noted to decline group-based and one-on-one restoration sessions. Staff observed that he tended to stay in his bed most of the day and to move and speak slowly. He also appeared to have lost weight since his admission. During his most recent treatment team meeting, Mr. Smith reported feeling sadness and hopelessness regarding his case, with the belief that he is likely to spend a year in jail for his charges, which would irreversibly disrupt his life. He also reported feeling as if he has no one in his corner because he often has difficulty reaching his lawyer directly. As a result of these factors, Mr. Smith had not engaged in competency restoration efforts.

Behavioral Activation

Due to Mr. Smith's tendency to isolate in his room, the competency restoration provider on his unit began to directly engage with him whenever possible (e.g., during mealtimes, from the doorway of his room when appropriate) to build rapport. During their brief discussions, the provider discovered that prior to this hospitalization, Mr. Smith greatly enjoyed and regularly watched movies. In the context of behavioral activation, the provider spoke with Mr. Smith about planning a specified time each day for films to be played in the unit common room. Mr. Smith was noted to engage in this activity regularly, even though he still declined other activities offered on the unit. After a couple of weeks, the provider spoke with Mr. Smith about watching movies involving legal cases, to which he agreed. After playing these films, the provider began asking defendants in the common room competency-based questions (e.g., about courtroom personnel, plea options, verdicts, and punishments) relevant to the movies and facilitated discussion about how they relate to actual legal concepts.

Cognitive Restructuring

In the context of growing rapport between the restoration provider and Mr. Smith, he agreed to participate in individual competency restoration sessions. During said sessions, the provider introduced Mr. Smith to the concept of cognitive distortions—or "unhelpful beliefs of ways of thinking." Subsequently, Mr. Smith was also introduced to a variation of a thought log (ABC worksheet; see "Changing Our Thoughts to Change Our Emotions & Behaviors" worksheets in Appendix B). Together, Mr. Smith and the clinician began to examine some of the events and beliefs leading to his distress. During this exercise, Mr. Smith detailed how often being unable to reach his attorney directly leads him to feel a decline in his mood. With encouragement, Mr. Smith was able to cite a belief of "if he doesn't answer, he doesn't care" as the thought leading to his feelings of depression. Additionally, he was able to identify this thought as an example of the cognitive distortion of "tunnel vision." Specifically, Mr. Smith reported that even though his attorney was not always readily available, he usually returned his calls in a timely manner. In this instance, Mr. Smith was able to replace the thought of "if he doesn't answer, he doesn't care" with "even though he's busy, he's still making time to help me." This, in turn, led to reduced feelings of distress.

Likewise, Mr. Smith's belief that he will receive the maximum sentence for his charges was also explored. Regarding this, Mr. Smith disclosed he sometimes tends to think of situations "in the worst possible light." Accordingly, he was able to identify his use of the cognitive distortion of *catastrophizing* in this specific case and to replace his thought of "I'm going to serve the maximum sentence" with "I'll know more about what might happen in my case after I speak to my lawyer and come up with a legal strategy." This change of perspective was noted to lead to more psychological flexibility and fewer feelings of depression.

Values Card Sorting Task

To promote further buy-in regarding restoration efforts, the unit provider introduced Mr. Smith to the values card sorting task (Hayes et al., 2012; Miller et al., 2001). During this exercise, Mr. Smith selected the *autonomy* and *family* cards among his top five, and the restoration provider asked how Mr. Smith knew these values were important to him. Mr. Smith was able to identify personal freedom and independent decision-making as key components of who he is as a person. He also identified his family as the strongest source of support in his life, though admitted he had been avoiding their visits due to symptoms of depression. In collaboration with the provider, Mr. Smith was also able to identify behaviors that might bring him closer to his values, such as working on his competency-related abilities to move toward eventual release/decision-making in his trial, as well as accepting visits from his family as a means of gaining emotional support.

REFERENCES

Abramowitz, J. S., Deacon, B. J., & Whiteside, S. P. (2019). *Exposure therapy for anxiety: Principles and practice.* Guilford Press.

Airaksinen, E., Larsson, M., & Forsell, Y. (2005). Neuropsychological functions in anxiety disorders in population-based samples: Evidence of episodic memory dysfunction. *Journal of Psychiatric Research, 39*(2), 207–214. doi:10.1016/j.jpsychires.2004.06.001

Airaksinen, E., Larsson, M., Lundberg, I., & Forsell, Y. (2004). Cognitive functions in depressive disorders: Evidence from a population-based study. *Psychological Medicine, 34*(1), 83–91. doi:10.1017/S0033291703008589

American Psychological Association. (2018, April 19). Schema. https://dictionary.apa.org/schema

American Psychiatric Association. (2022). *Diagnostic and statistical manual of mental disorders* (5th ed., text rev.).

American Psychological Association. (2018a, April 19). Behavioral activation. https://dictionary.apa.org/behavioral-activation

American Psychological Association. (2018b, April 19). Token economy. https://dictionary.apa.org/token-economy

American Psychological Association. (2017). What is exposure therapy? https://www.apa.org/ptsd-guideline/patients-and-families/exposure-therapy

American Psychological Association. (2023a, November 15). Cognitive restructuring. https://dictionary.apa.org/cognitive-restructuring

American Psychological Association. (2023b, November 15). Executive functioning. https://dictionary.apa.org/executive-functions

American Psychological Association. (2023c, November 15). Socratic dialogue. https://dictionary.apa.org/socratic-dialogue

Austin, M.-P., Mitchell, P., & Goodwin, G. M. (2001). Cognitive deficits in depression: Possible implications for functional neuropathology. *British Journal of Psychiatry, 178*(3), 200–206. doi:10.1192/bjp.178.3.200

Barlow, D. H., & Craske, M. G. (2006). *Mastery of your anxiety and panic.* Oxford University Press.

Basso, M. R., Lowery, N., Ghormley, C., Combs, D., Purdie, R., Neel, J., . . . Bornstein, R. (2007). Comorbid anxiety corresponds with neuropsychological dysfunction in unipolar depression. *Cognitive Neuropsychiatry, 12*(5), 437–456. doi:10.1080/13546800701439854

Beck, A. T. (1963). Thinking and depression: I. Idiosyncratic content and cognitive distortions. *Archives of General Psychiatry, 9*(4), 324–333. doi:10.1001/archpsyc.1963.01720160014002

Beck, A. T. (1970). Cognitive therapy: Nature and relation to behavior therapy. *Behavior Therapy, 1*(2), 184–200. doi:10.1016/S0005-7894(70)80030-2

Beck, A. T. (1979). *Cognitive therapy and the emotional disorders.* Penguin.

Beck, A. T., Rush A., Shaw, B., & Emery, G. (Eds.). (1979). *Cognitive therapy of depression.* Guilford Press.

Beck, J. S. (1995). *Cognitive behavior therapy: Basics and beyond*

Beck, J. S. (2011). *Cognitive behavior therapy: Basics and beyond* (2nd ed.). Guilford Press.

Beck, J. S., & Fleming, S. (2021). A brief history of Aaron T. Beck, MD, and cognitive behavior therapy. *Clinical Psychology in Europe, 3*(2), e6701. doi:10.32872/cpe.6701

Chase, J. A., Houmanfar, R., Hayes, S. C., Ward, T. A., Vilardaga, J. P., & Follette, V. (2013). Values are not just goals: Online ACT-based values training adds to goal setting in improving undergraduate college student performance. *Journal of Contextual Behavioral Science, 2*(3–4), 79–84. doi:10.1016/j.jcbs.2013.08.002

Clark, D. A. (2013). *Cognitive Restructuring. In The Wiley Handbook of Cognitive Behavioral Therapy* (pp. 1–22). John Wiley & Sons, Ltd. doi:10.1002/9781118528563.wbcbt02

Cloyes, K. G., Lovell, D., Allen, D. G., & Rhodes, L. A. (2006). Assessment of psychosocial impairment in a supermaximum security unit sample. *Criminal Justice and Behavior, 37*(12), 1361–1378. doi:10.1177/0093854806288143

Craske, M. G., & Barlow, D. H. (2007). *Mastery of your anxiety and panic: Therapist guide* (Vol. 2). Oxford University Press.

Dahl, J., Plumb, J., Stewart, I., & Lundgren, T. (2009). *The art and science of valuing in psychotherapy: Helping clients discover, explore, and commit to valued action using acceptance and commitment therapy.* New Harbinger.

DeLuca, A. K., Lenze, E. J., Mulsant, B. H., Butters, M. A., Karp, J. F., Dew, M. A., . . . Reynolds, C. F., III. (2005). Comorbid anxiety disorder in late life depression: Association with memory decline over four years. *International Journal of Geriatric Psychiatry, 20*(9), 848–854. doi:10.1002/gps.1360

Derakshan, N., & Eysenck, M. W. (2009). Anxiety, processing efficiency, and cognitive performance: New developments from attentional control theory. *European Psychologist, 14*(2), 168–176. doi:10.1027/1016-9040.14.2.168

Fernando, D. S., & Fernando, S. (2004). *Cultural Diversity, Mental Health and Psychiatry: The Struggle Against Racism.* United Kingdom: Taylor & Francis.

Fledderus, M., Bohlmeijer, E. T., Smit, F., & Westerhof, G. J. (2010). Mental health promotion as a new goal in public mental health care: A randomized controlled trial of an intervention enhancing psychological flexibility. *American Journal of Public Health, 100*(12), 2372–2378. doi:10.2105/AJPH.2010.196196

Gifford, K. A., Liu, D., Damon, S. M., Chapman, W. G. IV, Romano, R. R. III, Samuels, L. R., . . . Alzheimer's Disease Neuroimaging Initiative. (2015). Subjective memory complaint only relates to verbal episodic memory performance in mild cognitive impairment. *Journal of Alzheimer's Disease: JAD, 44*(1), 309–318. doi:10.3233/JAD-140636

Harris, R. (2009). *ACT made simple: An easy-to-read primer on acceptance and commitment therapy*. New Harbinger.

Harris, R. (2019). *ACT made simple: An easy-to-read primer on acceptance and commitment therapy* (2nd ed.). New Harbinger.

Hayes, S. C., Barnes-Holmes, D., & Roche, B. (2001). *Relational Frame Theory: A Post-Skinnerian Account of Human Language and Cognition.* Springer Science & Business Media. doi:10.1016/S0065-2407(02)80063-5

Hayes, S. C., & Brownstein, A. J. (1985, May). Verbal behavior, equivalence classes, and rules: New definitions, data, and directions. *Annual Meeting of the Association for Behavior Analysis*, Columbus, OH.

Hayes, S. C., Luoma, J. B., Bond, F. W., Masuda, A., & Lillis, J. (2006). Acceptance and commitment therapy: Model, processes and outcomes. *Behaviour Research and Therapy, 44*(1), 1–25. doi:10.1016/j.brat.2005.06.006

Hayes, S. C., & Smith, S. (2005). *Get out of your mind and into your life: The new acceptance and commitment therapy.* New Harbinger.

Hayes, S. C., Strosahl, K. D., & Wilson, K. G. (1999). *Acceptance and commitment therapy* (Vol. 6). Guilford Press.

Hayes, S. C., Strosahl, K., & Wilson, K. G. (1999). *Acceptance and commitment therapy: Understanding and treating human suffering.* New York: Guilford.

Hofmann, S. G., Asnaani, A., Vonk, I. J., Sawyer, A. T., & Fang, A. (2012). The efficacy of cognitive behavioral therapy: A review of meta-analyses. *Cognitive Therapy and Research, 36*(5), 427–440. doi:10.1007/s10608-012-9476-1

Iwamoto, D. K., Gordon, D., Oliveros, A., Perez-Cabello, A., Brabham, T., Lanza, S., and Dyson, W. (2012). The role of masculine norms and informal support on mental health in incarcerated men. *Psychology of Men & Masculinities, 13*(3), 283–293. doi:10.1037/a0025522

Kizilbash, A. H., Vanderploeg, R. D., & Curtiss, G. (2002). The effects of depression and anxiety on memory performance. *Archives of Clinical Neuropsychology, 17*(1), 57–67. doi:10.1016/S0887-6177(00)00101-3

Kaczkurkin, A. N., & Foa, E. B. (2015). Cognitive-behavioral therapy for anxiety disorders: An update on the empirical evidence. *Dialogues in Clinical Neuroscience, 17*(3), 337–346. doi:10.31887/DCNS.2015.17.3/akaczkurkin

Kanter, J. W., Manos, R. C., Bowe, W. M., Baruch, D. E., Busch, A. M., & Rusch, L. C. (2010). What is behavioral activation?: A review of the empirical literature. *Clinical Psychology Review, 30*(6), 608–620. doi:10.1016/j.cpr.2010.04.001

Knapp, P., & Beck, A. T. (2008). Cognitive therapy: Foundations, conceptual models, applications and research. *Brazilian Journal of Psychiatry, 30*(Suppl. 2), s54–s64. doi:10.1590/s1516-44462008000600002

Kohler-Hausmann, I. (2013). Misdemeanor justice: Control without conviction. *American Journal of Sociology, 119*(2), 351–393. doi:10.1086/674743

Karekla, M., Kasinopoulos, O., Neto, D. D., Ebert, D. D., van Daele, T., Nordgreen, T., . . . Berking, M. (2019). Best practices and recommendations for digital interventions to improve engagement and adherence in chronic illness sufferers. *European Psychologist, 24*(1), 49–67. doi:10.1027/1016-9040/a000349

Kuyken, W., Padesky, C. A., & Dudley, R. (2009). *Collaborative case conceptualization: Working effectively with clients in cognitive-behavioral therapy.* Guilford Press.

Leahy, R. L. (2003). *Cognitive therapy techniques: A practitioner's guide.* Guilford Press.

Li, Z., Shang, W., & Yang, K. (2022). Characteristics and trends in acceptance and commitment therapy research: A bibliometric analysis. *Frontiers in Psychology, 13,* Article 980848.

Masuda, A., Twohig, M. P., Stormo, A. R., Feinstein, A. B., Chou, Y. Y., & Wendell, J. W. (2010). The effects of cognitive defusion and thought distraction on emotional discomfort and believability of negative self-referential thoughts. *Journal of Behavior Therapy and Experimental Psychiatry, 41*(1), 11–17. doi:10.1016/j.jbtep.2009.08.006

Mayer, R. E., & Moreno, R. (2003). Nine ways to reduce cognitive load in multimedia learning. *Educational Psychologist, 38*(1), 43–52. doi:10.3389/fpsyg.2022.980848

Mazzucchelli, T., Kane, R., & Rees, C. (2009). Behavioral activation treatments for adults: A meta-analysis and review. *Clinical Psychology: Science and Practice, 16*(4), 383–411. doi:10.1111/j.1468-2850.2009.01178.x

Massoglia, M., & Remster, B. (2019). Linkages between incarceration and health. *Public Health Reports, 134*(1 Suppl.), 8S–14S. https://journals.sagepub.com/home/phr

Miller, W. R., C'de Baca, J., Matthews, D. B., & Wilbourne, P. L. (2001). *Personal values card sort.* University of New Mexico.

Mouta, S., Fonseca Vaz, I., Pires, M., Ramos, S., & Figueiredo, D. (2023). What do we know about pseudodementia? *General Psychiatry, 36*(4), Article e100939. doi:10.1136/gpsych-2022-100939

NAMI. (2024, May 6). *Mental health treatment while incarcerated.* https://www.nami.org/advocacy/policy-priorities/improving-health/mental-health-treatment-while-incarcerated

Newman, C. E. (2016). Cognitive restructuring/cognitive therapy. In C. M. Nezu & A. M. Nezu (Eds.), *The Oxford handbook of cognitive and behavioral therapies* (pp. 118–141). Oxford University Press.

Newman, M. G., Zainal, N. H., & Hoyer, J. (2020). Cognitive-behavioral therapy (CBT) for generalized anxiety disorder (GAD). In A. L. Gerlach & A. T. Gloster (Eds.), *Generalized anxiety disorder and worrying: A comprehensive handbook for clinicians and researchers* (pp. 203–230). Wiley Blackwell. doi:10.1002/9781119189909.ch10

Pearlin, L. I., & Bierman, A. (2013). Current issues and future directions in research into the stress process. In C. S. Aneshensel, J. C. Phelan, & A. Bierman (Eds.), *Handbook of the sociology of mental health* (2nd ed., pp. 325–340). Springer Science + Business Media. doi:10.1007/978-94-007-4276-5_16

Quigley, L., & Dobson, K. S. (2017). Behavioral activation treatments for depression. In A. W. Hayes & S. G. Hofmann (Eds.), *The science of cognitive behavioral therapy.* https://www.sciencedirect.com/science/article/abs/pii/B978012803457600012X

Reddy, Y. C. J., Sudhir, P. M., Manjula, M., Arumugham, S. S., & Narayanaswamy, J. C. (2020). Clinical practice guidelines for cognitive-behavioral therapies in anxiety disorders and obsessive-compulsive and related disorders. *Indian Journal of Psychiatry, 62*(Suppl. 2), S230–S250. doi:10.4103/psychiatry.IndianJPsychiatry_773_19

Schnittker, J., & John, A. (2007). Enduring stigma: The long-term effects of incarceration on health. *Journal of Health and Social Behavior, 48*(2), 115–130. doi:10.1177/002214650704800202

Skinner, B. F. (1971). *Beyond Freedom and Dignity: B.F. Skinner.* United States: Alfred A. Knopf.

Stancliffe, R. J., & Frantz, B. L. (2024). Criminal justice and people with intellectual and developmental disabilities. *Intellectual and Developmental Disabilities, 62*(3), 211–224. doi:10.1352/1934-9556-62.3.211

Sue, D. W., & Sue, D. (2016). *Counseling the culturally diverse: Theory and practice*. John Wiley & Sons.

Sugie, N. F., & Turney, K. (2017). Beyond incarceration: Criminal justice contact and mental health. *American Sociological Review*, *82*(4), 719–743. doi:10.1177/0003122417713188

Viskovich, S., Pakenham, K. I., & Fowler, J. A. (2021). A mixed-methods evaluation of experiential intervention exercises for values and committed action from an acceptance and commitment therapy (ACT) mental health promotion program for university students. *Journal of Contextual Behavioral Science*, *22*, 108–118. doi:10.1016/j.jcbs.2021.10.001

Willner, P. (2009). Psychotherapeutic interventions in learning disability: Focus on cognitive behavioural therapy and mental health. *Psychiatry*, *8*(10), 416–419. doi:10.1016/j.mppsy.2009.06.018

Wilson, K. G., & DuFrene, T. (2009). *Mindfulness for two: An acceptance and commitment therapy approach to mindfulness in psychotherapy*. New Harbinger.

Wolff, N., Shi, J., & Siegel, J. A. (2009). Patterns of victimization among male and female inmates: evidence of an enduring legacy. *Violence and Victims*, *24*(4), 469–484. doi:10.1891/0886-6708.24.4.469p

7

Religion and Spirituality (RS) and Competency Restoration

MEREDITH CAIN MUNSON, PSYD ■

INTRODUCTION TO THE TERMS

This chapter will consider the intersectionality of religion, spirituality, mental health, and competency restoration. As religion and spirituality are complex topics, the following definitions are provided to ensure thorough understanding.

The American Psychological Association (APA) defines *religion* as "a system of spiritual beliefs, practices, or both, typically organized around the worship of an all-powerful deity (or deities) and involving behaviors such as prayer, meditation, and participation in collective rituals" (2018c, Religion section). Buddhism, Christianity, Hinduism, Islam, and Judaism are examples of predominant religions. According to the Pew Research Center (2012), there are 5.8 billion people with RS beliefs around the world, making up 84% of the population (6.9 billion in 2010). Thus, it is important to understand that having a basic understanding of an individual's specific religion is a starting point. The above-mentioned religions may only partially explain a defendant's religious framework if they identify with a specific sect or denomination. Given the variance in practices even within the same religion, clinicians should attempt to understand how the individual practices.

Another important term to understand is *religiosity*. Religiosity refers to one's commitment to and practice of religion. In contrast, *hyperreligiosity* can be understood as harboring intense faith-based beliefs that negatively impact one's functioning. The beliefs go beyond what another practicing member of their faith would deem typical. For example, a person may pray as part of their faith practices, but it becomes hyperreligious when their prayer practices interfere with their social life, employment, education, etc. beyond what would be considered normative.

Similar to religion, *spirituality* is "a concern for or sensitivity to things of the spirit or soul, especially as opposed to materialistic concerns," which may or may not include religious practices (APA, 2018d, Spirituality section). The practice of spirituality can include, but is not limited to, prayer, meditation, and/or connecting with the earth or a higher being. Practices such as yoga and the use of crystals may come to mind, but such practices may or may not be connected to one's spirituality.

Considering the overlap in definitions for religion (R) and spirituality (S), and as the terms are often used interchangeably in the literature, the initialism RS will be utilized moving forward. The remainder of the chapter will cover *what* is RS integration, *why* it is important to educate ourselves about RS when providing competency restoration services,

Meredith Cain Munson, *Religion and Spirituality (RS) and Competency Restoration*. In: *The Competency Restoration Handbook*. Edited by: Laura M. Grossi, Oxford University Press. © Laura M. Grossi (2025). DOI: 10.1093/9780197768075.003.0007 *when* integration of RS and competency restoration may be appropriate or contraindicated, *how* RS can impact competency restoration, and *how* to begin integrating our work.

WHAT IS RS INTEGRATION

To better understand the inclusion of this chapter in this volume, one must first understand what it means to integrate RS into competency restoration. The APA defines integration as "the coordination or unification of parts into a totality" (2018a, Integration section). Considering the consistent finding throughout the literature that RS is a significant component of the lives of many people, including individuals with serious mental illnesses (Grover et al., 2014; Hodge, 2018; Huguelet et al., 2006; Hustoft et al., 2013; Milner et al., 2020; Mohr et al., 2007), RS integration with competency restoration is the unification of an important "part." Integration may include conducting an RS assessment, discussing an individual's RS belief system, and consulting and collaborating with RS leaders (e.g., chaplains, pastors, rabbis, ministers, imams). RS integration does not critique, attempt to convert, or eliminate an individual's belief system. Instead, the goal is to aid in coordinating or unifying an individual's RS beliefs in an adaptive manner that is conducive to their success in competency restoration. Due to unique RS beliefs, even between individuals in the same faith system, integration is likely to look different with each defendant.

WHY CLINICIANS SHOULD DEVELOP RS SKILLS

Ethical Considerations

One may wonder why it is important when providing competency restoration services. The APA (2017) *Ethical Principles of Psychologists and Code of Conduct*, section 2.01b states:

> *Where scientific or professional knowledge in the discipline of psychology establishes that an understanding of factors associated with . . . religion . . . is essential for effective implementation of their services or research, psychologists have or obtain the training, experience, consultation, or supervision necessary to ensure the competence of their services, or they make appropriate referrals.*

In other terms, RS is deemed as one of the core components of diversity that psychologists should explore when providing services. RS is also mentioned in the ethics codes for counseling, music therapists, psychiatry, and social work. A working knowledge of RS factors is thus formally established as an aspect of professional competency. Hodge (2018) proposes the term *spiritual competence*, which is defined as "a form of cultural competence that deals with spirituality and religion, specifically clients' individually constructed spiritual worldviews" (What Is Spiritual Competence section). Similarly, this author posits RS humility, with ongoing humbleness and willingness to learn, should be the standard for competency for subjects as complex as RS.

RS plasticity, or "flexibility and adaptability" (APA, 2018b, Plasticity section), further supports the idea that clinicians should have ongoing RS education. According to Dudek et al. (2019), Krzystanek et al. (2012), and Mohr et al. (2010), RS topics have plasticity; beliefs and practices may change over time. Individuals' beliefs may fluctuate for a plethora of reasons, and sometimes a person may choose to convert their faith altogether. Of relevance,

Drinnan and Lavender (2006) found that changes in participants' RS beliefs impacted the content of their delusions.

On cultural and societal levels, RS trends and beliefs may change or adapt according to historical events or environmental or systemic situations. RS ideas may shift, practices may be outlawed, and new belief systems can evolve. For example, it is possible that the study by Krzystanek and colleagues (2012) was impacted by the state of Poland's government at that time. The government was attempting to control access to RS information and practices, possibly sparking more fixed RS beliefs in the study sample. Thus, having a single class or lecture on RS is likely insufficient. Instead, clinicians should be encouraged to regularly seek resources that keep them up to date on RS research and information.

As the ethics codes call for an understanding of RS, this is likely the simplest reason that clinicians should develop these skills. Further implications are drawn from the research.

Therapeutic Engagement

Incorporating RS into competency restoration, as other interventions, may contribute to improved therapeutic engagement (Glorney et al., 2019). As many competency restoration providers know, encouraging a defendant to engage in services can be challenging. Thus, creating an environment for RS discussions and practices may aid in improving a defendant's restoration efforts if RS is important to their identity.

Additionally, those with well-grounded RS systems have been found to engage in more active and adaptive coping skills (Das et al., 2018). As such, removing judgment while providing feedback about one's RS beliefs as related to restoration success may increase self-esteem, reduce their symptoms, manage stress more efficiently, and improve the RS component of their coping processes (Das et al., 2018; Iyassu et al., 2014). Moreover, participants who chose to participate in RS groups tend to be more hopeful and utilize more positive coping strategies (Revheim et al., 2010). Lucchetti and colleagues (2021) considered several studies that indicated improved symptoms, better social outcomes, and a more positive prognosis when individuals engaged in healthy RS practices. Each of these benefits could lead to a defendant's improved engagement in competency restoration and increase the possibility of them attaining competence. While the sole goal of competency restoration is to aid defendants in moving forward with their charges, focusing on RS and related mental health components (e.g. quality of life) would likely improve their overall functioning and decision-making.

As mentioned above, the literature consistently asserts that RS is an important aspect of the lives of many individuals with serious mental illness (Grover et al., 2014; Hodge, 2018; Huguelet et al., 2006; Hustoft et al., 2013; Milner et al., 2020; Mitchell & Romans, 2003; Mohr et al., 2007). According to Mohr and colleagues (2007), individuals with schizophrenia, in particular, engage in RS practices more than the general public. RS practices (e.g., prayer, meditation, reading religious texts, attending RS services) may be used as coping skills that lead to less symptomology and improved mental health, fewer instances of substance abuse and suicide attempts, increased social support and feelings of inclusion, and a stronger sense of identity (Das et al., 2018; Glorney et al., 2019; Grover et al., 2014; Hodge 2018; Iyassu et al., 2014; Mohr et al., 2006; Mohr et al., 2010; Mohr & Huguelet, 2004). As each of these impacts may aid in restorative success, addressing RS may be a beneficial component of competency restoration when the defendant has identified RS as important to them.

Intervention in the Absence of Medication Adherence

Another way defendants might cope and demonstrate durable stability is through medication adherence (see Chapter 3). However, medication acceptance can be impacted by one's RS beliefs (Kate et al., 2012; Mohamed et al., 2009; Mohr et al., 2006; Morken et al., 2008; Vernon et al., 2010). For example, Khokhar et al. (2015) discuss how those who adhere to Judaism, Islam, Hinduism, Buddhism and Seventh-Day Adventism may have concerns due to medication ingredients containing animal products/byproducts (e.g., gelatin). While some religions prohibit the consumption of specific animals (e.g., Islam disallows eating pork), others do not consume animal products at all (e.g., Hinduism). Other religions disallow treatment with psychotropic medications altogether, with a hardline stance on pharmaceuticals and/or encouragement to use other interventions (e.g., prayer) as an alternative to medication.

It is important to understand that such beliefs may not be communicated by defendants verbally but through behaviors that meet their needs without having to disclose or explain their beliefs. For example, a defendant may consistently refuse a medication containing animal products, subsequently impacting their mood, impulse control, and other psychiatric symptoms—without providing a verbal explanation of that decision. This behavior may be viewed as antisocial or being resistant to treatment, when in the patient's mind they are adhering to their belief guidelines. It should be emphasized that these beliefs arise via the individual's interpretation of their RS beliefs; not everyone within the same religion holds the same views.

In the study by Mohr and colleagues (2007), 32% of participants were inconsistent or nonadherent with their medication regimen, with some reporting that taking medication was not in line with their RS beliefs. In contrast, almost half of the study participants in the study by Kate and colleagues (2012) believed that prayer was adequate for managing symptoms. Mitchell and Romans (2003) highlighted significant inconsistencies between the recommendations of healthcare providers and RS leaders, to the extent that some RS leaders suggested that individuals were spiritually cured and no longer in need of prescribed medication.

Medication inconsistency can be detrimental to those with serious mental illness, as not adhering to one's medication regimen could lead to a relapse of psychiatric symptoms and cognitive decompensation (Mohamed et al., 2009; Morken et al., 2008; Vernon et al., 2010). Considering that medication is an important component of restoration to competency (Lemons et al., 2022) and that RS could be a driving force in medication acceptance, clinicians should attempt to understand the impact of RS on an individual's medication adherence. RS may otherwise be an unknown barrier, resulting in longer terms of restoration efforts and less effective patient care.

DEVELOPING RS HUMILITY

This section will incorporate the three major components of spiritual competency as written in the article by Hodge (2018). These components include (1) configuring our own worldview, (2) working to understand the defendant's worldview, and (3) developing "the ability to design and implement intervention strategies that are appropriate, relevant, and sensitive to the client's spiritual worldview" (p. 3, What Is Spiritual Competence section).

The latter will be broken into three subcomponents: (A) RS assessment, (B) discussing RS, and (C) consultation and collaboration.

Configuring Our Own Worldview

Anyone who has ever flown on an airplane has been instructed to put their own oxygen mask on, before assisting others with their mask, in a crisis. The same is true for many in the helping field—it is imperative for a clinician to wrestle with their own internal traumas, current beliefs, worldviews, etc. before, and in the midst of, providing mental health services to others. This may be especially true when working with defendants with RS beliefs.

Hodge (2018) points out that there is no completely objective way of interpreting reality. That is, we utilize our lived experiences to inform our truth and create our own normal. As this usually occurs on an unconscious level, clinicians should take the time to use introspection (looking within oneself) to determine what or who influences our realities. For example, are you more scientifically minded, or do you entertain realities that are thus far not proven by hard facts? Do different settings or people bring about different thought processes for you? How strong are your RS beliefs? Will you over-identify with those with the same beliefs, or struggle in developing rapport with those who have vastly different RS? Do strong emotions arise, or are you willing to accept others' beliefs for what they are? These are a few questions that would likely be beneficial to ask yourself, whether addressing RS in competency restoration or not.

Working to Understand the Defendant's Worldview

To thoroughly understand a person's belief system, ask them. Clinicians should directly assess RS as they would inquire about any other domain of life. For example, just as one would ask the open-ended question, "What was your childhood like?," they could ask, "What religious or spiritual practices do you engage in?" Another way to inquire about a defendant's RS is to utilize a structured or semi-structured spiritual assessment. Appropriately assessing RS can aid in avoiding over-pathologizing or misdiagnosing a defendant. Established spiritual assessments can also provide guidance on appropriate questions and suggested verbiage. Just as there is not one "correct" or perfect measure for assessing personality or psychopathology, there is not a perfect measure for RS assessment. The spiritual assessment provided in Appendix B is the author's preferred, informal way to assess RS.

Assessment selection should focus on the information desired. For example, the Spiritual Health Locus of Control Scale (Holt et al., 2003) focuses on the patient's perceived control of health outcomes. This would be useful when working with a defendant who has been treatment hesitant, possibly due to RS beliefs. Of note, this assessment also utilizes the verbiage "God" and "Lord." As the assessment was normed with this verbiage, it may or may not translate quantitatively if those terms are substituted by terms for other chosen higher powers. However, collecting the qualitative information may still be informative for treatment.

When utilizing any spiritual assessment, clinicians should monitor their personal assumptions and biases. It is important to remember that simply sharing the same religion does not mean that beliefs and practices are identical. For example, one should not assume that their own Islamic experiences are the same as any other Muslim's experiences.

Additionally, recall that television, film, and incidental encounters with other religions or spiritual practices are not reflective of each individual's practices. It is also possible that assessment will be uncomfortable and that strong feelings will arise on either side. As the clinician, be sure to monitor your facial expressions, body language, and tone. This is not a place for judgment nor expert advice or problem-solving. Instead, RS assessment should be patient centered. Such an approach signals that the clinician is open and willing to provide a safe space for honest RS expression. Another way to develop rapport while assessing for and discussing RS is to utilize their RS language.

Even when clinicians believe that they are familiar with a defendant's RS, they may have a distorted understanding of, or make incorrect assumptions about, their RS beliefs and practices. Generally, clinicians tend to overestimate their awareness of a patient's RS (Grover et al., 2014; Huguelet et al., 2006). This may be due to a lack of assessment or RS-related discussion (Grover et al., 2014; Huguelet et al., 2006). Throughout the recovery process, it is pivotal that clinicians correctly perceive and have respect for clients' RS beliefs. This is especially important when one's RS beliefs are a perceived barrier to achieving competency.

Hodge (2018) suggests familiarizing oneself with moral foundation and epistemological humility. Moral foundation considers that, despite cultural and RS variance, most beliefs have a similar underlying moral basis. Epistemological humility recognizes that there are many ways to know or understand the world. Being able to appreciate a defendant's worldview or RS beliefs does not mean that a clinician must accept those beliefs as their own. Instead, they are simply willing to recognize that the defendant has a different way of understanding the world and making efforts to understand how that is impacting their life.

Developing Intervention Strategies

The literature suggests that RS is an area of functioning that is often under-addressed during treatment (Cain Munson, 2024; Glorney et al., 2019; Grover et al., 2014; Hill & Kilian, 2003; Huguelet et al., 2006; Milner et al., 2020; Mohr et al., 2007). In many instances, RS is poorly tended to or altogether ignored. Possible reasoning may include clinician discomfort in discussing RS and a lack of empirical support for RS guidance and competence (Grover et al., 2014; Huguelet et al., 2006). In this chapter, we illustrate how to design and implement competency restoration interventions that are appropriate, relevant, and sensitive to the client's RS worldview.

HOW RS CAN IMPACT COMPETENCY RESTORATION

RS can present as a barrier to competency, especially when one's beliefs or practices become entangled with delusional ideation. In turn, this affects one's understanding of their case, decision-making, and/or behaviors related to their legal situation. RS delusions may be partially based on their faith's truth, though the extent of the delusion may go beyond the norm. Just as an individual may have generalized that everyone is out to harm them after making enemies with only one person or group of people, someone with an RS delusion may have taken a normative belief (e.g., that everyone is made in God's image) and atypically interpreted that belief (e.g., that they *are* God in a literal sense). While such a delusion would likely cause one's competence to come into question, RS delusions may or may not impact a defendant's competency-related abilities. If the defendant believes that they are God, but understands their case and does not believe that being God prevents them from being tried fairly in court, they may be competent. It is not until the belief impacts their competency-related knowledge or abilities that it becomes a concern to be addressed in competency restoration.

RS delusions that would not necessarily impact competence may include, but are not limited to, seeing angels, demons, or prophets (unless these cause significant distraction, etc.); hearing the voice of their higher power or adversaries (except when these issue commands or suggestions that affect legal decision-making, etc.); or believing that they are a prophet (if their message is unrelated to their legal situation). More likely to impact competency-related abilities are RS delusions that continue to alter the defendant's interpretation of the crime (e.g., they were fighting a deity or were being controlled by a demon) or would make it difficult for them to rationally consider a realistic legal strategy (e.g., their strategy includes speaking on their prophecy in court, or if they believe that they will be martyred). When RS impacts a defendant's competency-related abilities, it is in everyone's (i.e., the court's, the defendant's, the hospital's or jail's, and the community's) best interest to address RS so that the legal situation can appropriately move forward.

If you have not worked with a client experiencing delusions, think about someone with whom you have strongly disagreed. Recall any attempts either side made to get the other person to understand their stance. It is likely that neither side ended up adopting the other side after just one conversation. If you have had a client that experiences delusions, think about your work with them. Ask yourself how difficult it was to reality check those delusions. Did it make it more difficult when even one small piece of the delusion was, or could have been, rooted in reality? This is a common challenge when working with those who experience RS delusions.

INDICATIONS AND CONTRAINDICATIONS OF RS AND COMPETENCY RESTORATION INTEGRATION

Simply put, RS-informed competency restoration may be warranted when a defendant identifies RS as important, when they have RS-based delusions (but are not so out of touch with reality that conversation is difficult), and/or if their beliefs are possibly impacting treatment (for better or worse). It is likely contraindicated if the defendant is acutely symptomatic (e.g., behaviorally unstable) or if they experience significant agitation when discussing RS. The defendant may first require other treatment and additional coping skills to appropriately engage in such discussion. Clinician lack of comfortability discussing RS is not an appropriate reason for not engaging in RS-based discussions. Instead, clinicians should seek formal training, consultation, and collaboration so that clinically indicated services can be provided.

It is important to remember that each case should be treated uniquely. There are protective and risk factors associated with RS (Borras et al., 2007; Cain Munson, 2024; Drinnan & Lavender, 2006; Grover et al., 2014; Hill & Kilian, 2003; Mohr et al., 2006; Mohr & Huguelet, 2004), with corresponding indications and contraindications for incorporating RS interventions in competence restoration. Specifically, RS can impact (positively or adversely) social interactions, views on illness, substance abuse, suicidality, symptomology, and treatment outcomes (Borras et al., 2007; Grover et al., 2014; Mohr et al., 2006; Mohr & Huguelet, 2004). To better understand the impact of RS on these factors, one must understand how they impact those with serious mental illness. Specifically, psychotic disorders (e.g., schizophrenia spectrum disorders) and bipolar disorder will briefly be discussed because they are common diagnoses among defendants receiving competency restoration services.

Schizophrenia Spectrum Disorders

Individuals with schizophrenia may experience "incoherent or illogical thoughts, bizarre behavior and speech, and delusions or hallucinations" (American Psychological Association, n.d., Schizophrenia section). Each of these symptoms may make it difficult to effectively interact with others. This may be exacerbated when the individual has strong RS beliefs, as those with RS-related symptoms tend to be assessed as more symptomatic and functionally impaired (Lucchetti et al., 2021; Siddle et al., 2002). At times, normative faith practices may be misperceived as evidence of psychosis, with observable behaviors appearing consistent.

For example, to someone unfamiliar with the Pentecostal faith, a patient speaking in tongues (a deeply religious or spiritual experience during which an individual feels connected to the Holy Spirit and speaks in an unknown or unfamiliar language) may appear incoherent, seem to have illogical thoughts, or seem to be engaging in bizarre behavior and speech. In such a case, a treatment provider would be advised to monitor their own biases and engage with the patient to ascertain the function of their behavior. Such an assessment would guide further intervention, whereas dissuading such behaviors would be culturally insensitive and *inappropriate*. Unfamiliar providers or evaluators may be hesitant to interact with the individual and engage with them about relevant RS considerations. In such instances, consulting with a provider trained in RS, a chaplain, family, or a clergy member of the defendant's faith may prove useful. Providers should work to understand each individual's RS experiences and how they may or may not impact their competency-related abilities.

As another example, defendants with a schizophrenia spectrum diagnosis may believe that they are a higher power (e.g., God), have special powers given to them (e.g., by a deity), or are in pursuit of a mission delineated by a higher power. In these circumstances, pending the defendant's informed consent, RS-informed competency restoration is likely *appropriate* and may even be required to fully explore their rational abilities.

Of relevance, Lucchetti and colleagues (2021) found that when RS was used negatively (i.e., when used in an unhealthy manner, such as avoiding dealing with a problem believing their higher power would handle it), individuals with schizophrenia presented with more symptoms, increased suicidality, and more conflicts with offered medical treatment. With increased symptomatology driven by RS, defendants may take longer to restore.

Bipolar Disorder

In those with bipolar disorder, experiences of mania may include RS themes. For example, one may believe that they were given supernatural powers by their higher power and, due to mania, lack the necessary impulse control to resist associated behaviors. They may believe they are invincible and thus engage in dangerous behaviors and/or refuse medications or other treatments. In such instances, RS-informed competency restoration would likely be *appropriate* after mania has subsided. Interestingly, one study indicated that higher RS importance was modestly associated with residual mania, while another noted negative RS coping predicted increased mania (Lucchetti et al., 2021). On the other side, depressive episodes may include a defendant feeling unmotivated to engage in competency restoration or being apathetic about their charges and associated possible sentences.

When the defendant has an RS system, the literature supports that discussing RS may lead to the improvement of mood-related symptoms, subsequently improving restoration capacity. Similar to those with schizophrenia, when using positive RS coping (i.e., utilizing healthy skills that address one's problems), individuals with bipolar disorder experienced better mental health outcomes, less suicidality, and a better prognosis (Lucchetti et al. 2021). Pesut and colleagues (2011) indicated that engagement in RS activities may aid in the daily management of bipolar symptoms, though over-engagement may suggest an increase in symptoms. This literature review also addressed the likelihood that maintaining healthy RS may be difficult for those with bipolar disorder due to the variability in mood. Individuals may find it easier to attend church, and pray or meditate when in euthymic or mixed states (i.e., when symptoms of both depression and (hypo)mania occur simultaneously or close together) as compared to manic and depressive states. Clinicians should be aware of either of these possibilities and if warranted, postpone or discontinue the RS component of restoration services when a treatment participant's mood is not conducive to intervention. Instead, medication or non-RS coping skills may be more appropriate as interventions.

INCORPORATING RS IN COMPETENCY RESTORATION

This section will provide guidance in developing RS humility, though it should not be a clinician's only resource. Further research, training, and continuing education courses are encouraged. How to develop foundational competency in competency restoration is described throughout this handbook; here we focus on gaining competency in RS intervention specifically. Gaining professional competence in each of these areas is necessary for informed and effective RS integration during the competency restoration process.

Developing Foundational Competency in RS and Competency Restoration

Ideally, clinicians should seek formal trainings on RS integration. This may be through a school or any credible resource that provides continuing education opportunities. As such trainings can be expensive, self-teaching via books and online resources may also prove beneficial. Researching this way may allow the clinician to narrow in on the information they desire most, such as reading about a religious practice with which they are not familiar. However, be cautious when taking this approach, especially when going down an internet search rabbit hole. That is, remember that it is important to select peer-reviewed articles and internet sites that stem from credible sources—blogs and social media videos should not be first choices.

Another way to gain experience in integrative work is to seek real-world training experiences. Such experiences may include volunteering and inquiring about practicum or clinical rotation experiences. Helpful settings may include places of religious worship (i.e., a church or mosque), hospitals affiliated with a particular faith, or private practices that include RS services. Many hospitals and jails also have access to chaplains. It may be beneficial to develop a relationship with local chaplains, as they are familiar both with RS and the population with which you serve.

RS Assessment

So how does a clinician develop an understanding of a defendant's RS in relation to competency restoration? The simple answer is to do research on the RS beliefs and ask the person directly. While not every defendant will want to discuss RS, it may prove beneficial to ask each patient if RS integration is something they would desire throughout competency restoration. This could easily fit into conversation during initial meetings, though it may be more appropriate when discussing rational knowledge or courtroom behavior. One way to inquire about RS integration at the onset of treatment would be to ask about their interest in integration, among all the essential information that is gathered (e.g., "What are your charges? How do you plan to cope with said charges? Are there any religious or spiritual practices that could help you along the way?"). Another method may involve introducing the possibility of RS integration when orienting the defendant to the plan for restoration services (e.g., "We will be discussing how to manage your anxiety in the courtroom. Are there any strategies you have found particularly helpful so far—breath meditation, drawing, prayer, or something else?"). It is important to remember that building rapport for RS discussions may take time, especially if the defendant is guarded about their faith. Initially, clinicians should be appropriately inquisitive and actively listen. Appropriate inquisition involves asking questions to better understand, not to demean or debunk one's RS. Active listening includes asking open-ended questions while making eye contact (usually), paraphrasing what you heard to assure mutual understanding, and recalling previously shared information as necessary. Best practice also includes doing one's own research on the defendant's RS outside of sessions to ensure thorough understanding.

That is, it may be beneficial to review records of the defendant's RS if available. This information may be directly available, or more subtle, within symptom descriptions in previous competency reports or past hospitalization notes. Utilizing only record review may be most appropriate when a defendant becomes overly defensive or psychiatrically destabilizes during RS discussions. However, as RS is fluid and can change over time, it is indicated to conduct a current RS assessment if possible. How much assessment is required will vary on a case-by-case basis. For example, someone utilizing RS as a positive coping skill will likely require significantly less assessment than someone whose RS is impacting their competency-related abilities. After the initial assessment, reassessment may only be necessary if there are significant shifts in the defendant's beliefs. Table 7.1 lists some assessments that may prove beneficial.

Engaging With the Defendant

RS-related discussion will be better informed after assessing a defendant's RS beliefs and practices. As appropriate, clinicians should use the defendant's RS language for higher power(s), places of worship, literature, and practices. Considering this language may be new, acknowledging mistakes as they arise will aid in rapport, which plays a large role in intervention productiveness (or lack thereof).

Table 7.1 Relevant RS Assessment Instruments

Name of Assessment	Description	Uses for Restoration
God Image Inventory (GII)	Versions include 156 items (8-point scale), 72 items (6-point scale), or 36 items (3-point scale) inquiring about one's image of God regarding belonging, goodness, and control	May be useful when RS is impacting treatment adherence or their ability to rationally address their charges, for those who believe in God
Heartland Forgiveness Scale (HSF)	18 statements about forgiving self, others, and situations using a 7-point scale	May be helpful to gain an understanding of those who are self-punitive or have negative views on court processes
Intrinsic Spirituality Scale (ISS)	6 statements about RS using an 11-point scale	May be helpful to aid in coping with stressors impacting their competency
Spiritual Assessment Inventory (SAI)	49 statements about one's relationship with God (awareness, disappointment, realistic acceptance, grandiosity, and instability) using a 5-point scale	May be particularly useful for those who have RS delusions or who present as hyperreligious

Facilitating Adaptive RS Coping

One area for engagement is discussing the usefulness of RS for the defendant. Inquiring about how RS helps cope with life stressors can be particularly helpful, especially for defendants who struggle to discuss their charges or attend legal hearings. As appropriate, encourage the defendant to attend their RS services or provide them with a video-based option, advocate for them to have their RS text, and generally support their RS practices. These supportive actions do not require clinician engagement in the RS. At the same time, a defendant's ability to tolerate and track lengthy RS services may speak to their ability to tolerate and track lengthy court hearings. To an extent, their ability to successfully read and focus upon RS literature may speak to their ability to do the same with competency restoration materials or legal paperwork.

Learning about the defendant's RS practices can also help direct interventions; RS can be integrated into common and empirically supported therapeutic skills. For example, if a defendant indicates that they prefer to pray when stressed, one could incorporate the IMPROVE (Imagery, Meaning, Prayer, One thing in the moment, Vacation, and Encouragement) skill from *dialectical behavior therapy* (see Chapter 10), which includes a prayer component. Loving kindness prayers (i.e., prayers that speak to love, positivity, or goodwill to self and/or others) may also be useful. When mantras or self-talk is helpful, possibly introduce tangible resources such as faith-based coping cards (i.e., individualized note cards that remind or encourage an individual to utilize their coping skills). Not only could creating these cards be useful, but placing them in frequently seen places (e.g., in their hospital room or jail cell) can also assist in recurrent coping. As defendants may not be able to bring coping cards or other paperwork from a restoration facility (e.g., hospital) to a secondary location, teaching how to utilize this skill in the future (e.g., using scrap paper in a courtroom) may be indicated.

From *cognitive behavioral therapy* (see Chapter 6), the ABC(DE) strategy (activating event, beliefs, consequences, disputation of beliefs, and effective manners of thinking or evaluate) to challenging one's thoughts can be altered to ABCD(R)E (R for religious or spiritual resources), which considers one's RS resources that aid in challenging thought distortion. In this exercise, the defendant should be instructed to identify the activating event that triggered the distorted thoughts. They should then consider their associated beliefs—whether religious or not. Next, the defendant should identify the consequences of their thoughts. The D and R sections can be combined, using secular or RS arguments that dispute their thoughts. Finally, they should evaluate their thoughts after considering all of the above information. Using such a strategy could both aid in an individual's ability to positively cope and in addressing competency barriers.

Consider a defendant whose alleged crime (e.g., murder of their family member) directly violates their RS beliefs. At the time of the crime, the defendant was experiencing significant symptoms of mental illness and thus had no recollection of the alleged offense. After a period of being medicated with antipsychotic medication, they begin to recall the incident. They subsequently begin to experience significant grief and self-loathing. The defendant informs his restoration provider that they plan to plead guilty, not because of the evidence against them, but due to their RS belief that they should not lie, and their feelings that they should be punished for their actions. In such a scenario, it would likely be beneficial to aid the defendant in exploring their underlying RS beliefs to improve their competency-related abilities. It may be beneficial to utilize ABCD(R)E and coping cards while encouraging them to utilize other healthy RS coping skills (e.g., prayer or speaking with RS leaders).

To illustrate the use of ABCD(R)E and coping cards, one could begin by discussing the (A) activating event, (B) the defendant's related beliefs, and (C) their perception of the consequences. Depending on the defendant's mental state and ability to tolerate such a discussion, this may take several minutes or multiple sessions. If significant distress is impeding the discussion, introducing coping cards may be appropriate. It may otherwise best fit after (D and R) disputing the beliefs with RS resources. For example, "When discussing the evidence against the idea of your crime being unforgivable, you mentioned that God is forgiving of your sins. That may be beneficial to write down on a coping card or on a scrap piece of paper when you are in court to help you cope if those negative thoughts come up." Following such discussions, restoration providers should have the defendant (E) evaluate or re-evaluate their thoughts. If their thoughts continue to negatively impact their competency abilities, further encouraging independent RS coping may help supplement treatment.

Addressing RS Barriers to Competence

If a defendant experiences RS-themed delusional beliefs, it is after RS assessment and rapport-building discussion that challenging those delusions is appropriate. Clinicians should have a thorough understanding of the defendant's RS belief system prior to challenging RS delusions, as assumptions and biases could be harmful, negatively impact rapport, or further instill said delusions. If enough information is available, using the facts to reality test may be helpful (e.g., "You previously told me that God is loving and gentle, but you also believe that He asked you to harm your family. Can you help me make sense of these two things?"). Especially if the delusions are deeply engrained, the defendant may try to rationalize or provide an altogether illogical understanding. It is unlikely that asking such a question will resolve the delusion in the moment, but similar questions over time may aid in re-establishing the defendant in reality. Such interventions are generally consistent with *cognitive behavior therapy for psychosis* (see Chapter 9).

In general, when an individual's major mental health symptoms are disruptive, medication likely needs to be titrated or changed, and RS-informed competency restoration may *not* be appropriate. In such circumstances, efforts to address RS may be futile as the individual is likely to have significant difficulty reasonably thinking through related concepts. Delusions, whether rooted in RS or not, tend to be fixed, so it may be beneficial to address them when symptoms of acute psychosis have improved. However, there may also be an argument that discussions when an individual is symptomatic would be beneficial for parallel documentation. That is, if a defendant is unable to rationally think through his or her RS, this may indicate similar difficulties in rationally considering legal information.

In a study on individuals with schizophrenia, Mohr and colleagues (2007) found that few participants engaged in an RS community, as their symptoms negatively impacted their ability to effectively participate in the RS practices. This could translate to a defendant's ability to effectively participate in their defense, by appropriately attending to court proceedings. Moreover, on an inpatient basis, defendants may feel that they are being judged for their RS beliefs or that these beliefs and practices are unimportant to providers (Glorney et al., 2019). Thus, providing RS-based groups or individual discussions would provide defendants with a safe space to express their faith while working on their ability to meaningfully participate and engage with others. Regarding social interactions, addressing RS may be indicated when a defendant with RS beliefs isolates, has limited interactions with others, or when they are hesitant to discuss their RS beliefs that are likely impacting competency domains.

It should also be considered that, as a result of their symptoms or legal involvement, individuals may have experienced alienation within their place of worship (Hustoft et al., 2013; Mohr et al., 2007). This in turn may influence their expectations for how they are perceived in a courtroom. In these circumstances, clinicians should consider exploring the depths of the RS and possibly cultural vigilance. Additionally, instead of consulting or collaborating with clergy following RS alienation, it may be beneficial to engage family or trusted others. However, clinicians should take caution when doing so, as individuals may pursue congruence between their beliefs and those of their caregivers, leading to increased distress and impeding recovery (Chan & Ho, 2017). Thus, the clinician should consult with other professionals who are well versed in RS and use clinical judgment when involving themselves and/or others when addressing RS with a defendant.

Additionally, when deciding on the appropriateness of RS-informed treatment, clinicians should consider the above-noted research as well as the defendant's individual treatment needs. For example, clinicians could aid in strengthening one's already existing positive RS coping skills and develop or strengthen their ability to engage in their legal circumstances by encouraging RS group attendance or making room for individual discussions about RS. Again, these discussions should *not* be a place of judgment or an attempt to change the defendant's beliefs, but simply a place to safely disclose. This is especially true when working with those without positive RS coping skills or with maladaptive RS skills. When such individuals are acutely symptomatic, it will likely be unproductive to have such complex discussions. Upon improvement of their symptoms, RS discussions may be more appropriate, especially to reduce the possibility of the impacts that negative RS coping can influence (e.g., increased symptoms, suicidality, and conflicts with treatment). In either scenario, addressing RS can aid in improving various components of mental health, which could in turn improve one's willingness and/or ability to effectively engage in competency restoration.

Further supporting the need for RS-informed clinical judgment is the finding that those with religiously based delusions may be perceived as having more symptoms and being lower functioning, resulting in being prescribed more medication than those without religious delusions (Lucchetti et al., 2021; Siddle et al., 2002). For competency restoration purposes, Lemons and colleagues (2022) found that those who were prescribed medium and high doses of antipsychotic medications were restored significantly slower than those on low doses. Thus, it may be beneficial for clinicians to address said RS delusions to possibly reduce the need for higher dosages. As those with delusional systems tend to have internal justifications and may be less open to considering alternative explanations (Iyassu et al., 2014), treatment will likely require RS-informed reality testing. Reality testing is the process of aiding the defendant in "distinguish[ing] between self and nonself and between fantasy and real life" (APA, 2023, Reality Testing section).

Consultation and Collaboration

Another strategy that may prove beneficial is consulting and collaborating with RS leaders and experts. For the purpose of this chapter, *consultation* refers to seeking supervision, information, and/or advice from others educated in RS. During consultation, defendant information should be de-identified and thus does not require defendant permission. Consultation tends to be brief and goal directed rather than an ongoing process. In contrast, *collaboration* is the process of working with others in developing a treatment plan or facilitating treatment sessions with defendants. RS consultation is likely necessary when one is learning about and working with RS for the first time(s). While this may also be the case when collaborating, collaboration is a more "hands-on" learning experience.

As previously mentioned, clinicians should seek consultation when learning about RS, whether that is general education or education about one particular RS system. When seeking general education, it is ideal to search for clinicians or educators who have specifically received training in RS integration. It should not matter whether these individuals adhere to RS in their personal lives; it is more important that they are familiar with a variety of RS structures and how that may impact treatment. Another beneficial consideration when seeking consultation is to find someone who is willing to challenge your biases and thought processes. This may include seeking someone with whom you are unfamiliar or with whom you do not share RS faith. Such efforts can help expand your mindset and produce ideas, conceptualizations, and strategies that may otherwise be missed.

As it is not always possible to find RS-trained clinicians or educators, another option may be to seek information from RS leaders. If working in a setting with a chaplain or similar provider, they may be an ideal resource, as they are likely familiar with the population. In other circumstances, consultation efforts may require reaching out to places of worship. Though defendant information should not be shared during consultation, avoid contacting the defendant's place of worship when possible. Otherwise, the leaders may be aware of the defendant's situation and make their own connections, breaching confidentiality. As finding other places of worship may be more difficult in rural settings or when a defendant's RS is not as common in the location, it may be best to obtain the defendant's permission prior to reaching out to their place of worship.

As collaboration would require sharing a defendant's information, the defendant should be asked to provide informed consent for collaborative efforts during competency restoration. Follow the requirements of your workplace for obtaining such permission. Without this permission, it is still possible to create a treatment plan for the defendant, though pertinent information may have to be withheld for privacy purposes. In-session collaboration, however, would not be ethical, as consent has not been provided. It is important to remember that defendants have the right to *not* consent to RS-informed treatment; withholding consent does not equate to antisocial behavior. Clinicians should remember that RS vigilance (i.e., an awareness of RS stigma, especially in secular settings) can be similar to cultural or racial vigilance. Addressing this vigilance may prove helpful to building rapport, aiding in reducing RS-related stress, and fostering eventual openness to collaborative efforts. The possibility of RS collaboration may be re-approached at a later time.

Assuming consent for collaboration is ultimately obtained, the next step is to reach out to the desired collaborator. This may include but is not limited to RS-trained clinicians and educators, chaplains, RS leaders (specific to the defendant's RS), clergy members, or family members. It is then that coordination of efforts begins. Coordination may include discussing boundaries with the defendant and collaborator, finding times and places to meet (in person or via phone or video), identifying information that will be discussed during the meeting(s), and strategizing for the future. As it is possible that the clinician and collaborator are unfamiliar with the other's work and ethics, discussing boundaries is important; typically boundaries may look different for each person involved. If agreeing on boundaries proves difficult, finding a common goal to work toward may be the simplest solution. Should collaboration become counterproductive (e.g., if the defendant's symptoms worsen during or after collaboration), consultation may be required and/or termination of the collaborative relationship may be appropriate.

TREATMENT CONSIDERATIONS

Restoration Service Location Considerations

Defendants receiving competency restoration services in the community likely have more direct access to their RS needs compared with those in a jail or hospital setting. For example, they may live near those with similar belief systems and have appropriate accommodations for their practices (e.g., allotted free time for Muslim prayer throughout the day, a kneeler for Catholic prayer, or religious attire such as a hijab). However, those in the community may also encounter barriers to RS practices, such as not having a means of transportation to or from their place of worship.

Those receiving services in jail and inpatient settings may encounter more challenges in practicing their faith. They cannot go to their preferred place of worship and may have lost contact with those within their RS community in the context of their arrest/incarceration. The jail or hospital may or may not have an appropriate area to practice their RS faith, and even when present, access to these areas may be limited. In hospital or jail settings, RS accommodations may be limited due to space or safety concerns (e.g., religious attire could pose choking concerns).

Particularly when it is indicated to integrate RS in competency restoration, clinicians should advocate for a defendant's RS needs. In an institutional setting, this could include educating other staff members, who do not understand the defendant's RS identity, and may mistakenly believe that the defendant's RS self-advocacy efforts are pathological. This may involve taking the defendant to the worship area before or after a restoration session or setting up a virtual meeting with RS leaders from the defendant's community. In community-based restoration, it may be worthwhile to aid the defendant in researching video-based (i.e., live or recorded) options or other alternative means of worship (e.g., a priest going to a home to offer communion). These options will likely vary depending on location and how common the RS is in that particular location. For example, Jewish services and resources may be more vast and readily available in areas with larger populations of those practicing Judaism (e.g., the Northeastern U.S.) than elsewhere.

Diversity Considerations

RS is a component of diversity that should be considered along with other common cultural components (e.g., race, ethnicity, gender, etc.). Examining the intersectionality of RS with other diversity components can be helpful in the course of competency restoration. Certain behavioral and interpersonal aspects of a defendant's presentation may be best understood, and addressed or accommodated, through this intersectional lens. RS attire, gendered interpersonal interactions, eye contact, and physical contact are among aspects that may come up during the course of competency restoration.

Consider the case of a female defendant who is unable to wear RS attire (i.e., a burqa or hijab) due to hospital or jail restrictions and whose RS beliefs provide strict guidelines on interactions with men, but she has been assigned a male restoration provider and defense attorney. If the defendant is used to having her hair and/or face covered, she may withdraw to avoid unnecessary interactions with others. Doing so could negatively impact the progress she is able to make in restoration efforts. On the other hand, the defendant may also engage in what may otherwise be viewed as an odd or rule-breaking behavior, such as covering herself with a blanket or towel despite redirection not to do so. This could lead to unnecessary behavioral plans or medication trials that may impact her restoration abilities. Furthermore, it may be beneficial to process any concerns about wearing or not wearing RS attire when in court. The defendant may feel unsafe or exposed if she does not wear the attire but may believe that she will be stigmatized if she does wear it. Discussing such concerns with the defendant may aid in reducing court-related anxiety that is impacting her competency. Regarding the gendered interpersonal interactions, the defendant may refuse to meet with her restoration provider or attorney. Thorough assessment of her RS may lead to the identification of accommodations to promote engagement. For example, perhaps a third party needs to be present during meetings with these individuals if it is not possible to have a same-sex provider or attorney assigned.

As another example, making eye contact generally shows that a person is paying attention and invested in the conversation. However, certain cultures and religions have differing positions on eye contact and body language. If you notice variable eye contact or that the defendant positions themselves in a peculiar manner, immediacy could be appropriate. For example, "I noticed that you have been avoiding eye contact, could you help me understand why that is?" If appropriate adjustments can be made, making those adjustments would likely improve competency restoration efforts. Responses may also yield useful information to pass along to their attorney if the defendant gives permission. On the other hand, the defendant may provide a response for which adjustments cannot be made. In such cases, discuss why you cannot adjust and explore their related emotions. It may also be useful to discuss how this may translate into court or trial proceedings and their plan to cope with lack of accommodation in the legal context.

Case Example

Spencer is a 29-year-old White male charged with first-degree murder. He is diagnosed with schizophrenia and experiences visual and auditory hallucinations, along with his delusions, as outlined below. Spencer would see shadow images, objects that he explained as "spirits" that would glisten or sparkle, and other "scary" images that he was unwilling to describe. He also heard growling, screaming, and other unpleasant noises. His symptoms proved to be medication resistant; he underwent various medication trials, though none completely resolved his symptoms. Spencer was admitted to an inpatient psychiatric hospital for restoration services. His assigned restoration provider was not on his treatment team in an attempt to avoid multiple relationships.

Spencer is a member of the Church of Jesus Christ of Latter-day Saints, otherwise known as the LDS Church or Mormon faith. It should be noted that the LDS faith is one practice under the umbrella of Mormonism (e.g., as Catholicism is a practice within Christianity). Spencer was guarded about his religious beliefs, sharing only limited insight into his faith with a select few providers. Over time, he shared that he believed that God told him to commit murder so that he and his loved one (the victim) could elevate to a higher plane of being (i.e., to be Godlike or immortal). As he believed this to be a command from God, this significantly impacted his ability to rationally think through his case—he believed that he could not be successfully prosecuted in a courtroom because God would protect him. This also impacted his ability to assist his attorney in his defense.

While Spencer was guarded in RS conversations with staff at the hospital, he desired and enjoyed conversations with visiting members of his faith. He indicated that he could truly express himself with other members of the Church, as they thoroughly understood his belief system. On the downside, his treatment team would often notice an increase in his symptoms after these visits. Complicating matters, Spencer would not sign a release of information for his treatment team members to speak to his visitors about his care. He also asked that his parents were not consulted about his faith.

When working with Spencer for individual restoration, a thorough assessment of his faith and how that impacted his life, specifically related to his case, was difficult. He would not complete any structured RS assessments. If Spencer was more willing to share his beliefs, the provider would have also utilized a formal RS assessment measure (see "Religion/Spirituality Assessment" in Appendix B), as well as consultation and/or collaboration with religious leaders or members of his faith. It is important to remember that, when integrating RS into one's work, assumptions about the defendant's faith should not be made, and clinician biases and judgments should be explored and checked when possible. As Spencer was unable/unwilling to participate in such an assessment, the restoration provider first sought additional resources to better understand the LDS faith. These included internet research (using credible sources) and talking with a coworker who previously practiced this faith (while keeping in mind they are not the expert on Spencer's specific beliefs). Most importantly, the clinician provided an open, supportive space for Spencer so that he was willing to share during competency restoration, even if minimally.

When Spencer was agreeable to discussing his faith, efforts were made to understand his preferred language (e.g., what to call his higher being—Heavenly Father, God, Jesus Christ, etc.). Over time, discussions also included how his RS beliefs impacted his thoughts on mental illness, medication, and his alleged offense. At times worksheets were utilized to facilitate discussion (see "Faith and Law" worksheet in Appendix B). It was sometimes more beneficial to use hypothetical scenarios instead of directly addressing his personal situation. For example, the restoration provider tried asking about how a person of his faith might feel about sitting through a court hearing for trespassing when they had permission from God to be on the property. While this did not directly relate to Spencer, it gave the provider insight into difficult feelings that might arise for him during court hearings, and then they could address them accordingly. This also presented the opportunity to explore other language use (e.g., church or temple, prayer or meditation) and appropriate ways and times to use Spencer's RS practices. Additionally, this presented the opportunity to explore Spencer's religious coping tools. Between intervention sessions, the provider also utilized supervision to process any countertransference that arose during sessions.

REFERENCES

American Psychological Association. (2017). *Ethical principles of psychologists and code of conduct.* https://www.apa.org/ethics/code/

American Psychological Association. (2018a). Integration. https://dictionary.apa.org/integration

American Psychological Association. (2018b). Plasticity. https://dictionary.apa.org/plasticity

American Psychological Association. (2018c). Religion. https://dictionary.apa.org/religion

American Psychological Association. (2018d). Spirituality. https://dictionary.apa.org/spirituality

American Psychological Association. (2023). Reality testing. https://dictionary.apa.org/reality-testing

American Psychological Association. (n.d.). Schizophrenia. https://www.apa.org/topics/schiz/

Borras, L., Mohr, S., Brandt, P. Y., Gilliéron, C., Eytan, A., & Huguelet, P. (2007). Religious beliefs in schizophrenia: Their relevance for adherence to treatment. *Schizophrenia Bulletin, 33*(5), 1238–1246. doi:10.1093/schbul/sbl070

Cain Munson, M. G. (2024). *The relationship between schizophrenia and clinically significant religious impairment.* [Doctoral dissertation, Regent University]. ProQuest Dissertations.

Chan, C. K. P., & Ho, R. T. H. (2017). Discrepancy in spirituality among patients with schizophrenia and family care-givers and its impacts on illness recovery: A dyadic investigation. *British Journal of Social Work, 47*(1), 28–47. doi:10.1093/bjsw/bcw156

Das, S., Punnoose, V. P., Doval, N., & Nair, V. Y. (2018). Spirituality, religiousness and coping in patients with schizophrenia: A cross sectional study in a tertiary care hospital. *Psychiatry Research, 265*, 238–243. doi:10.1016/j.psychres.2018.04.030

Drinnan, A., & Lavender, T. (2006). Deconstructing delusions: A qualitative study examining the relationship between religious beliefs and religious delusions. *Mental Health, Religion and Culture, 9*(4), 317–331. doi:10.1080/13694670500071711

Dudek, A., Krzystanek, M., Krysta, K., & Górna, A. (2019). Evolution of religious topics in schizophrenia in 80 years period. *Psychiatria Danubina, 31*, 524–529. https://www.psychiatria-danubina.com/articles

Glorney, E., Raymont, S., Lawson, A. and Allen, J. (2019). Religion, spirituality and personal recovery among forensic patients. *The Journal of Forensic Practice, 21*(3), 190–200. doi:10.1108/JFP-05-2019-0021

Grover, S., Davuluri, T., & Chakrabarti, S. (2014). Religion, spirituality, and schizophrenia: A review. *Indian Journal of Psychological Medicine, 36*(2), 119–124. doi:10.4103/0253-7176.130962

Hill, P. C., & Kilian, M. K. (2003). Assessing clinically significant religious impairment in clients: Applications from measures in the psychology of religion and spirituality. *Mental Health, Religion & Culture*, *6*(2), 149. doi:10.1080/1367467021000038192

Hodge, D. R. (2018). Spiritual competence: What it is, why it is necessary, and how to develop it. *Journal of Ethnic & Cultural Diversity in Social Work*, *27*(2), 124–139. doi:10.1080/15313204.2016.1228093

Holt, C. L., Clark, E. M., Kreuter, M. W., & Rubio, D. M. (2003). Spiritual Health Locus of Control Scale. *APA PsycTests*. doi:10.1037/t19819-000

Huguelet, P., Mohr, S., Borras, L., Gillieron, C., & Brandt, P.-Y. (2006). Spirituality and religious practices among outpatients with schizophrenia and their clinicians. *Psychiatric Services*, *57*(3). doi:10.1176/appi.ps.57.3.366

Hustoft, H., Hestad, K. A., Lien, L., Møller, P., & Danbolt, L. J. (2013). "If I didn't have my faith I would have killed myself!": Spiritual coping in patients suffering from schizophrenia. *International Journal for the Psychology of Religion*, *23*(2), 126–144. doi:10.1080/10508619.2012.688003

Iyassu, R., Jolley, S., Bebbington, P., Dunn, G., Emsley, R., Freeman, D., . . . Garety, P. (2014). Psychological characteristics of religious delusions. *Social Psychiatry and Psychiatric Epidemiology*, *49*(7), 1051–1061. doi:10.1007/s00127-013-0811-y

Kate, N., Grover, S., Kulhara, P., & Nehra, R. (2012). Supernatural beliefs, aetiological models and help seeking behaviour in patients with schizophrenia. *Industrial Psychiatry Journal*, *21*(1), 49–54. doi:10.4103/0972-6748.110951

Khokhar, W. A., Dein, S. L., Qureshi, M. S., Hameed, I., Ali, M. M., Abbasi, Y., . . . Sood, R. (2015). When taking medication may be a sin: Dietary requirements and food laws in psychotropic prescribing. *BJPsych Advances*, *21*(6), 425–432. doi:10.1192/apt.bp.114.012534

Krzystanek, M., Krysta, K., Klasik, A., & Krupka-Matuszczyk, I. (2012). Religious content of hallucinations in paranoid schizophrenia. *Psychiatria Danubina*, *24*, 65–69. https://www.psychiatria-danubina.com/articles

Lemons A., Iuppa C. A., Kriz C. R., Diefenderfer L. A., Nelson L. A., Lang S. E., . . . Sommi, R. W. (2022). Antipsychotic factors related to time to competency for forensic inpatients in a state psychiatric facility. *The Mental Health Clinician*, *12*(3), 175–180. doi:10.9740/mhc.2022.06.175.

Lucchetti, G., Koenig, H. G., & Lucchetti, A. L. G. (2021). Spirituality, religiousness, and mental health: A review of the current scientific evidence. *World Journal of Clinical Cases*, *9*(26), 7620–7631. doi:10.12998/wjcc.v9.i26.7620

Milner, K., Crawford, P., Edgley, A., Hare-Duke, L., & Slade, M. (2020). The experiences of spirituality among adults with mental health difficulties: A qualitative systematic review. *Epidemiology and Psychiatric Sciences*, *29*(34), 1–10. doi:10.1017/S2045796019000234

Mitchell, L., & Romans, S. (2003). Spiritual beliefs in bipolar affective disorder: Their relevance for illness management. *Journal of Affective Disorders*, *75*(3), 247–257. doi:10.1016/s0165-0327(02)00055-1

Mohamed, S., Rosenheck, R., McEvoy, J., Swartz, M., Stroup, S., & Lieberman, J. A. (2009). Cross-sectional and longitudinal relationships between insight and attitudes toward medication and clinical outcomes in chronic schizophrenia. *Schizophrenia Bulletin*, *35*(2), 336–346. doi:10.1093/schbul/sbn067

Mohr, S., Borras, L., Rieben, I., Betrisey, C., Gillieron, C., Brandt, P., . . . Huguelet, P. (2010). Evolution of spirituality and religiousness in chronic schizophrenia or schizo-affective disorders:

A 3-years follow-up study. *Social Psychiatry and Psychiatric Epidemiology, 45*(11), 1095–1103. doi:10.1007/s00127-009-0151-0

Mohr, S., Brandt, P.-Y., Borras, L., Gilliéron, C., & Huguelet, P. (2006). Toward an integration of spirituality and religiousness into the psychosocial dimension of schizophrenia. *American Journal of Psychiatry, 163*(16), 1952–1959. doi:10.1176/ajp.2006.163.11.1952

Mohr, S., Gillieron, C., Borras, L., Brandt, P.-Y., & Huguelet, P. (2007). The assessment of spirituality and religiousness in schizophrenia. *The Journal of Nervous and Mental Disease, 195*, 247–253. doi:10.1097/01.nmd.0000258230.94304.6b

Mohr, S., & Huguelet, P. (2004). The relationship between schizophrenia and religion and its implications for care. *Swiss Medical Weekly, 134*(25–26), 369–376. doi:2004/25/smw-10322

Morken, G., Widen, J. H., & Grawe, R. W. (2008). Non-adherence to antipsychotic medication, relapse and rehospitalisation in recent-onset schizophrenia. *BMC Psychiatry, 8*(1), 32–32. doi:10.1186/1471-244X-8-32

Pesut, B., Clark, N., Maxwell, V., & Michalak, E. E. (2011). Religion and spirituality in the context of bipolar disorder: A literature review. *Mental Health, Religion & Culture, 14*(8), 785–796. doi:10.1080/13674676.2010.523890

Pew Research Center (2012). *The global religious landscape*. https://www.pewresearch.org/religion/2012/12/18/global-religious-landscape-exec/

Revheim, N., Greenberg, W. M., & Citrome, L. (2010). Spirituality, schizophrenia, and state hospitals: Program description and characteristics of self-selected attendees of a spirituality therapeutic group. *Psychiatric Quarterly, 81*(4), 285–292. doi:10.1007/s11126-010-9137-z

Siddle, R., Haddock, G., Tarrier, N., & Faragher, E. B. (2002). Religious delusions in patients admitted to hospital with schizophrenia. *Social Psychiatry and Psychiatric Epidemiology, 37*(3), 130–138. doi:10.1007/s001270200005

Vernon, M. K., Revicki, D. A., Awad, A. G., Dirani, R., Panish, J., Canuso, C. M., . . . Kalali, A. H. (2010). Psychometric evaluation of the medication satisfaction questionnaire (MSQ) to assess satisfaction with antipsychotic medication among schizophrenia patients. *Schizophrenia Research*, 118(1-3), 271–278. doi:10.1016/j.schres.2010.01.021.

PART V

Serious Mental Illness (SMI) as a Barrier to Competency

8

Music Therapy (MT) and Competency Restoration

KENDALL JOPLIN, MME, MT-BC AND KATE STANLEY, MMT, MT-BC

OVERVIEW OF MUSIC THERAPY

Music therapy has been defined by the American Music Therapy Association as "the clinical and evidence-based use of music interventions to accomplish individualized goals within a therapeutic relationship by a credentialed professional who has completed an approved music therapy program" (2023, AMTA Official Definition of Music Therapy section). To become a music therapist, one must obtain a degree from an accredited music therapy program and complete at least 1,200 clinical hours. Following training, one must pass the board examination to become a board-certified music therapist (MT-BC). Music therapists are often trained in four different types of musical interventions that take into consideration the cognitive, physical, and emotional arousal levels required to engage in the intervention—receptive music, re-creative music, improvisation, and composition (Bruscia, 2014). These different intervention types will be further explained along with specific examples in the next section. Because music is a complex medium, each intervention type should take into account which music elements are present and utilized to develop the most appropriate intervention for the task. These musical elements include timbre, rhythm, tempo, pitch, melody, dynamics, lyrics, form, harmony, and style (Hanson-Abromeit, 2015). While the training offered by a music therapy program allows music therapists to have a nuanced, in-depth understanding of the mechanisms of change that can exist through music's uses in a therapeutic setting (Kazdin, 2006), they are not the only helping professionals capable of purposefully drawing upon them. If not specifically trained in how the various elements of music (e.g., rhythm, instrumentation, dynamics, harmony, melody, timbre, lyric content, etc.) might be helpful or harmful in treatment, clinicians should use music with caution.

As of this writing, the most recent Workforce Survey indicated that 19.85% of music therapists work in forensic settings (American Music Therapy Association, 2021). However, specific education on competency restoration services is not often covered in music therapy education. While this chapter will serve as a tool for music therapists working in forensic settings, it will also serve as a guide for how non-music therapists can integrate creative intervention designs into their competency restoration services. While reading this chapter, note that music therapists come from an array of backgrounds, identities, and theoretical orientations. As with other forms of treatment, these personal differences often affect how treatment services are provided, including the way music's role is conceptualized and implemented in sessions. This chapter should be read with the knowledge that it is written by the authors, who describe themselves and their clinical work in the author biographies in

Kendall Joplin and Kate Stanley, *Music Therapy (MT) and Competency Restoration*. In: *The Competency Restoration Handbook*.
Edited by: Laura M. Grossi, Oxford University Press. © Laura M. Grossi (2025). DOI: 10.1093/9780197768075.003.0008

this chapter (see "Authors' Sociocultural Statements"); these recommendations may differ from another music therapist's practice. If you are a music therapist, consider how your individual experiences and understanding of the world show up in the work you do. If you are not a music therapist, we encourage you to see if one works in your setting and to consult with them about how they conceptualize the use of music interventions in competency restoration services.

Because this chapter is written for music therapists and non-music therapy clinicians, a framework for an intervention design process that utilizes music is presented as a model for how clinicians can work through the process of being creative in treatment. Portions of this chapter have been adapted from author Kate Stanley's unpublished final project for completion of a master's in music therapy through Temple University: a treatment manual titled "Music Therapy, Serious Mental Illness and Adjudicative Competence—An Intervention Manual."

SERIOUS MENTAL ILLNESS AND COMPETENCE

Serious mental illness (SMI) is defined by the Substance Abuse and Mental Health Services Administration as having "a diagnosable mental, behavior, or emotional disorder that causes serious functional impairment that substantially interferes with or limits one or more major life activities" (2023, Mental Health and Substance Use Disorders section). SMI is determined by severity and duration, and diagnoses can include thought, mood, anxiety, and personality disorders. Schizophrenia and bipolar disorder are the SMIs most frequently encountered in adjudicative competence cases, often with constellations of complex symptoms.

Psychosis and other SMI symptomology alone are not enough to warrant an evaluation for competence, though, in the past, the presence of psychotic symptoms and incompetence were seen as synonymous (Roesch et al., 2014). An attempted meta-analysis of the competency literature showed that patients with psychotic disorders were "eight times more likely to be found incompetent" (Pirelli et al., 2011, p. 1). However, forensic evaluators and researchers are working to ensure that evaluations accurately assess a defendant's adjudicative competence, rather than assuming the presence of SMI equates to incompetence.

RELEVANT EVIDENCE BASE FOR MUSIC THERAPY

Current evidence seems to point to the inclusion of varied educational and therapeutic resources—a multimodal approach—in creating successful restoration programs. Music has been shown to be effective in the management of mental health difficulties in and out of forensic and correctional settings (Chen et al., 2016; Tseng et al., 2016; Wang et al., 2023), and music therapy is often conceptualized as an adjunctive treatment for competency services in forensic settings. Therefore, it would stand to reason that music therapy may prove to be an effective addition to existing competency restoration programming when introduced with intentionality.

One example of the need for intentionality within music intervention design to address specific goal areas can be seen in the use of music for memory. As memory—recall of factual information—is a component of adjudicative competence, understanding the specific components of music that assist with recall can be a valuable tool in treatment. Within the literature there is contradicting evidence, with research that supports music to assist with memory (Swanson, 2020), and research that indicates it divides attention, creating worse outcomes (Musliu et al., 2017). This contradiction within the literature has been shown to be due to the specific ways in which music interacts with memory. Literature that investigates the use of background music (i.e., playing live or recorded music in the space without specific focus on the music) during memory tasks shows music is contraindicated for memory goals. However, the use of tailored, live music, which deliberately utilizes music-responsive systems in the brain, has been shown to be an effective form of treatment (Ferreri & Rodriguez-Fornells, 2017). Because music is composed of many different elements, intentionally considering and utilizing each element can have an impact on its efficacy toward memory-related goals. Ferreri and Verga (2016) identified specific musical components that assist with recall, including singing instead of speaking the information, use of simple melodies with symmetric contours, use of moderate tempos, stimulation of emotional responses, and instrumentation that is not too simplistic nor too complex.

Another relevant area of research examined the use of music therapy for schizophrenia and schizophrenia-like disorders in a systematic review. Geretsegger and colleagues (2017) concluded that when added to standard treatment, music therapy appears to "improve the global state, mental state (including negative and general symptoms), social functioning, and quality of life of people with schizophrenia or schizophrenia-like disorders" (p. 2). However, those authors cautioned that the included studies are of low to moderate quality and more research is needed. Jia and colleagues (2020) had similar results in their meta-analysis. The authors found that music therapy as an addition to treatment as usual "significantly improved the total symptoms, negative symptoms, and depression symptoms" (p. 8), with the same caution that the evidence quality indicates a need for further research with larger groups. Because the most frequent symptoms that may impact or cause deficits in competence-related abilities are those that occur along the schizophrenia spectrum (Ryba & Zapf, 2011), it is significant that music therapy affects such symptoms.

When designing interventions for individuals with SMI, it is essential to take a trauma-informed approach in competency restoration services, and when using music it is important to understand and consider the impacts of each of these musical elements. Research shows that individuals with SMI who have a history of trauma or a diagnosis of post-traumatic stress disorder (PTSD) have worse outcomes in symptom management and more frequent hospitalizations (Corrigan et al., 2024). Along with decreased symptom management, trauma responses lead to hyperarousal, decreasing the activation of an individual's prefrontal cortex and overall cognitive processing, and increasing the risk of emotional decompensation (Andrewes & Jenkins, 2019). Music has been shown to be an effective intervention to treat most symptom clusters in PTSD (Landis-Shack et al., 2017). Specifically, music has been shown to significantly increase heart rate variability and decrease cortisol levels (McPherson et al., 2019; Parizek, 2021). However, there is variation in the efficacy of music as an intervention for PTSD based on the volume (do Amaral et al., 2016), music preferences (Archana, 2016), tempo (Thakare et al., 2017), genre (da Silva et al., 2014), and level of active musical engagement (McPherson et al., 2019).

MUSICAL CONSIDERATIONS

Screening

Should you choose to utilize prerecorded music as part of your intervention's design, it is clinically and ethically imperative to first listen to it and become familiar with its content. Take note of your personal reactions to the music and explore how those reactions may differ from the individuals you serve. Explore how you can set aside your personal biases to use music that connects to your client's or clients' personal lives and experiences. Prerecorded music is not only about the lyrics and thematic content. It also includes all the other musical elements such as the instruments used, the speed at which the music is played, the volume of the music and each instrument, the song's structure, the timbres of each component, the cultural context of the music, etc. All the aspects work together to create the song and contribute to the listener's experience of it. Considering how these elements might impact you and your clients is a crucial part of planning for the use of music in any intervention. Additionally, it is important to know your facility's guidelines about music content. Specific facilities may have rules regarding songs with explicit content or guidance on specific styles of music.

Censorship

Censorship may be an area of consideration where emotional safety is prominent, as described in the "What Tools Do I Have Access to and Can Safely Bring?" subsection. Any censorship of lyric content, printed lyric sheets, styles of music/artists, etc. should be done purposefully, based on clinical needs, and in accordance with the therapist's facility guidelines. The decision about censoring should be rooted in ensuring safety in the therapeutic space, not the therapist's personal judgments and beliefs about the music. Additionally, censorship should be implemented with music quality in mind; aesthetic considerations need to be made to ensure censoring causes the least amount of interruption in the musical experience. This can include a sound effect over the content, clean versions of songs, muting certain content, replacing words, or only playing portions of a song. When considering whether and to what extent to censor music, think about what message censoring sends to your clients about their preferences, lived experiences, and cultural identities.

When considering not censoring music, also think about the importance of the emotional well-being of all individuals in the space—particularly ensuring the music is not triggering for anyone. Triggers in music can be thematic content such as substance use or violence, words that may be offensive, or based on an individual's personal associations with a piece of music. This means any music has the potential to be triggering for someone based upon their relationship to the music. Clinicians should always be actively monitoring clients' reactions to music and be ready to make in-the-moment decisions about the music.

Additionally, be ready to have conversations with your clients about your choice to censor or not censor, so they are aware of your therapeutic decisions and can be a part of informed decisions about the treatment they are receiving. For example, you can ask the client if they prefer the clean or not clean version of a song, give a content warning before the music, or start the experience by saying you already chose to remove some content because of a particular reason. Non-music therapists are encouraged to consult music therapists about how to facilitate such discussions and what to look for in musical responses. For more information on censorship in music therapy, see Joplin and Dvorak (2017).

Interpretation

For music therapists reporting on client progress in restoration groups, there is an additional layer of translation that must occur to help other clinicians make connections between engagement in music therapy services and adjudicative competence. It is especially important to tie together psycholegal abilities and their possible counterparts in music therapy interventions. For example, a client who is able to accurately repeat a drum beat modeled for them by the music therapist can be said to demonstrate time-oriented behavior or the ability to track and respond contextually to events in the group room. This may generalize or translate into the ability to track and engage in courtroom proceedings. Translating specific musical and music-related engagement can help highlight the functional and psycholegal skills that are the basis of adjudicative competence, as well as provide additional insight for those writing reports or collaborating with non-music therapists about a client's competence to proceed.

TRANSFERENCE OF SKILLS POST-TREATMENT

Music therapy services should always be treated as temporary. Clients should be able to transfer the skills they learned and used in sessions after services are terminated. Most clients probably will not have access to instruments while they are in jail or in a holding cell awaiting a court appearance. However, some of the musical skills they have hopefully learned can be used without instruments. For example, clients may have a song list they built for coping or grounding. The client can sing or hum (in their head or out loud) the songs on this list without an instrument. To increase active musical engagement they can add physical responses such as swaying, bilateral tapping, or playing air drums along with the song. In sessions centered on songwriting, clients may have written a chant that includes affirmations, and they can use this chant outside of sessions. Part of services might include teaching clients how they can adapt interventions to spaces where they have less access to the musical tools they had in sessions.

Technology

Part of services might include teaching and engaging in music technology so the clients can practice these skills and be able to use them independently after termination. Some clients may have access to listening devices or a tablet while in jail. Building playlists (e.g., playlists for different emotions) can be done during sessions, and client(s) can download these songs to their own device. If they have a tablet, plenty of apps allow for music creation. These include digital audio workstations and apps that display instruments such as guitar, piano, or drums. Clients can write their own songs to process thoughts and emotions, engage in their own improvisations, or practice structured leisure through learning to play instruments. Additionally, there are apps that allow for the creation of relaxation music by providing a variety of sound clips (e.g., waterfalls, rain, birds, white noise, simple melodies, etc.), which can be added to or subtracted from a track. This customization can allow clients to make adjustments to calming music in real-time, as needed.

CREATIVE INTERVENTION DESIGN

There are many ways in which music can be used to address the competency restoration needs of your client(s). Building the best intervention involves thorough planning and creativity. To help make decisions during intervention design, consider following this creative intervention design framework. The primary factor is the needs of the client(s), followed by what current barriers to competence exist. However, the next steps are crucial for deciding your course of treatment. What is motivating for one person may or may not be motivating for the next. Thinking about what motivates your clients and what you can safely bring to the session that aligns with those motivators will assist in deciding which intervention might be the most successful.

Cultural Context and Considerations

As a profession, music therapists are becoming increasingly aware that the therapeutic space is impacted by social structures including the intersections of gender, race, age, dis/ability, socioeconomic status, heteronormativity, and colonialism. The profession has been calling for an expansion in our understanding of music therapy to engage in anti-oppressive practices (Baines, 2021). Inpatient mental health and competency restoration services have a history of reinforcing the oppression of non-majority groups of individuals. Sociocultural factors impacting competency restoration services include disparities based on immigration status (Cabeldue et al., 2021) and gender (Dirks-Linhorst et al., 2019). Harm caused by racial inequities has even been formally acknowledged by the American Psychological Association (2021). Similar to psychology, these, and other, inequities are seen in music therapy. Music therapy has the added context that music therapists are largely educated in European classical music, leading to Western ideals of what music can be valuable within the therapeutic space (Goodman, 2023).

Equivalently, adjudicative competence is said to be "socially constructed and represents an open-textured, context-specific construct" and literature has yet to find a "best practice" or "gold standard" for treatment (Pirelli et al., 2011, p. 4). If this is accepted as true, it seems implied that both competence evaluation and restoration must be tailored to meet the contextual and cultural setting of the therapeutic work. Indeed, it is these authors' opinions that clinicians are ethically and morally obligated to understand how the systems in which we operate and exist impact the restoration process. All clinicians are implored to consider the unique components of the individuals they serve, to develop interventions that are anti-oppressive, trauma informed, and motivating. This is one way to help dismantle oppressive forms of treatment, as is encouraged by Baines (2021) and others.

It may be worth noting that frontline staff members in inpatient and correctional facilities in the U.S. tend to be a more diverse group than clinicians with more formal education. Frontline clinicians have the unique opportunity to craft innovative and tailored interventions to meet their clients' strengths, needs, cultures, and preferences. Only music therapists can provide music therapy, but professionals across disciplines can leverage their innate creativity to develop interventions that are trauma informed, anti-oppressive, and motivating to reach a variety of individuals. This section is for both music therapists and non-music therapists to work through the process of developing creative clinical interventions.

What Is the Goal Being Addressed?

The primary consideration when building interventions should always be the goal that is addressed. In competency restoration, a logical start is identifying which of the *Dusky* prongs the needs of your clients fall under. From there, a creative therapeutic task can then be purposefully chosen and shaped to support progress toward the goal. For example, if factual knowledge is needed, clinicians may design a songwriting experience that utilizes specific musical elements such as rhythm, melody, and rhyming schemes that can assist with memorization of the material. If working with an attorney is the primary need, clinicians may choose a lyric analysis intervention that explores the complexity of interpersonal relationships and assertive communication skills.

For assistance in identifying specific areas of need, these authors recommend referring to Zapf and Roesch (2009). In their article, the authors present a table (pp. 181–183) that combines the domains and subdomains addressed by all the existing formal assessments utilized for competence to proceed. By basing the interventions around these commonly assessed areas, a music therapist, as well as other clinicians utilizing nontraditional interventions, can make direct, concrete connections between the creative processes observed in groups and the psycholegal abilities sought by the court system.

What Are the Current Barriers to This Goal?

Though all the individuals one is working with are receiving competency restoration services and may have the same or similar diagnoses, they will each have individualized experiences of what their barrier to competency is. Additionally, they may have a list of barriers generated by clinical assessment. As unique individuals, clients have complex histories that impact treatment. This includes their diagnoses and symptoms, their past experiences with the judicial system, personal trauma histories, and intergenerational trauma including systemic bias directly related to the judicial and healthcare systems. For example, a client's frustration tolerance can be impacted by emotional lability stemming from mental illness, interpersonal skills that are maladaptive in a judicial setting, *and* intergenerational trauma related to the court system.

What Motivates the Individual(s) I'm Working With?

As unique individuals, clients will have myriad interests and motivators that should be incorporated into treatment. These motivators should be considered and validated within interventions not only because it may help with increased investment in treatment, but also because it is a way to practice respect for their individuality. Thinking of motivators, clinicians may want to consider a client's preferred leisure activities, strengths, and future goals. Music therapists, and other clinicians who incorporate music into interventions, may want to consider the level of musical engagement provided by Bruscia (2014). Specifically, clinicians should recognize that listening to, improvising, re-creating, and composing music each require different amounts of physical, emotional, mental, relational, and spiritual arousal and engagement. During intervention design, each type of engagement and the amount required should be contextualized with what would be most motivating for clients. For example, if individuals are motivated by more physically active musical engagement, then listening to music with lyric analysis may not be the best choice; however, improvisation might be highly motivating for the clients.

What Skills or Interests Do I Have That Align With Motivators for the Individual(s) I'm Working With?

Each clinician providing treatment is as unique as the client receiving services. Those intersecting identities, lived experiences, worldviews, interests, and personal strengths are part of the therapeutic foundation and process. Drawing upon those "unrelated" skills and interests can help a clinician to brainstorm and create specifically tailored interventions that meet their clients' and their own interests and also contribute to rapport building. This can potentially lead to greater engagement in, and gains from, treatment services. For example, a non-creative-arts-therapy clinician who is particularly interested in, and skilled at, working with plastic building blocks/bricks may be able to bring this into a competency-specific group, with the competency-related goals of problem-solving, sequencing/following directions, collaboration, communication, or frustration tolerance. In processing the experience of building with the blocks, the clinician can help clients make connections between those competency-related skills exhibited in the process and their court-specific counterparts. Similarly, non-music therapists may have musical backgrounds that can assist them in bringing music-based interventions to sessions that help clients connect to the competency-specific material. Disclosing their musical backgrounds may also help to build rapport.

What Tools Do I Have Access to and Can Safely Bring?

Once you have determined a specific goal, barriers to this goal, what strengths and interests your clients have, and what skills you have that align with clients' interests, it is time to consider all the things you have access to. Common tools of creativity include musical instruments, electronic musical equipment (e.g., a midi or digital audio workstation), art supplies, game pieces, or a video player. A simple piece of paper can be used to write down lyrics, create a court album, take a test covering competency-related information, or act as a handout that includes information for the clients. Other than only being a tool for reading and writing, a piece of paper can be used creatively as a means of practicing mindfulness (see also Chapter 10) while creating origami, a paper football for a competency-related game, a paper flute, and beyond. Think of the items you have and use every day, and think of every possible way it could be creatively utilized.

For music therapists, you likely have access to a variety of musical instruments. As such, safety may be of greater concern than access. Considerations of safety can include the obvious potential to physically harm oneself or others with various instruments, but it also includes the emotional safety of instruments. For example, the difficulty of using a certain acoustic or electronic instrument in a way that is aesthetically pleasing to a group of clients may not feel emotionally safe to a client who is already emotionally dysregulated. Thinking about culture and intersectional identities—certain songs, genres, or instruments may be perceived differently based on who is presenting them, how they are presented, and the historical context of the musical components. For example, as white music therapists, these authors are keenly aware that while rap is the most commonly preferred genre of our clients, creating an intervention centered on us rapping, or using only the rap genre in musical examples of crimes being committed, has significant and harmful implications. Physical and emotional safety always need to be considered in every aspect of creative intervention design.

Can I Address Multiple Treatment Areas With a Single Intervention?

Individuals with SMI are often not receiving psychiatric treatment for the first time, and they are often facing complex recovery needs. While defendants with SMI may have been mandated specifically for competency restoration, that is rarely the only area in which therapeutic effort can be made. What are the ways in which a creative intervention might meet multiple treatment needs at once, effectively "stacking" the possible gains? Finding the connections between a person's competency-related barriers and other psychiatric treatment goals can help build interventions that, in theory, have the ability to disrupt the cycle of re-hospitalization and recidivism.

For example, a client struggling with emotional regulation may exhibit inappropriate courtroom behavior (e.g., yelling at the judge, throwing items in the courtroom, etc.). That same difficulty may also factor into the client's substance use or difficulty communicating with others. By explicitly focusing a creative intervention on building the client's emotional awareness and management, such as improvisation that switches between different musical elements (e.g., varying tempo, dynamics, etc.), those same skills may generalize into areas unrelated to adjudicative competence. Relatedly, helping clients make connections between competence-specific skills and life outside of the courtroom can provide opportunities for progress toward other treatment goals.

Reassess—Is My Current Intervention Working?

Once you have implemented an intervention, either once or over a period of time, it is important to assess the individual's reactions to the intervention and progress toward competency goals. If there has been limited progress, or if the intervention is not received well, ask yourself what may be impacting success. It may be as simple as changing one thing about the intervention. For example, music therapists may want to consider the individual music elements of their intervention through the lens of the therapeutic functions of music by using the "Therapeutic Function of Music Plan" worksheet (Hanson-Abromeit, 2015). By thinking about each music element, music therapists can make small changes to the music used without changing the entire intervention. However, reconsideration of an intervention as a whole may be needed. If this is the case, restart the process outlined here to build a new intervention based on the information you have gained about client responses to what you previously tried.

MUSIC-BASED INTERVENTIONS IN COMPETENCY RESTORATION

Music therapists often conceptualize treatment through the specific ways in which they are using music to address individualized treatment goals. In the field, these different uses of music are called interventions. Following is a description of interventions commonly used by these authors during the course of competency restoration.

Receptive Interventions

Receptive music-based interventions, as defined by Bruscia (2014), involve the client receiving and responding to music. This often includes but is not limited to listening to prerecorded or live songs. The listening experience may be paired with verbal prompts, relaxation, movement, or creative tasks. It may be followed by discussion, movement, visual art creation, or active music-making. In utilizing prerecorded music, the clinician should select the playback method that is most appropriate for their practice and facility. For example, in a facility where CDs are not allowed, using a tablet with a wireless speaker may be required. In a facility where Wi-Fi is limited, songs should be pre-downloaded to ensure a seamless listening experience. For all clinicians, it is important to ensure the speaker conveys enough musical detail so that all the musical elements can be heard clearly. Safety and contraband policies should be taken into consideration when identifying what technology, instruments, etc. should be used in session.

***Dusky*-Specific Song Discussion**

For this receptive intervention, the therapist creates a list of songs that specifically relate to the musical preferences and needs of the client. Depending on the targeted need area, songs may be selected based on any of the musical elements, such as rhythm, instrumentation, dynamics, harmony, melody, timbre, or lyric content. Artists or styles of music preferred by the client should be emphasized, keeping in mind trauma-informed care as illustrated above. Using music that clients are familiar with can help build rapport, create a feeling of validation and safety, acknowledge the culture and lived experiences of the individuals in treatment, and help minimize the effects of bias and systemic oppression in the therapeutic space. As emphasized above, it is recommended that all clinicians be thoroughly familiar with the songs they will use in this intervention, prior to using them, and consider the role the music is serving. For a music therapist, it is suggested that all of a song's musical elements be considered to create individualized song lists. For other clinicians, a sample song list can be found in Appendix B ("Sample Competency Song List").

Following music listening, facilitated discussions can be centered on or structured around specific musical elements and their relationship to the targeted need area. For example, a song with lyrics that center on the story of a person who admits to committing a crime can be used to review factual information, such as the type of charge, or might lead to a rationally focused discussion on hypothetical legal strategies the person in the song might take.

Due to the receptive nature of this intervention, interpreting responses to this intervention will largely be non-musical (e.g., verbal/nonverbal, engagement in discussion), though there may be some behaviors that occur that are directly linked to or a result of the music (e.g., tapping feet, dancing, singing/rapping along, clapping, etc.). These behaviors may be tied to specific psycholegal abilities, such as reality orientation/ability to track events (e.g., following along with lyrics on a printed page), or emotional regulation. For example, if a client is very loudly singing along while others listen quietly, it might be reasonable to interpret this as an example of a limit in their capacity to regulate behaviors based on environmental/social cues. For an outline of this intervention see "*Dusky*-Specific Song Discussion" in Appendix B.

Courtroom Discography

For this receptive intervention, clients will engage in a creative process during the session to demonstrate their understanding of each component of a prompt and create artwork that represents their comprehensive understanding. Clinicians should select a prompt based on the needs of the clients then give them a square sheet of paper to write their song list on one side and create their album cover on the other side. Prompts commonly used by these authors include songs representing a timeline of the legal process from a crime being committed to sentencing, songs that correlate with the emotions one might experience while going through the legal process, and songs that explore interpersonal relationships (e.g., between a defendant and court personnel). This song list can be created entirely by the client, can be selected from a list brought in by the therapist, or can be co-created by client and therapist. Making the song list can be paired with listening to the songs, re-creating them with instruments, or re-recording the songs selected. Additionally, discussions can be held exploring how clients related songs to the topic.

This intervention allows clinicians to assess the client's ability to follow the prompt given and demonstrate their understanding of the concepts. For example, if the prompt is to choose songs that represent court personnel, a client choosing "Tell You Everything" by Robyn Ottolini for the prosecutor demonstrates a potential lack of understanding regarding the prosecutor's role (i.e., with open disclosure encouraged by the song's title and lyrics).

Because this intervention requires limited theoretical knowledge of music from the clinician, it is easily facilitated by clinicians with any background. When considering if you want to play music that was identified by the client, it is important to consider your knowledge of the song(s) to be played during the session. Considerations of lyrical content along with the impact of other musical components should be highlighted. If a therapist is unsure they are able to facilitate a therapeutic discussion related to the musical elements of songs used in the session, then not playing any musical examples or playing only well-known songs is suggested. An example of a court-related album is shown in Figure 8.1; templates are available in Appendix B under "Courtroom Discography & Timeline."

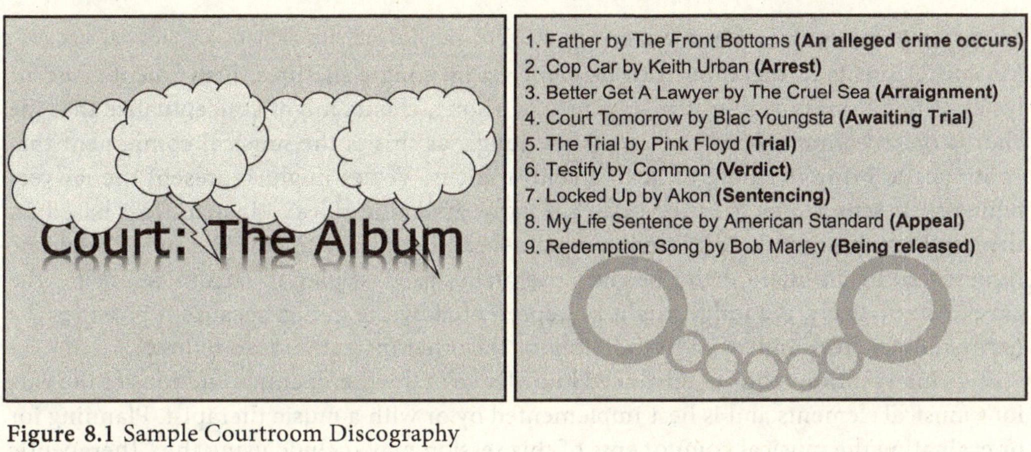

Figure 8.1 Sample Courtroom Discography
Source: Authors (Joplin & Stanley)

Re-Creative Interventions

Playing, singing, or musically reproducing preexisting music is the basis of re-creative music-based interventions (Bruscia, 2014). Often during re-creative interventions, the client and music therapist work together to play instruments, sing, or otherwise reproduce a piece of music. This active music-making experience can include client-preferred music and instruments.

Competency-Related Song Re-Creation

Re-creating a song is taking an existing song and reproducing it with instruments and/or voice. Therapists can select songs that are directly linked to the *Dusky* prongs or more closely related to other goal areas such as emotional regulation, communication, reality orientation, decision-making, frustration tolerance, etc. Additionally, the re-creative aspect of this intervention provides many opportunities for a music therapist to craft an active music-making experience to help clients build upon those related competency-specific and adjacent skills. For example, accurately re-creating snare drum hits on beats 2 and 4 during song re-creation may indicate a capacity to track events, while moderating dynamics along with the group may indicate a capacity to manage emotions given contextual and social cues. The re-creation process can also be paired with a song discussion before/after the re-creation process.

Because this intervention requires extensive theoretical knowledge of the music used, as well as the capability to both re-create songs and interpret the musical responses of clients, it should be facilitated by or with a music therapist. In addition to considerations regarding song selection (e.g., client preferences, censorship, etc.), music therapists should also purposefully consider the instruments offered, the role the music serves within this intervention, and the connection between music creation and the treatment goals. As with other music therapy methods, while there is not a guarantee of the transfer of musical skills/responses to the non-musical realm, a client's ability to engage with these skills in a musical context may indicate the capacity for related non-musical skills to be present. Therefore, the music creation aspect of this intervention needs to be purposefully and specifically crafted to provide multiple, varied opportunities for clients to engage with musical skills that have a psycholegal analog or connection. For an outline of this intervention, see "Competency-Related Song Re-Creation" in Appendix B.

Musical Elements as Metaphor

Musical elements as metaphor can be centered on song structures, instruments, and/or lyrics. When thinking about the structure of a song, clients might conceptualize that the chorus or repeating refrain represents the judge, as this is the musical component that continues to bring the song back to a central focus. Verses might represent the lawyers telling their separate facts in the case. Similarly, assigning roles to instruments based on the qualities and functions of court personnel can be the metaphor. The judge might be represented by a buffalo drum because the mallet used to play the drum resembles the gavel. Alternatively, the judge might be represented by the guitar because it provides the harmonic structure and lays a foundation for the other instruments to follow.

This intervention requires advanced knowledge of the therapeutic functions of the various musical elements and is best implemented by or with a music therapist. Planning for or evaluating the musical components of this session may include using the "Therapeutic

Function of Music Plan" worksheet (Hanson-Abromeit, 2015). Taking time to conceptualize the abstract representations of the musical elements will assist with prompting, facilitating, and evaluating client responses to this intervention.

Once the metaphor is decided on and a discussion has been held to identify which musical element represents which roles, song re-creation can serve as a musical mock trial (see "Musical Mock Trial" in Appendix B). Through the song re-creation, clients might demonstrate their level of understanding based on how they play their instruments. For example, if a client intentionally plays their part of the music poorly it could represent their understanding that the prosecutor is bad, at least in terms of the defendant's relationship to the prosecutor. Contrastingly, if they are playing loudly because their role is the defendant and they believe the defendant should be the loudest in a courtroom, it may demonstrate a poor understanding of courtroom behaviors.

This intervention can evoke conversation about the roles of court personnel, and the role of the defendant, allowing clinicians to assess the client's understanding of the factual component of the court process. Additionally, to engage in music with others requires orientation to time and situation, demonstrating the level of reality orientation they have during the music playing. Frustration tolerance and emotional regulation are needed during discussion and in response to the aesthetics of the music played. Lastly, interpersonal interactions are easily assessed based on the client's verbal and musical engagement in this intervention. For an outline of this intervention, see "Musical Elements as Metaphor" in Appendix B.

Improvisational Interventions

During an improvisational music-based intervention, clients and therapists spontaneously create music utilizing musical instruments, which may also include the voice and body percussion (Bruscia, 2014). This active music-making may be based around a non-musical theme or idea and can have varying levels of musical structure.

Court-Specific Freestyle

Freestyling is a form of vocal improvisation where clients can speak, sing, or rap over an instrumental track or acapella. For individuals with factual needs a word bank of court-related terms can be given to clients as reference points for what they could discuss. Based on a client's lyrics the clinician can assess the factual understanding of the court process. For individuals with rational needs the ability to freestyle demonstrates abilities such as orientation to time and linear thought processes. If facilitating this intervention in a group, turn-taking demonstrates an ability to maintain self-regulation and display courtroom behaviors while others are freestyling.

An important component of deciding if this intervention can be used with your client is determining whether or not you can musically support the client in any way that might be needed. If done acapella, only basic knowledge of the musical elements is needed from the clinician, and this intervention can be successfully facilitated by any clinician confident in their ability to do it. If further musical layers are added, this intervention requires basic knowledge of the musical elements and intermediate knowledge of music production and is best facilitated by a music therapist. Common musical needs include how you musically redirect those who are getting off-topic or not following lyrical or musical boundaries you have set; how you create supportive music for them to freestyle over; how you use music technology to enhance the musical components; how you aesthetically use music technology to censor if needed (i.e., mute, add a sound effect, or record different lyrics over the content); and how you mix and master recorded pieces. For an outline of this intervention see "Court-Specific Freestyle" in Appendix B.

Instrumental Improvisation

There are many options to structure an instrumental improvisation to meet adjudicative competence goal areas. Often the authors will utilize variations of referential improvisation (Bruscia, 2014) based on court-specific or psycholegal skill-specific prompts such as using instruments to represent different aspects of the plea deal process or creating client-identified relaxing music for emotional regulation. The reference, theme, or prompt can be created based on the specific competency-related needs of their clients. Impairments in the factual domain may result in a prompt that is more concrete and tied directly to factual information, such as instruments representing the courtroom personnel or musical elements being shaped to represent the severity of a charge. Impairments in the rational and consult with counsel domains may be more abstract or focus on competency-related skills like decision-making, communication, self-expression, or stress management. The approach and customization of this intervention is as unique as the music therapist implementing it. For clients unfamiliar with improvisation, it may be important to introduce the concept of spontaneous music creation and discuss their level of comfort with the instruments available to help clients be successful in this intervention.

As this intervention requires an extensive theoretical understanding of the use of instruments and music in a therapeutic setting, it should be facilitated by or with a music therapist. Music therapists should carefully and purposefully consider the instruments offered as part of this intervention, specifically their relationship to the goal(s), as well as the strengths, needs, preferences, and cultures of the client. Music technology or body percussion could be utilized if appropriate, and a variety of timbres can be offered. The level of structure should also be purposefully considered, both musical and non-musical. For example, if using tonal instruments, will the options offered be limited by key/tonality (e.g., all in the key of G major)? Will there be a meter/time signature? Will this improvisation have an established musical form? Music therapists can utilize the "Therapeutic Function of Music Plan" worksheet (Hanson-Abromeit, 2015) to help make decisions about the type and level(s) of structure needed.

Assessing musical responses is similar to the re-creative interventions previously described and can be directly or indirectly linked to *Dusky* prongs or related psycholegal abilities. Instrumental, referential improvisations for relaxation, emotional and self-regulation, and/or frustration tolerance are often used by music therapists, especially in psychiatric and forensic settings. The ways in which a music therapist conceptualizes musical responses for these goals would also apply in a competency-specific setting. For an outline of this intervention see "Instrumental Improvisation" in Appendix B.

Compositional Interventions

Whereas receptive and re-creative interventions typically rely on preexisting songs or pieces of music, compositional music-based interventions involve the creation of a "musical product" (Bruscia, 2014, p. 133) such as a song or lyrics. The music is shaped by the musical skills of both the therapist and client and can include active music-making, lyric creation, and verbal discussion.

Original Courtroom Song

Like the freestyle improvisation described above, an original courtroom song (compositional intervention) can be utilized for a variety of adjudicative competence-specific and related need areas. By creating original music and lyrics, clients can engage in decision-making and, when in a group setting, negotiation and conflict management processes. The song created can focus on the *Dusky* prongs or other psycholegal domains, such as motivation, communication, frustration tolerance, and/or experience of incarceration and treatment. For a non-music therapist, there are myriad sources of instrumental music that can be found online to serve as the musical foundation for the song's lyrics. For a music therapist, all components of the songwriting process can be tailored to meet the client's strengths, needs, cultures, and preferred music(s).

Music therapists can utilize the "Therapeutic Function of Music Plan" worksheet (Hanson-Abromeit, 2015) to help make decisions about the type and level(s) of structure needed, as well as the relationship between the musical elements and the clinical goals selected. Music therapists can use the preferences of the clients to help dictate the type of song written, which can then inform choices about musical elements offered (e.g., instruments, meter, form, etc.) and ways to craft those elements to help clients meet their goals.

For music therapists, compositional interventions are commonly used for a wide variety of clinical goals, and the same interpretation of musical responses can be applied to competency-specific and competency-supportive goals. For other clinicians, the content of song lyrics can offer insight into the client's understanding of *Dusky*-specific information. Client engagement in the process, especially when in a group setting, can also provide opportunities for the clinician to assess competency-supportive goals such as communication, emotional regulation, motivation, etc. For an outline of this intervention see "Original Courtroom Song" in Appendix B.

Song Rewrite

Rewriting new lyrics to an existing song can be a way for clients to be motivated by the music they know and enjoy while being able to tailor the lyrical content to treatment goals. The new lyrics could be written with the clients during a session, or the clinician could bring lyrics already written and blanks for the clients to fill in. An example of a fill-in-the-blank song rewrite can be found on the page titled "Song Rewrite: To the Tune of 'Folsom Prison Blues' by Johnny Cash" in Appendix B.

This intervention requires the clinician to be able to re-create a song, which likely includes the ability to sing and play an accompanying instrument. If rewriting the song during a session, the clinician should be prepared to make musical decisions such as adjusting melodic rhythms for lyrics that do not fit the original rhythmic structure of the song. Once a song is re-created the clinician can increase and expand the effectiveness of the intervention by playing the song in different ways and processing how the musical components change the feeling and understanding of the song. For example, if a pop song is sung as a blues song, how does it change one's perception? If a song in a major key is performed in a minor key, what does it do to the emotional interpretation of the song? Thinking about how each musical element impacts the client's experience of the music will help facilitate a deeper dive into the therapeutic function of this intervention. This intervention can be facilitated by any clinician with musical abilities to address the factual components through lyrical content. However, if changing musical components other than lyrics, this intervention should be conducted by or with a music therapist.

CONCLUSION

Music therapists are trained to use music in intentional ways that address related goals. Music therapists can adapt interventions used in other settings to their competency restoration groups such as memory recall, emotional regulation, and reality orientation. However, music therapists are not the only creative clinicians, and non-music therapists can, and should, utilize creative intervention design in competency restoration services. Currently, there is a dearth of research on the efficacy of music therapy in competency restoration services specifically, as well as effective interventions for adjudicative competence using other therapeutic approaches/modalities. While music therapists currently practicing within this population work to conduct experimental research on the topic, it is important for the field to continually utilize existing knowledge in related areas while developing treatment interventions. Further research on the efficacy of music therapy for competency restoration is warranted and should continue to be explored.

AUTHORS' SOCIOCULTURAL STATEMENTS

Kendall Joplin is a board-certified music therapist (MT-BC) with a decade of experience working in mental health settings, most of which has been in forensic hospitals. Kendall identifies as a disabled, white, cisgender female who is privileged in her education level and current socioeconomic status. When considering her work, Kendall tries to utilize post-humanistic, critical psychology as a basis to continually think about the how her privilege and power may impact the therapeutic relationships and services provided. Additionally, these frameworks are used to assist with identifying the ways in which being educated in Eurocentric ideals of music therapy has shaped the way she views her work.

Kate Stanley is a board-certified music therapist (MT-BC) with over a decade of experience working in a state forensic mental health hospital. Kate identifies as a cisgender, heterosexual female, who is white and able-bodied. She has benefited from these privileged identities, as well as through her education and socioeconomic status. Kate conceptualizes her own and the music's role in the therapeutic space through concepts central in both humanistic and object relations/attachment theories, with the client's preferences, strengths, and voice at the center of treatment services.

Case Example

Below is a case example of a fictional music therapy competency group. The example takes place inpatient at a forensic psychiatric hospital and serves as an example of how music therapy can be used in competency restoration services. This fictitious group has four members.

Cameron is diagnosed with schizophrenia and has had this diagnosis for 10 years. They have often been involved with the criminal justice system for lesser offenses—such as public urination, simple assaults, or theft—and as a result has had multiple admissions to the hospital for competency restoration. Cameron's symptoms include frequent responses to internal stimuli and disorganized behaviors. Cameron has impairments in all three *Dusky* prongs due to symptoms from their mental illness.

Kai is diagnosed with schizoaffective disorder and has had this diagnosis for 20 years. They have been involved with the criminal justice system several times for varying offenses and have been found unlikely to be restored in their previous two admissions. Kai has borderline intellectual functioning in addition to their psychiatric diagnosis and has difficulty with abstract concepts and memory. Kai's most frequent psychiatric symptoms include mood lability, selective mutism, and inappropriate social skills (e.g., touching others without permission, difficulty reading and responding to social cues, and an incongruent affect).

Carter is diagnosed with schizophrenia and has had this diagnosis for five years. This is their first involvement with the criminal justice system and as such, their first competency restoration. Carter's symptoms include both persecutory and grandiose delusional thought content and disorganized, often pressured speech. These delusional beliefs are rigid, fixed, and highly detailed. Carter has impairments in their rational understanding of the proceedings against them, as well as their ability to consult with counsel.

Ezra is diagnosed with bipolar disorder with psychotic features and has had this diagnosis for three years. This is not their first involvement with the criminal justice system; they have been arrested several times while experiencing manic symptoms. Ezra's symptoms include pressured speech and movements, reduced need for sleep, racing thoughts, extreme mood lability, and poor impulse control. Ezra has impairments in their rational understanding of the proceedings against them, as well as their ability to consult with counsel.

All four clients were present in a music therapy competency restoration group session. The intervention chosen by the music therapist for the group was "Musical Elements as Metaphor," in order to address impairments in both the factual and rational *Dusky* prongs.

Prior to the session the music therapist set chairs in a circle and placed a variety of instruments in the middle of the circle. Aurally, the instruments included a variety of timbres, different resonant qualities, varying pitches and frequencies, and wide dynamic capabilities. Kinesthetically, the instruments required different physical movements to play, such as a mallet to strike an instrument, shaking, scraping, and strumming strings. Additionally, the resonant qualities of the instruments provide differing levels of sensory feedback, and the physical textures of the instruments can also contribute to the sensory experience of playing. Visually, the instruments include those that are paired (e.g., two maracas, a mallet and a drum), are composed of different materials (e.g., metal, wooden, plastic), some have no pattern and others have artistic designs, and the sizes varied.

To begin the session the music therapist initiated an unstructured music-making warm-up by inviting clients to choose an instrument, then join in while the therapist provides a steady beat with a cajon. During this warm-up, Kai chose the tambourine and played it intermittently at a loud volume that was incongruent with the rest of the group. The tempo of Kai's playing was inconsistent, at times aligning with the group and at other points playing faster than the other group members. Despite musical, visual, and verbal prompts from the music therapist, Kai was unable to regulate their playing to consistently match the group's music.

After the warm-up the music therapist asked clients to name and review courtroom personnel and their roles. The music therapist then asked the clients which instrument could represent each person in the courtroom based on their role. Carter was able to list the judge, bailiff, and prosecutor, but they required education on the roles of these personnel as well as verbal redirection and reality orientation regarding their paranoid delusions of the judge "transmitting messages through the TV" and "putting poison in their food." When selecting an instrument for the judge, Carter suggested a single high-pitched tone chime because it "sounds like the messages in the TV." After reflecting the client's suggestion and the previously stated role of the judge, the music therapist asked the group if they felt that was the best choice. Cameron suggested that the loudness and piercing nature of the chime's tone allowed it to be heard over everything else, matching the judge's job of enforcing rules and order in the courtroom.

Once all courtroom personnel had an instrument selected to represent their role the music therapist led the group in an improvisation structured by time (e.g., with a five-minute limit) and meter and tempo by providing a consistent 4/4 ostinato pattern. Group members were encouraged to play their instruments in a way that reflected the roles of the courtroom personnel, as well as their relationship to the other instruments in the room (e.g., how to musically represent the difference between the prosecutor responding to the judge compared to the defense attorney).

During the improvisation Ezra, whose instrument represented the defense attorney, required several musical and verbal prompts in order to remain focused on the music-making task due to attempting to play other group members' instruments and getting up and dancing around the room. With multiple prompts, Ezra began actively engaging in the intervention. Kai did not begin the improvisation with the rest of the group and required direct prompting to begin playing an instrument. Kai's instrument, the djembe, was chosen to represent the prosecutor. They played a repetitive pattern on the djembe, not changing in rhythm, volume, or phrasing, and not engaging in a call-and-response pattern initiated by Carter, who was playing the tone chime to represent the judge.

After bringing the improvisation to a close, the music therapist began verbal processing of the music and music-making experience. During the discussion Cameron was observed responding to internal stimuli as evidenced by talking to unseen persons and laughing without an obvious stimulus. Kai verbalized not understanding ("What's going on?"). With further exploration, Kai discussed not knowing how to "make the instrument sound like a person." This was consistent with Kai's difficulty with abstract concepts, and the music therapist asked prompting questions (e.g., "Would the prosecutor be loud or soft?" "Would they engage in discussions with the defendant?") while making concrete connections between the answers they gave and the instruments representing those personnel. After providing further processing and education, the music therapist repeated the improvisation to reassess the group's engagement and understanding.

During the second improvisation Cameron was able to remain reality oriented and track events. Their instrument, the xylophone, represented the defendant, and they played the instrument quietly throughout the improvisation, with moments of "talking" quietly with Ezra. Cameron's playing was time-oriented through tempo, meter, and rhythm, and they used stepwise scale patterns moving up and down the xylophone, demonstrating organized musical behaviors. Ezra required fewer verbal redirections and was more able to engage in collaborative, responsive music-making with the group compared to the first improvisation. Kai's playing mirrored the examples given during the verbal discussion, without additions or adaptations. Carter continued to play the tone chime, encouraging musical dialogue between the tone chime and the djembe, similar to the first improvisation. Carter demonstrated an ability to track events and was time oriented through tempo, meter, and rhythm throughout the second improvisation.

After the second improvisation the music therapist reinforced the progress demonstrated between the two improvisations. The group engaged in a discussion about the roles of courtroom personnel to reinforce the information covered in group that day. Following the review, the music therapist ended the session.

In this group, Cameron showed limited ability to manage symptoms of mental illness outside of active music-making. While the music appears to offer an organizing stimulus that allows Cameron to remain reality oriented, when it ends, these effects do not last long.

Kai showed limited ability to apply concrete information (e.g., the role of courtroom personnel) to a symbolic or more abstract form (e.g., representing said personnel with musical sounds), which is consistent with their cognitive impairments. With assistance, Kai was able to create and repeat musical representations of courtroom personnel, but not spontaneously.

Carter's music-making could be interpreted as accurately reflecting the role of the judge. During both improvisations Carter initiated call-and-response style "musical conversations" with other group members and was able to track and respond to musical changes made by the group. In verbal discussion Carter was able to identify specific musical moments and make connections between the music and what it represented.

Ezra initially required redirection to remain focused and engaged. Following redirection Ezra also was able to engage in similar "musical conversations" with other group members and make connections between the music-making and competency-specific information. Ezra struggled with connections between their early behavior and appropriate courtroom behavior.

REFERENCES

American Music Therapy Association. (2023). *What is music therapy?* https://www.musictherapy.org/about/musictherapy/

American Music Therapy Association. (2021). *Workforce analysis: A descriptive, statistical profile of the 2021 AMTA membership and music therapy community.* https://www.musictherapy.org/assets/1/7/2021_Workforce_Analysis_final.pdf

American Psychological Association. (2021). *Apology to people of color for APA's role in promoting, perpetuating, and failing to challenge racism, racial discrimination, and human hierarchy in U.S.* https://www.apa.org/about/policy/racism-apology

Andrewes, D. G., & Jenkins, L. M. (2019). The role of the amygdala and the ventromedial prefrontal cortex in emotional regulation: Implications for post-traumatic stress disorder. *Neuropsychology Review, 29*(2), 220–243. doi:10.1007/s11065-019-09398-4

Archana R., & Mukilan R. (2016). Beneficial effect of preferential music on exercise induced changes in heart rate variability. *Journal of Clinical and Diagnostic Research, 10*(5), 9–11. doi:10.7860/JCDR/2016/18320.7740

Baines, S. (2021). Anti-oppressive music therapy: Updates and future considerations. *Arts in Psychotherapy, 75*, 101828. doi:10.1016/j.aip.2021.101828

Bruscia, K. E. (2014). *Defining music therapy* (3rd ed.). Barcelona Publishers.

Cabeldue, M., Green, D., McGrath, R. E., & Belfi, B. (2021). Factors related to repeat forensic hospital admissions for restoration of competency to stand trial. *Journal of Forensic Psychology Research and Practice, 21*(2), 91–117. doi:10.1080/24732850.2020.1834834

Chen, X., Leith, H., Aarø, L., Manger, T., & Gold, C. (2016). Music therapy for improving mental health problems of offenders in correctional settings: Systematic review and meta-analysis. *Journal of Experimental Criminology, 12*(2), 209–228. doi:10.1007/s11292-015-9250-y

Corrigan, P. W., Twiss, M., Nieweglowski, K., & Sheehan, L. (2024). Recovery and trauma among urban African Americans with serious mental illness. *Psychiatric Rehabilitation Journal, 47*(2), 157–166. doi:10.1037/prj0000602

Da Silva, S. A. F., Guida, H. L., Dos Santos, A. M., de Abreu, L. C., Monteiro, C. B. M., Ferreria, C., . . . Valenti, V. E. (2014). Acute auditory stimulation with different styles of music influences cardiac autonomic regulation in men. *International Cardiovascular Research Journal, 8*(3), 105–110. PMID: 25177673

Dirks-Linhorst, P. A., Linhorst, D. M., & Loux, T. M. (2019). Criminal court-ordered psychiatric evaluations: Does gender play a role? *Women & Criminal Justice, 29*, 303–322. doi:10.1080/08974454.2018.1520673

Do Amaral, J. A. T., Guida, H. L., de Abreu, L. C., Barnabé, V., Vanderlei, F. M., & Valenti V. E. (2016). Effects of auditory stimulation with music of different intensities on heart period. *Journal of Traditional and Complementary Medicine, 6*(1), 23–28. doi:10.1016/j.jtcme.2014.11.032

Ferreri, L. & Rodriguez-Fornells, A. (2017). Music-related reward responses predict episodic memory performance. *Experimental Brain Research, 235*(12), 3721–3731. doi:10.1007/s00221-017-5095-0

Ferreri, L., & Verga, L. (2016). Benefits of music on verbal learning and memory: How and when does it work? *Music Perception: An Interdisciplinary Journal, 34*(2), 167–182. doi:10.1525/mp.2016.34.2.167

Geretsegger, M., Mössler, K. A., Bieleninik, Ł., Chen, X. J., Heldal, T. O., & Gold, C. (2017). Music therapy for people with schizophrenia and schizophrenia-like disorders (Review). *Cochrane Database of Systematic Reviews, 5*, 1–101. doi:10.1002/14651858.CD004025.pub4

Goodman, K. D. (2023). *Developing issues in world music therapy education and training: A plurality of views.* Charles C. Thomas Publisher.

Hanson-Abromeit, D. (2015). A conceptual methodology to define the therapeutic function of music. *Music Therapy Perspectives, 33*(1), 25–38. doi:10.1093/mtp/miu061

Jia, R., Liang, D., Yu, J., Lu, G., Wang, Z., Wu, Z., . . . Chen, C. (2020). The effectiveness of adjunct music therapy for patients with schizophrenia: A meta-analysis. *Psychiatry Research, 293*. doi:10.1016/j.psychres.2020.113464

Joplin, K., & Dvorak, A. (2017). A survey exploring the current state of censorship in adult psychiatric music therapy practice. *Music Therapy Perspectives, 35*(2), 199–208. doi: 10.1093/mtp/miw032

Kazdin, A. E. (2006). Mechanisms of change in psychotherapy: Advances, breakthroughs, and cutting-edge research (do not yet exist). In R. R. Bootzin & P. E. McKnight (Eds.), *Strengthening research methodology: Psychological measurement and evaluation* (pp. 77–101). American Psychological Association. doi:10.1037/11384-005

Landis-Shack, N., Heinz, A. J., & Bonn-Miller, M. O. (2017). Music therapy for posttraumatic stress in adults: A theoretical review. *Psychomusicology: Music, Mind, and Brain, 27*(4), 334–342. doi:10.1037/pmu0000192

McPherson, T., Berger, D., Alagapan, S., & Fröhlich, F. (2019). Active and passive rhythmic music therapy interventions differentially modulate sympathetic autonomic nervous system activity, *Journal of Music Therapy, 56*(3), 240–264. doi:10.1093/jmt/thz007

Musliu, A., Berisha, B., Musaj, A., Latifi, D., & Peci, D. (2017). The impact of music in memory. *European Journal of Social Science Education and Research, 4*(4), 138–143. doi:10.26417/ejser.v10i2.p222-227

Parizek, D., Sladicekova, K., Tonhajzerova, I., Veterník, M., & Jakus, J. (2021). The effect of music on heart rate variability (review). *Acta Medica Martiniana, 21*(1), 1–8. doi:10.2478/acm-2021-0001

Pirelli, G., Gottdiener, W. H., & Zapf, P. A. (2011). A meta-analytic review of competency to stand trial research. *Psychology, Public Policy and Law, 17*(1), 1–53. doi:10.1037/a0021713

Roesch, R., Zapf, P., Golding, S. L., & Skeem, J. L. (2014). *Defining and assessing competency to stand trial.* U.S. Department of Justice. https://www.justice.gov/sites/default/files/eoir/legacy/2014/08/15/Defining_and_Assessing_Competency_to_Stand_Trial.pdf.

Ryba, N. L., & Zapf, P. A. (2011). The influence of psychiatric symptoms and cognitive abilities on competence-related abilities. *International Journal of Forensic Mental Health, 10*, 29–40. doi:10.1080/14999013.2010.550982

Substance Abuse and Mental Health Services Administration (2023). *Mental and substance use disorders.* https://www.samhsa.gov/disorders

Swanson, A. L. (2020). Music therapy in schools: Stimulating the mind and body to create positive change. In C. Maykel & M. A. Bray (Eds.), *Promoting mind–body health in schools: Interventions for mental health professionals.* (pp. 233–244). American Psychological Association. doi:10.1037/0000157-016

Thakare A. E., Mehrotra R., & Singh A. (2017). Effect of music tempo on exercise performance and heart rate among young adults. *International Journal of Physiology, Pathophysiology, and Pharmacology, 9*(2), 35–39. PMID: 28533890 PMCID: PMC5435671

Tseng, P. T., Chen, Y. W., Lin, P. Y., Tu, K. Y., Wang, H. Y., Cheng, Y. S., . . . Wu, C. K. (2016). Significant treatment effect of adjunct music therapy to standard treatment on the positive, negative, and mood symptoms of schizophrenic patients: A meta-analysis. *BMC Psychiatry, 16*, 1–11. doi:10.1186/s12888-016-0718-8

Wang, S. M., Chan, S. T., Wong, Y. L., Hsu, H. M., Lee, C. Y., Check, C. Y., & Leung, C. K. (2023). Rhythmic auditory stimulation incorporated in training improved movements in individuals with psychotic-like experiences. *European Archives of Psychiatry & Clinical Neuroscience, 273*(4), 995–1005. doi:10.1007/s00406-022-01524-3

Zapf, P. A. & Roesch, R. (2009). *Evaluation of competence to stand trial.* Oxford University Press.

Cognitive Behavior Therapy for Psychosis (CBTp) and Competency Restoration

LAURA M. GROSSI, PHD, ABSMIP AND ALEXANDRA BRERETON, PHD ■

PSYCHOSIS AS A BARRIER TO COMPETENCY

Specific symptoms of psychosis, alone or in combination, are at times a major or minor barrier to a defendant's adjudicative competence. Psychotic symptoms can arise in the presence of a formal psychotic disorder, as a secondary symptom of a major mood disorder, or in atypical presentations of other major mental illnesses. In addition, defendants who experience residual effects of substance use may present with psychotic symptoms (American Psychiatric Association, 2022).

Psychotic symptoms are typically classified as positive, disorganized, and negative symptoms of psychosis (Gur, 2014). Positive symptoms are those which are present in addition to a normative experience of the world (e.g., hallucinations, delusions). Hallucinations may, for example, present as a barrier to competency if what the defendant perceives causes major distraction (e.g., such that they cannot focus on court proceedings), or distress (e.g., such that they cannot tolerate discussing their legal situation), or if atypical perceptions inform their decision-making (e.g., command auditory hallucinations). Delusional beliefs are another positive symptom that may prohibit a defendant from making reasoned and reality-based decisions about their legal case. For example, a defendant may hold misperceptions about courtroom personnel or others involved in their case due to persecutory delusions. Disorganized symptoms of psychosis are those which appear more erratic (e.g., disorientation, thought disorganization, bizarre behaviors, inappropriate affect). These may interfere with competency if they render the defendant unable to track court proceedings, communicate clearly, and maintain appropriate behaviors in a courtroom. Negative symptoms are those which involve a decrease in typical functioning (e.g., impaired neurocognitive functioning, thought blocking, avolition). These might interfere with a defendant's competency by impairing their ability to understand their legal situation or advocate for themselves effectively. Further, such deficits may impair a defendant's ability to benefit from new information and guidance provided by their defense attorney. Individuals with full-fledged psychotic disorders commonly present with some combination of the aforementioned symptoms and may experience other mental health symptoms as well (e.g., anosognosia).

The experience of psychotic symptoms varies greatly from individual to individual, and given the nature of the symptoms, they can be exceptionally difficult for any particular individual to describe. Clinicians working with defendants who experience psychosis may benefit from reading first-person accounts of psychosis, such as *The Quiet Room: A Journey*

Laura M. Grossi and Alexandra Brereton, *Cognitive Behavior Therapy for Psychosis (CBTp) and Competency Restoration.*
In: *The Competency Restoration Handbook*. Edited by: Laura M. Grossi, Oxford University Press.
 DOI: 10.1093/9780197768075.003.0009

out of the Torment of Madness (Schiller & Bennett, 1994) and *The Center Cannot Hold: My Journey Through Madness* (Saks, 2007). Similar benefits may be acquired by reviewing fictional literature that illustrates and simulates the experience of serious mental illness (e.g., *I Never Promised You a Rose Garden*, Greenberg, 1964).

It is worth emphasizing here that a defendant can still be found competent to proceed while experiencing symptoms of psychosis, as long as the symptoms they experience do not interfere with their competency-related abilities (Dusky v. United States, 1960; Drope v. Missouri, 1975; Viljoen et al., 2003). For example, auditory hallucinations may quiet or become less frequent, such that they no longer pose a major distraction. Delusional beliefs may loosen, such that the defendant becomes able to entertain alternative beliefs. However, even with some symptom reduction, treatment-refractory psychotic symptoms may also continue to impair the defendant's ability to engage in a focused, organized, and reality-based manner about their pending legal situation. Symptoms may also interfere with their ability to learn necessary information about the court system. Research has consistently found that defendants with psychotic disorders are less likely to be restored to competency than other defendants (Danzer et al., 2019; Gay et al., 2017; Pirelli & Zapf, 2020) largely due to treatment-refractory psychotic symptoms.

This absolutely does not mean that defendants should be taught to "stop reporting" their psychotic symptoms or "stop talking about" their delusional beliefs for the purpose of being found competent. As explained at the start of this handbook, the purpose of competency restoration is to protect a defendant's legal rights and ensure that they have the opportunity to meaningfully and knowingly assist in their defense. The purpose of competency restoration is not to help a defendant "pass" a competency evaluation. Psychotic symptoms that present as a barrier to competency, and are masked or downplayed during the course of competency restoration and/or a competency evaluation, still interfere with the defendant's competency-related abilities. Masked symptoms could actually present as a greater barrier to competency than openly acknowledged symptoms, with treatment providers, defense counsel, and the court unable to appropriately treat, advocate for, and accommodate the defendant. Defendants benefit more from learning strategies to help them reduce their symptoms, manage the distress associated with their symptoms, and communicate effectively about their symptoms, versus learning to mask their symptoms.

CULTURAL CONSIDERATIONS AND RULE OUTS

It is of course possible for individuals to have unusual experiences, or hold atypical beliefs, that are not a result of psychosis. It is also possible for a person to present with unusual experiences or atypical beliefs in addition to psychotic symptoms. As only psychotic symptoms are expected to remit with antipsychotic medications and related interventions, it is especially important for clinicians to clarify what is "psychosis" and what is not. For example, a defendant may present with unusually structured speech, neologisms, and/or latencies in responding because English is not their first language (i.e., as opposed to disorganized or negative symptoms). A defendant from another country may verbalize rigidly held misperceptions about the court system because they are used to a different nation's system; the barrier in that case may be acculturation (i.e., rather than delusional beliefs). Sometimes defendants originally from the U.S. also rigidly hold atypical beliefs that must be ruled out as possible delusions. For example, sovereign citizens commonly believe that the U.S. government is illegitimate and may resist the idea that they are facing real penalties for alleged behaviors. Alternatively, Indigenous persons might make statements about distrusting the police or justice system that may sound paranoid but are actually rooted in cultural/generational trauma. Black Americans, who disproportionately face legal charges in the U.S., may verbalize similar concerns that are rooted in very valid personal/vicarious experiences with the justice system rather than psychosis. At the same time, identification with a certain group does not exclude a person from developing psychotic symptoms; both psychotic and nonpsychotic beliefs may influence a person's decision-making. Competency restoration providers must learn to disentangle these potential influences so that effective interventions can be implemented.

TREATMENT AS USUAL FOR DEFENDANTS EXPERIENCING PSYCHOSIS

Treatment with psychotropic (e.g., antipsychotic) medications is typically the frontline intervention for defendants experiencing psychosis who undergo competency restoration, as it is the frontline treatment for psychosis more broadly (see Chapter 3). For defendants who are experiencing psychosis as a residual effect of substance use, their symptoms may simply remit with time, as neurotoxins are processed out of the defendant's body. Regardless of the specific diagnosis or etiology, it is often the case that psychotic symptoms do not fully remit and continue to present as barriers to competency and to progress in competency restoration. This may be the situation even with aggressive and sustained psychiatric intervention, particularly for those defendants with a history of poor medication adherence.

Other interventions for symptom management must therefore be considered. Individualized and targeted interventions aimed at improving a defendant's insight into their mental illness, developing skills for differentiating between their perceptions and reality, teaching skills for controlling one's symptoms, and practicing skills for coping with those symptoms should they return may be key in getting the defendant the last few yards toward competency attainment (Grossi et al., 2021a). Anecdotally, this appears true in particular for defendants for whom treatment as usual (see Section 3) is insufficient for competency attainment (Herbel & Stelmach, 2007; Ladds et al., 1993).

INTRODUCTION TO CBTp

Cognitive behavior therapy for psychosis (CBTp), a variant of *cognitive behavioral therapy* (CBT), is empirically supported for the treatment of individuals who experience psychotic symptoms (Jauhar et al., 2014; Turner et al., 2020). As the name implies, CBTp involves adapting general CBT concepts and skills (see Chapter 6) for individuals who experience psychosis. The overarching goal of CBTp is to improve the participant's quality of life and reduce the distress they experience as a result of their psychotic symptoms (Hardy, 2017). Distress is reduced by arming treatment participants with information about psychotic symptoms and related disorders, introducing and reviewing skills for identifying and coping with such symptoms, and otherwise instilling in participants some sense of control over their illness. CBTp can be administered in conjunction with or in the absence of psychotropic medications. The literature suggests that CBTp is beneficial in remediating residual symptoms while a treatment recipient adheres to a psychotropic medication regimen (Dixon et al., 2009; National Institute for Health and Care Excellence, 2014). As with many treatments, the best treatment progress and outcomes are found when CBTp participants are also consistently receiving psychotropic medications (e.g., Morrison et al., 2014).

To date, there is not a gold-standard protocol for the implementation of CBTp as individual therapy, although there is significant empirical support for some group protocols (e.g., LeComte et al., 2016). There is also a degree of consistency among the various manuals and related resources available to clinicians looking to use CBTp-based interventions with their clients (e.g., Beck et al., 2008; Fowler et al., 1995; Landa, n.d.; Smith et al., 2003). Developed protocols tend to directly address positive psychotic symptoms (i.e., hallucinations and delusions) and secondary symptoms (e.g., depression and anxiety) but not the negative and disorganized symptoms of psychosis.

Generally speaking, the conceptual framework and core components for CBTp are consistent with traditional CBT (Morrison & Barratt, 2010). Cognitive-behavioral formulations inform interventions, and active collaboration between the treatment provider and treatment participant is emphasized. As a specialized form of CBT, case conceptualization in CBTp focuses on patterns in the treatment participant's thoughts, feelings, and behaviors (cognitive triad) and the factors maintaining those patterns. Psychoeducation is provided to inform the treatment participant about general mental health concepts, their own mental illness, and interventions that might be helpful in mitigating their symptoms and/or reducing their distress. However, the clinician does not identify as an "expert," particularly with respect to the symptoms the client is experiencing. Rather, the CBTp clinician and treatment participant approach and consider the client's situation collaboratively. Rapport is essential, as the treatment provider and treatment participant join to evaluate the participant's experiences and perceptions. Skills for coping with ongoing symptoms are introduced and practiced, and the therapeutic dyad plans for the treatment participant to make use of skills that are found to be helpful moving forward.

As in traditional CBT, in the intervention phase of CBTp there is an examination of the interaction between the treatment participant's thoughts, feelings, and behaviors as related to their experiences (psychotic or nonpsychotic). Unique to CBTp is a focus on positive symptoms of psychosis (i.e., hallucinations and delusions) that may have a major impact on one's thoughts, feelings, and behaviors. Use of the *ABC model* (focusing on antecedents/activating events, beliefs/perceptions, and consequences/outcomes) is extended to experiences involving possible psychotic symptoms. Normalization of experiences is encouraged; it can be helpful to draw parallels between psychotic symptoms and more common problems (See Table 9.1 for examples). Treatment participants may require affirmation that their symptoms are separate from their identity and assistance in distinguishing between internal and external experiences (e.g., what is their own thought versus an auditory hallucination versus what they believe is a telepathic message or some similar experience). Strategies for considering and challenging one's own thoughts (metacognition), changing one's emotions, and/or engaging in adaptive behaviors are explored, particularly as related to the experience of psychotic symptoms.

As a future-oriented approach, planning for how to maintain treatment gains is also important in CBTp. This aspect tends to be fairly holistic, with emphasis on consistent sleep, a healthy diet, regular exercise, and medication compliance (when applicable), along with making use of the skills developed during the course of treatment. As an empirically based intervention, CBTp protocols typically include an early treatment assessment and post-treatment assessment; much of the efficacy research is based on this test-retest. These assessments help the treatment provider evaluate possible gains in insight, distress reduction, etc. and may guide further treatment.

There is some evidence to suggest that CBTp as an early intervention can help prevent or delay the escalation from early/prodromal symptoms of psychosis to a full-fledged psychotic disorder (e.g., Stafford et al., 2013). Traditional CBTp administered in outpatient

Table 9.1 Examples of Symptom Parallels

Psychotic Symptom (CBTp)	Symptom/Bias (CBT)	Category
Agitation	Anxiety	Affect
Paranoia	Fear	Affect
Grandiosity	Excessive optimism, overconfidence	Affect
Isolation	Social withdrawal	Behavior
Disorganized speech, tangential speech	Problems with effective communication	Behavior
Thought blocking	Word-finding difficulties (e.g., tip-of-the-tongue phenomenon)	Cognition
Anosognosia	Lack of understanding/insight	Cognition
Rigid thinking	"All or nothing thinking"	Cognition
Delusions	Maladaptive thinking, phobias, jumping to conclusions, "mind reading" bias, "attribution" bias	Cognition
Hallucinations	Situational stress, interpersonal problems	Experience

settings has led to a reduction in symptoms for treatment participants experiencing medication-resistant psychosis (e.g., Burns et al., 2014). Low-intensity CBTp involving no more than 16 hours of intervention was also shown to be effective in reducing psychotic symptoms (Hazell et al., 2016). Meta-analyses have also found that CBTp has desirable secondary effects on treatment participants' level of social anxiety, mood, and functioning generally (Wykes et al., 2008). This in particular has some implications for defendants who are tasked with performing in an objectively stressful situation (i.e., assisting in their legal defense).

In summarizing their meta-analysis of CBTp research to date, Turner and colleagues (2020) indicated that practice-based research examining the efficacy of CBTp "may be better directed toward novel approaches" (p. 12), given the wealth of support for traditional CBTp to date. We contend that using CBTp as an adjunct to competency restoration is one such novel approach deserving of further exploration. While there is no research yet published that examines the efficacy of CBTp as an adjunct to competency restoration (Kois, 2023), there is much data to support the general efficacy of CBTp in helping people manage their psychotic symptoms. Given the lack of formal efficacy studies to date, use of CBTp in competency restoration at this point should be considered empirically informed rather than empirically supported.

THE CASE FOR USING CBTp AS AN ADJUNCT TO COMPETENCY RESTORATION

Many emerging adults are arrested in the U.S., having incurred charges while in the phase of life when psychotic symptoms typically first emerge (e.g., American Psychiatric Association, 2022). For those who were not already symptomatic in the time leading up to their arrest, the stress of pretrial incarceration can contribute to a psychotic break (i.e., considering the diathesis-stress or stress-vulnerability model). Individuals with first or early episode psychosis, and limited experience with the adult criminal court system, are therefore often recommended for competency restoration due to both lack of knowledge of the court system and suspected symptoms of mental illness that present as a barrier to assisting in their defense. As noted, research consistently suggests that individuals experiencing first or early episode psychosis often experience significant long-term clinical benefit from cognitive behavioral interventions such as CBTp (e.g., Addington & Gleeson, 2005). Introducing CBTp during competency restoration early on in the course of illness, while mental health services are available to the defendant, could potentially have long-term effects for this subpopulation (i.e., particularly for those with trouble accessing outpatient mental health care).

Also admitted for competency restoration are individuals who have been living long-term with serious mental illness, who experienced a psychiatric relapse in the time leading up to, or shortly after, their arrest. The baseline functioning of individuals living with psychotic disorders tends to decrease over time (Maxmen et al., 2009). For those individuals with poor medication adherence in particular, it may be especially difficult for an effective medication regimen to be identified during the course of competency restoration. The education provided and skills developed in CBTp may help such individuals make clinical gains that are not possible through medication alone.

It is worth noting here that, in addition to presenting as a barrier to adjudicative competence, psychotic symptoms may present as a barrier to a defendant's ability to engage in the competency restoration process itself. It may go without saying that studying takes a degree of organization, focus, and self-discipline; these skills and abilities may be limited for a defendant who is actively experiencing psychosis (Keepers et al., 2020). A defendant may therefore experience significant difficulty learning, understanding, retaining, and integrating new information about the court system generally or their case(s) specifically due to interference from psychotic symptoms. Defendants may be similarly limited in their ability to benefit from CBTp interventions while experiencing active psychotic symptoms, depending on the severity of symptoms they experience.

In short, competency restoration providers have a unique opportunity to provide psychoeducation and skills that may improve both short- and long-term outcomes for the defendants with whom they work by supplementing traditional competency restoration with CBTp. Use of adjunctive interventions such as CBTp may help improve restorability rates for defendants. As noted elsewhere, some have proposed that CBTp in particular can improve a defendant's competency-related abilities and strengthen the durability of an improved clinical presentation (i.e., such that the defendant is more likely to remain competent until their legal case is resolved; Grossi et al., 2021a), when psychotic symptoms are identified as a barrier to competency. Although there is not outcome research available to support or disconfirm those specific hypotheses, CBTp has been recommended for use with this subset of the forensic population as it is an evidence-based treatment that can be introduced in conjunction with, or in lieu of, psychotropic medications (Grossi et al., 2021a; Kois, 2023). In particular, this is the case when patients are experiencing an early episode of psychosis or who are at increased risk for developing psychotic symptoms given their history (Gur, 2014).

MODIFICATIONS AND TECHNOLOGY FOR INCORPORATING CBTp

Traditional or full CBTp is designed to be implemented over a period of at least six months in the format of individualized one-on-one sessions run by a cognitive behavioral therapist with CBTp-specific training. However, most individuals who undergo competency restoration are restored in under six months, and many attain competency in significantly less time (see Chapter 1). The integration of CBTp-informed interventions and the introduction of CBTp skills are what we propose as viable for defendants with psychosis participating in competency restoration. There has been a call to modify empirically supported treatments for use with forensic patients for decades (e.g., Jeglic & Calkins, 2018; Ladds, 1996). There is also precedent for modifying CBTp in different settings and implementing the treatment modality to varying degrees.

Specific protocols exist for providing targeted CBTp interventions, as outlined in *Cognitive Therapy for Command Hallucinations: An Advanced Practical Companion* (Meaden et al., 2013) and *Individual Resiliency Training* (Penn et al., 2014) among other manuals. The relevant skills can be practiced verbally, using a whiteboard, and using standardized worksheets for consistency (i.e., with predictability being helpful when working with individuals with severe and persistent mental illness). Technological advances have allowed for more creative and less structured CBTp-informed interventions as well. For example, *avatar therapy* (Leff et al., 2014; Aali et al., 2020) is a computer-based intervention that has been adapted for use with virtual reality technology. The avatar therapy protocol allows patients to directly engage their persistent auditory hallucinations in a discussion (i.e., with the role of the hallucinations played by the therapist), with the goal of increasing the participant's sense of control over their symptoms. Whether and to what extent competency restoration providers can incorporate such technology in competency restoration will vary depending on funding/resources and where competency restoration is conducted; it is unclear whether such technology will be more accessible in the foreseeable future.

CBTp AND COMPETENCY RESTORATION IN PRACTICE

It goes without saying that not all competency restoration providers are cognitive behaviorally oriented therapists, and it is unclear what proportion have CBTp training or experience. In order for CBTp to be incorporated into competency restoration effectively, restoration providers are first encouraged to seek training experiences and gain professional competency in CBTp before proceeding. Treatment providers who see the utility in introducing CBTp interventions in the competency restoration process are encouraged to seek out manuals, webinars, in-person trainings, and practical experiences where they can be instructed in relevant theory and techniques. Proficiency in CBT, as well as competency in CBTp specifically, is important for efficacious implementation of the treatment modality and its components. A practical understanding of how to implement CBTp skills is necessary but not sufficient.

In CBTp and competency restoration, collaboration and mutual respect between the clinician and treatment participant are essential. As in general CBT, rapport building and the establishment of a therapeutic relationship is a first and foundational step. Rapport can be difficult to establish when working with those defendants experiencing paranoia or those who have a reality-based mistrust of treatment providers and/or legal professionals.

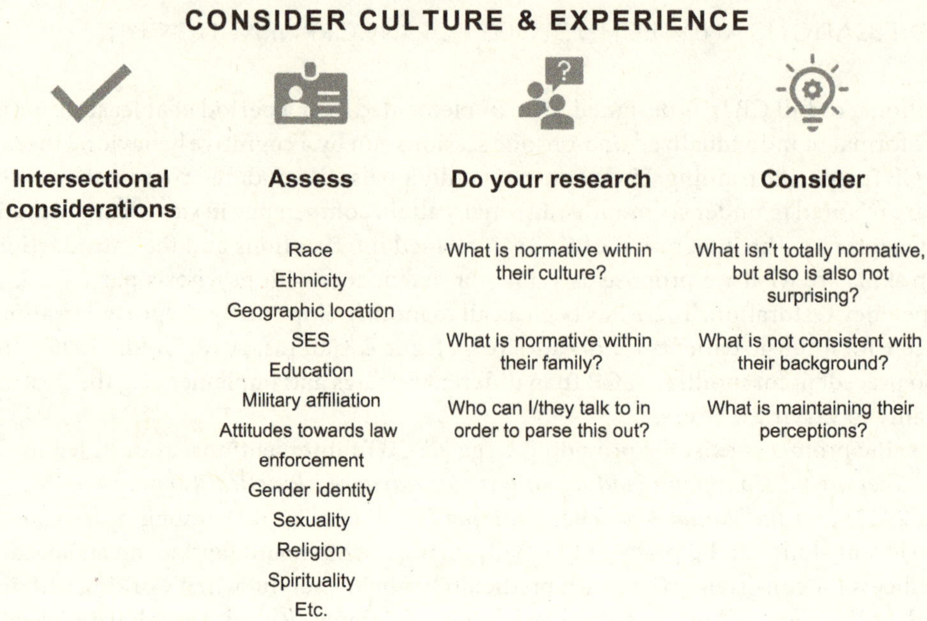

Figure 9.1 Culturally Humble Assessment

Source: Author (Grossi)

An earnest, transparent, and consistent approach may be helpful in working with such individuals. This may involve transparency in what the restoration provider does not know (i.e., rather than providing misinformation, even with caveats) and encouraging the treatment participant to do their own fact-checking of what is discussed (e.g., with available resources or by asking trusted others).

Early assessment is essential (Figure 9.1), so that the clinician has an awareness of problems in the defendant's life (including and beyond their legal situation), their perception of their own mental health, and their views on mental illness generally. The assessment should involve inquiry about "culturally unacceptable interpretations, selective attention, control strategies, positive beliefs about psychotic phenomena, imagery in relation to psychotic phenomena, and metacognitive beliefs" (Morrison, 2008, p. 228). Aspects of a defendant's culture, including race, religion/spirituality, gender/sex, and socioeconomic status, should thus be addressed in a clinical interview. This is imperative, as a person's cultural background and identity informs their view of the legal system and relevant legal personnel. A thorough assessment may be necessary to differentiate between clinical paranoia, extreme overvalued beliefs, and reality-based concerns about the legal system. Cultural and related demographic information may also speak to the defendant's comfort with certain treatment interventions, such as those involving technology.

The Positive and Negative Syndrome Scale (PANSS; Kay et al., 1987) is considered the gold-standard tool for evaluating the efficacy of antipsychotic medications (Opler et al., 2017) and as such may be considered for pre- and post-intervention assessment in the context of CBTp. Less complex tools such as the Birchwood Insight Scale (Birchwood et al., 1994) and Beck Cognitive Insight Scale (Beck et al., 2004) may also be of use when assessing one's view of their own mental health, among other measures designed to assess one's self-perception and understanding of psychosis. In interpreting assessment responses, the treatment provider must consider the cultural context and environmental factors that may be contributing to or maintaining adverse experiences. This data should inform the clinician's case conceptualization, and the conceptualization should in turn inform interventions. Assessment should also be ongoing throughout the course of treatment, so that the conceptualization and treatment plan consistently reflects the current situation. Changes may reflect progress or regression; a defendant may simply be able to provide more accurate information about their background and experiences as their symptoms clear (e.g., as they experience benefits of psychiatric medications).

In the intervention phase, psychoeducation about the treatment participant's mental illness, and mental health generally, is indicated. The defendant's prior, recent, and current experiences of potential mental health symptoms (psychotic and nonpsychotic) should be explored. As a kind of parallel process, given the legal context, regularly exploring the defendant's prior, recent, and current experiences with the justice system is also indicated; this is elaborated upon below. As in traditional CBT, the clinician should engage the defendant in a discussion about their thoughts, feelings, and behaviors, particularly as related to the experience of possible or likely symptoms of psychosis (Morrison, 2008). Worksheets (e.g., skill-building worksheets; see Appendix B) are commonly used intervention tools that can be completed in session or independently and discussed later. CBTp manuals typically include modules on providing cognitive therapy for hallucinations and cognitive therapy for delusional beliefs, as those are common experiences among individuals with psychotic disorders. The clinician helps the treatment participant learn to track and examine their possible hallucinations (e.g., perhaps by keeping a journal, similar to a thought log) and consider and reattribute the source of auditory hallucinations (e.g., brainstorming where voices might have originated). This is done as much as possible in a neutral and collaborative manner. Techniques traditionally used to address unhelpful thinking (e.g., listing and comparing the advantages and disadvantages of holding a specific belief) in CBT can be used to critically examine delusional beliefs (Morrison, 2008).

CBTp also involves some degree of behavioral skills training, and competency demands a certain level of behavioral control. Using CBTp as an adjunct to competency restoration, the treatment provider introduces skills for coping that are within the treatment participant's control (e.g., identifying what exacerbates or reduces psychotic experiences). Distraction skills (e.g., talking to others), relaxation skills (e.g., breathing exercises), and more physical activities (e.g., workouts) can be practiced during the treatment sessions or independently as homework.

The application of CBT skills to secondary symptoms (e.g., distress, depression) is also encouraged, particularly as these can exacerbate psychotic symptoms (Bebbington & Kuipers, 2008; Dvoskin et al., 2020) and are commonly experienced by individuals with legal involvement. The treatment provider may wish to specifically discuss and review with the defendant what coping skills they can use in other contexts that might be stressful; particular coping skills may be more or less accessible in different settings. For some defendants, stressful situations might involve transferring to a correctional setting or having their case heard in court. For others, the idea of interacting with their social supports (e.g., given their legal context) or returning to the community (e.g., for those who are more institutionalized) may be more distressing. For many, CBTp in itself is inherently threatening. For that reason alone, it may be helpful to practice coping skills during competency restoration sessions, either at the start or on an as-needed basis. For defendants undergoing competency restoration, it may be of greatest benefit to explicitly focus on honing coping skills that can be utilized while in a courtroom without causing disruption (e.g., paced breathing, progressive muscle relaxation).

Regardless of the specific focus of a CBTp session occurring in the context of competency restoration, the treatment provider should at some point check in with the defendant about their pending legal case. This may involve asking about recent contact with their attorney, for any news about their case, or about any changes in their thoughts on the case. This is a supportive intervention that may help ensure that the treatment provider has an up-to-date understanding about the person's legal situation and/or changes in the defendant's psychotic symptoms as related to their legal situation. In addition, it may help remind both parties about the reason for meeting and may facilitate the defendant making connections between what is otherwise discussed (e.g., reality testing, coping skills) and their legal situation. The hope is that defendants will come to an accurate conclusion about how their mental health may have influenced their behaviors at the time of the alleged offense and how it is affecting them presently, in their own time. Gains in cognitive insight may be imperative for those defendants who are slated to complete a sanity evaluation once opined as competent or who may be advised to communicate their perspective to the fact finder in court (i.e., through personal testimony).

Toward the end of treatment, CBTp traditionally involves planning for using the information and skills learned in therapy in the future, with the goal of maintaining treatment gains. For CBTp as part of competency restoration, this maintenance phase should be used to ensure that the defendant's improved presentation is durable. The restoration provider may assess the defendant's psychiatric stability by inquiring as to their medication adherence, sleep schedule, stressors (including legal updates in particular), use of coping skills, and perhaps asking the defendant candidly about their mental health functioning. Any issues that come up during this maintenance phase should be addressed; this may involve reverting to an earlier phase of CBTp interventions. How a defendant presents during this phase of intervention may inform when they are referred for a post-restoration competency evaluation. Even after being referred for evaluation, CBTp interventions should continue; without CBTp-informed restoration sessions to continue orienting the defendant, they may revert to more unhelpful habits in their thinking, emotions, or behaviors.

CBTp is not necessarily linear, although the information provided and skills introduced tend to build on each other. The treatment provider is permitted, and even encouraged, to cease forward progress to review concepts and strategies presented earlier in the process. In general, it can be helpful to move from general and less threatening topics (e.g., one's overall well-being) to more specific and distress-inducing topics (i.e., particular pending legal allegations). CBTp interventions can be also discontinued and resumed as demanded by the situation. For example, if a defendant is restored to competency on an inpatient basis, discharged, and later readmitted for competency restoration, they can resume CBTp interventions. Services can also be transferred through coordinated discharge planning. For example, the same defendant could continue to receive services that they received in a hospital upon transfer to a jail facility, if the need for such services is relayed and a qualified provider is available in that context.

In CBTp there is typically a post-treatment assessment, which may involve the re-administration of the early assessment tools (i.e., alone or in conjunction with additional assessment measures). As noted above, much of the efficacy research involves examining whether improvements in insight are quantifiably different between early assessment and post-treatment assessment (i.e., using test-retest methodology). When CBTp is integrated with competency restoration, the initial competency evaluation and post-restoration competency evaluation may serve as their own kind of pre-test/post-test with respect to the nexus of symptom severity and functional impairment. Given that defendants commonly cease competency restoration services as soon as they are opined as having attained competency, and in some cases may be immediately discharged from the location where they are receiving restoration services, there may not be an opportunity for a more traditional post-test regardless of the restoration provider's best intentions/plans.

PRACTICAL TIPS FOR INDIVIDUALIZED INTERVENTIONS

While every clinician has their own style of interacting with treatment participants, CBTp is designed to be more collaborative than didactic. The treatment provider is expected to be unassuming and neutral, helping the treatment participant come to their own conclusions about what they experience that may be perceived by others as mental health symptoms. This may align well with an approach to competency restoration that is intentionally nonjudgmental and generally supportive, including when addressing the defendant's legal situation. Relatively neutral and collaborative prompts such as, "What do other people say might be a symptom of psychosis?" and "What do you think other people might have to say if X comes up as evidence in court?" reflect similar processes intended to facilitate alternative perspective-taking. Sometimes, CBTp may involve examining whether an experience is delusional, although the clinician personally believes the experience to be reality based and perhaps culturally informed. For example, a competency restoration provider using CBTp techniques might explore the idea "my attorney should not be trusted" by discussing the defendant's prior personal and secondhand experiences with defense attorneys to date, typical demands on public defenders, and common practice in their jurisdiction. Not all "scientific" examination of a belief or experience must result in a conclusion that what is being explored is a symptom (in that case, paranoid ideation); at times it actually may be more useful for the participant to also learn the skills to identify what is not a symptom. A more balanced and collaborative approach can help build trust and rapport and allow more opportunities for education to be provided.

Physical handouts used to provide information to a treatment participant may also have a secondary function in rapport building. Printed handouts, particularly those which include references (e.g., from a known organization such as the National Alliance on Mental Illness [NAMI]), may help signal to a participant that the information being provided is trustworthy and legitimate. Seemingly standard handouts related to mental health may also have a normalizing effect on treatment participants (Grossi et al., 2021a), improving their ability to tolerate and accept education about their mental illness. Use of up-to-date legal information as a visual aid (electronic or hard copy) can at times be key in helping a defendant evaluate and modify their beliefs about their legal situation. For example, a defendant who insists their charge has been dismissed, and is not swayed by the fact that they remain incarcerated, may benefit from reviewing a current court case information website that contains data to challenge their belief; in many states/jurisdictions such websites are publicly accessible. Clinically informed restoration providers may also take this a step further: It may be helpful to orient the defendant to the website more broadly and demonstrate how to find it, so that they or trusted others with internet access can find and correctly interpret the same information on their own time (i.e., as verification that the restoration provider did not manipulate the information therein). This approach is particularly relevant when the defendant experiences paranoia but may also be received well by defendants undergoing restoration more broadly.

Whether in print or verbally, it is necessary to establish common language that can be used by the treatment provider and the defendant. Competency restoration providers and evaluators commonly opt to use one term or another (e.g., prosecutor, district attorney, DA, or commonwealth attorney) depending on the language used by the defendant. This helps make the defendant more comfortable, feel heard, and reduce the likelihood that the interaction is perceived as adversarial. The same benefits may be achieved by using common language to discuss potential symptoms of mental illness. A treatment provider may actively opt to not use the defendant's language if that language reinforces their perception that a symptom was not a symptom; in such cases, a more neutral alternative might be suggested. For example, rather than referring to a delusional belief as a "delusion" (as the clinician might be thinking) or "fact" (as the treatment participant might be thinking), "belief" may be a neutral term that both parties find acceptable; both parties can collaboratively identify and operationally define the neutral term. Eventually, it may be helpful to ensure that the competency evaluator and subsequently relevant courtroom personnel (in particular the defense attorney) are made aware of this common language so that the defendant is not later perceived to be more symptomatic presently than they truly are. The defendant may have to participate in an evaluation to see if they qualify for the insanity defense, discuss whether they wish to pursue that defense with their attorney, and perhaps testify about their mental health at the time of the alleged offense(s) upon being restored to competency. If they are misperceived as more symptomatic while engaging in such tasks, they may be unnecessarily re-ordered to participate in competency restoration.

TREATMENT FORMATS

Opportunities may arise to incorporate CBTp in competency restoration in a variety of formats, or in a combination of formats, depending on the resources available. CBTp skills may also be reinforced by non-clinicians (e.g., attorneys, floor staff, correctional officers) and through environmental stimuli (e.g., posters, slideshows on televisions in common areas). Competency restoration providers, including those who incorporate CBTp in the restoration process, should be transparent about their role in helping the defendant achieve their treatment goals.

CBTp Group Therapy

Traditional CBTp can be administered in a group format, whether that is in a hospital, jail, or in the community. A group setting facilitates discussion about mental health symptoms amongst individuals who may share similar experiences, perspectives, and power. For some, such discussions are more palatable than being told about "reality" by professionals, who they may perceive to be aligned with the courts or otherwise not on their side. Group-based CBTp provides the opportunity for practicing CBTp skills in a supportive and collaborative setting. Moreover, group sessions allow multiple individuals to receive services at once; this is an important consideration when limited resources are a concern.

General CBTp groups may yield clinical benefit for treatment participants undergoing restoration, with empirically supported treatment implementation adapted for the setting. Without directly addressing the legal context, certain participants may be more receptive to the treatment and independently extrapolate how the concepts discussed might apply to their current legal situation. CBTp groups conducted with individuals undergoing competency restoration can also make use of hypothetical examples that involve legally involved individuals, or otherwise encourage discussions that reference the legal system, as a relevant adaptation.

One-on-One CBTp interventions

Individualized one-on-one sessions provide the opportunity for a defendant to express their thoughts about their personal legal situation and their mental health, without the stress of a group setting (e.g., safety concerns, impression management due to the presence of peers) and with as much privacy and respect as can be ensured. A clinician can conduct one-on-one CBTp sessions with a defendant undergoing competency restoration, parallel to the competency restoration being provided (see section "Simultaneous Interventions"). Alternatively, a defendant may be exposed to CBTp interventions during competency restoration sessions while working with a designated competency restoration provider. A case example[1] at the end of this chapter illustrates how a competency restoration provider might incorporate CBTp into their one-on-one competency restoration sessions.

Simultaneous Interventions

Defendants who are on bond in the community may have the opportunity and preference to participate in CBTp services through a private practice or other agency while undergoing court-ordered competency restoration services. Defendants in jail or hospital settings may have the opportunity to participate in traditional CBTp with a therapist, separate from standard competency restoration services. In such cases, the competency restoration provider might reinforce what is learned and practiced in CBTp and help the defendant apply the skills and knowledge learned elsewhere to their legal context. The competency restoration provider is encouraged to obtain permission (e.g., with a signed release of information) to consult with the CBTp therapist(s) to coordinate care.

Team-Based Interventions

When a restoration provider intending to use CBTp is a member of, or consultant to, a treatment team or care team, team members should be made aware of the CBTp services being provided. Communication can help ensure that a defendant's barriers to competency are being appropriately addressed from an interdisciplinary perspective. For example, progress in one-on-one sessions may inform potential medication changes. Teams can also be provided with suggestions for supporting a competency restoration provider's CBTp interventions when they meet (i.e., collectively or individually) with the defendant.

1. See Grossi et al. (2021a) for an additional case example.

THE TREATMENT CONTEXT

As both CBTp and competency restoration can occur in a variety of different settings, it is important to be mindful of contextual factors that may impact how such interventions are provided. Each setting has its own limitations in resources (e.g., electronic devices, staffing, meeting rooms) that can impact when and how interventions are delivered (see Lehman et al., 2010 and Danzer et al., 2019 for additional commentary on considerations). Regardless of the specific modifications made to provide restoration services, competency restoration providers should adhere to relevant practice and ethical guidelines.

Considerations for Inpatient Hospital-Based Interventions

Psychiatric hospitals are specifically designed to facilitate mental health treatment and typically have established avenues for psychiatric treatment over objection. Given the intended function of the facilities, hospitals are arguably better equipped than alternative institutions to provide treatment, including that which is necessary for competency restoration (Danzer et al., 2019; Kapoor, 2011). For example, staff at psychiatric hospitals regularly run therapeutic groups (e.g., CBTp groups, given that psychosis is a common presenting problem in such settings), and such groups are typically a core component of the hospital's schedule. Service availability may be limited depending on staffing and intermittent unit/facility quarantines, however. Since the start of the COVID-19 pandemic, psychiatric hospitals have seen more quarantines that temporarily prevent particular patients, groups of patients, or whole units from receiving scheduled treatment services including competency restoration interventions. Such disruptions may pose an extra challenge to group leaders attempting to work through a group protocol at a steady pace.

A number of safety and logistical considerations for clinical interventions in state psychiatric hospitals, including CBTp and competency restoration, are described by Grossi and colleagues (2021b). It is worth reiterating here that inpatient hospitals typically have restrictions on what items can be brought into the facility and onto a unit. When facilitating CBTp activities, the therapist may need to consider alternative methods or means for interventions. For example, many units will not allow inpatients to use common pens due to safety concerns; clinicians need to consider using alternative writing implements (e.g., flexi-pens, crayons, markers). As a result of the dehospitalization movement, hospital facilities are often crowded; meeting space can often be limited on inpatient units, and thus groups or individual sessions may be conducted in suboptimal spaces. For example, meetings may need to take place in a milieu/common area, which is likely to be louder and less private than a dedicated meeting space. There may also be more distractions, with other patients and staff in the immediate vicinity and/or staff monitoring the defendant engaged in a restoration session. Such interference, including lack of privacy, may affect a defendant's ability and willingness to engage in the CBTp interventions and the competency restoration process more broadly.

Considerations for Jail-Based Interventions

In correctional settings, mental health symptoms can be exacerbated without access to sufficient treatment (Jennings & Bell, 2012). Although correctional institutions are often tasked with providing mental health treatment, jails are typically not designed to supply mental health treatment, including for inmates experiencing psychosis. Often jails do not have mechanisms in place to medicate inmates over their objection, even if the inmate is experiencing significant mental health problems (e.g., psychosis) and lacks medical decision-making capacity. Verbal interventions for psychosis (e.g., CBTp) become the frontline clinical intervention for some inmates by default.

In addition to quarantine-related and staffing-related barriers to competency restoration that appear in other settings, jails intermittently experience full or partial lockdowns that restrict movement and inmate access to services (e.g., Felthous & Bloom, 2018; Kapoor, 2011). Jails also typically have stricter limitations than hospitals with regard to contraband restrictions and meeting space availability; this may demand more adaptations to CBTp interventions. It has been hypothesized that the relative discomfort of incarceration in jails may incentivize participation in mental health treatment in hopes of being released faster (Danzer et al., 2019; Kapoor, 2011). This may mean that some incarcerated defendants put in extra effort to attain competency quickly, even if it means masking genuine psychotic symptoms. For other defendants, there may be evidence of feigned mental health symptoms (e.g. psychosis), with motivation to be transferred to a more desirable setting (e.g. a psychiatric hospital or mental health unit). Jail-based competency restoration providers may have a key role in differentiating between those who genuinely need more intensive mental health services and those who do not.

Considerations for Community-Based Interventions

Community-based competency restoration is a viable option for pretrial defendants on bond, assuming there is infrastructure for outpatient restoration in their jurisdiction. Individuals participating in outpatient treatment, including community-based interventions, tend to be "psychiatrically stable and take medications voluntarily" (Gowensmith et al., 2016, p. 298). However, community-based restoration may not be suited for defendants with current severe psychotic symptoms, particularly if they lack insight into their need for treatment. That said, there are multiple established CBTp protocols for use on an outpatient basis with individuals who are more stable, as described above; this means less demand for protocol modification because of the environment.

Outside of a controlled setting such as a hospital or jail, defendants have greater personal responsibility when it comes to attendance and engagement in competency restoration services and related treatment. Where in-person treatment is standard practice, defendants typically have to travel to attend treatment programming, which can adversely affect attendance rates. Compounding this issue, individual and group-based interventions may occur less frequently than in more controlled settings. Sometimes community-based interventions are implemented in residential settings, which can help mitigate barriers to attendance. Some services may also be provided virtually via HIPAA-compliant telehealth platforms. However, defendants in need of those services may not have the consistent internet/technology access necessary to participate in those services. Defendants who experience psychotic symptoms (e.g., disorganized symptoms) may also not be able to navigate the technology they can access, given associated functional impairments.

Moreover, defendants have greater access to illicit substances in the community than in more controlled settings, which can impede the success of competency restoration

(Danzer et al., 2019). This may mean that discerning between defendants not responding to antipsychotic medication and those who present with substance-induced psychosis is more difficult.

Case Example

Jess is a 19-year-old defendant, who was attending college and studying political science in the time leading up to the alleged offenses. Jess identifies as Dominican American, both Black and Hispanic, non-binary, and of middle-class socioeconomic status. Jess was raised Roman Catholic but typically describes themself as agnostic. Jess's mother has been diagnosed with bipolar disorder, and a paternal cousin has been treated for schizophrenia. However, that was the extent of Jess's knowledge of their mental health difficulties, given mental health stigma within the family and culture.

In the time leading up to their arrest, Jess began hearing voices that others could not hear. When Jess started hearing just one voice, they thought it was the voice of God. Eventually Jess began to hear two other voices, which at times gave commands; Jess perceived these as an angel and demon who were fighting for Jess's soul. As a typically nonreligious person, Jess became more religiously preoccupied than ever before. They began seeing "signs" around them to guide their behaviors and affirm their decisions. Jess believed that if they made a decision that was "too good," the demon would become angry and vice versa; this led to significant distress, paranoia, and near paralysis at times. Jess became intentionally isolated, afraid to involve others in their predicament. Jess had no prior history of psychosis; this episode was conceptualized as being brought on by school-related stress and inadequate sleep.

Jess was initially charged with trespassing (misdemeanor), after pacing outside a church and frightening some of the parishioners. Soon after, Jess was charged with breaking and entering (felony), petit larceny (misdemeanor), and obstruction of justice (misdemeanor). Specifically, Jess was accused of breaking into a church, stealing holy water and a candle, and attempting to flee from the law enforcement officers who responded to the incident. Once apprehended, Jess told the law enforcement officers that the angel said that the items taken were needed to keep the demon at bay. Upon receiving the police reports, Jess's attorney immediately referred them for a competency evaluation (i.e., before they had even met). The initial competency evaluator flagged religious preoccupation, likely delusional beliefs, auditory hallucinations, distress, and lack of insight as major barriers to competency.

Jess was hospitalized on an inpatient basis for competency restoration. Jess did not believe that they had a mental illness and did not want to provide their treatment team with any contact information for family members. Jess was court ordered to receive treatment with psychotropic medications as indicated, and they began receiving antipsychotic medications regularly. They were encouraged to study printed materials about the court system and participate in general competency restoration groups. As a bright college student with an interest in politics, it was not difficult for them to learn factual information about the court system and their personal legal situation. After some time on medications, Jess stopped hearing the voices; they were unsure of how to interpret that change, however. Jess continued verbalizing mistrust of their defense attorney, whom they had still not met. During competency restoration, the attorney was not returning phone calls from Jess or their assigned competency restoration provider. Further, Jess still struggled to discuss their personal legal situation in a meaningful way, given their understanding of what had transpired in the time leading up to their arrest.

As Jess's treatment team monitored the extent to which Jess responded to the medications initially prescribed, Jess began attending scheduled groups. Their group schedule included a mental health education group, wherein education was provided about various mental health conditions including major mood and psychotic disorders. Additionally, Jess was enrolled in group-based CBTp. During that group, a formal protocol was followed, and the results of Jess's baseline assessment were shared with the primary competency restoration provider. Information from those groups (running parallel to individualized competency restoration) was integrated into the competency restoration sessions. That is, individualized restoration sessions reinforced the skills and information from those groups, showing Jess how to apply the information in a more personalized way. Targeted restoration efforts shifted the focus from building Jess's factual knowledge to improving Jess's rational understanding of their legal situation and ability to assist in their defense.

During the individualized sessions, standardized worksheets were used to facilitate "scientific experiments" (see Appendix B) to evaluate Jess's unique (possibly delusional) beliefs related to their legal situation. Jess and the restoration provider were able to conclude that Jess had some valid concerns about defense counsel, which upon evaluation (if not earlier) were reality based to an extent that was inconsistent with paranoia. With Jess's perspective validated, rapport improved, and the therapeutic dyad were more able to discuss other possible symptoms; the restoration provider occasionally checked in about Jess's relationship with the defense attorney, monitoring for any changes that might merit further discussion. Similar worksheets were used to facilitate discussions of whether the potential hallucinations Jess experienced in the time leading up to their arrest were true experiences or psychotic symptoms. Jess and the restoration provider agreed to call these "experiences" or "voices" rather than "hallucinations" or "messages," given the more loaded connotations. Jess was encouraged to keep a journal of any similar such "experiences" moving forward so that they could also be examined in therapy. Jess typically did such "homework" activities but often had nothing new to report. In such cases, they were encouraged to identify and consider a particular unusual experience that happened in the past. The restoration provider also processed with Jess what it would mean to them if they were experiencing hallucinations and/or related symptoms of a thought disorder at the time of the alleged offenses. Psychoeducation about Jess's diagnosis of record was provided, and they discussed how Jess might communicate about their unusual experiences to others (including Jess's family, defense attorney, and forensic evaluators) moving forward. Jess consistently indicated that they were not interested in pursuing an insanity defense, but collateral information suggested that it would be a forthcoming discussion with defense counsel regardless; Jess was slated to complete a sanity evaluation upon attaining competency. As the competency restoration provider did not feel competent to fully engage Jess in a discussion of the religious aspects of Jess's presentation while symptomatic, a referral was made to the hospital chaplain to lead adjunctive faith-based discussion. As Jess maintained that they were not personally religious, they declined those services.

For the future, Jess was encouraged to relay any unusual experiences to a family member of their choice (their sister), who could be on lookout in the future for beliefs not consistent with their culture/religion. A specific plan for Jess to respond to and cope with symptoms in the case of a re-emergence was also developed and reviewed (e.g., what Jess could do if they started hearing the voices again while in jail or in court, in the moment and otherwise). Healthy habits and coping skills, to help Jess maintain their current level of functioning, were also regularly reviewed (e.g., reminding Jess to pay attention to their sleep schedule and actively practice good sleep hygiene, given their history), and coping skills at times were practiced in vivo.

Jess appeared to be making clinical gains quickly, and their treatment team began to consider making a referral for a post-restoration competency evaluation before Jess could complete the CBTp group protocol. This was discussed with the restoration provider in consultation, and they mutually agreed that an additional session was indicated to ensure that barriers to competency were overcome. During that session, Jess participated in a mock competency evaluation. In addition, the assessment measures originally administered in group were re-administered by the restoration provider as a means of more formally assessing for therapeutic gains (e.g., in insight). The assessment tools supported the hypothesis that Jess had made some substantial gains in insight, consistent with other data in the hospital record. Jess did well in their formal competency evaluation, although they were surprised to find the evaluator actually asked about their plans for responding to possible hallucinations moving forward.

REFERENCES

Aali, G., Kariotis, T., & Shokraneh, F. (2020, May). Avatar therapy for schizophrenia or related disorders. *Cochrane Database of Systematic Reviews, 2020*(5), published online. doi:10.1002/14651858.CD011898

Addington, J., & Gleeson, J. (2005). Implementing cognitive-behavioural therapy for first episode psychosis. *British Journal of Psychiatry, 187*(48), s72–s76. doi:10.1192/bjp.187.48.s72

American Psychiatric Association (2022). *Diagnostic and statistical manual of mental disorders* (5th ed., text revision). Washington, DC: Author.

Bebbington, P., & Kuipers, E. (2008). Psychosocial factors. In K. T. Mueser & D. V. Jeste (Eds.), *Clinical handbook of schizophrenia* (pp. 226–239). Guilford Press.

Beck, A. T., Baruch, E., Balter, J. M., Steer, A. S., & Warman, D. M. (2004). A new instrument for measuring insight: The Beck Cognitive Insight Scale. *Schizophrenia Research, 68*, 319–329. doi:10.1016/S0920-9964(03)00189-0

Beck, A. T., Rector, N. A., Stolar, N., & Grant, P. (2008). *Schizophrenia: Cognitive theory, research, and therapy.* Guilford Press.

Birchwood, M., Smith, J., Drury, V., Healy, J., Macmillan, F., & Slade, M. (1994). A self-report insight scale for psychosis: Reliability, validity and sensitivity to change. *Acta Psychiatrica Scandinavica, 89*, 62–67. doi:10.1111/j.1600-0447.1994.tb01487.x

Burns, A. M. N., Erickson, D. H., & Brenner, C. A. (2014). Cognitive-behavioral therapy for medication-resistant psychosis: A meta-analytic review. *Psychiatric Services, 65*(7), 874–880. doi:10.1176/appi.ps.201300213

Danzer, G. S., Wheeler, E. M. A., Alexander, A. A., & Wasser, T. D. (2019). Competency restoration for adult defendants in different treatment environments. *Journal of the American Academy of Psychiatry and the Law, 47*(1), 68–81. https://jaapl.org/

Dixon, L., Perkins, D., & Calmes, C. (2009). *Guideline watch (September 2009): Practice guideline for the treatment of patients with schizophrenia.* Arlington: American Psychiatric Association.

Drope v. Missouri, 420 U.S. 162 (1975).

Dusky v. United States, 362 U.S. 402 (1960).

Dvoskin, J. A., Knoll, J. L., & Silva, M. (2020). A brief history of the criminalization of mental illness. *CNS Spectrums, 25*(5), 638–650. doi:10.1017/S1092852920000103

Felthous, A. R., & Bloom, J. D. (2018). Jail-based competency restoration. *Journal of the American Academy of Psychiatry and the Law, 46*(3), 364–372. https://jaapl.org/content/jaapl/46/3/364.full.pdf

Fowler, D. R., Garety, P. A., & Kuipers, L. (1995). *Cognitive behaviour therapy for psychosis: Theory and practice.* Wiley.

Gay, J. G., Vitacco, M. J., & Ragatz, L. (2017). Mental health symptoms predict competency to stand trial and competency restoration success. *Legal and Criminological Psychology, 22*(2), 288–301. doi:10.1111/lcrp.12100

Gowensmith, W., Frost, L. E., Speelman, D., & Therson, D. (2016). Lookin' for beds in all the wrong places: Outpatient competency restoration as a promising approach to modern challenges. *Psychology, Public Policy, & the Law, 22*, 293–305. doi:10.1037/law0000088

Greenberg, J. (1964). *I never promised you a rose garden.* Henry Holt.

Grossi, L. M., Cabeldue, M., & Brereton, A. (2021a). Cognitive behavior therapy for psychosis (CBT-p) as an adjunct to competency restoration. *Journal of Forensic Psychology: Research and Practice, 21*(4), 317–337. doi:10.1080/24732850.2021.1877022

Grossi, L. M., Osborn, L. Joplin, K., & O'Connor, B. (2021b). Clinical interventions in state psychiatric hospitals: Safety and logistical considerations. *Journal of Forensic Psychology Research and Practice, 21*(2), 152–170, doi:10.1080/24732850.2020.1843105

Gur, R. E., (2014). Early detection of psychosis: Challenges and opportunities. *Current Behavioral Neuroscience Reports, 1*, 117–124. doi:10.1007/s40473-014-0012-3

Hardy, K. V. (2017). *Cognitive behavioral therapy for psychosis: A factsheet.* National Association of State Mental Health Program Directors. https://www.nasmhpd.org/sites/default/files/DH-CBTp%20Fact%20Sheet.pdf

Hazell, C. M., Hayward, M., Cavanagh, K., & Strauss, C. (2016). A systematic review and meta-analysis of low intensity CBT for psychosis. *Clinical Psychology Review, 45*, 183–192. doi:10.1016/j.cpr.2016.03.004

Herbel, B. L., & Stelmach, H. (2007). Involuntary medication treatment for competency restoration of 22 defendants with delusional disorder. *Journal of the American Academy of Psychiatry and the Law, 35*, 47–59. http://jaapl.org/content/jaapl/35/1/47.full.pdf

Jauhar, S., McKenna, P. J., Radua, J., Fung, E., Salvador, R., & Laws, K. R. (2014). Cognitive-behavioural therapy for the symptoms of schizophrenia: Systematic review and meta-analysis with examination of potential bias. *The British Journal of Psychiatry, 204*, 20–29. doi:10.1192/bjp.bp.112.116285

Jeglic, E. L., & Calkins, C. (Eds.) (2018). *New frontiers in offender treatment: The translation of evidence-based practices to correctional settings.* Springer. doi: 10.1007/978-3-030-01030-0

Jennings, J. L., & Bell, J. D. (2012). The "ROC" model: Psychiatric evaluation, stabilization and restoration of competency in a jail setting. In *Mental Illnesses: Evaluation, Treatments and Implications* (pp. 75–88). Intech. https://www.intechopen.com/

Keepers, G. A., Fochtmann, L. J., Anzia, J. M., Benjamin, S., Lyness, J. M., Mojtabai, R., Servis, M., Walaszek, A., Buckley, P., Lenzenweger, M. F., Young, A. S., Degenhardt, A., & Hong, S. H. (2020). The American Psychiatric Association practice guideline for the treatment of patients with schizophrenia. *The American Journal of Psychiatry, 177*(9), 868–872. doi:10.1176/appi.ajp.2020.177901

Kapoor, R. (2011). Commentary: Jail-based competency restoration. *Journal of the American Academy of Psychiatry and the Law Online, 39*(3), 311–315. https://jaapl.org/content/39/3/311

Kay, S. R., Fiszbein, A., & Opler, L. A. (1987). The Positive and Negative Syndrome Scale (PANSS) for schizophrenia. *Schizophrenia Bulletin, 13*(2), 261–276. doi:10.1093/schbul/13.2.261

Kois, L. (2023). Improving competency to stand trial services amid a national "competency crisis" [Training]. Institute of Law, Psychiatry, and Public Policy. https://www.ilppp.org/trainings/improving-competency

Ladds, B., Convit, A., Zito, J., & Vitrai, J. (1993). Involuntary medication of patients who are incompetent to stand trial: A descriptive study of the New York experience with judicial review. *Bulletin of the American Academy of Psychiatry and the Law, 21*, 529–545. http://jaapl.org/

Ladds, B. (1996). Forensic treatment and rehabilitation: The growing need for more services and more research. *International Journal of Mental Health, 25*(4), 3–10. www.jstor.org/stable/41344796

Landa, Y. (n.d.). *Cognitive behavioral therapy for psychosis (CBTp): An introductory manual for clinicians.* Mental Illness, Research, Education, and Clinical Center, U.S. Department of Veterans Affairs. https://www.mirecc.va.gov/visn2/docs/CBTp_Manual_VA_Yulia_Landa_2017.pdf

LeComte, T., Leclerc, C., & Wykes, T. (2016). *Group CBT for psychosis: A guidebook for clinicians.* Oxford University Press. doi:10.1093/med:psych/9780199391523.001.0001

Leff, J., Williams, G., Huckvale, M., Arbuthnot, M., & Leff, A. P. (2014). Avatar therapy for persecutory auditory hallucinations: What is it and how does it work? *Psychosis, 6*(2), 166–176. doi:10.1080/17522439.2013.773457

Lehman, A. F., Dixon, L. B., McGlashan, T. H., Miller, A. L., & Perkins, D. O. (2010). Treatment of patients with schizophrenia. *American Psychiatric Association, 1*, 104–113.

Maxmen, J. S., Ward, N. G., & Kilgus, M. (2009). *Essential psychopathology and its treatment* (3rd ed.). W. W. Norton.

Meaden, A., Keen, N., Aston, R., Barton, K., & Bucci, S. (2013). *Cognitive therapy for command hallucinations: An advanced practical companion.* Routledge/Taylor & Francis Group. doi:10.4324/9780203086544

Morrison, A. P. (2008). Cognitive-behavioral therapy. In K. T. Mueser & D. V. Jeste (Eds.), *Clinical handbook of schizophrenia* (pp. 226–239). Guilford Press.

Morrison, A. P., & Barratt, S. (2010). What are the components of CBT for psychosis? A Delphi study. *Schizophrenia Bulletin, 36*(1), 136–142. doi:10.1093/schbul/sbp118

Morrison, A. P., Turkington, D., Pyle, M., Spencer, H., Brabban, A., Dunn, G., Christodoulides, T., Dudley, R., Chapman, N., Callcott, P., Grace, T., Lumley, V., Drage, L., Tully, S., Irving, K., Cummings, A., Byrne, R., Davies, L. M., & Hutton, P. (2014). Cognitive therapy for people with schizophrenia spectrum disorders not taking antipsychotic drugs: A single-blind randomised controlled trial. *Lancet, 383*, 1395–1403. doi:10.1016/S0140-6736(13)62246-1

National Institute for Health and Care Excellence. (2014). *Psychosis and schizophrenia in adults: The NICE guideline on treatment and management (NICE Clinical Guideline 178).* National Collaborating Centre for Mental Health. https://www.nice.org.uk/guidance/cg178/evidence/full-guideline-490503565

Opler, G. A., Yavorsky, C., & Daniel, D. G. (2017). Positive and Negative Syndrome Scale (PANSS) training. *Innovations in Clinical Neuroscience, 14*(11-12), 77–81. https://innovationscns.com/

Penn, D. L., Meyer, P. S., & Gottlieb, J. D. (2014). *Individual resiliency training (IRT)* [NAVIGATE program for first episode psychosis].

Pirelli, G., & Zapf, P. A. (2020). An attempted meta-analysis of the competency restoration research: Important findings for future directions. *Journal of Forensic Psychology Research and Practice, 20*(2), 134–162. doi:10.1080/24732850.2020.1714398

Saks, E. R. (2007). *The center cannot hold: My journey through madness.* Hachette Books.

Schiller, L. & Bennett, A. (1994). *The quiet room: A journey out of the torment of madness.* Grand Central Pub.

Smith, L., Nathan, P., Juniper, U., Kingsep, P., & Lim, L. (2003). *Cognitive behavioural therapy for psychotic symptoms: A therapist's manual.* Perth, Australia: Centre for Clinical Interventions.

Stafford, M. R., Jackson, H., Mayo-Wilson, E., Morrison, A. P., & Kendall, T. (2013). Early interventions to prevent psychosis: Systematic review and meta-analysis. *BMJ (Clinical Research Ed.), 346*, f185. doi:10.1136/bmj.f185

Turner, D. T., Burger, S., Smit, F., Valmaggia, L. R., & van der Gaag, M. (2020). What constitutes sufficient evidence for case formulation-driven CBT for psychosis? Cumulative meta-analysis of the effect on hallucinations and delusions. *Schizophrenia Bulletin, 46*(5), 1072–1085. doi:10.1093/schbul/sbaa045

Viljoen, J. L., Zapf, P. A., & Roesch, R. (2003). Diagnosis, current symptomatology, and the ability to stand trial. *Journal of Forensic Psychology Practice, 3*(4), 23–37. doi:10.1300/J158v03n04_02

Wykes, T., Steel, C., Everitt, B., & Tarrier, N. (2008). Cognitive behavior therapy for schizophrenia: Effect sizes, clinical models, and methodological rigor. *Schizophrenia Bulletin, 34*(3), 523–537. doi:10.1093/schbul/sbm114

PART VI

Personality Disorders as a Barrier to Competency

Dialectical Behavior Therapy (DBT) and Competency Restoration

LYNDSAY BROOKS, PSYD AND MOLLIMICHELLE MCCLENDON, PHD ■

PERSONALITY DISORDERS AND THE SOCIOCULTURAL CONTEXT

The *Diagnostic and Statistical Manual of Mental Disorders* (currently *DSM-5-TR*) describes personality disorders as an "enduring pattern of inner experience and behavior that deviates markedly from the norms and expectations of the individual's culture, manifested in at least two areas including: cognition, affectivity, interpersonal functioning, or impulse control" (American Psychiatric Association, 2022, p. 733). Personality disorders vary widely in terms of clinical presentation, but symptoms may include marked impulsivity, poor social functioning, rigid thinking, unstable mood or frequent mood shifts, pronounced relationship difficulties, and behavioral disturbances. Defendants with personality disorders may experience difficulties interacting with their attorneys in a collaborative manner, difficulty establishing a trusting relationship with their attorneys, problems managing behavioral and emotional distress in courtroom settings, and challenges coping with the stressors surrounding their legal situations, as some examples.

There are a number of sociocultural and contextual factors to consider in case formulation and treatment planning with respect to personality disorders in forensic settings. Individuals with personality disorders are overrepresented in forensic and correctional settings (Rodwell & Frith, 2024; Johnson & Elgoben, 2013). This may be due to a variety of factors, but some studies suggest that racial and gender biases impact clinicians' decision-making when diagnosing personality disorders, particularly antisocial personality disorder (Garb, 2021; Bozzatello et al., 2024). This appears to be a particularly salient issue in correctional settings, where it is estimated that 10% to 15% of inmates are incorrectly categorized with respect to mental health conditions, and where antisocial personality disorder and borderline personality disorder are more likely to be diagnosed, regardless of other individual patient factors (LaRue, 2020; Martin et al., 2016). In addition, when working with individuals with personality pathology, it is important to note that this may often include individuals who have experienced profound trauma. Individuals with personality disorders, particularly those with borderline personality disorder, have often experienced trauma-related issues (MacIntosh et al., 2015), making a trauma-informed approach crucial to working with this population in any setting.

There are also prevalent myths among mental health and correctional personnel regarding the treatability of personality disorders, negative stigma, countertransference, etc. For example, there are misconceptions that personality disorders cannot be treated, despite evidence of new and more established treatment approaches for various personality disorders.

Lyndsay Brooks and Mollimichelle McClendon, *Dialectical Behavior Therapy (DBT) and Competency Restoration*.
In: *The Competency Restoration Handbook*. Edited by: Laura M. Grossi, Oxford University Press.
 DOI: 10.1093/9780197768075.003.0010

Limited resources are focused on accurately assessing, diagnosing, and treating personality disorders in the community. There are greater limitations on resources in correctional settings, suggesting the need for further research and attention to this area.

PERSONALITY DISORDERS AND THE LAW

The inclusion of personality disorders in the *DSM* appears to acknowledge them as a form of "mental disorder." However, legal and medical definitions often conflict, and it continues to be argued among legal and psychiatric scholars that a personality disorder may not necessarily qualify as a serious "mental disease or defect,"[1] as is required by federal and most state competency statutes and standards (see Part I of this volume). Highlighting the differences between legal and medical definitions of various conditions and sets of behaviors, the *DSM-5* and its revisions include a cautionary statement for the forensic use of the manual, stating, "Although the DSM-5[-TR] diagnostic criteria and text are primarily designed to assist clinicians in conducting clinical assessment, case formulation, and treatment planning, DSM-5[-TR] is also used as a reference for the courts and attorneys in assessing the legal consequences of mental disorders. As a result, it is important to note that the definition of mental disorder included in DSM-5[-TR] was developed to meet the needs of clinicians, public health professionals, and research investigators rather than the technical needs of the courts and legal professionals" (American Psychiatric Association, 2022).

Federal and state courts have struggled to clearly define the significance of personality disorders in legal arenas, including in decisions related to an individual's adjudicative competence. On the one hand, it can be argued that personality disorders should not be accepted in the courtroom in the same way as other mental illnesses. Personality disorders may be less amenable to treatment and are not thought to remove a person's volitional choice to act (Johnson & Elbogen, 2013; Lee, 2021). On the other hand, it can be argued that diagnosable personality disorders should be considered a "disease of the mind," just as any other major mental illness, in part, because the symptoms are associated with significant distress and impairment (Slovenko, 2009). This perspective is supported by emerging research that has identified brain abnormalities in neuroimaging of patients with personality disorders, suggesting the presence of neurobiological underpinnings for personality pathology in the same way that psychotic and mood disorders are associated with functional or structural brain abnormalities (Slovenko, 2009; Jiang et al., 2017; Johanson et al., 2020; Wong, 2023; Chan et al., 2020; Lee, 2021).

Legal findings on issues related to personality disorders are varied, and it remains unclear whether personality disorders can or should qualify as a mental illness in the courtroom. Legal outcomes have often depended on case-by-case decisions made by courts. Confusion around this topic is further complicated by the fact that legal standards (e.g., for adjudicative competence and sanity) vary by jurisdiction, as well as the lack of precision in diagnosing personality disorders. Many courts have found that personality disorders cannot be considered a mental illness for the purposes of adjudicative incompetence or other psycholegal questions before the court. However, there has not been a clear consensus.

1. Throughout the remainder of this chapter, unless specifically quoted by another party, we have used the terms "mental illness," or "mental condition," as opposed to the legal term "mental disease or defect," given the clinical focus intended.

For example, in *United States v. Veatch* (1993), the Supreme Court held that while the defendant in question was capable of understanding his proceedings, his personality disorder "wrought with paranoid, narcissistic and antisocial traits, rendered him incapable of effectively assisting counsel in his defense or conducting his own defense." Other cases have similarly resulted in courts finding that there is no practical difference between a mental illness and a personality disorder. In *United States v. DeShazer* (2009), the defendant argued that a distinction should not have been made between a mental illness and a personality disorder during his initial competency proceedings, where he was found competent on the basis of having a personality disorder and not another (i.e., Axis I[2]) condition. The court accepted his argument, asserting that the question before the court related to the degree of functional impairment being experienced by a defendant, and whether they had the ability to rationally assist counsel. In that case, the court noted that whether Mr. DeShazer was diagnosed with an Axis I or Axis II condition was "irrelevant."

However, in *State v. Halder* (2008), the appellate court findings—including both the majority and dissenting opinions—implied that a personality disorder could qualify as a mental condition for the purposes of competence to stand trial in Ohio (Reisner & Piel, 2018). In *Falcone v. State (2010)*, the court determined that Mr. Falcone was not competent to proceed pro se due to his personality disorder. The court of appeals' opinion stated, "Falcone presented pleadings and courtroom objections that were neither rational nor coherent. His personality disorder and obstreperous courtroom conduct suggested that his trial presentation would be similarly unintelligible. Based on these factors, [the judge] could reasonably conclude that Falcone could not present his defense in a rational and coherent manner."

Despite these findings, many legal statutes and courts at various levels have held that personality disorders should be considered separate and distinct from primary mental illnesses and do not qualify as a reason for a finding of incompetence to proceed or to represent oneself. For example, in United States v. Armstrong (2008), the Court asserted, "While bipolar disorder is considered a serious 'mental disease or defect' for purposes of establishing an individual's mental incompetence, a personality disorder is not." Though not related to adjudicative competence, it is relevant to note that in *Foucha v. Louisiana (1992)*, the Supreme Court accepted expert witness testimony that antisocial personality disorder was not considered a "mental illness" for the purposes of hospitalizing someone after being found not guilty by reason of insanity. In *United States v. McKinney*, the defendant argued that the district court erred by "[taking] the position that a personality disorder could not qualify as a 'serious mental illness.'" However, the Court of Appeals for the District of Columbia found that the defendant had provided no basis to determine that a "personality disorder can, in a clinical sense, constitute a serious mental illness." In *State v. Klein* (2005), the defendant petitioned the court to determine whether her "polysubstance dependence" and "personality disorder not otherwise specified" legally qualified as mental conditions under the insanity law in Washington state. The court asserted that a mental illness is not synonymous with

2. Prior versions of the *DSM* included a multi-axial system that asked clinicians to classify mental conditions according to five distinct categories or "axes." Axis I required coding of primary psychiatric and substance use disorders. Axis II was used for coding pervasive conditions, including personality disorders and intellectual disability (previously "mental retardation"). Axis III included general medical conditions, Axis IV was for documentation of psychosocial and environmental problems (e.g., legal or housing problems), and Axis V involved an assessment of global functioning known as the GAF. This system was discontinued in the most recent editions of the DSM (Substance Abuse and Mental Health Services Administration, 2016).

the term "disorder" and went on to state, "Not all disorders defined therein will rise to the status of 'disease or defect' under our statutes."

It has been suggested that the narrow definition of mental illness most commonly used by courts (i.e., excluding personality disorder as a qualifying diagnosis) has left individuals with personality disorders at risk of receiving unfair trials or biased legal outcomes (Collins, 2019; Slovenko, 2009; Lee, 2021).

PERSONALITY DISORDER SYMPTOMS AS A BARRIER TO ADJUDICATIVE COMPETENCE

Many studies suggest that individuals with personality disorder diagnoses may be more likely to be perceived as competent. This aligns with the literature that suggests the majority of individuals opined incompetent to stand trial are diagnosed with primary psychotic disorders rather than personality disorders (Cochrane et al., 2021). However, others have suggested that the presence of personality pathology may actually present as a barrier to restoration and negatively impact the length of time to competency attainment in some cases (Morris & DeYoung, 2012; Secarea et al., 2021). For example, personality pathology may interfere with individuals' ability to interact effectively with their attorneys or participate in competency restoration programming. Given that personality pathology may interfere with competency restoration for some individuals, it may be clinically indicated to target personality pathology for incompetent defendants (Secarea et al., 2021). Although it varies by jurisdiction whether an individual may be found incompetent to stand trial based solely on a personality disorder diagnosis, personality disorder symptoms may have a negative impact on individuals' ability to consult with their attorney, maintain appropriate behavior in court, and manage emotional lability when faced with stressors. In some cases, symptoms may even rise to the level of losing touch with reality (e.g., dissociation, derealization). For defendants with a comorbid mental health condition, a personality disorder may not be the primary reason they were found incompetent to proceed. Diagnostic overlap is common in forensic settings, with many individuals presenting with both primary psychiatric conditions and co-occurring personality disorders. Individuals with comorbid personality and mood or psychotic disorders may experience a higher severity of pathology and poorer outcomes (Williams et al., 2020; Schandrin et al., 2022; Wang et al., 2021).

The presence of personality disorder traits may also interfere with an individual's ability to participate in competency restoration programming in inpatient and outpatient settings. For example, individuals with personality disorders may have difficulty accepting help, may interact with mental health staff in hostile or turbulent ways, and may avoid or decline to participate in recommended treatment programming (Moore, 2012). Personality pathology may manifest in challenging behaviors in forensic settings, such as significant levels of emotional distress and lability, frequent interpersonal conflict, aggression, or involvement with contraband, all of which could negatively interfere with an individual's engagement in competency restoration education and programming (Moore, 2012; Rodwell & Frith, 2024; Katakis et al., 2023). While there are effective evidence-based therapies that have emerged for some personality disorders (i.e., with a particular focus in the literature on treating borderline personality disorder), there is a lack of definitive evidence regarding the ideal treatment for people with personality disorders in general (Katakis et al., 2023). Treatment guidelines and recommendations across different countries vary widely, and there is no FDA-approved medication or "treatment as usual" for personality disorders (Zhan Yuen Wong et al., 2023).

One area that has received rigorous investigation is the use *of dialectical behavior therapy* (DBT) to treat borderline personality disorder. DBT has some of the most robust data supporting it as an evidence-based approach for treating borderline personality disorder, it and offers one potential approach to providing adjunctive services for individuals with personality traits that are contributing to their difficulty achieving competency and/or going through the process of competency restoration. DBT is not the only treatment approach that shows promise or has empirical support for use with personality disorders. For example, mentalization-based treatment (e.g., McGowan et al., 2021) and schema-focused therapy (e.g., Zhang et al., 2023) have both shown promise in treating personality disorders. However, DBT offers one possible approach to working with incompetent defendants with personality disorder traits to improve the likelihood of restoration and will be the focus of this chapter. *It is certainly not being suggested that DBT-informed interventions alone are likely to lead a defendant with a personality disorder to attain competence.* However, these interventions may help address some of the clinical concerns that are often present in incompetent defendants.

INTRODUCTION TO DBT

DBT is an empirically supported cognitive behavioral treatment, developed by Marsha M. Linehan, PhD, ABPP. The intervention program was designed for individuals with borderline personality disorder, particularly those who engaged in high-risk self-injurious behaviors (Linehan, 1987; Rizvi et al., 2013). Consistent with *cognitive behavioral therapy* (CBT; see Chapter 6), DBT focuses on the interaction of thoughts, emotions, and behaviors. Above and beyond CBT, DBT emphasizes use of mindfulness, acceptance, and relevant skills training (O'Connell & Dowling, 2014).

The theoretical framework of DBT is important to its implementation and practice. According to Dr. Linehan (1987, 1993), the driving forces guiding DBT include (1) the biosocial theory of development and maintenance of behaviors typical of borderline personality disorder, (2) behavioral theory, and (3) dialectical philosophy. The biosocial theory suggests that one major feature of borderline personality disorder is emotion dysregulation. Dr. Linehan (1987, 1993) theorized that emotion dysregulation develops based on interaction between biological irregularity in emotion regulation abilities (e.g., heightened emotional sensitivity) and an invalidating environment (Crowell et al., 2009; Linehan 1993). The invalidating environment most commonly refers to surroundings where an individual's emotions are not recognized or affirmed and, therefore, cannot be adequately and appropriately expressed (Rizvi et al., 2013). Put more plainly, some individuals are predisposed to feel emotions more deeply than others. They may be more likely to become dysregulated in the face of strong emotions including anger, grief, jealousy, and anxiety, among others. If an individual experiencing strong feelings of anxiety is in a validating environment (e.g., if they are consoled, listened to, or respected), they may be able to process their emotions in a helpful manner or may be able to implement skills to assist in regulating emotions. However, if they are met in an invalidating environment (e.g., if they are put down, belittled, lectured, or judged for their reactions), where they are unable to process their emotions in a healthy manner, they may utilize unhealthy coping mechanisms and may become further dysregulated, contributing to additional problematic outcomes (e.g., aggression, self-harm, substance use, impaired relationships). The idea of dialectics—understanding two things, which may feel like opposites, can be true at the same time—is also foundational to DBT. For example, a common dialectic utilized in DBT is accepting where someone currently is ("I'm doing the best I can") while embracing improvement and change ("I need to do better").

Comprehensive DBT intervention includes wrap-around services and is provided through several modalities. For example, individuals participating in comprehensive DBT engage in group skills training (further described below) as well as individual therapy, where the skills learned in groups are directly applied to their own personal life circumstances. Additionally, comprehensive DBT includes access to phone coaching, which includes the ability to call an individual's therapist between sessions, at any time, when additional support is needed. Comprehensive DBT is designed for implementation on an outpatient basis. Individuals completing comprehensive DBT intervention are generally involved in treatment for six months to a year. Therapists that provide comprehensive DBT intervention receive formal certification. DBT therapists also participate in consultation groups with other trained DBT therapists to discuss challenging cases, receive support, and consult about issues that arise in treatment. Although comprehensive DBT is ideal, in some situations it is not feasible; DBT-informed interventions or skills may still be helpful.

Much of what is referred to as "DBT" treatment, particularly in correctional and forensic psychiatric settings, is DBT-informed intervention focused on skills training. *DBT skills training* centers on four modules: (1) Mindfulness (accepting and remaining in the present moment), (2) Interpersonal Effectiveness (learning to express needs and set boundaries), (3) Emotion Regulation (improving baseline emotions), and (4) Distress Tolerance (handling crises effectively). Each of the modalities and skills training modules serve to address the goals of DBT in theory, which include increasing patient motivation to change their behavior, enhancing patient capabilities, helping the patient generalize progress in treatment to other settings, creating an environment to help reinforce patient progress, and building and maintaining therapist motivation and competence (Rizvi et al., 2013).

Currently, the *DBT Skills Training Manual* (Linehan, 2015a) is in its second edition, as is the accompanying spiral-bound book with handouts and worksheets (Linehan, 2015b). The *Skills Training Manual* includes numerous learning activities that help teach and reinforce the overarching modules. Additionally, it helps place the activities in the context of the principles that frame DBT, such as the biosocial theory. The accompanying spiral-bound DBT book includes handouts and worksheets that can be utilized in groups. Many of these can be adapted to be used in a legal context. For example, one DBT activity within the Emotion Regulation module focuses on identifying emotions that an individual is feeling. This skill, and other related skills in this module, may help an individual focus on the emotions they are experiencing in relation to their legal case and how those emotions may affect them in the courtroom or in meetings with their attorney.

EVIDENCE FOR USING DBT IN FORENSIC TREATMENT

In the past three decades, DBT as a treatment modality has been validated and adapted for use with additional populations, including forensic populations. Research on DBT implementation and adaptation in forensic settings is growing but remains limited to only a handful of studies.

For example, Evershed and colleagues (2003) examined outcomes of an 18-month DBT treatment to reduce anger and violence with male forensic patients diagnosed with borderline personality disorder in a high security hospital. A group of eight patients participated in a DBT program inclusive of weekly skills group and individual sessions with a psychologist adhering to DBT principles. Overall, when compared to those patients who received treatment as usual (general CBT), patients receiving DBT had fewer violent incidents, lower self-reports of anger, and fewer outward expressions of anger. It could certainly be hypothesized that decreasing such behaviors may improve a defendant's courtroom behavior, ability to manage stressors associated with legal cases, and improved communication with one's legal team.

More recently, a descriptive outcome study (Moulden et al., 2020) with offenders in a specialty forensic mental health unit in Canada investigated the impact of DBT treatment over a one-year period. Although much research in the DBT realm excludes patients with psychosis, patients with psychotic disorders were included in this study, as long as symptoms did not interfere with learning and group functioning and so long as patients also had problems with self-harm (i.e., suicidal and self-injurious behaviors, substance use, and disordered eating) or other harm behaviors (i.e., interpersonal conflict, disruptive behaviors, or violence). Participants completed a group focused on DBT skills, as well as individual work focused on the four core areas of mindfulness, emotion regulation, interpersonal effectiveness, and distress tolerance. Overall, outcomes were overwhelmingly positive, with results showing that participants had improved insight into their mental health and improved self-awareness. Certainly, improved self-awareness and increased insight could assist an individual in the competency restoration process. Although the post-treatment assessment indicated increased anger and "wish for vengeance" scores, the authors suggested this was likely due to increased openness and willingness to acknowledge long-standing problems, rather than actual increases in those domains.

In short, there is a plethora of evidence suggesting that DBT is useful in managing symptoms that could impact adjudicative competence (e.g., frustration tolerance, impulsivity, managing emotions). However, there is no empirical research that has addressed the efficacy of DBT as an adjunct to competency restoration. Therefore, use of DBT-based theory and interventions in competency restoration should be considered empirically informed rather than empirically supported. Although there is no research directly examining the effectiveness of DBT in a competency restoration population to date, use of DBT skills training as an adjunct to traditional competency restoration services appears to be a growing practice and is supported by optimistic outcomes of the use of DBT-informed interventions in forensic settings.

USING DBT AS AN ADJUNCT TO COMPETENCY RESTORATION

Treatment as usual for competency restoration (see Part II of this volume) varies by treatment setting, facility, and perhaps even by unit, but it typically involves the administration of psychiatric medication, psychoeducational groups, and individualized legal education. Improving psychiatric stability is often a key focus of competency restoration, particularly when an individual's symptoms have impacted competency abilities. Many defendants who are hospitalized for competency restoration attend groups focusing on legal issues, social skills, and mental illness education. DBT may be an additional treatment group that individuals attend and may assist in improving skills necessary for successful competency attainment.

In addition to targeting specific aspects of adjudicative competence with DBT, DBT components may have utility with the competency restoration population in terms of long-term outcomes. For example, the introduction and practice of DBT skills may increase the durability of a defendant's competency and perhaps help break the cycle of arrest/incarceration for a person secondary to improved impulse control. In turn, DBT interventions with pretrial defendants may benefit the criminal justice and mental health systems more broadly. By forestalling unnecessary admissions, psychiatric hospital beds may be more readily available for other forensic patients, in the midst of a nationwide competency crisis.

Applying DBT Skills Training to Adjudicative Competence Domains

Each of the modules in DBT skills training has relevance to common concerns observed in incompetent defendants. Some examples of proposed applications of DBT-informed skills for incompetent defendants are outlined below.

Mindfulness

One of the core domains of DBT involves a focus on *mindfulness*, which refers to maintaining an evolving awareness of one's internal state (i.e., thoughts, feelings, sensations) and one's external surroundings (Linehan, 2015a; VandenBos, 2007). Through mindfulness skills, an individual can learn to observe their thoughts and feelings in a nonjudgmental manner and be fully present, despite what may be going on around them. Mindfulness can be achieved through a number of skills including guided meditations, breathing exercises, body scans (i.e., noticing and observing cues in the body), and journaling as a few examples. One of the most well-known mindfulness practices involves mindfully eating a raisin, during which individuals are prompted to notice and observe characteristics of the raisin such as texture, weight, and color (to name a few) as well as bodily sensations such as salivation.

Mindfulness skills taught in DBT can be useful in managing impulsive tendencies and fostering a thoughtful approach to one's behaviors. Impulsivity often presents as a maladaptive personality trait that could inhibit defendants' ability to engage productively with their defense attorney and maintain decorum in a courtroom. Defendants may benefit from using mindfulness skills in the context of stressful experiences, such as meeting with treatment providers, discussing the legal case with their attorney, going to court, or testifying. There are numerous mindfulness activities that exist that defendants may find useful in different legal situations. For example, see "Mindfulness in the Courtroom" in Appendix B. This worksheet prompts individuals to practice mindfulness skills using their five senses to observe their surroundings, which in this case, is the courtroom. This activity may be particularly useful for an individual who has previously acted in a disruptive manner in the courtroom due to distress or anxiety. It may also be useful for an individual who has reported anxiety about an upcoming court date. A clinician could introduce this activity for practice with the defendant prior to an upcoming court appearance and provide a copy of the worksheet so the individual can refer to it as needed. It may be particularly useful for an individual to use while they are waiting for their case to be called.

Interpersonal Effectiveness

Another core focus of DBT involves *interpersonal effectiveness*, which refers to the skills needed to interact effectively with others (Linehan, 2015a). These skills can help individuals maintain positive relationships, communicate competently and assertively, and manage conflict appropriately. Meta-analytic research indicates that individuals with personality disorder diagnoses experience significant interpersonal issues (i.e., issues with other people; Wilson et al., 2017). This could present in the context of impacting a defendant's relationship with their attorney and also with treatment providers, depending on the setting they are in. Interpersonal effectiveness skills taught via DBT may be helpful for combatting these tendencies and improving general communication.

There are a number of skills included in the module of interpersonal effectiveness that focus on helping an individual to assertively express their needs and set boundaries with other individuals. A commonly used skill in this module is referred to as *DEARMAN*, which is taught to help improve interpersonal communication in a way to help get one's needs met. The acronym DEARMAN is made up of the words *describe* (describe the current situation using facts only); *express* (express to the other person your feelings and opinions about the situation); *assert* (assert yourself by either asking for what you want or saying no); *reinforce* (reinforce or reward the person by explaining the positive impacts for them based on what you are asking for); *mindful* (mindfully stay focused on your goals without becoming distracted); *appear* (appear confident and consider your body language including eye contact); and *negotiate* (negotiate if necessary; you may have to reduce your request or ask for other solutions). After an individual is introduced to this skill in treatment, they may be able to practice making a request of their attorney in a neutral manner, with a greater likelihood of receiving a positive response. In the case example at the end of this chapter, there are two examples of DEARMAN.

Additionally, see "Effective Communication Skills" in Appendix B for a worksheet that is designed to help a defendant improve communication skills and manage their emotions when talking to their lawyer and other relevant professionals (e.g., treatment team, judge). This worksheet can be introduced during treatment as a way to help an individual plan for a future conversation with their lawyer. It may be useful for a clinician to use this worksheet to help troubleshoot issues that might arise in future conversations, based on the presenting issue of an individual. For example, this worksheet prompts individuals to consider things such as feelings they might anticipate experiencing during a talk with their lawyer (e.g., anxiety, anger), goals for the conversation, and questions they want to ask their lawyer, among others. An individual could be assisted in filling out this worksheet before an upcoming meeting with their attorney and then encouraged to refer to it during the conversation as a way to improve the communication.

Distress Tolerance

Distress tolerance is another core focus in DBT and refers to being able to tolerate painful emotional states in a healthy and productive manner (Linehan, 2015a). Skills in this domain are designed to help an individual manage a crisis without making things worse. DBT skills may be useful for defendants who are experiencing stress associated with legal proceedings, regardless of personality pathology. For example, poor distress tolerance is a common barrier to incompetent defendants being able to cope with discussions about their legal situation and to engage in such discussions productively. Individuals with personality disorder diagnoses may struggle with tolerating distress in an adaptive manner, which could be particularly problematic while having to navigate legal proceedings. More effective distress tolerance skills may help a defendant better navigate a stressful conversation with their attorney or an actual criminal trial. In addition, targeting an individual's ability to manage their emotions and improving their ability to tolerate negative emotions and distress may help a defendant more effectively make decisions, particularly those decisions that require consideration of long-term implications (e.g., risks involved in accepting a plea bargain).

For example, one commonly used distress tolerance skill is taught through the acronym *TIPP*. The letters in TIPP are broken down to mean *temperature* (e.g., change your temperature; some ideas include splashing cold water on your face, holding an ice cube, standing in front of an air conditioner); *intense exercise* (e.g., do an intense exercise to match your intense emotion; some ideas include sprinting to the end of the sidewalk, swimming laps in a pool, doing jumping jacks in place); *paced breathing* (e.g., controlling your breathing with any type of breathing exercise; a common breathing exercise is called "box breathing" and includes repetitions of taking in air for four seconds, holding for four seconds, breathing out for four seconds, and holding for four seconds); and *paired muscle relaxation* (e.g., a technique that involves tightening a voluntary muscle, which will help it relax; it can be done with various muscles throughout your body). While not all of these activities can be done in the midst of major legal event such as a trial, certainly an individual could incorporate paced breathing or paired muscle relaxation in that situation. An individual could also use a brief recess to step into the bathroom to splash cold water on their face as referenced in the temperature prompt of TIPP.

See "Managing Big Emotions" in Appendix B for a sample worksheet that could be used for helping defendants manage emotions as related to stressful legal situations. This worksheet is designed to prompt individuals to use coping skills in the face of distressing emotions instead of resorting to negative behaviors that could lead to additional problems or consequences such as violence. For example, coping skills such as sketching a drawing, deep breathing, and doing a short exercise (e.g., jumping jacks) are included. Many of these coping skills can be done from small spaces (e.g., a hospital room, a jail cell, a courtroom bathroom) and do not require a lot of materials/equipment. Additionally, there is space for individuals to brainstorm personalized coping strategies to write in. For example, the individual described in the case example at the end of this chapter uses coping skills from this worksheet and writes in one of her own. Clinicians could introduce this worksheet during competency restoration treatment and help defendants practice these skills to determine which work best for them. Then, an individual can be provided a copy of the worksheet to refer to during future stressful situations, such as during conversations with their lawyer or during a court hearing.

Emotional Regulation

The final domain of DBT focuses on skills in *emotion regulation*, which assist an individual in recognizing and understanding emotions and decreasing negative or distressing emotions (Linehan, 2015a). When individuals struggle to regulate their emotions, they often act in harmful ways or ways that make the situation worse. Emotion dysregulation and reactivity are common barriers to the ability to work cooperatively with a defense attorney and maintain appropriate behavioral control during court proceedings, which are inherently stressful. The ability of a defendant to hold their own perception of the time leading up to their arrest and consider the possibly conflicting description provided in court documentation (e.g., criminal complaints, video evidence, witness testimony) may also be improved through DBT, as it poses a legally focused dialectic (i.e., holding and managing two opposing ideas) related to rational understanding. For example, an individual may need to be able to manage their own beliefs about the allegations against them, while still maintaining an understanding of the evidence that could be presented in court, even if those two perspectives do not align. They must also be able to tolerate hearing the alternative perspective in court, maintaining both appropriate behavior and focus.

One example of a skill that could be applied to competency restoration is the skill of *opposite action*, which teaches individuals to use an action that is the opposite of their urge in situations where acting on emotions may be unhelpful or even harmful. For example, using opposite action may be useful for an inpatient incompetent defendant who is feeling depressed about his legal situation and stays in bed all day and refuses participation in competency education classes, declines to meet with his treatment team, and does not engage in any hospital programming. Encouraging the use of opposite action for this individual might include helping him identify the emotion of sadness—and then act in an opposite manner by getting out of bed and attending at least one class per day or one meeting with his treating psychiatrist, despite the urge to stay in bed. Continuing to use opposite action could help this defendant improve his mood, increase his engagement in competency restoration treatment, and collaborate with his treatment team to enhance progress.

While the "Effective Communication Skills" worksheet in Appendix B is designed to help an individual improve communication skills with relevant professionals, it also targets emotion regulation, as strong emotions often interfere with effective communication. This worksheet prompts individuals to consider which emotions they might experience leading up to a specific interaction (e.g., an upcoming conversation with their attorney) and how they might cope with those emotions. Clinicians can utilize this worksheet during treatment with an individual and then provide a copy for an individual to refer to during future interactions.

MODIFICATIONS FOR FORENSIC IMPLEMENTATION OF DBT

DBT has been successfully implemented in a variety of settings, including inpatient forensic hospitals, jails, and outpatient settings. Thus, DBT may be a useful consideration for the restoration process in various settings where competency restoration is provided. Cautions and considerations are offered for clinicians intending to use DBT in the competency restoration process, generally and in setting-specific terms.

As suggested above, a trained therapist familiar with DBT theory and intervention is necessary for comprehensive DBT treatment administration. First, the level of training for clinicians conducting competency restoration varies across settings. Competency restoration providers may have less training in providing DBT treatment than general clinical providers with specialized skills and experience, particularly as many forensic treatment providers receive on-the-job training (McCann et al., 2000). McCann and colleagues suggested that this may be the most common threat to effectively implementing DBT in forensic settings. On the other hand, there are likely clinicians providing forensic treatment who are not making full use of their clinical training (e.g., clinical psychologists providing competency restoration services). In such cases, the incorporation of more applied clinical treatment interventions such as DBT in competency restoration also has the potential to improve job satisfaction and retention of clinically trained staff who provide restoration services regularly. Overall, clinicians should follow the ethical guidelines set out by their respective discipline relating to practicing within their boundaries of competence.

Another important consideration for forensic implementation of DBT is consideration for higher rates of learning-related problems among justice-involved individuals (e.g.,

Samuelsson et al., 2003; Slaughter et al., 2003). Regardless of setting, individuals may benefit from materials written at an adapted reading level and use of pictures to aid in learning. Further, justice-involved individuals would benefit from content and examples that are relevant to their experience. Choosing examples to use during skills training that are relevant to legal issues is one of the most straightforward ways to adapt DBT to competency restoration treatment. For example, encouraging the use of Emotion Regulation reskills in the face of relevant stressors such as not being able to contact their attorney, becoming frustrated in court, or disliking or disagreeing with a potential plea bargain. However, it may be useful to focus on less distressing topics/examples when first introducing the skills before transitioning to using specific legal examples. For example, discussing communication skills with an employer may be a place to start for some individuals, who may later benefit from examples focusing on communication skills with a psychiatric provider, family member, or peer support specialist.

Outpatient Competency Restoration

Comprehensive DBT was originally developed for use in outpatient settings. Thus, it may be a good fit to either implement traditional wrap-around DBT or to introduce and review DBT skills with defendants who are receiving outpatient competency restoration. Outpatient competency restoration is designed for individuals who are out on bond while awaiting a disposition of their cases; these defendants do not require inpatient-level mental health care and are perceived as able to present to court-mandated events (e.g., court dates, restoration sessions) as scheduled. Outpatient competency restoration programs vary widely in terms of clinical services provided, with some focusing primarily on medication management, and with others incorporating legal education or other psychosocial therapeutic treatment. While we are not aware of existing studies that have specifically applied DBT in outpatient competency restoration programs, there is emerging support for the use of DBT for justice-involved individuals in community settings, including community-based rehabilitation programs and other outpatient programs designed to reduce recidivism (Nyamathi et al., 2018; Edwards et al., 2022).

On an outpatient basis, there is likely more opportunity to provide the traditional wrap-around services of comprehensive DBT (e.g., through intervention parallel to traditional competency restoration), as opposed to focusing only on the skills training. However, the availability of resources and qualified providers is likely to impact what can be offered in outpatient restoration programming. For example, a defendant may not be able to afford (i.e., with respect to time or financing) DBT treatment parallel to outpatient competency restoration, and their competency restoration provider(s) may not be competent to incorporate DBT skills into their interventions. Additionally, the structure of the programming may impact the type of DBT treatment that can be offered. For example, some outpatient competency restoration programs are limited to weekly or monthly check-ins with a psychiatric provider for the purpose of medication management; such sessions are infrequent compared to traditional DBT. In this situation, a trained provider could offer skills training during individual check-ins as an adjunct to medication management. Other outpatient competency programming may be more comprehensive with individuals receiving various forms of clinical treatment in addition to medication management. In this situation, they could be enrolled in traditional wrap-around DBT programming or in a DBT skills group.

Outpatient competency restoration is less likely to be subject to some of the restrictions relevant to implementing DBT in an inpatient setting (see "Inpatient Competency Restoration"). For example, individuals may have less limitations in the coping skills they can utilize outside of an institution. For example, they may be able to use a favorite snack in a mindful eating exercise, or they may be able to go for a walk when feeling particularly stressed. Additionally, teaching DBT skills in an outpatient setting may greatly improve ecological validity, as individuals are able to learn and practice skills while coping with real-world stressors; opportunities for this are somewhat limited in inpatient and correctional settings.

Inpatient Competency Restoration

Although comprehensive DBT was developed for use in outpatient settings, inpatient hospitalization is often the primary modality for competency restoration. Individuals in inpatient treatment programming are more likely to have a comorbid serious mental illness or more severe personality pathology, as opposed to individuals who were deemed appropriate for outpatient restoration. More severe pathology, as well as the presence of psychotic symptoms, may impact the implementation of DBT. However, at least one study (Moulden et al., 2020) has implemented DBT in an inpatient population without fully excluding individuals with psychotic disorders. While floridly psychotic individuals will likely require medication management prior to engaging in DBT treatment groups, DBT does not appear contradicted for psychosis. In fact, some skills, particularly those in the Mindfulness module, may even assist in treating residual psychotic symptoms.

Treatment duration of DBT programming is an important consideration to forensic inpatient settings (Bloom et al., 2012). The literature suggests that 75%–90% of defendants admitted to psychiatric hospitals for competency restoration are hospitalized no longer than six months (Pinals, 2005; Zapf & Roesch, 2011), with most defendants attaining competency in less time. As original DBT studies implemented treatment programs consisting of 12-month protocols, modifications due to length of hospitalization for a more short-term intervention would be required and dependent on the average length of stay for the targeted population. Tomlinson (2018) also identified high patient turnover in forensic settings, and unexpected release in general, among major barriers to research examining the effectiveness of DBT interventions in those settings; such disruptions could theoretically also impact the effectiveness of DBT intervention in forensic settings. Relatedly, discontinuity/turnover of unit staff in forensic settings may also be disruptive, if not countertherapeutic, given DBT's emphasis on structure and environmental predictability.

Further, the standard protocol for DBT consists of weekly, one-hour individual sessions and weekly one-and-a-half- to two-and-a-half-hour group skills training sessions. This practice may not be feasible in inpatient settings, given systemic barriers such as limited staff availability and scheduling parameters (i.e., to include the roles/boundaries of staff), and more individualized factors such as the patient's legal status, hospital privileges, and assigned unit. Treatment for forensic patients tends to be primarily offered in group contexts in inpatient settings (Koukourikos & Pasmatzi, 2014) to best make use of resources and to provide treatment to many patients simultaneously. Modified DBT programs often range from daily to weekly skills groups based on what a facility can accommodate (Bloom et al., 2012).

The content of the group sessions in forensic settings may vary as well, depending on frequency of the group sessions, training of clinical staff, and institutional rules. For example, during the skills-based training module on mindfulness, clinicians using traditional DBT often utilize food as a tool during mindfulness exercises. In some settings, patients are allowed to practice this skill while eating a snack (e.g., raisins) in group; however, in many inpatient and correctional institutions this may be prohibited due to dietary concerns related to health (e.g., diabetes, allergies) or other factors (e.g., contraband policies). Additionally, patients may be limited in the resources they are provided for use during the group. For example, they likely require a flexi-pen to fill out worksheets.

As an adjunct to DBT skills training groups, it may be useful to use environmental cues in inpatient settings to assist defendants in practicing and utilizing skills. Although inpatients may lack access to real-world stressors, they may benefit from the opportunity to practice using interventions that will assist in future situations. For example, it may be useful to hang posters describing DBT skills to prompt inpatients to practice their skills outside of the group (McCann et al., 2000). This may also be useful for individuals who cannot leave the unit due to unit restrictions or other safety protocols (e.g., one-on-one monitoring/supervision, suicide watch). While these individuals are likely to derive great benefit from DBT skills training, they may not be able to attend off-unit programming, including DBT groups for safety reasons, yet they would still benefit from environmental cues in the unit. Additionally, staff members who are more regularly accessible (e.g., nurses) may be included in treatment and used to prompt patients to use skills as needed when a therapist was not available. This may be especially relevant for patients who are required to be followed one on one by staff, who could assist in promoting skill use. In the event that patients on one-on-one monitoring are able to attend a group (on or off the unit), hospital regulations may require that one-on-one staff accompany patients to the group. Many hospitals may have rules about staff members being present in or near treatment groups for safety purposes, even for individuals not on one-on-one monitoring. Although confidentiality is highly valued in treatment settings, forensic settings inevitably lack privacy given the legal status of patients. Further, it may be of use to have staff members involved in DBT skills training groups as they may benefit from learning the skills patients are using so that they can encourage skill use outside of the group.

Jail-Based Competency Restoration

Promising research has suggested that DBT treatment can be implemented in jail settings, especially considering the high rate of impulsivity and aggressiveness observed in jail-based settings. This suggests that it may be a useful consideration for jail-based competency restoration programming, which is promising, as jail-based competency restoration programs are growing in number. Trestman and colleagues (2004) developed and evaluated the effectiveness of a "corrections-modified" version of DBT, which focuses on skills training. In consideration of learning-related problems among incarcerated populations, the corrections-modified version of DBT was written at a fifth grade reading level with use of numerous visual aids. As such, their manual may be a valuable resource for clinicians looking to integrate DBT in competency restoration. For further study, the interested reader is also directed to a chapter entitled "Adapting Dialectical Behavior Therapy for Use in Correctional Settings" (Galietta, 2018), which addresses correctional adaptations of DBT, the research base for DBT in corrections, and suggestions for successful implementation in correctional settings.

As detailed by Sampl and colleagues (2010), jail settings may have security procedures in place, including "keep separate" orders that restrict certain inmates from interacting, which could affect group distribution. A higher need for flexibility in treatment provision may also be needed, as correctional facilities are often subject to lockdowns and other limitations on movement, such as isolation or suicide watch. Additionally, individuals on suicide watch, or those engaging in self-harm, may be the very population who would benefit most from DBT interventions; in the jail setting these individuals are often placed in isolation and are unable to participate in group programming. It may be useful to have alternative activities prepared in case of group disruption and for those who are temporarily restricted from attending group. For example, providing individuals with a worksheet or activity they can complete on their own may be helpful until the group can resume.

Technology Considerations

According to Dr. Linehan's official website,[3] there is promising research in the area of remote DBT services. However, there is an absence of formal guidelines for conducting DBT via telehealth, particularly given the high-risk nature of the work, including suicidal behavior and dissociation (Zalewsky, 2021). Although studies are still being conducted in the area of DBT and telehealth, technology could certainly be incorporated in various settings as an adjunct to competency restoration. Treatment providers may set up videoconferencing calls between a defendant and their attorney, so that a defendant can practice using communication skills. Additionally, this would allow a treatment team to ascertain whether any remaining deficits in communication assist. Some attorneys cease contact with a defendant while they are undergoing competency restoration; however, videoconferencing technology may allow defendants to simulate or practice a conversation with their attorney with another support person. As technology continues to advance, it may become possible to use virtual reality or other such technologies to simulate being in a courtroom as a way to allow individuals to practice skills in a courtroom environment.

Additionally, increased use of technology in inpatient and correctional settings may allow defendants an opportunity to practice various DBT skills with support persons as a way of translating the skills they have learned into real-world situations. For example, being able to call a friend or family member may be an effective distress tolerance skill for an individual in an inpatient or correctional facility. Further, many treatment programs may not have DBT services in place but may have defendants who would benefit from such programming. In these situations, it may be useful to identify community-based programming that would allow a defendant to participate via videoconferencing. This would be particularly useful if the group was local to the area where a defendant would be discharged or plans to live in the future, so that they could continue their participation after discharge, during community supervision, or after the resolution of their court case for continued skills building. Participation in existing telehealth DBT programming would also provide service access for individuals with transportation and other logistical issues limiting their participation in an in-person group.

3. Website: https://dbt-lbc.org/

Cultural Considerations

DBT appears suitable for use with a wide range of individuals across a variety of settings, including with individuals participating in competency restoration treatment. However, it is imperative that clinicians thoroughly assess individuals' beliefs, worldview, and history during the pretreatment phase of DBT (i.e., when determining whether it is a good fit or whether any adaptations need to be made). A recent systematic review by Haft and colleagues (2022) provides several recommendations for implementing culturally responsive DBT, including consideration of language, accessibility, context, and adaptations to the content and materials.

Of relevance, language should be a primary consideration when implementing DBT, including when providing therapy interventions, skills groups, and handouts or any other written materials in the individual's native language. This may be particularly challenging in forensic settings, such as jails, where many languages other than English are spoken and often not many clinical staff are bilingual. Utilizing professional interpretation services when providing DBT may be a viable alternative in cases where clinicians who speak the client's native language are not available.

Relatedly, DBT worksheets and handouts may need to be adapted for individuals with limited reading comprehension or literacy skills. Specifically, more visual elements, pictures, and verbal cues may be helpful to incorporate. For example, this may involve adaptations such as showing defendants pictures of a defendant in a courtroom sitting next to their attorney when teaching communication skills they might use to speak with their attorney if they do not understand something being said in court. As another example, it may be useful to show videos of someone doing a body scan in order to help visualize the application of that skill, as opposed to providing a written description of the skill.

Accessibility issues have also frequently been cited as barriers to DBT treatment for many individuals, including transportation difficulties, scheduling issues, and financial barriers. In addition, there may be stigma around telling others that they are attending therapy. Some examples of adaptations to address these barriers may include offering virtual sessions, arranging for transportation, providing bus vouchers or ride-share credits to assist individuals with attending their DBT sessions in outpatient competency restoration settings, and offering a wide range of times for sessions. Justice-involved individuals who are participating in outpatient competency restoration while residing in the community may have to adhere to other strict requirements, which can contribute to accessibility issues. These can include reporting to probation officers, attending work, attending mandatory court dates, curfews, or other scheduling requirements. Making accommodations is imperative for attendance, engagement, and best outcomes.

When presenting the biosocial theory underlying DBT, it has been recommended that clinicians include discussions of the impact of racism, intergenerational trauma, discrimination, and other systemic and historical factors that have contributed to many individuals' invalidating environments, which directly impact levels of distress (Cancian et al., 2019; Haft et al., 2022; Kinsey et al., 2014). Many individuals in the mental health and legal systems in the United States have a higher likelihood than the general population of having faced negative interactions with law enforcement, stigma related to mental illness, discrimination, and trauma (Laniyonu & Goff, 2021; McKenna et al., 2019; Tomlin & Völlm, 2023). Expanding the concept of an "invalidating environment," beyond early family experiences to include larger societal experiences of invalidation and trauma, provides a framework that allows for a more holistic view of the individual's needs.

The literature on culturally responsive DBT has consistently recommended that clinicians ensure that specific concepts, metaphors, and examples being used in DBT are culturally congruent for the individual being treated. It may be helpful for some individuals to add culturally bound proverbs or imagery when discussing the concepts in each DBT module. For example, using metaphors related to nature, such as breathing with the rhythm of the wind, may be more consistent with the Native American worldview than traditional DBT metaphors (Haft et al., 2022; Kinsey, 2014). A study in Nepal found that the concept of "wise mind" (referenced in the Mindfulness module) was best captured by instead referring to "heart-mind" and "brain-mind" (Ramaiya et al., 2018). DBT is based, in part, on Eastern philosophies and is likely to be a good fit for individuals who practice Buddhism or similar religious traditions. Comparing DBT mindfulness practices to Christian practices of prayer may be useful for other individuals. Regardless of religious or cultural background, incorporating clients' unique beliefs, worldviews, or cultural practices into the concept of creating "a life worth living" (a primary goal of DBT) may help clinicians apply DBT in a culturally congruent manner (see also Chapter 7).

Clinicians should also consider whether their clients have adequate financial and physical resources to practice the skills being taught based on socioeconomic status, living environment, and access to material resources. For instance, some of the coping skills suggested throughout the DBT materials reference activities that may not be possible or accessible for some. Suggestions of taking a long bath, going for a walk around your neighborhood, or noticing smells while cooking may not be feasible for someone living in a shelter, jail, or forensic hospital or is unhoused. Many individuals participating in competency restoration programs in locked hospital settings or jails, for example, may not have access to certain foods, may not have the ability to take walks whenever they would like, and may not have private use of a bathroom or bathtub. Suggesting some of these common DBT coping skills without recognition of important contextual factors may negatively impact rapport and treatment progress. In these instances, providing more accessible suggestions for coping skills is recommended, such as reading, showering, eating mindfully (regardless of the food type), and meditation.

Clinicians should use caution when considering the use of interventions in the Interpersonal Effectiveness module when teaching "assertiveness" skills in cases where this is not a culturally accepted way of interacting with others (Haft et al., 2022; O'Grady et al., 2022). In some cultures, assertive styles of communicating one's requests, needs, or opinions could be damaging or even unsafe, depending on the context of family, gender, societal, and religious norms and expectations. Clinicians may need to consider the dynamics of a client's relationships when determining how best to approach this module. This may involve consideration of how elders are treated in one's community and weighing the pros and cons of using the interpersonal effectiveness strategies (Cheng & Merrick, 2017). In the context of competency restoration, these interpersonal effectiveness strategies may be more useful when focused on the defendant's ability to communicate effectively with their attorney or members of their treatment team, rather than familial or other personal relationships where this style of assertive communication is not culturally congruent or is not an accepted practice. Similarly, hierarchical relationships, which exist in many jail settings for example, may not always call for highly assertive strategies. Clinicians should acknowledge that there are times when nonassertive approaches may be necessary or more effective (Haft et al., 2022).

In sum, clinicians implementing DBT in competency restoration treatment settings should work to bring self-awareness to their own beliefs, biases, and attitudes while also fully assessing each defendant's sociocultural context, needs, and values before proceeding.

They should work to ensure that the DBT interventions being implemented are aligned with the client's unique set of beliefs, values, and individualized needs.

Case Example

Ms. N is a 26-year-old woman facing a serious felony charge. She is a single, straight, Mexican American, Catholic woman of low socioeconomic status. She has had numerous negative encounters with the police and had been injured during her most recent arrest. Ms. N's defense attorney requested a competency evaluation due to concerns about her ability to assist in her defense. Specifically, he reported that he had been unable to have any sort of rational conversation with Ms. N. The state had proposed a plea deal, which Ms. N's attorney believed to be worth consideration. However, he had not been able to discuss it with Ms. N productively, as she was struggling to identify pros of the proposed deal and could only articulate cons in a hostile manner.

Ms. N was denied bond and incarcerated at the time of her initial competency evaluation. Ms. N had the capacity to make her own medical decisions and was refusing all pharmacological intervention at the jail. At the time of her initial competency evaluation, she demonstrated a good factual understanding of the court system. However, when discussing possible outcomes of her case, she became highly agitated and angry, to the point of yelling and cursing during the evaluation, such that it had to be discontinued. She was unwilling to consider any outcomes other than having her charges dismissed, given what she attributed as maltreatment by the police during her arrest.

Ms. N had been diagnosed with bipolar disorder a few years earlier and had been psychiatrically hospitalized on at least one occasion, on an emergency detention order. The initial competency evaluator diagnosed her with unspecified mood disorder and opined that her mood instability was impacting her ability to make rational legal decisions and communicate effectively with her attorney. The initial evaluator also noted concern about Ms. N's ability to engage in appropriate courtroom behavior, particularly as she had created a disturbance during a pretrial hearing. Although the judge had not held Ms. N in contempt, her behavior certainly warranted it.

After being opined incompetent to stand trial, Ms. N was hospitalized pursuant to a court order for competency restoration on an inpatient basis. She was transferred to a secure forensic facility. After several weeks of working with her treatment team, Mr. N agreed to try a low dose of a mood stabilizer, and many of her mood instability symptoms improved. Particularly helpful to her treatment was her treatment team's willingness to discuss her symptoms of trauma and the traumatic impact of negative interactions with the police. Ms. N acknowledged that the trauma-informed care had made it such that she could trust her treatment providers a bit more easily.

Despite progress, Ms. N's treatment team became concerned about possible personality pathology as she continued to demonstrate instances of emotional instability that seemed related to borderline personality disorder. For example, Ms. N had a tendency to become dysregulated when her requests were denied. They, in fact, wondered if Ms. N had been misdiagnosed with bipolar disorder several years prior. Despite decent rapport with the treatment team, Ms. N walked out of a treatment team meeting when she did not agree with suggestions her psychiatrist made. Despite some improvements to her mood, the ongoing emotional instability suggested continued concern about her ability to work with her attorney and showcase appropriate courtroom behavior.

Ms. N's treatment team referred her to an eight-week DBT skills group, which met for 45 minutes, twice per week on the unit. Each week, the group leader introduced a new skill from one of the main modules of DBT. The group leader provided context for the importance of the skill, linking it back to some of the overarching principles of DBT. The group leader demonstrated the skills and then had the group members practice among themselves. They also discussed ways that the skills may be helpful in various legal situations. For example, when discussing emotion regulation skills, the group leader prompted group members to identify emotions they had experienced during prior conversations with their attorneys. This allowed the group leader to showcase how specific skills might be useful for certain emotions that group members identified.

Initially, Ms. N was resistant to participation and did not believe it would be useful. However, she was intent on doing anything she could to facilitate her release from the hospital. Her attention peaked in the second week of group when the group facilitator introduced DEARMAN, an interpersonal effectiveness skill, which helped individuals make requests in a more assertive manner, improving the chances that the request would be granted. Ms. N acknowledged that she had had difficulty communicating with others in an effective manner in the past, which often resulted in her needs going unmet. She was reluctant to participate in the group and practice the skill. However, when the group leader provided copies of the DEARMAN handout (from the official DBT materials) and suggested that she practice using it at a later time, Ms. N decided to try it. She used the handout to write out some thoughts about how to handle a conversation she had been planning to have with her treatment team. The next day, she was successful in using the skill in a treatment team meeting to request a medication adjustment.

DESCRIBE: "*Last week we upped my dose of my anti-anxiety medication. I would like to discuss this.*"

EXPRESS: "*I have been having difficulty sleeping since then. I do not like the way the dosage increase makes me feel.*"

ASSERT: "*I would like to go back to the previous dose.*"

REINFORCE: "*I would be better able to participate in my treatment groups if I was sleeping better at night and not experiencing negative side effects.*"

MINDFUL: *Although Ms. N had other things she wanted to discuss with the team (such as setting up a call with her attorney), she did not become distracted and remained focused on the current request.*

APPEAR: *Ms. N made good eye contact and sat up straight in her chair while speaking clearly.*

NEGOTIATE: *Ms. N was prepared to negotiate if needed, by asking for a smaller reduction in dose or trying a different anti-anxiety medication.*

Ms. N was surprised at how receptive her treatment team members were, and they complimented her assertiveness. Additionally, a few days later, Ms. N used the skill to effectively ask her roommate to turn down her radio at night, as it had been disturbing her and had almost led to a fight on one occasion. Further, with some assistance from the psychologist on her treatment team, Ms. N filled out the DEARMAN worksheet in preparation for a conversation with her attorney about the proposed plea deal she had been opposed to initially.

She was not sure when she would get a chance to talk with her attorney, as he had been difficult to get a hold of, but she wanted to be prepared to talk with him when they met, even if that was not until her next court date. She planned to keep the filled-out worksheet with her personal belongings so she could refer to it as needed.

After Ms. N recognized the helpfulness of the DEARMAN skill, she was somewhat more open to participating in the remaining sessions of the DBT group. In addition to sessions on interpersonal effectiveness, she seemed to enjoy some of the sessions focused on emotion regulation, as she was willing to admit that sometimes her temper got the best of her. In one session, the group leader provided a worksheet designed to help manage "Big Emotions" (see Appendix B). The worksheet included a list of coping skills that could be used when an individual is experiencing strong emotions such as anger, anxiety, etc. Ms. N reviewed the coping skills ideas while in group and circled a few that she might try in the future, including splashing cold water on her face, giving herself a pep talk in a funny voice, and hugging her pillow. There was a space to fill in her own skill, and she added "pray the rosary." Her Catholic faith was very important to her, and she was given permission from her treatment team to keep a small rosary (approved because it had a break away clasp and was small enough not to be a ligature risk) with her while at the hospital. She had one at home as well but had never thought to use it in stressful situations before, largely because her anger would take over so quickly that she did not have time to use any sort of skills. Over the past few weeks, she had noticed that her new mood-stabilizing medication was useful in keeping her mood more regulated. This meant that even when she experienced a strong emotion such as anger, it did not overwhelm her, and she actually had time to think about using coping skills, such as praying her rosary. She planned to keep her rosary in her pocket during upcoming treatment team meetings and future court dates to use in case she became upset.

By the end of the group, Ms. N's treatment team noted that she had made improvements in emotional stability and in effective communication. They set up a phone call with Ms. N's attorney, finding out in the process that her defense attorney assignment had changed since competency restoration began. The treatment team and Ms. N's new attorney observed that Ms. N was able to engage in an effective, calm, and rational conversation about how she wanted to move forward in her case. Ms. N held her rosary while on the phone call and noted that it helped her keep calm. Although Ms. N was still resistant to the aforementioned plea deal, she wanted to discuss it with her attorney and ask assertive questions, including why her attorney believed it was worth considering, and what other options she would have if she turned down the plea deal. She did this by referring to the DEARMAN handout she had made notes on in preparation for the phone call.

DESCRIBE: "*I would like to discuss the plea deal that has been offered in my case.*"

EXPRESS: "*It makes me very anxious to think about accepting prison time. I'm also concerned about having a felony on my record.*"

ASSERT: "*I would like to discuss why you think it is a good deal AND what other options I might have if I decline the plea deal.*"

REINFORCE: "*If I can understand your thinking about the plea deal, that will help me to consider it further. Having all the information will help me make an informed decision.*"

MINDFUL: *Ms. N noticed that she felt anxious during the call, but she remained focused on holding her rosary as a coping skill, which helped her to concentrate on the conversation. She had written "ROSARY" on her worksheet as a reminder.*

APPEAR: *Ms. N did her best to show her attorney that she was calm and focused during the conversation. She maintained good attention by taking notes on a notepad provided by her treatment team. She spoke clearly so her attorney could understand her. At one point, she thought she might cry but remembered to take two deep breaths. Her DBT treatment provider had suggested that she write "BREATHE!" on her worksheet as a reminder.*

NEGOTIATE: *Ms. N was prepared to ask her attorney to continue the conversation at a later time if she got too upset to continue. However, this was not necessary, as the conversation went fairly smoothly, and she handled her distressing feelings with her coping skills.*

Following the conversation, Ms. N's attorney provided positive feedback to Ms. N's treatment team. She was particularly impressed with the way Ms. N had assertively communicated her concerns about having a felony on her record. She had been worried that Ms. N would become dysregulated and angry when informed that it was unlikely a better plea deal would be offered. They had agreed that Ms. N would continue thinking about the offer and they would discuss it further at her next court date. Following the feedback from Ms. N's attorney, the treatment team referred Ms. N for her final competency evaluation. Prior to the final evaluation, Ms. N's treatment team made sure that she had copies of the DBT materials and worksheets that had been most helpful to her. Additionally, they gave her a folder so she could keep the materials together, and they encouraged her to take them with her when she was discharged from the hospital and transferred back to jail. They also allowed her to keep the small rosary she had been given at the hospital after confirming that it would not be confiscated at the jail.

REFERENCES

American Psychiatric Association (2022). *Diagnostic and statistical manual of mental disorders* (5th ed., text rev.).

Bloom, J. M., Woodward, E. N., Susmaras, T., & Pantalone, D. W. (2012). Use of dialectical behavior therapy in inpatient treatment of borderline personality disorder: A systematic review. *Psychiatric Services*, *63*, 881–888. doi:10.1176/appi.ps.201100311

Bozzatello, P., Blua, C., Brandellero, D., Baldassarri, L., Brasso, C., Rocca, P., & Bellino, S. (2024). Gender differences in borderline personality disorder: A narrative review. *Frontiers in Psychiatry*, *15*, 1320546. doi:10.3389/fpsyt.2024.1320546

Cancian, A. C. M., de Souza, L. A. S., Liboni, R. P. A., de Lara Machado, W., & da Silva Oliveira, M. (2019). Effects of a dialectical behavior therapy-based skills group intervention for obese individuals: A Brazilian pilot study. *Eating and Weight Disorders-Studies on Anorexia, Bulimia and Obesity*, *24*, 1099–1111. doi:10.1007/s40519-017-0461-2

Chan, C. C., Vaccaro, D. H., Rose, N. L. J., Kessler, L. E., & Hazlett, E. A. (2020). Neuroimaging in personality disorders. In C. W. Lejuez & K. L. Gratz (Eds.), *The Cambridge handbook of personality disorders* (pp. 3–19). Cambridge University Press.

Cheng, P. H., & Merrick, E. (2017). Cultural adaptation of dialectical behavior therapy for a Chinese international student with eating disorder and depression. *Clinical Case Studies, 16*, 42–57. doi:10.1177/1534650116668269

Cochrane, R. E., Laxton, K. L., Mulay, A. L., & Herbel, B. L. (2021). Guidelines for determining restorability of competency to stand trial and recommendations for involuntary treatment. *Journal of Forensic Sciences, 66*(4), 1201–1209. doi:10.1111/1556-4029.14746

Collins, D. (2019). Re-evaluating competence to stand trial. *Law and Contemporary Problems, 82*, 157–198. https://scholarship.law.duke.edu/lcp/vol82/iss2/7

Crowell, S. E., Beauchaine, T. P., & Linehan, M. M. (2009). A biosocial developmental model of borderline personality disorder: Elaborating and extending Linehan's theory. *Psychological Bulletin, 135*, 495–510. doi:10.1037/a0015616

Edwards, E. R., Dichiara, A., Epshteyn, G., Snyder, S., Linzer, S., Riglietti, K., . . . Goodman, M. (2022). Dialectical behavior therapy for justice-involved veterans (DBT-J): Feasibility and acceptability. *Psychological Services, 20*(Suppl 2), 108–121. doi:10.1037/ser0000691

Evershed, S., Tennant, A., Boomer, D., Rees, A., Barkham, M., & Watson, A. (2003). Practice-based outcomes of dialectical behaviour therapy (DBT) targeting anger and violence, with male forensic patients: A pragmatic and non-contemporaneous comparison. *Criminal Behaviour and Mental Health, 13*, 198–213. doi:10.1002/cbm.542

Falcone v. State, 227 P.3d 469 (Alaska Ft. App. 2010).

Foucha v. Louisiana, 504 U.S. 71 (1992).

Galietta, M. (2018). Adapting dialectical behavior therapy for use in correctional settings. In E. Jeglic & C. Calkins (Eds.), *New frontiers in offender treatment* (pp. 147–169). Springer. doi:10.1007/978-3-030-01030-0_8

Garb, H. N. (2021). Race bias and gender bias in the diagnosis of psychological disorders. *Clinical Psychology Review, 90*, 102087. doi:10.1016/j.cpr.2021.102087

Haft, S. L., O'Grady, S. M., Shaller, E. A. L., & Liu, N. H. (2022). Cultural adaptations of dialectical behavior therapy: A systematic review. *Journal of Consulting and Clinical Psychology, 90*(10), 787–801. doi:10.1037/ccp0000730

Jiang, W., Shi, F., Liao, J., Liu, H., Wang, T., . . . Shen, D. (2017). Disrupted functional connectome in antisocial personality disorder. *Brain Imaging Behavior, 11*(4), 1071–1084. doi:10.1007/s11682-016-9572-z

Johanson, M., Vaurio, O., Tiihonen, J., & Lähteenvuo, M. (2020). A systematic literature review of neuroimaging of psychopathic traits. *Frontiers in Psychiatry, 10*, 1027. doi:10.3389/fpsyt.2019.01027

Johnson, S. C., & Elbogen, E. B. (2013). Personality disorders at the interface of psychiatry and the law: Legal use and clinical classification. *Dialogues in Clinical Neuroscience, 15*(2), 203–211. doi:10.31887/DCNS.2013.15.2/sjohnson

Katakis, P., Schlief, M., Barnett, P., Rains, L. S., Rowe, S., Pilling, S., & Johnson, S. (2023). Effectiveness of outpatient and community treatments for people with a diagnosis of 'personality disorder': Systematic review and meta-analysis. *BMC Psychiatry, 23*(1). doi:10.1186/s12888-022-04483-0

Kinsey, K. M. (2014). *A critical ethnography of the compatibility of a culturally modified dialectical behavior therapy with Native American culture and context* [Doctoral dissertation, University of Arizona]. UA Campus Repository. https://repository.arizona.edu/handle/10150/321004

Koukourikos, K., & Pasmatzi, E. (2014). Group therapy in psychotic patients. *Health Science Journal, 8*, 400–408. http://www.hsj.gr

Laniyonu, A., & Goff, P. A. (2021). Measuring disparities in police use of force and injury among persons with serious mental illness. *BMC Psychiatry, 21*, 1–8. doi:10.1186/s12888-021-03510-w

LaRue, G. C., & Dragon, W. R. (2020). *Misdiagnosing borderline personality disorder: Does setting bias and gender bias influence diagnostic decision-making?* [Unpublished doctoral dissertation]. Wright State University, Dayton, OH.

Lee, J. S. (2021). Borderline personality disorder in the courtroom. *Psychiatry, Psychology and Law, 2*, 206–217. doi:10.1080/13218719.2020.1767718

Linehan, M. M. (1987). Dialectical behavior therapy for borderline personality disorder: Theory and method. *Bulletin of the Menninger Clinic, 51*, 261–276. https://pubmed.ncbi.nlm.nih.gov/3580661/

Linehan, M. M. (1993). *Cognitive-behavioral treatment of borderline personality disorder*. Guilford Press.

Linehan, M. M. (2015a). *DBT® skills training manual* (2nd ed.). Guilford Press.

Linehan, M. M (2015b). *DBT skills training handouts and worksheets* (2nd ed.). Guilford Press.

MacIntosh, H. B., Godbout, N., & Dubash, N. (2015). Borderline personality disorder: Disorder of trauma or personality, a review of the empirical literature. *Canadian Psychology/Psychologie Canadienne, 56*(2), 227. doi:10.1037/cap0000028

Martin, M. S., Hynes, K., Hatcher, S., & Colman, I. (2016). Diagnostic error in correctional mental health. *Journal of Correctional Health Care, 22*(2), 109–117. doi:10.1177/1078345816634327

McCann, R. A., Ball, E. M., & Ivanoff, A. (2000). DBT with an inpatient forensic population: The CMHIP forensic model. *Cognitive and Behavioral Practice, 7*, 447–456. doi:10.1016/s1077-7229(00)80056-5

McGowan, N. M., Syam, N., McKenna, D., Pearce, S., & Saunders, K. E. (2021). A service evaluation of short-term mentalisation based treatment for personality disorder. *BJPsych Open, 7*(5), e140. doi:10.1192/bjo.2021.974

McKenna, G., Jackson, N., & Browne, C. (2019). Trauma history in a high secure male forensic inpatient population. *International Journal of Law and Psychiatry, 66*, 101475. doi:10.1016/j.ijlp.2019.101475

Moore, E. (2012). Personality disorder: Its impact on staff and the role of supervision. *Advances in Psychiatric Treatment, 18*(1), 44–55. doi:10.1192/apt.bp.107.004754

Morris, D. R., & DeYoung, N. J. (2012). Psycholegal abilities and restoration of competence to stand trial. *Behavioral Sciences & the Law, 30*(6), 710–728. doi:10.1002/bsl.2040

Moulden, H. M., Mamak, M., & Chaimowitz, G. (2020). A preliminary evaluation of the effectiveness of dialectical behaviour therapy in a forensic psychiatric setting. *Criminal Behaviour and Mental Health, 30*(2–3), 141–150. doi:10.1002/cbm.2158

Nyamathi, A., Shin, S. S., Smeltzer, J., Salem, B., Yadav, K., Krogh, D., & Ekstrand, M. (2018). Effectiveness of dialectical behavioral therapy on reduction of recidivism among recently incarcerated homeless women: A pilot study. *International Journal of Offender Therapy and Comparative Criminology, 62*(15), 4796–4813. doi:10.1177/0306624X18785516

O'Connell, B., & Dowling, M. (2014). Dialectical behaviour therapy (DBT) in the treatment of borderline personality disorder. *Journal of Psychiatric & Mental Health Nursing, 21*, 518–525. doi:10.1111/jpm.12116

O'Grady, S. M, Haft, S. L., Esme, A. L., Shaller, E. A. L., & Liu, N. H. (2022). Cultural adaptations of dialectical behavior therapy: Cultural recommendations. *DBT Bulletin, 6*, 4–6. https://

static1.squarespace.com/static/62e933212ea2a15419c196cd/t/63763102725422641fc7b7c8/1668690179847/DBTBulletin_V7.pdf

Pinals, D. (2005). Where two roads meet: Restoration of competence to stand trial from a clinical perspective. *New England Journal on Criminal and Civil Confinement, 31*, 81–108. https://pdfs.semanticscholar.org/a959/8c4f38b9b6dcb911f37e2c85c540665e1511.pdf

Ramaiya, M. K., McLean, C., Regmi, U., Fiorillo, D., Robins, C. J., & Kohrt, B. A. (2018). A dialectical behavior therapy skills intervention for women with suicidal behaviors in rural Nepal: A single-case experimental design series. *Journal of Clinical Psychology, 74*, 1071–1091. doi:10.1002/jclp.22588

Reisner, A. D., & Piel, J. L. (2018). Mental condition requirement in competency to stand trial assessments. *The Journal of the American Academy of Psychiatry and the Law, 46*(1), 86–92. https://jaapl.org/content/46/1/86

Rizvi, S. L., Steffel, L. M., & Carson-Wong, A. (2013). An overview of dialectical behavior therapy for professional psychologists. *Professional Psychology: Research and Practice, 44*, 73–80. doi:10.1037/a0029898

Rodwell, D., & Frith, H. (2024). Using a trauma-informed care framework to explore social climate and borderline personality disorder in forensic inpatient settings. *International Journal of Mental Health Nursing, 33*, 1139–1150. doi:10.1111/inm.13300

Samuelsson, S., Herkner, B., & Lundberg, I. (2003). Reading and writing difficulties among prison inmates: A matter of experiential factors rather than dyslexic problems. *Scientific Studies of Reading, 7*(1), 53–73. doi:10.1207/S1532799XSSR0701_04

Sampl, S., Wakai, S., & Trestman, R. L. (2010). Translating evidence-based practices from community to corrections: An example of implementing DBT-CM. *The Journal of Behavior Analysis of Offender and Victim Treatment and Prevention, 2*(2), 114. doi:10.1037/h0100463

Schandrin, A., Francey, S., Nguyen, L., Whitty, D., McGorry, P., Chanen, A. M., & O'Donoghue, B. (2022). Co-occurring first-episode psychosis and borderline personality pathology in an early intervention for psychosis cohort. *Early Intervention in Psychiatry, 17*(6), 588–596. doi:10.1111/eip.13352

Secarea, C. M., Cleary, S. D., & Candilis, P. J. (2021). Factors influencing adjudicative competence and length of time to restoration. *The Journal of Forensic Sciences, 66*, 982–991. doi:10.1111/1556-4029.14669

Slaughter, B., Fann, J. R., & Ehde, D. (2003). Traumatic brain injury in a county jail population: Prevalence, neuropsychological functioning and psychiatric disorders. *Brain Injury, 17*(9), 731–741. doi:10.1080/0269905031000088649

Slovenko, R. (2009). Commentary: Personality disorders and criminal law. *The Journal of the American Academy of Psychiatry and the Law, 37*, 182–185. https://jaapl.org/content/37/2/182

State v. Halder, No. 87974, Ohio Ct. App. (2008).

State v. Klein, 156 Wn. 2d 102 (Wash. 2005).

Substance Abuse and Mental Health Services Administration (2016). *DSM-5 changes: Implications for child serious emotional disturbance.* Substance Abuse and Mental Health Services Administration. https://www.ncbi.nlm.nih.gov/books/NBK519711/

Tomlin, J., & Völlm, B. (Eds.). (2023). *Diversity and marginalisation in forensic mental health care.* Routledge. doi:10.4324/9781003184768

Tomlinson, M. F. (2018). A theoretical and empirical review of dialectical behavior therapy within forensic psychiatric and correctional settings worldwide. *International Journal of Forensic Mental Health, 17*, 72–95. doi:10.1080/14999013.2017.1416003

Trestman, R. L., Gonillo, C., & Davis, K. (2004). Dialectical behavior therapy—Corrections—Modified (DBT-CM) skills training manual. Unpublished treatment manuscript. University of Connecticut Health Center.

United States v. Armstrong, 517 U.S. 456 (2008).

United States v. DeShazer, 554 F.3d 1281 (2009).

United States v. McKinney, 737 F.3d 772 (D.C. Cir. 2013).

United States v. Veatch, 842 F. Supp. 480 (1993).

VandenBos, G. R. (Ed.). (2007). *APA dictionary of psychology*. American Psychological Association.

Wang, Q., Zhang, L., Zhang, J., Ye, Z., Li, P., Wang, F., . . . Zhao, N. (2021). Prevalence of comorbid personality disorder in psychotic and non-psychotic disorders. *Frontiers in Psychiatry, 12*, 800047. doi:10.3389/fpsyt.2021.800047

Williams, R., Farquharson, L., Rhodes, E., Dang, M., Fitzpatrick, N., Quirk, A., . . . Crawford, M. J. (2020). Impact of co-morbid personality disorder on quality of inpatient mental health services for people with anxiety and depression. *Personality and Mental Health, 14*(4), 336–349. doi:10.1002/pmh.1484

Wilson, S., Stroud, C. E., & Durbin, C. E. (2017). Interpersonal dysfunction in personality disorders: A meta-analytic review. *Psychological Bulletin, 143*, 677–734. doi:10.1037/bul0000101

Wong, R. S. (2023). Psychopathology of antisocial personality disorder: From the structural, functional and biochemical perspectives. *The Egyptian Journal of Neurology, Psychiatry and Neurosurgery, 59*, 1–14. doi:10.1186/s41983-023-00717-4

Zalewski, M., Walton, C. J., Rizvi, S. L., White, A. W., Gamache Martin, C., O'Brien, J. R., & Dimeff, L. (2021). Lessons learned conducting dialectical behavior therapy via telehealth in the age of COVID-19. *Cognitive and Behavioral Practice, 28*(4), 573–587. doi:10.1016/j.cbpra.2021.02.005

Zapf, P. A., & Roesch, R. (2011). Future directions in the restoration of competency to stand trial. *Current Directions in Psychological Science, 20*, 43–47. doi:10.1177/0963721410396798

Zhang, K., Hu, X., Ma, L., Xie, Q., Wang, Z., Fan, C., & Li, X. (2023). The efficacy of schema therapy for personality disorders: A systematic review and meta analysis. *Nordic Journal of Psychiatry, 77*(7), 641–650. doi:10.1080/08039488.2023.2228304

Zhan Yuen Wong, N., Barnett, P., Sheridan Rains, L., Johnson, S., & Billings, J. (2023). Evaluation of international guidance for the community treatment of "personality disorders": A systematic review. *PLoS One, 18*(3), e0264239. doi:10.1371/journal.pone.0264239

APPENDICES

APPENDIX A

General Competency Restoration Games and Activities

Courtroom Illustration

Courtroom Scene Activity

Use this diagram to label or draw who and what you can find in a courtroom.

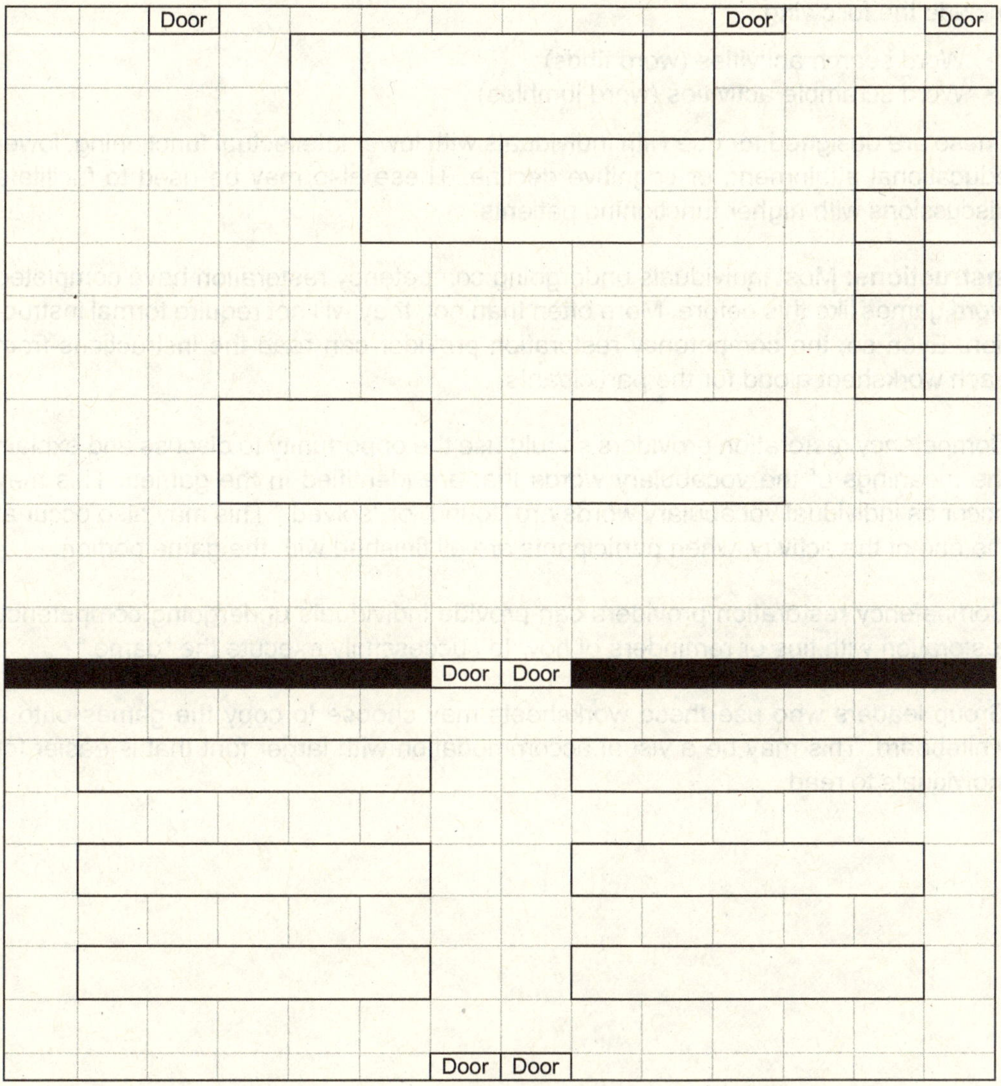

Legal Vocabulary Games

In this section, you will find a series of games designed to assess and expand upon the legal vocabulary of an individual undergoing competency restoration. These include the following:

- Word search activities (word finds)
- Word scramble activities (word jumbles)

These are designed for use with individuals with lower intellectual functioning, lower educational attainment, or cognitive decline. These also may be used to facilitate discussions with higher functioning patients.

Instructions: Most individuals undergoing competency restoration have completed word games like this before. More often than not, they will not require formal instruction. Even so, the competency restoration provider can read the instructions from each worksheet aloud for the participants.

Competency restoration providers should use the opportunity to discuss and explain the meanings of the vocabulary words that are identified in the games. This may occur as individual vocabulary words are "found" or "solved." This may also occur at the end of the activity, when participants are all finished with the game portion.

Competency restoration providers can provide individuals undergoing competency restoration with tips or reminders of how to successfully execute the "game."

Group leaders who use these worksheets may choose to copy the games onto a whiteboard. This may be a visual accommodation with larger font that is easier for individuals to read.

Competency Restoration Word Search #1

Find the vocabulary words so that we can talk about what each one means. The topic for this puzzle is "Competency Restoration."

U	E	L	B	A	R	O	T	S	E	R	N	U	C
P	C	L	A	S	J	A	C	K	S	O	N	L	O
E	A	O	A	W	S	F	J	C	A	R	I	A	M
O	P	R	N	W	U	E	P	J	P	A	G	N	P
M	A	S	T	T	Y	C	L	I	J	D	R	O	E
E	C	C	N	I	I	E	P	U	A	A	O	I	T
D	I	L	F	F	C	N	R	R	R	N	U	T	E
I	T	A	A	A	I	I	U	V	O	T	P	A	N
C	Y	S	C	A	C	S	P	A	I	V	S	R	T
A	D	V	O	C	A	T	E	A	N	S	E	C	F
T	T	R	O	F	F	E	U	P	T	C	I	E	E
I	D	S	T	U	D	Y	R	A	A	I	E	T	D
O	V	A	S	S	I	S	T	T	L	C	O	O	C
N	E	D	I	S	C	U	S	S	I	O	N	N	I

Word Bank:

ADVOCATE
ASSIST
CAPACITY
COMPETENT
CONTINUANCE
DISCUSSION
EFFORT
FACTUAL
GROUPS
JACKSON
JAIL
LAWYER VISIT
MEDICATION
PARTICIPATION
PROCEED
RATIONAL
RULES
STUDY
UNRESTORABLE

Competency Restoration Word Search #2

Find the vocabulary words so that we can talk about what each one means. The topic for this puzzle is "People at Court."

E	S	S	N	P	K	C	U	J	E	T	B	U	Y
N	T	S	A	Y	R	P	P	C	U	I	E	F	Y
S	E	E	M	T	E	R	U	S	A	R	O	F	E
E	N	N	S	I	L	O	B	N	L	E	Y	I	Y
E	O	T	D	R	C	S	L	N	I	I	X	T	E
W	G	I	N	U	T	E	I	F	B	D	R	N	W
B	R	W	O	C	R	C	C	J	I	S	L	I	I
A	A	T	B	E	U	U	I	U	W	H	P	A	T
I	P	R	L	S	O	T	T	D	I	E	Y	L	N
L	H	E	I	I	C	O	A	G	T	R	B	P	E
I	E	P	A	L	X	R	L	E	N	I	I	R	S
F	R	X	B	T	N	A	D	N	E	F	E	D	S
F	P	E	T	F	F	O	W	B	S	F	A	F	A
E	L	A	W	Y	E	R	S	R	S	A	I	E	W

Word Bank:

ALIBI WITNESS
BAIL BONDSMAN
BAILIFF
COURT CLERK
DEFENDANT
EXPERT WITNESS
EYEWITNESS
JUDGE
JURY
LAWYERS
PLAINTIFF
PROSECUTOR
PUBLIC
SECURITY
SHERIFF
STENOGRAPHER

Competency Restoration Word Search #3

Find the vocabulary words so that we can talk about what each one means. The topic for this puzzle is "A Defendant's Role & Rights."

N	E	N	T	E	R	P	L	E	A	S	I	D	T
U	I	E	G	E	L	I	V	I	R	P	A	S	P
N	I	A	G	R	A	B	A	E	L	P	P	C	L
A	A	N	K	U	G	K	A	P	P	E	A	L	U
Y	U	N	D	E	R	S	T	A	N	D	I	N	G
R	F	A	I	R	T	R	I	A	L	E	A	U	L
U	T	I	L	I	S	T	E	N	I	N	G	T	T
J	R	E	T	A	C	I	N	U	M	M	O	C	R
R	C	O	N	S	U	L	T	I	N	G	E	S	U
E	W	A	I	V	E	R	I	G	H	T	S	U	T
P	U	B	L	I	C	T	R	I	A	L	L	C	H
K	N	O	W	L	E	D	G	E	L	T	T	O	D
L	A	I	R	T	Y	D	E	E	P	S	I	F	I
G	G	T	L	A	I	R	T	Y	R	U	J	A	U

Word Bank:

APPEAL
CONSULTING
DEFENSE LAWYER
ENTER PLEA
FAIR TRIAL
FOCUS
JURY TRIAL
KNOWLEDGE
LISTENING
PERJURY
PLEA BARGAIN
PRIVILEGE
PUBLIC TRIAL
SPEEDY TRIAL
TESTIFY
TRUTH
UNDERSTANDING
WAIVE RIGHTS

Competency Restoration Word Search #4

Find the vocabulary words so that we can talk about what each one means. The topic for this puzzle is "Court Proceedings & Jargon."

C	S	M	A	R	R	A	I	G	N	M	E	N	T
R	O	B	J	E	C	T	I	O	N	N	A	N	A
O	G	A	E	V	E	R	D	I	C	T	P	O	R
S	A	A	D	I	R	E	C	T	A	T	P	I	G
S	D	P	H	G	T	Y	G	N	P	A	E	T	U
S	M	P	E	N	G	N	N	P	R	O	A	A	M
C	I	E	A	I	N	O	I	T	E	R	L	N	E
G	S	A	R	R	I	M	C	N	T	I	B	I	N
N	S	R	S	A	S	I	N	R	R	A	I	M	T
I	I	A	A	E	O	T	E	A	I	G	Y	A	S
N	B	N	Y	H	L	S	T	L	A	I	D	X	P
E	L	C	C	O	C	E	N	P	L	N	O	E	E
P	E	E	I	B	B	T	E	P	O	A	E	L	P
O	O	M	N	I	B	U	S	B	I	L	E	I	N

Word Bank:

ADMISSIBLE
APPEAL
APPEARANCE
ARGUMENTS
ARRAIGNMENT
BAIL
BOND
CLOSING
CROSS
DIRECT
EXAMINATION
HEARING
HEARSAY
OBJECTION
OMNIBUS
OPENING
PLEA
PRETRIAL
SENTENCING
TESTIMONY
VERDICT

Competency Restoration Word Search #5

Find the vocabulary words so that we can talk about what each one means. The topic for this puzzle is "Pleas, Verdicts, & Penalties."

I	U	Q	E	S	O	R	P	E	L	L	O	N	L
L	E	N	P	N	O	S	I	R	P	E	S	D	R
A	L	F	O	R	D	P	L	E	A	R	E	E	E
T	O	M	N	E	O	C	S	V	P	D	N	V	G
I	R	O	R	N	R	B	P	O	P	N	T	R	I
P	A	L	I	A	J	N	A	O	U	E	E	E	S
S	P	N	I	N	I	O	G	T	N	T	N	S	T
O	R	M	R	C	R	C	T	D	I	N	C	E	R
H	B	E	P	G	G	O	R	E	S	O	E	M	A
G	T	N	E	C	O	N	N	I	H	C	N	I	T
Y	T	L	I	U	G	T	O	N	M	O	N	T	I
T	R	E	A	T	M	E	N	T	E	L	G	H	O
D	E	S	S	I	M	S	I	D	N	O	R	I	N
I	N	S	A	N	I	T	Y	L	T	N	I	A	T

Word Bank:

ALFORD PLEA
DISMISSED
GBMI
HOSPITAL
INNOCENT
INSANITY
JAIL
NGRI
NO CONTEST
NOLLE PROSEQUI
NOLO CONTENDRE
NOT GUILTY
PAROLE
PRISON
PROBATION
PUNISHMENT
REGISTRATION
SENTENCE
SVP
TIME SERVED
TREATMENT

Word Search Answer Key

1

U	E	L	B	A	R	O	T	S	E	R	N	U	C
P	C	L	A	S	J	A	C	K	S	O	N	L	O
E	A	O	A	W	S	F	J	C	A	R	I	A	M
O	P	R	N	W	U	E	P	J	P	A	G	N	P
M	A	S	T	T	Y	C	L	I	J	D	R	O	E
E	C	C	N	I	I	E	P	U	A	A	O	I	T
D	I	L	F	F	C	N	R	R	R	N	U	T	E
I	T	A	A	A	I	I	U	V	O	T	P	A	N
C	Y	S	C	A	C	S	P	A	I	C	S	R	T
A	D	V	O	C	A	T	E	A	N	S	E	C	F
T	T	R	O	F	F	E	U	P	T	C	I	E	E
I	D	S	T	U	D	Y	R	A	A	I	E	T	D
O	V	A	S	S	I	S	T	T	L	C	O	O	C
N	E	D	I	S	C	U	S	S	I	O	N	N	I

2

E	S	S	N	P	K	C	U	J	E	T	B	U	Y
N	T	S	A	Y	R	P	P	C	U	I	E	F	Y
S	E	E	M	T	E	R	U	S	A	R	O	F	E
E	N	N	S	I	L	O	B	N	L	E	Y	I	Y
E	O	T	D	R	C	S	L	N	I	I	X	T	E
W	G	I	N	U	T	E	I	F	B	D	R	N	W
B	R	W	O	C	R	C	C	J	I	S	L	I	I
A	A	T	B	E	U	U	I	U	W	H	P	A	T
I	P	R	L	S	O	T	T	D	I	E	Y	L	N
L	H	E	I	I	C	O	A	G	T	R	B	P	E
I	E	P	A	L	X	R	L	E	N	I	I	R	S
F	R	X	B	T	N	A	D	N	E	F	E	D	S
F	P	E	T	F	F	O	W	B	S	F	A	F	A
E	L	A	W	Y	E	R	S	R	S	A	I	E	W

3

N	E	N	T	E	R	P	L	E	A	S	I	D	T
U	I	E	G	E	R	I	V	I	R	P	A	S	P
N	I	A	G	R	A	B	A	E	L	P	P	C	L
A	A	N	K	U	G	K	A	P	P	E	A	L	U
Y	U	N	D	E	R	S	T	A	N	D	I	N	G
R	F	A	I	R	T	R	I	A	L	E	A	U	L
U	T	I	L	I	S	T	E	N	I	N	G	T	T
J	R	E	T	A	C	I	N	U	M	M	O	C	R
R	C	O	N	S	U	L	T	I	N	G	E	S	U
E	W	A	I	V	E	R	I	G	H	T	S	U	T
P	U	B	L	I	C	T	R	I	A	L	L	C	H
K	N	O	W	L	E	D	G	E	L	T	T	O	D
L	A	I	R	T	Y	D	E	P	P	S	I	F	I
G	G	T	L	A	I	R	T	Y	R	U	J	A	U

4

C	S	M	A	R	R	A	I	G	N	M	E	N	T
R	O	B	J	E	C	T	I	O	N	N	A	N	A
O	G	A	E	V	E	R	D	I	C	T	P	O	R
S	A	A	D	I	R	E	C	T	A	T	P	I	G
S	D	P	H	G	T	Y	G	N	P	A	E	T	U
S	M	P	E	N	G	N	N	P	R	O	A	A	M
C	I	E	A	I	N	O	I	T	E	R	L	N	E
G	S	A	R	R	I	M	C	N	T	I	B	I	N
N	S	R	S	A	S	I	N	R	R	A	I	M	T
I	I	A	A	E	O	T	E	A	I	G	Y	A	S
N	B	N	Y	H	L	S	T	L	A	I	D	X	P
E	L	C	C	O	C	E	N	P	L	N	O	E	E
P	E	E	I	B	B	T	E	P	O	A	E	L	P
O	O	M	N	I	B	U	S	B	I	L	E	I	N

5

I	U	Q	E	S	O	R	P	E	L	L	O	N	L
L	E	N	P	N	O	S	I	R	P	E	S	D	R
A	L	F	O	R	D	P	L	E	A	R	E	E	E
T	O	M	N	E	O	C	S	V	P	D	N	V	G
I	R	O	R	N	R	B	P	O	P	N	T	R	I
P	A	L	I	A	J	N	A	O	U	E	E	E	S
S	P	N	I	N	I	O	G	T	N	T	N	S	T
O	R	M	R	C	R	C	T	D	I	N	C	E	R
H	B	E	P	G	G	O	R	E	S	O	E	M	A
G	T	N	E	C	O	N	N	I	H	C	N	I	T
Y	T	L	I	U	G	T	O	N	M	O	N	T	I
T	R	E	A	T	M	E	N	T	E	L	G	H	O
D	E	S	S	I	M	S	I	D	N	O	R	I	N
I	N	S	A	N	I	T	Y	L	T	N	I	A	T

Competency Restoration Word Scramble #1

Unscramble the vocabulary words so that we can talk about what each one means.

_ _ _ _ UJRY	_ _ _ _ _ _ CUSACE
_ _ _ _ _ _ _ IIBAFFL	_ _ _ _ _ IUTGL
_ _ _ _ _ _ _ _ RRRETOPE	_ _ _ _ _ _ _ _ _ ITNEMYTSO
_ _ _ _ IFEN	_ _ _ _ _ _ _ _ _ _ NCCPOEETMY
_ _ _ _ _ _ _ _ _ IOBTJOCEN	_ _ _ _ _ _ _ _ _ NEEDTNFAD
_ _ _ _ _ _ FNOYLE	_ _ _ _ _ _ _ _ _ IURTCENDO
_ _ _ _ _ CRTUO	_ _ _ _ _ _ _ _ _ CENNIENOC
_ _ _ _ _ _ _ _ ENICEDEV	_ _ _ _ _ _ _ ISFEHRF
_ _ _ _ _ _ _ _ TNECNEES	_ _ _ _ HTOA
_ _ _ _ _ _ _ _ _ _ _ RADIEEOMNSM	_ _ _ _ _ _ _ EIGAHRN

Competency Restoration Word Scramble #2

Unscramble the vocabulary words so that we can talk about what each one means.

________________ CRNAECRINITAO	____________ DEDEFERN
______ ROSCS	________ RYAWLE
______________ ENTXOIANMIA	________ TYGIUL
_______ EAPPLA	_____ WKOR
_________ SEWSNTI	__________ ALEREES
_______ PCLIOE	_______ IRTAL
______ DJUEG	_____ JILA
_________ ATAWRRN	________ RITSGH
_______ DITERC	_______ MECRI
_________ ONORBOP	__________________ NSARGEVITITSO

Competency Restoration Word Scramble #3

Unscramble the vocabulary words so that we can talk about what each one means.

_ _ _ _ A I B L	_ _ _ _ _ H N B C E
_ _ _ _ _ _ _ _ _ _ O I S M O N S I C M	_ _ _ _ _ _ _ _ _ _ _ _ _ M N A N I C I I R O N T I
_ _ _ _ W S A L	_ _ _ _ _ A T L U F
_ _ _ _ _ _ O R D C R E	_ _ _ _ _ _ _ _ _ _ _ _ A N T R H O P S E R G E
_ _ _ _ _ _ C H G E R A	_ _ _ _ _ _ _ _ _ D A L I S S M I S
_ _ _ _ _ _ _ _ _ _ M I N S P N U H E T	_ _ _ _ _ _ _ _ M O N T P C T E
_ _ _ _ _ _ _ _ T T A E N O Y R	_ _ _ _ _ _ _ _ N I S N I T A Y
_ _ _ _ _ _ _ R U R E Y P J	_ _ _ _ _ _ _ _ _ _ _ A G A T E S T M R I
_ _ _ _ _ _ _ _ _ _ P E R R S C T O U O	_ _ _ _ _ _ _ _ _ _ D E I S M R E V E T
_ _ _ _ _ _ L I P C U B	_ _ _ _ _ _ _ _ _ _ C A P P A R A N E E

Word Scramble Answer Key

Number 1	Number 2	Number 3
JURY **UJRY**	INCARCERATION **CRNAECRINITAO**	BAIL **AIBL**
BAILIFF **IIBAFFL**	CROSS **ROSCS**	COMMISSION **OISMONSICM**
REPORTER **RRRETOPE**	EXAMINATION **ENTXOIANMIA**	LAWS **WSAL**
FINE **IFEN**	APPEAL **EAPPLA**	RECORD **ORDCRE**
OBJECTION **IOBTJOCEN**	WITNESS **SEWSNTI**	CHARGE **CHGERA**
FELONY **FNOYLE**	POLICE **PCLIOE**	PUNISHMENT **MINSPNUHET**
COURT **CRTUO**	JUDGE **DJUEG**	ATTORNEY **TTAENOYR**
EVIDENCE **ENICEDEV**	WARRANT **ATAWRRN**	PERJURY **RUREYPJ**
SENTENCE **TNECNEES**	DIRECT **DITERC**	PROSECUTOR **PERRSCTOUO**
MISDEMEANOR **RADIEEOMNSM**	PRO BONO **ONORBOP**	PUBLIC **LIPCUB**
ACCUSE **CUSACE**	DEFENDER **DEDEFERN**	BENCH **HNBCE**
GUILT **IUTGL**	LAWYER **RYRYAWLE**	INCRIMINATION **MNANICIIRONTI**
TESTIMONY **ITNEMYTSO**	GUILTY **TYGIUL**	FAULT **ATLUF**
COMPETENCY **NCCPOEETMY**	WORK **WKOR**	STENOGRAPHER **ANTRHOPSERGE**
DEFENDANT **NEEDTNFAD**	RELEASE **ALEREES**	DISMISSAL **DALISSMIS**
INTRODUCE **IURTCENDO**	TRIAL **IRTAL**	CONTEMPT **MONTPCTE**
INNOCENCE **CENNIENOC**	JAIL **JILA**	INSANITY **NISNITAY**
SHERIFF **ISFEHRF**	RIGHTS **RITSGH**	MAGISTRATE **AGATESTMRI**
OATH **HTOA**	CRIME **MECRI**	TIME SERVED **DEISMREVET**
HEARING **EIGAHRN**	INVESTIGATORS **NSARGEVITITSO**	APPEARANCE **CAPPARANEE**

Legal Flashcard Activities

Both formal legal flashcards and homemade flashcards (i.e., made by competency restoration providers or by defendants) can be used for more than memorization of terms. Here are some ideas for making use of those visual aids:

One-on-One Restoration Activities

1. **Traditional flashcard use**—Sort and/or shuffle the flashcards. Show the defendant the flashcards one at a time, and have them explain the term listed on the card. Provide additional education as each card is reviewed.
2. **Extended flashcard use**—Engage in traditional flashcard use, but ask more extensive follow-up questions. For example, rather than just having the defendant explain what a defendant is, review the role of a defendant, how a defendant should act in court, the legal rights of a defendant, and/or who the "defendant" is. Provide additional education as each card is reviewed.
3. **Open hand flashcard use**—Sort and/or shuffle the flashcards. Lay out the flashcards on a table. Describe a term, and have the defendant locate and identify the card that matches the term described. For individuals with cognitive limitations, it may help to organize the cards by category on the table. At times, some of the cards on the table may have to be "eliminated" by the restoration provider to help the defendant identify the correct card. Provide additional education as each card is reviewed.
4. **Whose side is it anyway?**—Select the flashcards that describe people, put the "defendant" card aside, and shuffle the remaining people cards. Review the "defendant" card with the actual defendant, and place the card in front of the defendant, slightly to the right or left of center. Then review the remaining cards one at a time, placing each card (A) on the same side as the defendant when they describe people aligned with the defense, (B) on the side opposite of the "defendant card" when they describe people aligned with the prosecution, or (C) in the middle for people who are considered neutral players at court. It can be helpful to keep the cards unobstructed (e.g., by lining them up), so that the defendant can see how the cards are being grouped. Provide additional education as each card is reviewed.
5. **Where do I go?** Select the flashcards that describe people, and shuffle the people cards. Review the cards with the defendant one at a time. When done with each card, have the defendant place the card on the table in a spot that corresponds with where they would be in a courtroom. It is certainly beneficial to place the cards on an image of a courtroom, but this can also be done without a courtroom image, using orienting landmarks (e.g., "this side of the table will be the back of the courtroom"). Provide additional education as each card is reviewed.

Group Restoration Activities

6. **Legal heads up**—Shuffle the flashcards. Draw 5–10 cards, and hand them to one group member without letting them see what is on the cards. Have the group member put the stack of cards to their forehead, term toward the rest of the group. When the group leader says "Go," group members should start to explain the word listed on the flashcard or otherwise give clues so that the person with the cards ("the *guesser*") can guess the term. When the *guesser* identifies the correct term (at the discretion of the group leader), they should place the card on the table. The process repeats with subsequent cards until there are none left. Each player can rotate in as the *guesser*. This can be played as a whole group or in teams, depending on the size of the group.
7. **Legal Pictionary**—Provide each group member a piece of paper and a writing implement. Shuffle the flashcards. Have each group member select 1 flashcard, without showing the others in the group. All at the same time have each group member do their best to draw the concept on their card. After a set amount of time, or when everyone is done, have the group members exchange papers so that they each have a peer's paper rather than their own (e.g., pass left, pass right, trade across, or a random exchange). Have each person guess what term the artist was trying to draw, with or without assistance from the rest of the group (at the discretion of the group leader).
8. **Memory game**—Shuffle and/or sort the cards. Lay out the cards on the table, either grouped by category or randomly, so that all group members can see. When everyone is ready, have the group members each cover their eyes and/or turn to face away from the table (e.g., looking up at the ceiling, or at a specific wall). Remove 1 card, and do not show which card has been removed. Instruct the group members to look at the cards and identify which card was removed. Once the answer is accurately guessed, return the card to the table. Once modeled, the person to remove a card can be rotated through the group members (at the discretion of the group leader).
9. **20 Questions**—Shuffle and/or sort the cards. Randomly select a card, and do not show the card to the group. One at a time, have each group member ask 1 question that will help the group identify which card was selected. For example, a group member may ask, "Is it a person?" or "Is it a verdict?" If a group member guesses an incorrect vocabulary word, they are out for the rest of the round. If a group member guesses the correct vocabulary word, they are the winner of the round. The group may be permitted to work collaboratively to brainstorm their next questions, as practicing communication and teamwork may be good practice for assisting in their defense. Once modeled, the person to select a card can be rotated through the group members (at the discretion of the group leader). The group leader may cap the number of questions that can be asked at 20, or much lower, given the limited options for terms.

Restoration providers are encouraged to think of other interactive uses for flashcards (e.g., charades). Additional flashcard games, designed for use in school settings, can also be found online.

Competency Restoration BINGO

Instructions:

1. Give each group member a blank BINGO board and *word bank* worksheet. They will also need a writing implement if they do not already have one.
2. The group leader should determine at the start of the game whether "the *caller*" will be calling numbers or vocabulary words. This may help the players decide whether they want to put numbers or vocabulary words on their BINGO boards.
3. Have each person design their own BINGO board using the *word bank* provided. They can either write the number of the term that would be called, or the associated number.
4. Identify the *caller*. The *caller* can be the group leader, a designated group member, or a rotating group member (i.e., round by round or turn by turn, to encourage engagement/participation).
5. *Caller* duties:
    a. If a traditional BINGO cage is being used: The *caller* will be the person to pull a ball from the cage with an identified number.
    b. If a BINGO cage is not available, or the group leader prefers: Numbers should be printed or written on slips of paper, folded, and placed in a box/bowl/cup that can be shaken up. The *caller* will be the person to pull a number from the box/bowl/cup.
6. There are several options for how to call numbers, depending on the functioning of the individuals playing the game and preference of those involved.
    a. Beginner: The *caller* can use the number they pull to refer to the *word bank* and call the associated vocabulary word. This will help the players become familiar with the vocabulary words by sight and sound. This approach may be easiest if the actual words are written on the boards rather than numbers.
    b. Advanced: The *caller* can use the number they pull to refer to the corresponding prompt on the *question list*. They can then read the prompt listed (not the vocabulary word), and leave it up to the participants to figure out the correct vocabulary word. If numbers are written on the board rather than words, they can use the word bank to figure out which box to mark.
7. Participants should mark the appropriate box on the board.
    a. If the boards will only be used for one group, participants can write on them and mark (e.g., X) on the box with a vocabulary word that has been called. A different marking can be used for subsequent rounds if the boards will be reused.
    b. If the boards will be reused, the group leader may want to laminate the boards or identify "chips" (e.g., pieces of paper) that can be temporarily placed on the boards.
8. Group leaders are encouraged to ask follow-up questions and engage participants in discussion about the vocabulary words during the game.

9. Traditional BINGO rules apply. The group leader should determine each round what the goal is for the game. Examples include the following:

- Standard Line (Across or Down)
- Top, Middle, or Bottom Line
- Outside Edge/Square
- 2 Lines
- 4 Corners
- Full Board/Full House
- X Marks the Spot
- Arrow

Competency Restoration

B	I	N	G	O
		FREE  SPACE		

Player Instructions:

Use the word bank to design your own BINGO board! Follow the instructions the group leader gives you for what to write on the board.

B—Pleas, Verdicts & Penalties (#1–15)
I—Court Proceedings (#16–27)
N—Legal Jargon (#28–39)
G—A Defendant's Rights (#40–51)
O—People at Court (#52–63)

Competency Restoration BINGO Word Bank

B - Pleas, Verdicts & Penalties

1. COMMUNITY SERVICE
2. GUILTY
3. HOUSE ARREST
4. INSANITY
5. JAIL
6. NO CONTEST
7. NOT GUILTY
8. PAROLE
9. PLEA BARGAIN
10. PRISON
11. PROBATION
12. SUSPENDED SENTENCE
13. SVP REGISTRATION
14. TIME SERVED
15. TREATMENT

I - Court Proceedings

16. ARRAIGNMENT
17. COMPETENCY RESTORATION
18. CLOSING ARGUMENTS
19. CROSS EXAMINATION
20. DIRECT EXAMINATION
21. EVIDENCE
22. INITIAL APPEARANCE
23. OPENING ARGUMENTS
24. PRETRIAL HEARING
25. SENTENCING HEARING
26. TESTIMONY
27. VERDICT

N - Legal Jargon

28. ADMISSIBLE
29. ALIBI
30. BAIL
31. BURDEN OF PROOF
32. CONTEMPT OF COURT
33. FAILURE TO APPEAR
34. HEARSAY
35. OBJECTION
36. OATH
37. PERJURY
38. PLEA
39. PRETRIAL

G - A Defendant's Rights

40. APPEAL
41. DEFENSE ATTORNEY
42. FAIR TRIAL
43. FIFTH AMENDMENT
44. DECIDE STRATEGY
45. KNOWLEDGE
46. JURY TRIAL
47. MIRANDA RIGHTS
48. ATTORNEY-CLIENT PRIVILEGE
49. PRESUMPTION OF INNOCENCE
50. PUBLIC TRIAL
51. SPEEDY TRIAL

O - People at Court

52. BAIL BONDSMAN
53. BAILIFF
54. COURT CLERK
55. DEFENDANT
56. EXPERT WITNESS
57. EYEWITNESS
58. JUDGE
59. PLAINTIFF
60. PROSECUTOR
61. SECURITY
62. SHERIFF
63. STENOGRAPHER

Competency Restoration BINGO Question List

B - Pleas, Verdicts & Penalties

1. **COMMUNITY SERVICE:** This is when a defendant has to spend a certain amount of hours helping the community to pay back for the crime that was done. This type of unpaid work would be considered "volunteer" work if the court was not ordering that they do it.
2. **GUILTY:** This is a plea that means that the defendant is admitting that they did the crime and are accepting a punishment. This is also a verdict that means the judge or jury believes the defendant committed the crime.
3. **HOUSE ARREST:** This is punishment that involves staying at home, unless you have special permission to go somewhere else (like work or a funeral). A person with this penalty may have to wear an ankle monitor to prove that they are staying where they are supposed to be.
4. **INSANITY:** This defense involves the defense arguing that the defendant did the crime because of a mental illness or related disability.
5. **JAIL:** This is a short-term correctional facility where people can be housed pretrial or as a punishment.
6. **NO CONTEST:** This plea means that the defendant is accepting a punishment, although they are not admitting that they did the crime. Usually when someone uses this plea, they know that there is evidence that makes it look like they did the crime.
7. **NOT GUILTY:** This is a plea that means that the defendant is saying that they did not do the crime. This is also a verdict that means that the judge or jury believes that you did not commit the crime.
8. **PAROLE:** This refers to a period of supervision when someone is released early from prison. When they are released early, they may have to follow some extra rules on top of following the law.
9. **PLEA BARGAIN:** This is an agreement that the prosecutor offers the defense. They can offer a reduced sentence, reduced charges, or they can drop some of your charges if you have more than one. In exchange the defendant usually must plead guilty.
10. **PRISON:** This is a correctional facility where people go long term after they are found guilty of a serious crime.
11. **PROBATION:** This penalty involves a period of supervision where you have to follow some extra rules above and beyond following the law. People start this penalty without going to prison first.
12. **SUSPENDED SENTENCE:** This punishment involves time in a correctional facility being held over you as a later consequence. You get a chance to demonstrate good behavior or be on probation at first. If you cannot complete that lighter requirement successfully, then you may have to serve the held time in jail or prison.
13. **SVP REGISTRATION:** This punishment involves being required by law to regularly provide your information to law enforcement after being found guilty of a sex offense.
14. **TIME SERVED:** This punishment means the defendant is being given credit for the time they already served before a sentence was officially

given. The court would be saying that you do not have to serve more jail time because of the time you were locked up already.

15. **TREATMENT:** Being ordered to receive help due to a health problem. For example, the court can order you take medications due to a mental illness.

I - Court Proceedings

16. **ARRAIGNMENT:** This is a court hearing where the defendant is told the charges and asked what plea they want to enter.
17. **COMPETENCY RESTORATION:** This refers to the process of preparing a defendant to go back to court. This can involve learning more about how the court system works, talking about your case, and maybe even taking medications to make sure that you are mentally healthy enough to think clearly about your case and act properly in court.
18. **CLOSING ARGUMENTS:** This refers to the final statements made by the attorneys in a trial, summarizing the case they made for the court. The prosecution goes first and then the defense.
19. **CROSS EXAMINATION:** This is when a witness is asked questions by the side that they are expected to help the least. These questions can be challenging to answer.
20. **DIRECT EXAMINATION:** This is when a witness is asked questions by the side that they are expected to help the most. The witness might have a chance to prepare answers to these questions.
21. **EVIDENCE:** This refers to facts, statements, or objects that are used to prove whether a defendant did or did not do the crime.
22. **INITIAL APPEARANCE:** This refers to the first court hearing a defendant has after they are arrested or charged with a crime. During this part of the process, the court may inform you of your charges, set bail, assign an attorney to your case, or schedule your next court date.
23. **OPENING ARGUMENTS:** This refers to the summary statements that the lawyers make to the court at the beginning of a trial about what the judge or jury should expect during a trial. The prosecution goes first and then the defense.
24. **PRETRIAL HEARING:** This refers to any hearing that happens before a trial begins. At this time, the lawyers talk to the judge about your case.
25. **SENTENCING HEARING:** This refers to the court date when the judge tells the defendant what their punishment will be.
26. **TESTIMONY:** This refers to any official statements that a witness makes while under oath.
27. **VERDICT:** This is the final decision from the court about whether the defendant is responsible for the crime. The judge or jury decide this depending on what kind of trial you have.

N - Legal Jargon

28. **ADMISSIBLE:** This means something is allowed as evidence in court.
29. **ALIBI:** This is proof that the defendant was somewhere else when the crime happened.

30. **BAIL:** When someone pays a bond so that the defendant is temporarily let out of jail.
31. **BURDEN OF PROOF:** This refers to how sure a judge or jury must be in order to find a defendant guilty. For example, in criminal cases, this is "beyond a reasonable doubt."
32. **CONTEMPT OF COURT:** This is a charge anyone can receive for acting up in court.
33. **FAILURE TO APPEAR:** This is a charge a defendant can receive for not showing up at court when scheduled to do so.
34. **HEARSAY:** This term describes when someone is talking about things that they heard second-hand.
35. **OBJECTION:** This term is used by lawyers when they take issue with something that is being said in court.
36. **OATH:** This is another word for a promise. For example, in court, they may make you take one of these to promise to tell the truth.
37. **PERJURY:** This is a charge that someone can get when they lie in court after swearing to tell the truth.
38. **PLEA:** This describes the defendant's response to the charges against them. It is a word or short phrase that tells the court whether they are willing to accept a punishment for the crime.
39. **PRETRIAL:** This is another way of saying "before your case is decided" or "before your trial is finished."

G - A Defendant's Rights

40. **APPEAL:** This refers to your right to ask a higher court to hear your case with the goal of getting a better outcome.
41. **DEFENSE ATTORNEY:** This is the lawyer who represents you and tries to prove that you should not get punished for the crime you are accused of. If you can't afford to pay for one, you'll get one assigned to you.
42. **FAIR TRIAL:** This is the process of proving whether the defendant actually committed the crime. It involves lawyers making arguments, evidence getting presented, and witnesses testifying.
43. **FIFTH AMENDMENT:** When people refer to this, they are talking about their right to stay silent and not tell on themselves for committing a crime.
44. **DECIDE STRATEGY:** The defendant has a right to pick what plea to enter and determine whether they will accept a plea bargain that is offered to them.
45. **KNOWLEDGE:** The defendant has a right to understand the charges against them and what consequences they are facing.
46. **JURY TRIAL:** If you have this, your case will be decided by 12 community members, who are asked by the court to make a unanimous decision about whether you are guilty of the crime.
47. **MIRANDA RIGHTS:** Police officers are supposed to give people a warning before they question someone as a suspect in a case. They may have read you these or given you a paper with the warning on it.
48. **ATTORNEY-CLIENT PRIVILEGE:** This means that the conversations you have with your defense lawyer are private, just like your conversations

with your doctors. You have the power to talk to whomever you want about your case, but your lawyer is limited in what they can say to other people without your permission.

49. **PUBLIC TRIAL:** You have a right to have community members in court during your trial to help make sure everything is fair.
50. **PRESUMPTION OF INNOCENCE:** This refers to the fact that the court is supposed to assume that the defendant is innocent, unless and until they are proven guilty.
51. **SPEEDY TRIAL:** This means that the court has to move your case along without unnecessary delays. They do consider competency restoration a necessary delay.

O - People at Court

52. **BAIL BONDSMAN:** This is someone who lends people money who cannot afford to pay their bond on their own. They make money by charging the borrower a percentage of the money borrowed.
53. **BAILIFF:** This is someone who acts as a security officer for the court. He makes sure everything is safe and orderly at the courthouse.
54. **COURT CLERK:** This person is an administrative assistant for the court. They keep court records organized, collect fees, and will help schedule your next court date.
55. **DEFENDANT:** This is the person who is accused of having broken the law. In court, this is the term used to describe you.
56. **EXPERT WITNESS:** A person who knows a lot about a certain topic and is approved to tell the court about that topic. For example, a psychiatrist may tell the court about mental health medications.
57. **EYEWITNESS:** This person is someone who testifies in court about what they saw, heard, or otherwise observed.
58. **JUDGE:** This person is responsible for keeping order in court, deciding the verdict in a bench trial, and deciding the punishment for a defendant who is found guilty.
59. **PLAINTIFF:** This is the person who brings the case against the defendant. In criminal court, this is often the state/commonwealth on behalf of the victim.
60. **PROSECUTOR:** This is the lawyer who represents the victim or the public. They try to prove that the defendant is responsible for the crime and make sure that the defendant gets the biggest punishment possible if they are found guilty.
61. **SECURITY:** When people enter a courthouse, they may be searched and/or go through a metal detector. This is the person who is responsible for making sure only items that are allowed enter the courthouse.
62. **SHERIFF:** This is a kind of law enforcement officer. This person helps keep order and maintains jail facilities, along with other responsibilities.
63. **STENOGRAPHER:** This is the person who keeps a record of everything that is said in court by typing or talking into a device.

Competency Restoration Board Game

Rules & Instructions

Game board: Group leaders are encouraged to draw their own game board on a poster board or some alternative. A mini board is provided as a sample. However, group leaders are encouraged to make a more or less complex board based on their expected play time and functioning of players.

Game pieces: If accessible and permitted, actual board game token pieces can be used. Otherwise, the group leader should make a player piece for each defendant or have them make them themselves. This may involve using a small piece of paper with their name on it. If accessible and permitted, dice can be used. Otherwise, the group leader should fold up small pieces of paper with the numbers 1–6 written on them and place them in a cup/container that is large enough to shake up the papers.

Game play: All players should start with their "game pieces" on or around the "Arrest (START)" spot. Players then take turns "rolling the dice" to identify how many spaces forward their piece can possibly move. The active player's piece should not move until the end of their turn. The first player to go can be identified at the group leader's discretion or randomly by having each player "roll the dice" and having the person who yields the highest number go first. The following turns should go in order based on seating clockwise around the game board. A player who lands on an "F" space should be read a prompt in the "Factual" category. A player who lands on an "R" space should be read a prompt in the "Rational" category. A player who lands on a "C" space should be read a prompt in the "Consult With Counsel" category. Players who answer the prompt correctly move ahead, with the number of spaces they move corresponding to the "dice." Players who answer the prompt incorrectly stay at their original location for that turn. Special spots labeled "Wild" reflect chance cards, which can lead a player to go forward or backward on the board. Instructions are specific to each prompt. The winning player is the first to land on the "Release" spot (an exact "roll" is not necessary). At the group leader's discretion, the rest of the players may complete the round, potentially yielding more than one winner.

Additional instructions: Group leaders may read the game space prompts to players aloud off of these activity sheets. It is not necessary to go in the order listed (i.e., the prompts can be "shuffled"). Group leaders can also contribute their own prompts/questions to the game.

For the smoothest gameplay, group leaders may wish to put the Factual, Rational, Consult With Counsel, and Wild prompts on index cards or board game cards. If this is done, the cards should be shuffled and stacked in separate piles by category. With index cards/board game cards, players can read their own prompts aloud for the group.

Players are permitted to talk to each other about the answer to each prompt. The player whose identified turn it is should ultimately decide the final answer to the prompt. The group leader may facilitate discussion about the prompt topic during or after the turn is done. The group leader will ultimately decide if the provided answer is adequate, with feedback from the group.

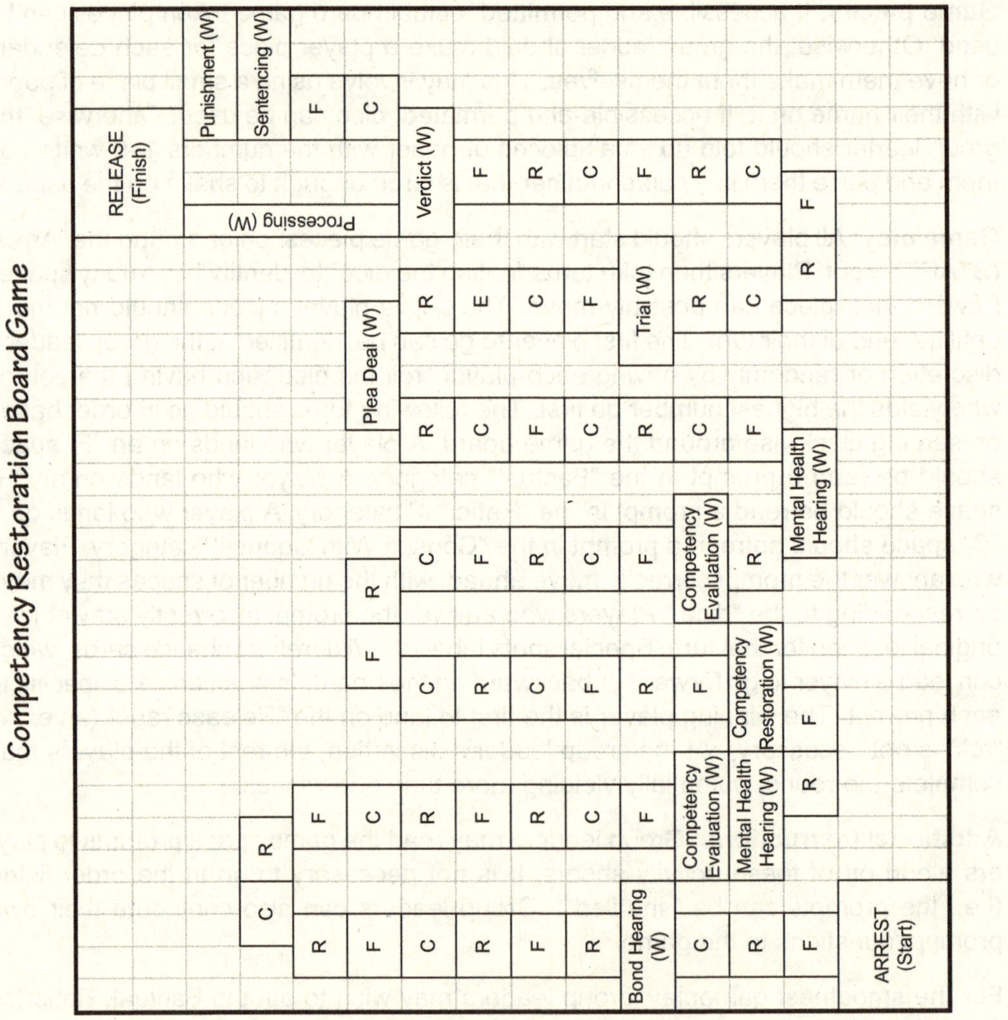
Competency Restoration Board Game
RELEASE (Finish)
Punishment (W)
Sentencing (W)
Processing (W)
Verdict (W)
Plea Deal (W)
Trial (W)
Mental Health Hearing (W)
Competency Evaluation (W)
Competency Restoration (W)
Competency Evaluation (W)
Mental Health Hearing (W)
Competency Evaluation (W)
Mental Health Hearing (W)
Bond Hearing (W)
ARREST (Start)

Competency Restoration Board Game Prompts

F - Factual Knowledge

- Where does a trial take place?
- Name 3 people that would be in the courtroom.
- What are two different names for the attorney who tries to make the defendant look guilty?
- How many classes of felony are there?
- How many classes of misdemeanor are there?
- What's the most serious kind of felony/misdemeanor
- What is a bench trial?
- What is a jury trial?
- What's the name of the type of lawyer that's on your side, as the defendant, in court?
- What's the judge's job?
- What's the stenographer's job?
- What 2 people help keep order in the court?
- Name 2 legal/Miranda rights.
- What is a verdict?
- What rights do you give up if you accept a plea deal?
- What are 2 more legal rights no one has mentioned yet?
- If someone is convicted of a felony for the first time, what rights can they lose?
- What are 3 examples of evidence?
- What is a continuance?
- What does this legal plea mean? (pick one: guilty, not guilty, no contest, Alford plea, not guilty by reason of insanity, guilty but mentally ill)

R - Rational Understanding

- Who can refer you for a competency evaluation?
- When can you be referred for a competency evaluation?
- What is the point of competency restoration?
- How do you know if your charge is serious or not?
- Are you charged with a felony or a misdemeanor?
- What class is your charge(s)?
- What's the maximum amount of time in jail/prison you could face if you were convicted?
- What's the biggest fine you could have to pay if you were convicted?
- Why might you want to take a plea deal?
- How would you decide if a plea-deal offer was good or not?
- How would a felony conviction affect your life?
- What's the difference between being sentenced to 1 year incarcerated for a felony versus being sentenced to 1 year incarcerated for a misdemeanor?
- Is the judge for you or against you? [trick question]
- Is the jury for you or against you? [trick question]
- If you decided to use the insanity defense, and it was successful, what would happen to you next?

- How much time do you serve in jail/prison if the court decides that you were insane at the time of the defense? [trick question]
- Does evidence help or hurt your legal case? [trick question]
- Who can bring evidence into court in your case?
- Why might you want a jury trial instead of a bench trial?
- What would happen to your case if the jury can't make a unanimous decision about it?

C - Consult With Counsel

- How should you behave in court?
- Name 2 things you should NOT do in court?
- What's your lawyer's name?
- How much information should you share with your attorney?
- Would you rather have a court-appointed lawyer or a paid lawyer, and why?
- Should you share or conceal information from your attorney?
- Name 1 plea option that you do NOT want to use and explain why.
- You just found out that you and your lawyer disagree about your legal strategy—he thinks you should take a plea deal, and you think you should go to trial. What do you do next?
- What does the color of your lawyer's clothing tell you about how well he will defend you?
- What should you do if you think the witness is on stand lying about your behavior on the day of the offense?
- What should you do if you have a question in court?
- Are you allowed to laugh if someone says something you think is really funny in court?
- Can you cry if you get upset in court?
- If you get really mad in court, what is 1 thing you can do to help yourself calm down?
- What should you do if you REALLY have to go to the bathroom while you're at court?
- What should you do if they're going to be speaking English in court, and you don't speak English as your first language?
- Why would your attorney want to know as much as possible about what happened leading up to your arrest?
- What should you do if you disagree with the recommendations of your attorney?
- Who makes the final decision on whether to take a plea deal?
- What can your attorney tell other people about your legal case or legal strategy without your permission?

W - Wild

- Come up with a legal question for the person to your RIGHT. If they get it wrong, you move forward 1 space. If they get it right, you move back 1 space.
- Come up with a legal question for the person to your LEFT. If they get it right, you move forward 1 space. If they get it wrong, you move back 1 space.
- You made bond! Move forward 1 space.
- Your application for bond got denied! Move back 1 space.

- Your appeal got approved! Move forward 1 space.
- Your application for appeal got denied! Move back 1 space.
- Evidence against you got thrown out! Move forward 1 space.
- You discovered evidence that will help your case! Move forward 1 space.
- You just found out they have a new witness to testify against you! Move backward 1 space.
- A pro bono lawyer agreed to take your case! Move forward 1 space.
- Your court-appointed lawyer got reassigned! Move back 1 space.
- Your lawyer answered your phone call! Move forward 1 space.
- Your lawyer says they won't talk to you about your case until you're restored to competency! Move back 1 space.
- Your case got continued, so your lawyer has more time to strategize! Move forward 1 space.
- Your case got continued, so you have to wait longer for your case to be resolved. Move backward 1 space.

Competency Vignettes for Discussion

Instructions: The purpose of these vignettes is to teach individual(s) undergoing competency restoration in group or one-on-one settings about what it means to be competent to stand trial. This may also help individual(s) undergoing competency restoration to process their personal barriers to competency in a less threatening manner.

Each vignette describes defendants in hypothetical scenarios. Each scenario includes some indication that the person described might be competent or might not be competent. These vignettes are designed to facilitate discussion rather than prompt participants to guess whether a person is "competent" or "not competent."

At the beginning of the activity, remind the individual(s) undergoing competency restoration about what it means to be competent to stand trial. In general:

> *In order to be competent to stand trial, a defendant must know basic information about how the court system works, understand their personal legal situation, and be able to help with their defense. They have to be able to work productively with their lawyer, pay attention and behave appropriately in court, and testify effectively about their side of the story, if needed.*

Read each vignette, one at a time, to the individual(s) undergoing competency restoration. Alternatively, have the individual(s) read each scenario aloud, being mindful of their reading ability and providing supportive assistance as needed. In a group setting, group members may take turns reading, as a means of promoting engagement and investment in the activity.

After reading a vignette, engage the individual(s) undergoing competency restoration in a discussion about the signs that the defendant in the scenario might be incompetent or competent. This may involve pointing out certain aspects of the scenario and asking participants what they think about it. In a group, try to get everyone to make some kind of comment or suggestion at some point in the activity.

Additional prompting can be used to facilitate broader discussion. It may be appropriate to ask the group questions such as "How would you feel if you were this person?" "How do you think this person would react if the judge decided that they were incompetent?" or "What do you think would help this person become competent?"

Competency Vignettes for Discussion #1

For each of these scenarios, we will discuss whether the defendant is competent or incompetent. We're also going to discuss what makes you think that they are competent and/or what makes you think they might not be competent.

- Barbara understands the roles of the judge, defense attorney, and the prosecutor. She believes that the defense attorney is a vampire and the prosecutor is a werewolf. She believes that the criminal justice system is unjust because these supernatural beings have control over the outcome at court. Based on this information, are they likely competent or incompetent? What other information would you want to know?
- Joe always speaks up while in court, raising his hand to ask the judge questions even after his lawyer tells him to wait. When Joe's lawyer talks to him about this, Joe says, "This is my life on the line—I speak up in court because I have to make sure I'm representing my best interests. I don't care if I get held in contempt." Based on this information, are they likely competent or incompetent? What other information would you want to know?
- Rita has a medical condition that leads her to have to go to the bathroom about every 15 minutes. This can be disruptive in court, since she has to leave the room frequently to use the bathroom. It also makes it challenging for her to have a long conversation with her attorney about her case. Based on this information, are they likely competent or incompetent? What other information would you want to know?
- Bob knows that there are 4 different pleas in his state. He understands that one means that he didn't do what he's accused of, one means that he did do it, and one means that he did do it but shouldn't be held accountable because of his mental illness. He says the other plea option doesn't matter because he's not going to use it. He can't remember the names of any of the pleas, but when someone uses the words in a sentence, he seems to understand what that person is talking about. Based on this information, are they likely competent or incompetent? What other information would you want to know?
- Sarah doesn't want to go forward with her court case. She thinks that the charges against her are not a big deal and believes that if she acts like she's incompetent for long enough, the charges against her will be dropped. She has a long history of mental illness and has been arrested several times in the past. At least once before, her legal charge was actually dropped. Based on this information, are they likely competent or incompetent? What other information would you want to know?

Competency Vignettes for Discussion #2

For each of these scenarios, we will discuss whether the defendant is competent or incompetent. We're also going to discuss what makes you think that they are competent and/or what makes you think they might not be competent.

- Rachel is facing serious charges that could result in a lot of prison time. She wants to take a plea bargain, even though the offer will probably involve a lot of time incarcerated, because she figures she could always appeal it while she's in prison, prior to finishing her time. Based on this information, are they likely competent or incompetent? What other information would you want to know?
- Anthony doesn't trust his defense lawyer. This is the first time they're working together, and they only met once, for about 5 minutes. The meeting seemed to go fine, but it was really short, and he didn't get as much time with his lawyer as he wanted. Anthony has had other lawyers in the past, and they weren't successful getting him out of jail. He is not hopeful about the outcome of his current case. Based on this information, are they likely competent or incompetent? What other information would you want to know?
- Maria feels as though she has to testify in court because that is the only way the court will hear her side of the story. She can recite her Miranda rights but doesn't think the right to remain silent applies to her because she's a prophet, and prophets need to speak the truth regardless of personal consequences. Based on this information, are they likely competent or incompetent? What other information would you want to know?
- Fred tells his lawyer that he is an undercover FBI agent and has been working undercover at psychiatric hospitals for most of his career. Fred has a history of receiving social security disability insurance, and during his time in psychiatric hospitals, he was diagnosed with schizophrenia. Fred believes that when he goes to court, the judge will find him guilty so that he can go undercover in the jail and uncover bad things that happen there for the FBI. Based on this information, are they likely competent or incompetent? What other information would you want to know?
- Steve tells his lawyer that he told the police that he committed the crime he's accused of, even though he didn't really do it. He tells his lawyer that he was really tired and confused at the time and told the police whatever they wanted to hear just so that they would stop bothering him and let him go home. His lawyer thinks that this is outrageous, and knowing that Steve has a history of depression, refers him for a competency evaluation. Based on this information, are they likely competent or incompetent? What other information would you want to know?

Competency Vignettes for Discussion #3

For each of these scenarios, we will discuss whether the defendant is competent or incompetent. We're also going to discuss what makes you think that they are competent and/or what makes you think they might not be competent.

- Elizabeth knows the legal system inside and out. She can explain the different legal pleas, the roles of everyone in the courtroom, and how to behave in court. She says she knows this information because she is the Queen of Virginia and helped write the policies and procedures for court and the legal process. She believes that if she goes to trial to face her legal charges, she will be treated just like any other person, without special treatment, because that is how the system is designed in Virginia. However, she hopes that the judge/jury will go easy on her because of her contributions to the legal system. Based on this information, are they likely competent or incompetent? What other information would you want to know?
- Juan has never gotten in trouble for his behaviors in court before. He understands that it is important to stay quiet in court and to let his attorney do most of the talking for him. English is not Juan's first language, and sometimes he does not understand the fancy legal words that are being used in the courtroom. He is not comfortable with asking his lawyer for help when he is confused about the language used in court. Based on this information, are they likely competent or incompetent? What other information would you want to know?
- Tonya does not believe that she needs psychiatric medications and is not taking any at the moment. However, people keep telling her that she is talking too fast or not making sense with her speech. She admits that she has been getting angry at the smallest things, including when being told to slow down or quiet her speech. When she is told those things, she usually ends up getting even louder. Based on this information, are they likely competent or incompetent? What other information would you want to know?
- Patrick has been arrested several times and has had some very bad interactions with police officers and people who work in the court system. He feels like everyone sees him as a criminal before they even get to know him. He does not think that he will get a fair trial for his current case because of how things have gone for him in past court cases. Based on this information, are they likely competent or incompetent? What other information would you want to know?
- Skylar keeps calling the prosecutor the "district attorney," calling competency to stand trial "fitness to stand trial," and calling people who are found unrestorable "Jacksoned." Those are the correct words for those concepts in New York but not in this state. Based on this information, are they likely competent or incompetent? What other information would you want to know?

Competency Vignettes for Discussion #4

For each of these scenarios, we will discuss whether the defendant is competent or incompetent. We're also going to discuss what makes you think that they are competent and/or what makes you think they might not be competent.

- Derrick confidently tells you that he is super smart and 100% smarter than his defense lawyer and everyone else at court. He says that he plans to act as his own lawyer and represent himself in court because he can do a better job than any lawyer. Based on this information, are they likely competent or incompetent? What other information would you want to know?
- Sasha is charged with child neglect and cannot discuss her legal situation without crying. She tries to hold it together, but she starts crying any time someone asks her about her family background, her charges, her legal strategy, or possible outcomes for her case. She is extremely worried that she will lose custody of her children if she is found guilty of the pending charge. Based on this information, are they likely competent or incompetent? What other information would you want to know?
- Steve just turned 19 and has never gotten into trouble with the law before. He is facing a felony "abduction" charge for allegedly locking his car doors and not letting his girlfriend out of the vehicle. He has never talked to someone with a felony on their record before and seems pretty naive about his charge and how the court system works. Based on this information, are they likely competent or incompetent? What other information would you want to know?
- Betsy thinks the conditions at the jail are horrible and finds the food disgusting. She is refusing to eat anything at the jail and refusing to talk to anyone besides her defense attorney. She has been trying to get her lawyer to advocate for her and other inmates at the jail and speak up to the court about the conditions there. Based on this information, are they likely competent or incompetent? What other information would you want to know?
- Drew is able to explain the roles of everyone at court and explain how court is adversarial. He knows that his defense lawyer is on his side and will argue that he is innocent and that the prosecutor is against him and will argue that he did the crime. It does not make sense to him that the prosecutor is the person who comes up with and offers plea deals, but he understands that is how things work. He believes that his defense lawyer will give him advice on whether to accept any plea deals that are offered and that he can ask his defense lawyer questions about any offers. Based on this information, are they likely competent or incompetent? What other information would you want to know?

Mock Court

Instructions:

1. This activity should begin with an explanation that the purpose of a *mock trial* or *mock court* is to help everyone get familiar with the court process and practice some of the skills they might need for court, like staying focused and speaking in front of others.

2. A brief printed summary of a case should be handed out to group participants or projected on a screen. The group leader, or a group member, should read the case summary aloud to the rest of the group. It is recommended that the case involve only 1 pending charge, rather than multiple charges, for simplicity.

   Example: Louie Charles is a 37-year-old man who is accused of shoplifting several packets of tuna and gallon of milk from a local grocery store in Virginia. It is alleged that on the day in question, he entered the store, sought the identified items, and placed them in a shopping cart. He then took the shopping cart and items past all points of sale, out of the store building, and walked down the street with just the grocery items toward his home. Video surveillance shows that store employees were mostly busy with other customers as he left the building, and they did not make efforts to stop Mr. Charles or prompt him to pay for the items. However, law enforcement did intercept Mr. Charles with the items in question. As part of the investigation, a store employee rang up duplicates of the items found with Mr. Charles and estimated the value of items taken to be under $20.

3. A brief definition of the crime in question, perhaps with the formal legal code for the crime in question, should also be distributed to defendants and/or projected on a screen. The group is encouraged to discuss the offense, including the specific elements of the crime, together in group. The group leader should emphasize that each of these elements must be proven *beyond a reasonable doubt* in order for the defendant to be convicted of a crime. This definition should be added to the provided script as part of the jury instruction.

   Example: Virginia Code § 18.2–103, Concealing or taking possession of merchandise; altering price tags; transferring goods from one container to another; counseling, etc., another in performance of such acts:

   > *Whoever, without authority, with the intention of converting goods or merchandise to his own or another's use without having paid the full purchase price thereof, or of defrauding the owner of the value of the goods or merchandise, (i) willfully conceals or takes possession of the goods or merchandise of any store or other mercantile establishment, or (ii) alters the price tag or other price marking on such goods or merchandise, or transfers the goods from one container to another, or (iii) counsels, assists, aids or abets another in the performance of any of the above acts, when the value of the goods or merchandise involved in the offense is less than $1,000,*

shall be guilty of petit larceny and, when the value of the goods or merchandise involved in the offense is $1,000 or more, shall be guilty of grand larceny. The willful concealment of goods or merchandise of any store or other mercantile establishment, while still on the premises thereof, shall be prima facie evidence of an intent to convert and defraud the owner thereof out of the value of the goods or merchandise.

4. Particularly if the group appears confused about how the allegations map onto the definition of the crime in question, facilitate discussion about what specific behaviors are alleged to be against the law. It may help to provide examples unrelated to the case in question but related to the same legal code.

   Example: Let's say an 18-year-old woman, Clover, is charged with shoplifting. In her case, she is accused of going to a thrift store and switching the price stickers of a high-value item (a winter coat) and low-value item (a scarf). She allegedly attempted to pay for the high-value item (the coat) at the lower price (the price of the scarf). In her case, the cashier noticed the incorrect price sticker at checkout. The cashier also remembered that something similar happened before with Clover and accused Clover of intentionally swapping the stickers on the day in question.

5. Collaboratively assign participants to roles. Higher functioning, or more actively engaged defendants, may be most appropriate for more demanding roles (e.g., lawyers). Lower functioning, or more passively engaged defendants, may be most appropriate for less demanding roles (e.g., jury members). If there are not enough participants to cast all jurors, the correct number of jurors in the current jurisdiction (e.g., 12) should be emphasized. It may be indicated to run a mock *bench trial* instead of a *jury trial* if the number of group members is quite limited.

6. Facilitate small group planning discussion, amongst (A) the prosecution team, including the prosecuting attorney(s), victim, and prosecution witness(es); (B) the defense team, including the defense attorney(s), defendant, defense witness(es); and (C) the fact finders (i.e., judge, jurors).

   (A) The prosecution team should discuss how to prove that the defendant committed the crime. This may involve identifying specific arguments to make in the opening/closing statements, identifying questions that can be asked to various witnesses, and what other evidence can be presented to build their case. The group facilitator should remind this team that the burden of proof is on the prosecution—it is up to their side to prove that the defendant deserves a punishment.

   (B) The defense team should discuss how to show that the defendant does not deserve a punishment for the crime. This may mean arguing that they did not do the crime, that the crime was not their fault, or that the crime did not happen. They should decide whether it is a good idea or a bad idea for the defendant to testify in their own defense. The group facilitator should remind this team that the defendant is innocent until proven guilty—they do not necessarily have to "prove" that the defendant is innocent.

(C) The fact finder team should discuss what they have already heard about the case and their thoughts about what evidence or testimony they would expect to see in this case. The group facilitator should remind this team that when they decide the case, they must focus on the elements of the crime and whether the prosecution team has proven each element. The group facilitator should also remind this group that in order to find the defendant guilty "beyond a reasonable doubt" they need to be 90%–100% sure that the defendant did the crime. This standard may be discussed by the group but not reduced/altered for the purpose of the mock trial.

7. Set up the room for a trial. Have the *judge* sit at the front of the room, behind a desk or podium if possible. Set up the *jury* box, with enough chairs for jurors at one side of the room. Set up the prosecution area, with chairs/table in front of the judge, on the side closest to the jury. Set up the defense area, with chairs/table in front of the judge but on the side further from the jury. Set up the *witness* box, with a chair to the side of the judge. Prepare the *bailiff* to stand next to the witness box. Prepare the *stenographer* to sit across from the jury. Have everyone take their designated places once ready to begin the mock trial.
8. Have the group act out the mock trial, reading the script and the lines they have created.
9. Debrief after the trial is complete. Ask each participant for their thoughts/feelings about participating in their designated role. Discuss whether the group agrees with the verdict and how difficult it was to come up with a verdict. Process whether the mock proceedings seemed fair or biased. Discuss the extent to which having a strong/weak lawyer, active/passive role in one's defense, etc. might affect the outcome of a trial based on the same evidence. Ask group members to consider whether the mock court experience made them think about, or rethink, how to approach their own cases. Prompt the group members to ask any questions they might have about court proceedings generally or the trial process in particular.

Competency restoration providers are encouraged to modify the following script for their jurisdiction. This script has been kept intentionally vague so that the forms can be used with various case examples (i.e., different charges, allegations, defendant names). A group facilitator may come up with a unique case example to be used for the purpose of a mock trial, or the mock trial case information can be decided by the group.

For lower functioning groups, it may be beneficial to have the group simply read a pre-created mock trial script that is already complete aloud with various group members assigned to different roles. In such cases, a designated *court reporter/stenographer* may take the role of a narrator.

Use of a mock trial may involve an opportunity to provide education that actual court experiences may occur at a faster pace and with more advanced vocabulary. It may help to troubleshoot and review what the defendant(s) can do if they feel lost or confused while in court.

Mock Court

Mock Court Role Assignments

Judge	
Jury members	
Bailiff	
Prosecutor	
Prosecution witness1	
Prosecution witness2	
Defendant	
Defense attorney	
Defense witness1	

Mock Court Script

Entrance

Bailiff: All rise. The ____________________________________ Court is now in session. The Honorable Judge ______________________ is presiding.

Judge: [walk to seat, and sit down] Thank you. Everyone but the jury may be seated. Bailiff, please swear in the jury.

Swearing In and Initial Instruction

Bailiff: Jurors, please all raise your right hands. [wait for hands to be raised] Do you solemnly swear that you will listen to the details of this case, and at the end of trial, decide a true and fair verdict?

Jury: Yes/I do.

Bailiff: Thank you. You can also be seated. [jury sits down]

Judge: For the record, what is the case we are hearing today?

Clerk: Your Honor, today's case is the State/Commonwealth v. ________________.

Judge: Members of the jury, your duty today is to determine whether the accused defendant, ________________________, did commit the crime of ______________________________________ as alleged. You will hear both sides of the argument today, starting with opening arguments. You will then hear facts and evidence presented that may help you answer the question before you today. You will then hear closing arguments from both sides. When closing arguments are finished, I will provide instructions regarding your deliberation. I will remind you of the specific law that is to be applied in this case. You will then leave the courtroom to meet privately, select a **foreperson**, deliberate, and arrive at a unanimous verdict. The **foreperson** will deliver the verdict to the court.
[to the **prosecutor**] Is the prosecution ready?

Prosecutor: [stand up] Yes, your Honor. [sit down]

Judge: Is the defense ready?

Defense attorney: [stand up] Yes, your Honor. [sit down]

Judge: Proceed.

Prosecutor's Opening Statement

Prosecutor: [stand up] Good day your Honor and members of the jury. I represent ________________________. In our time today, we the prosecution plan to show that on or about ____________ (date): ____________________

____

____

As you listen to this case, I urge you to consider:

1. ____

 ____

2. ____

 ____

3. ____

 ____

I am confident that you will hear these facts and decide a verdict in favor of ________________________. Thank you. [sit down]

Defense Attorney's Opening Statement

Defense attorney: [stand up] Hello your Honor and members of the jury. Thank you for your time today. I represent ____________________, who I will argue should not be punished for the crime you will hear about today. The defense plans to show:

____

____

As you listen to this case, I beg you to consider:

1. ____

 ____

2. ____

 ____

3. ____

____

I am confident that you will hear these facts and come to a ______________ verdict. Thank you. [sit down]

Presentation of Evidence

Judge: Thank you. Prosecution, you may call your first witness.

Prosecutor: [stand up] Thank you, your Honor. We call to the stand ____________________.

Judge: Will ______________________ please approach the witness stand? [Witness walks towards witness box and is escorted/directed to sit by bailiff]

Bailiff: [to witness] Please raise your right hand. Do you swear to tell the truth, the whole truth, and nothing but the truth?

Witness: Yes/I do.

Bailiff: You can be seated. [**Witness** sits down]

Prosecutor: Can you please state your name for the court? [**Witness** answers] [Prosecutor asks direct examination questions, and **witness** answers]

1. ____

____

2. ____

____

3. ____

____

Thank you. Your honor, no further questions. [sit down]

Judge: Defense counsel may cross-examine the witness.
[Defense attorney stands and asks cross-examination questions; **witness** answers]

1. ____

____

2. ____

____

3. ____

____

Judge: Does the prosecution have questions for re-direct?

Prosecutor: No, your Honor. [sit down]/Yes, your Honor. [if yes, ask follow-up questions quickly, and **witness** answers] [when done, sit down]

Judge: [to witness] You may step down. The prosecution may call their next witness.

Prosecutor: [stand up] Thank you, Your Honor. We call to the stand ____________________.

Judge: Will ____________________ please approach the witness stand? [Witness walks towards witness box, and is escorted/directed to sit by bailiff]

Bailiff: [to witness] Please wear your right hand. Do you swear to tell the truth, the whole truth, and nothing but the truth?

Witness: Yes/I do.

Bailiff: You can be seated. [**Witness** sits down]

Prosecutor: Can you please state your name for the court? [**Witness** answers] [Prosecutor asks direct examination questions, and **witness** answers]

1. ____

____

2. ____

____

3. ____

____

Thank you. Your Honor, no further questions. [sit down]

Judge: Defense counsel may cross-examine the witness.
[Defense attorney stands and asks cross-examination questions; **witness** answers]

1. ____

____

2. ____

____

3. ____

____

Judge: Does the prosecution have questions for re-direct?

Prosecutor: [stand up] No, your Honor. [sit down]/Yes, your honor. [if yes, ask follow-up questions quickly, and **witness** answers] [when done, sit down]

Judge: [to witness] You may step down. Does the prosecution have a third witness?

Prosecutor: [stand up] No, your Honor. [sit down]

Judge: Okay, the defense may call their first witness.

Defense attorney: [stand up] Thank you, Your Honor. We call to the stand ____________________.

Judge: Will ______________________ please approach the **witness** stand?
[Witness walks towards witness box, and is escorted/directed to sit by bailiff]

Bailiff: [to witness] Please wear your right hand. Do you swear to tell the truth, the whole truth, and nothing but the truth?

Witness: Yes/I do.

Bailiff: You can be seated. [**Witness** sits down]

Defense attorney: Can you please state your name for the court? [**Witness** answers]
[Defense attorney asks direct examination questions, and **witness** answers]

1. ____

____

2. ____

____

3. ____

____

Thank you. Your honor, no further questions. [sit down]

Judge: The prosecution may cross-examine the witness.
[Prosecutor stands and asks cross-examination questions; **witness** answers]

1. ____

____

2. ____

____

3. ____

____

Judge: Does the defense have questions for re-direct?

Prosecutor: No, your Honor. [sit down]/Yes, your honor. [if yes, ask follow-up questions quickly, and **witness** answers] [when done, sit down]

Judge: [to witness] You may step down. Do you have an additional witness?

Defense attorney: No, your Honor. *[if the defense team has decided that the defendant should not testify]* [sit down]/Yes, your honor. We call to the stand ____________________. *[if the defense team has decided that the defendant should testify]*
(if the defendant is testifying, continue. If not, skip to Prosecutor's Closing Argument.)

Judge: Will the defendant, _________________ please approach the witness stand?

[Defendant walks towards witness box, and is escorted/directed to sit by bailiff]

Bailiff: [to defendant] Please wear your right hand. Do you swear to tell the truth, the whole truth, and nothing but the truth?

Defendant: Yes/I do.

Bailiff: You can be seated. [Defendant sits down]

Defense attorney: Can you please state your name for the court? [Defendant answers]
[Defense attorney asks direct examination questions, and **witness** answers]

1. ____

   ____

2. ____

   ____

3. ____

   ____

Thank you. Your honor, no further questions. [sit down]

Judge: The prosecution may cross-examine the witness.
[Prosecutor stands and asks cross-examination questions; **defendant** answers]

1. ____
____
2. ____
____
3. ____
____

Judge: Does the defense have questions for re-direct?

Defense attorney: No, your Honor. [sit down]/Yes, your Honor. [if yes, ask follow-up questions quickly, and **defendant** answers] [when done, sit down]

Judge: [to defendant] You may step down. Do you have an additional witness?

Defense attorney: No, your Honor. [sit down]

Prosecutor's Closing Argument

Judge: Okay, the prosecution may begin their closing argument.

Prosecutor: Honorable judge and members of the jury. Today you heard:
____
____
____
____
____

I believe that you will find, beyond a reasonable doubt, that the defendant ________________ did in fact ______________________________. Thank you.

Defense Attorney's Closing Argument

Judge: Defense, you may make your closing argument.

Defense attorney: Members of the jury and the honorable judge. Today you heard:

____

____

____

____

____

I urge you to find that the defendant ______________ is not guilty of the crime of _________________________. I strongly hope that law enforcement is able to find the person who did commit this crime—but that person is not my client, _____________(defendant). Thank you.

Jury Instructions and Deliberation

Judge: Members of the jury. You have heard all the arguments, testimony, and other evidence for this case. It is now up to you to determine whether the facts presented today prove beyond a reasonable doubt that a crime was committed and that the defendant _______________ committed that crime. I remind you that the law in question is defined as such:

(*Legal Code*) ____

____

____

____

____

In a moment, the **Bailiff** will escort you to the jury room where you can deliberate and decide the verdict. All of you must be in agreement on that verdict—it must be unanimous. The first thing you will do is select a **foreperson**. The **foreperson**'s duty will be to sign down the verdict statement from the jury when you have come to an agreement and to read that statement to the court when you return to the courtroom. The **Bailiff** will now escort you to the deliberation room.

Bailiff: All rise. [everyone stands, **Judge** exits, **Bailiff** leads jury to deliberate] [The **Jury** has ______ minutes to deliberate. This involves discussing what they heard in the case about the allegations, evidence, and law. They may vote and re-vote until they come to a unanimous decision. Then the **Bailiff** is called to escort them back to the courtroom.]

Judge: Have to reached a verdict?

Foreperson: [stands up] We have your honor.

Judge: What have you decided?

Foreperson: We the jury, in the case of the State/Commonwealth v. ______________, find the defendant ______________________(verdict) with respect to the charge of ______________________________. [The **foreperson** hands the **Bailiff** the signed verdict form]

Judge: Thank you **foreperson**, and thank you to the jury for your service to-day. [if guilty] A sentencing hearing will be held next Tuesday at 8:00 a.m. in this courtroom. OR: Court is adjourned. [if not guilty]

APPENDIX B

Clinically-Focused Competency Restoration Materials

Medication Worksheets

Instructions: The worksheets in this section are designed to accompany verbal information about a defendant's treatment with psychotropic medications during competency restoration. These worksheets are designed to be completed by a defendant (A) taking notes as education is provided to them or (B) independently as "homework." Alternatively, a prescriber may complete a form such as this for use as a visual aid when educating a defendant undergoing competency restoration about their medications.

A defendant's ability to understand and remember information about their mental health treatment is parallel to competency. For example, an individual who is able to learn about their rights as a patient in an inpatient setting should be able to learn about their rights as a defendant in the legal context. Therefore, these worksheets may be used as tools to gather information about parallel knowledge and abilities.

If intended for use as a parallel data-gathering tool, these worksheets should not be completed by a clinician for the defendant. Responses should also not be copied verbatim (duplicated) from a previously completed worksheet, so that their current understanding can be accurately assessed.

My Medication Information

1. Today I am prescribed medication by this person:

   Name: ______________________________

   Job: ______________________________

2. Today I am prescribed this medication:

   (A)

   (B)

   (C)

3. The medication is supposed to help me with:

   (A)

   (B)

   (C)

4. Because I am diagnosed with:

   (A)

   (B)

   (C)

5. This means that mental health staff think I have these symptoms:

   ____

   ____

   ____

Medication Over Objection

1. I am getting mental health treatment at (where):

   ____

2. If they decide that I am not able to make my own medical choices, I trust these people to make medical decisions for me.

   (A) Name: ______________________________

   Relationship: ______________________________

   Contact Information:

   (B) Name: ______________________________

   Relationship: ______________________________

   Contact Information: ______________________________

   (C) No one

3. If there is not a trusted person who is able to make medical choices for me, I may have to go to court about medications. This is the court that would hear my case:

   ____

4. At court, a ______________________ will decide if I should be given medications. They will decide this based on:

   ____

   ____

5. If I disagree with their decision, I have a right to ______________________. This means that I would have to:

   ____

   ____

Slater Method Modified Workbook

Instructions: Restoration providers are strongly encouraged to refer to the Slater Method manual's Part I: Instructional Manual for more detailed instructions on how to use this tool and related resources:

Wall, B., Krupp, B., & Guilmette, T. (2003). *Returning your client to court: The Slater Method: An educational tool to restore competence to stand trial in mentally retarded defendants*. Department of Mental Health, Retardation and Hospitals, Eleanor Slater Hospital.

The following workbook is a modified version of the workbook from Section II of the Slater Method manual; permission to partially reproduce the manual was granted by Dr. Barry Wall on behalf of Eleanor Slater Hospital of the Rhode Island Department of Mental Health, Retardation and Hospitals. The authors of the original manual encouraged competency restoration providers making use of the Slater Method to modify language based on the needs of defendants in their jurisdiction, etc. In this version, we attempt to include updated language that is more widely applicable across jurisdictions, with additional suggestions for prompts and answers. Space is included for restoration providers to document the responses provided by defendants during interventions without needing a separate response sheet. Additionally, a column is included for scoring responses so as to remove the need for a separate score sheet.

In this workbook packet, modified Column A (related to factual knowledge) prompts from the original Slater Method workbook are listed numerically (e.g., 1, 2, 3). Modified Column B (related to rational understanding) prompts from the original workbook are listed alphabetically (e.g., A, B, C). As in the original workbook, all questions are *examples*. Restoration providers are encouraged to adapt questions, elaborate upon them, and to add additional questions to foster discussion. Prompts/questions that we recommend reading verbatim are in **bold.** Samples of acceptable answers are in (parentheses). Prompts to assist the restoration provider are in [brackets].

In the space provided, restoration providers are encouraged to document the defendant's response to each prompt provided and note any additional prompts/questions that are provided.

In the right-most column (Rating), restoration providers are encouraged to score responses on a 3-point scale: Poor (P), Fair (F), or Good (G). The creators of the Slater Method provide the following guidelines for ratings: A rating of Poor is assigned if "the defendant does not answer questions, erroneously articulates a concept, or says 'I don't know' or 'I don't remember,' in response to questions." A rating of Fair is assigned to responses that provide a limited description of a concept or include some confused information and is somewhat understandable. A rating of Good is assigned if the client provides a generally complete and understandable answer. These ratings should be used to identify whether a defendant has demonstrated an acceptable level of knowledge in that area or if this topic should be reviewed in another session. All answers should ideally be scored as Fair or Good before moving on to the next module.

Slater Method: Modified Module 1

Question/Prompt (Answer) [Instruction]	**Rating**
1. **Who sent you for restoration?** (The judge; a doctor; a competency evaluator.) [Provide education about the cause for restoration if necessary]	
2. **Why did they send you for restoration?** (Because the judge says I'm not able to stand trial; Because the doctor says I have to learn about court; Because I'm not competent.) [Provide education about the function of competency restoration if necessary]	
3. **A charge is the thing people say you did that is against the law. If someone says you broke the law, the police might charge you with a crime. What is/are your charge(s)?** [Provide education about charge name(s) if necessary] **What does it mean if I was accused of [crime]? What might I have been accused of doing?**	
4. **What does the charge mean?** (E.g., if the charge is arson, a correct response would be, "They said I set a fire.") [Provide education about the charge definition if necessary]	
5. **What crime did the police say you did? What were you accused of doing to break the law?** [Provide education about the allegations if necessary]	
6. **When did this happen? On what date? What month/year? About what time?** [Provide education about the date of the offense if necessary]	
7. **What is a crime?** (It's when you do something bad and break the law.)	

A. **How come you're in trouble?** (Some people say I did something bad. They say I did a crime; They said I broke the law; They said I did [offense].)	
B. **Just because you're in trouble, does that mean you go to jail?** (No.) **How come?** (Because I have to tell them I'm guilty or they have to prove I'm guilty before they can punish me. They have to prove it first.) **Just because you got arrested for [crime], does that mean you will get punished? Does everyone who gets arrested get sent to jail or prison?** (No. I'm not guilty yet. I only get a punishment if they say I'm guilty.)	
C. **Is it a crime to steal a candy bar? Alt: Is it a crime to go into someone's house without permission?** (Yes.) **Why?** (Because you didn't pay for it. Because it's against the law.) Another way to ask this line of questioning at a later time may be: **Is it a crime to buy a candy bar? Alt: Is it a crime to go into someone's house if they invite you?** (No.) **Why?** (Because you paid for it; Alt: Because they said you could go inside.)	
8. **When someone gets charged with a crime, they have to enter a plea. What is a plea?** (It's the answer I give when the judge asks me if I did it; It's if I say I did it or not.)	
9. **You get to choose what answer (or plea) you want to give/enter. How many pleas can you choose from?** (jurisdiction specific: ___) [Provide multiple choice options if needed]	

10. **What are they?** (jurisdiction specific, but may include guilty, not guilty/innocent, no contest/nolo contendre, not guilty by reason of insanity/guilty except for insanity/guilty but mentally ill/the insanity defense.)	
11. **What does it mean to say you're guilty? Alt: What does it mean if you plead guilty?** (When they ask me if I did it, I tell them that I did it.)	
D. **Why might someone decide to say they are guilty?** (Because they did it; Because there is a lot of proof.)	
12. **What does it mean to say you're innocent? Alt: What does it mean if you plead not guilty?** (When they ask me if I did it, I tell them I did not do it.) E. **Why might someone want to say they are innocent/not guilty?** (Because they didn't do it. Because they want to fight the charges. Because they think they can win.)	
13. **What does it mean to plead nolo contendre/no contest?** (When they ask me if I did it, I tell them I'll take a deal; I'm not going to fight the charges. I am not going to say I did it or didn't do it; I'll just let the judge decide.)	
F. **Why does somebody have to tell the judge their plea? Why does someone have to choose between [list plea options in jurisdiction]?** (Because you have to give the judge an answer to the question before the judge or jury can decide your case; I am answering the question about whether I did it or not.)	

G. **Is what you tell the judge the same thing as what the judge or jury finally decides? Is a plea the same thing as a finding/verdict?** (No.) **Why is it not the same? What's the difference?** (The finding is what the judge decides about my case. They will decide if I'm guilty or innocent.) **Just because you say you are innocent, does that mean the judge will automatically believe you?** (No.)	
14. **What does it mean to be <u>found</u> guilty? What does it mean if the judge says I am guilty?** (The other side shows that I did it. The judge or jury says that I really did do it.)	
15. **What does it mean to be <u>found</u> not guilty?** (The judge or jury says that I really didn't do it. The other side couldn't show that I did it.)	
16. **What would happen to you if they said you were guilty?** (I get some kind of a punishment. I *may* have to go to jail.)	
17. **What would happen to you if they said you were not guilty?** (I get to go home [or other living arrangement]. They set me free; I get released.)	
18. **What is probation?** (I get to go home, but if I do something bad, I have to go back to jail; I have to follow rules, and I can't get in trouble again.) **Where would you live if you were on probation: in jail, in a hospital, or at home/in the community?** (Home/community.) **What is it called when you get a punishment, but you don't have to go to jail or prison, you get to go home but you have to follow rules?** (Probation.)	

H. **Why do some people like/want probation?** (Because they aren't locked up.)	
I. **Why do some people not like/want probation?** (Because it's hard to follow all the rules; Because they have no place to live.)	
19. **What is a sentence?** (It's my punishment if they say I did it. It's how long I have to stay in jail, or how long I have to be on probation.)	
J. **When would you get a sentence?** (If the judge says I'm guilty.)	
K. **Does everyone who is accused of a crime get a sentence?** (No.)	

In/after reviewing this module, provide the defendant with printed or clearly written information about their charge(s) and sentencing guidelines in simplified form. If this has already been provided, see if they need a new copy.

Slater Method: Modified Module 2

In reviewing this module, show the defendant a courtroom illustration, diagram, or photo(s). Ask them who sits where. As they name the judge, jury, lawyer, etc., ask them the following questions.

Question/Prompt (Answer) [Instruction]	**Rating**
1. **What is the job of the judge? What is the judge supposed to do? What decisions can the judge make?** (Make sure that everybody plays fair; Decides the verdict and sentence; Decides if I am innocent or guilty in a bench trial.)	
2. **Can you talk to the judge?** (Yes.) **When can you talk to the judge?** (Only if they ask me a question; When I have permission.)	
3. **What is the job of the jury?** (Decides whether I am guilty or innocent; Decides the verdict in a jury trial.)	
4. **Can you talk to the jury?** (No.) **When can you talk to the jury?** (Never.)	
A. **How come the jury listens to your side of the story?** (They are supposed to listen to my side and to the other side, then decide whom they believe.)	
5. **What is the job of your defense lawyer?** (Tries to help me out; Talks to me; Listens to me when I talk to him; Gives me legal advice; Helps me figure out what to do and what to say.)	
6. **Can you talk to your defense lawyer?** (Yes.) **When can you talk to your lawyer?** (Before I go to court. When I am in court.)	

7. **What is the job of the other side's lawyer?** (Tries to convince the judge or jury that I did it; Tries to convince the court that I should be punished; Tries to make me look guilty.)	
8. **Can you talk to the other side's lawyer?** (Yes.) **When can you talk to the other side's lawyer?** (Only when he asks me a question when I am on the witness stand.)	
B. **How come the other side's lawyer wants to make you look bad?** (His job is to try to make the judge or jury put me in jail; He is against me)	
C. **Who is on your side in the court?** (My lawyer; My family [depending on the charge]; Some witnesses may be on my side.)	
D. **Who is not on your side?** (The other lawyer; Some witnesses may not be on my side.)	
E. **Is the judge on your side?** (No. She is in the middle/neutral. She does not take sides until the end.)	
F. **Who is neutral? Who is on no one's side?** (The jury and the judge until the end when one of them decides my case; the bailiff; the clerk; the stenographer.)	
9. **What is a witness?** (Somebody who was there when it happens; They come in and talk about what they saw; Someone who is an expert; Someone who can tell the court about how I am.)	

10. **Can you talk to a witness?** (No.) **When can you talk to a witness?** (Never.) **Who can ask witnesses questions?** (The lawyers. The judge.)	
11. **If another person sits in the box, what are they called?** (A witness.) **Are you allowed to talk to them?** (No.)	
12. **What do you do when someone is sitting in the box talking?** (Sit quietly; Listen to what they say; Quietly tell my lawyer if I get upset or if I think they are lying.)	
13. **What is your job when you go to court?** (To stay calm and behave well; To pay attention; To listen to everything that is happening; To quietly tell my attorney if I don't understand something; Maybe to be a witness.)	
14. **Can you be a witness?** (Yes.) **When are you a witness?** (When I sit in the witness box; When I tell my side of the story.) **What is it called when you tell your side of the story?** (Testify.)	
G. **Who gets to ask you questions when you tell your story/testify?** (My attorney; The prosecutor/other attorney.)	

H. **What is the other side's lawyer trying to do when he asks you questions?** (To get me in trouble; Catch me in a lie; To make a mistake; To make me look bad.)	
15. **What is your job if you sit in the (witness) box?** (To tell the truth; To answer the questions the lawyers and the judge ask me; To tell the judge or my lawyer if I don't understand the question.)	
I. **Can anyone force you to be a witness in your case?** (No.) **Why not**? (I have the right to remain silent; I can plead the fifth.)	

In/after reviewing this module, show the defendant a photograph of a witness testifying. Ask them who is sitting where. As they name the judge, attorney, and witness, review the above questions with them to make sure that they understand the scenario.

Slater Method: Modified Module 3

Question/Prompt (Answer) [Instruction]	**Rating**
1. **What happens when you get to court?** (People at court talk about what happened; Your case is presented; They look at evidence.)	
A. **How come you have to go to court?** (Because they say I did something wrong, and when they say you did something wrong, they give you a charge and they take you to court; At court they'll decide if I'm guilty or not guilty.)	
2. **Having a trial is different from just going to court. There is a trial only if you plead not guilty [innocent]. If you plead guilty or nolo contendre, there is no trial—instead, the judge just gives you the sentence.** **If you say you're guilty, is there a trial?** (No.) **If you say [plead] innocent, is there a trial?** (Yes.) **If you say [plead] nolo, is there a trial?** (No.) [Because these are yes/no questions, repeat from a different perspective to make sure the client knows. For example: What are your possible pleas? Which plea is it where they would have a trial?]	
3. **What happens during a trial?** (Both sides get to tell their story; One side gets to go first, then the other side gets to go; Each side asks questions; The judge and jury listen to both sides; Then they decide whether you are guilty or innocent.)	
4. **There might not be a trial. For example, if you tell them you are guilty or take a plea deal, then you don't need a trial. If there is no trial, what happens?** (I get the plea/deal; The judge gives me a sentence; They don't hear both sides. There is no jury.)	

B. **Why don't you need a trial if you plead guilty or take a deal?** (Because if I plead guilty everyone knows I'm getting a punishment; Because if I plead guilty I'm telling them I'm not fighting my case; Because they already have an answer to the question.)	
5. **Taking a plea deal means that you admit you did something bad. People make a deal to get an easier punishment. What's good about taking a plea?** (It might keep me out of jail; They might lower my charge; They could drop a charge; It might let me go home.)	
6. **There are also some bad things about taking a plea deal (making a deal). You must give up some rights. If you take a deal, you give up the chance to go to trial and let the jury decide your case. You have to admit that you did something bad; You're not fully able to tell your side of the story at court; You don't get the chance to go back to court and have them listen to your story again (an appeal); You will definitely get some kind of a punishment, but you might get no punishment if they found you not guilty at trial. What are the bad things about taking a deal?** (I may have to tell them I did something bad, even if I didn't do it or if I don't want to; I don't get a second chance to talk about the charge; Nobody gets to listen to my side of the story in court.)	
7. **Will you go to trial?** (Maybe; If I want to; I won't know until I talk with my lawyer.) [*The answer depends on the charge.*]	
C. **How come you probably won't go to trial?** (My lawyer might want me to take a plea deal.)	
D. **What is a possible bad thing about going to trial? What is a risk?** (I could lose; I could get punished.)	

E. **What is something good about going to trial?** (I can tell my side of the story; I could win and go home.)	
8. **What happens when you take a plea deal (make a deal)?** (I have to say I did something bad; I don't get a trial; I don't get a chance to go back to court if I don't like how everything turns out.)	
F. **When is there is no jury?** (When I take a deal; When I plead guilty; When it's a bench trial.) **Why is that?** (Because when I take a deal, there is no trial; Because in a bench trial the judge decides.)	
G. **What's in it for you if you take a deal?** (I probably won't have to go to jail; I won't have to go to jail for so long; I might get probation; I might get time served.)	
H. **When could you go to court and not have a trial?** (Other hearings; When you go to court, they talk about your case and your court dates; If you say you are innocent, they have a trial so they can listen to both sides before the judge/jury decides who they believe; If you say you're guilty or take a deal.)	

Slater Method: Modified Module 4

Question/Prompt (Answer) [Instruction]	Rating
1. **Who will you talk to before you go into the courtroom?** (My lawyer.)	
2. **Who can you talk to in court whenever you want to?** (My lawyer.)	
3. **You can also speak to other people in court, but only when they ask you a question. Who are these people?** (I can only talk to the judge when they ask me a question; I can only talk to the other side's lawyer when they ask me a question while I am on the witness stand.)	
4. **Who can you never talk to in court?** (I can't talk to the jury; I can't talk to a witness; My lawyer will talk to them for me.)	
5. **If you have to go to the bathroom while you are in court, who can you tell this to?** (My lawyer.)	
6. **If you don't understand what is being said about you in court, who can you tell this to?** (My lawyer.)	
7. **What do you say to him if you don't understand what is being said?** (I say, "I don't know what is going on" or "I'm confused, please help.")	
A. **Why is it important to tell your lawyer if you don't understand what is being said?** (Everybody goes to court to talk about me; My job is to make sure that I know what people are saying about me and my case; I might miss something important.)	

8. **What are the things you need to tell your lawyer?**	
[Ask the client to tell you their story of what happened. If important parts are left out, help them make it fluent but don't add new material and don't write down incriminating information. Review law enforcement records so you can help them make sense of the situation]	
9. **Let's go over the story of what happened**. [Review their version; Paraphrase; Highlight important details.]	
B. **Let's talk about what you just told me** (question 9). **What are the most important things that you told me?** **Why are these things important?**	
10. **What do you do if a witness tells a lie about you?** (Tell my lawyer.)	
C. **Why do you tell your lawyer if somebody lies about you?** (I'm not supposed to talk to the witness myself; The lie might make me look bad; My lawyer can ask them about it)	
11. **What do you do if a witness says a mean thing about you or something about you that you don't like?** (Tell my lawyer.)	
D. **Why do you tell your lawyer, if somebody says things about you that you don't like?** (I'm not supposed to talk to the witness myself; I need to tell my attorney because I want to look as good as possible.)	

12. **What do you do if your lawyer tells you to do something that you don't like? For example, what if your lawyer wants you to change your story?** (Tell my lawyer I'm uncomfortable, so we can talk about it; Ask them why; Tell somebody that I know, like [name of family member, staff person].)	
E. **Why is that important?** (Because my lawyer should help me; I want to trust my lawyer; If I don't feel comfortable with my lawyer, I should tell somebody.)	
13. **What would you do if your lawyer wants you to take a plea deal, but you don't want to?** (Tell them; Talk to them about it; Explain why.)	
14. **If you talk with your lawyer about a deal, and he still wants you to take it, and you aren't happy about it, who else can you talk to?** (Family member; staff member.)	
F. **Why is that?** (Because it's my choice about whether I want to take a deal if they offer me a deal. I have my rights.)	
15. **The other side's attorney may try to confuse you on the witness stand. When they ask you a question that you don't understand, what would be the wrong thing to say?** (Yes, I understand; To just answer the question.) **What will you say instead?** (I could say "I don't understand what you're saying," or "Ask me again please.")	
[Take the client through several examples of leading questions. Try to get them to follow your lead, and then show them how they are being led so that they will recognize the pattern themselves. Then work with them to resist answering leading questions, and have them practice asking for clarification if they do not understand a question.]	

G. **If somebody you know got arrested for stealing, and he really didn't do it, but he wants to take the deal, why is that a problem?**	
[Then go through examples (e.g., "This is John. He is the defendant. This is Mr. Smith, his lawyer. What is John accused of?")]	

Slater Method: Modified Module 5

Question/Prompt (Answer) [Instruction]	**Rating**
1. **How are you supposed to behave in court?** (Be nice; Pay attention; Listen; Don't yell; Talk to my lawyer.)	
2. **Can you laugh in court?** (No.) [Repeat yes/no questions from a different perspective.]	
3. **Is it good to sit quietly in court?** (Yes.)	
4. **Does that mean you can never talk in court?** (No; I can talk in court sometimes.)	
A. **When can you talk in court?** (When the judge asks me a question.)	
5. **Can you tell jokes/yell/etc. in court?** (No.) [Repeat yes/no questions from a different perspective.] **Why not?** (Because going to court is serious; Because it is important to show the judge/jury respect.)	
6. **Is it good to talk quietly in court?** (Yes.)	
7. **Can you get mad in court?** (Yes; But I can't yell or scream.) **What do you do if you are getting very upset?** (Tell my lawyer; Ask to take a break; Take deep breaths. Use my coping skills.) **[This is a good time to review/teach coping skills to manage distress in a courtroom setting.** Explain and discuss why some may not be appropriate (e.g., pacing the room)]	

B. **Why can't you laugh/yell/scream in court?** (Because that won't make me look good; Because going to court is serious.)	
C. **Why is it important to speak up in court?** (Because they are talking about me; Because I have to stand up for myself; Because I have to understand what is going on.)	
8. **Can you walk around in court?** (No; Not while they are talking about my case.) [Repeat yes/no questions from a different perspective.] **Why not?** (Because I have to stay in my area; Because it's not allowed.)	
9. **What would happen if you got up and talked directly to the judge?** (They would tell me I have to sit down; They might get upset; I might get in trouble.)	
10. **What would happen if you got angry and screamed and yelled in court?** (They would tell me to stop; They might take me out of the courtroom; I might get in trouble.)	
D. **Why is it important to not stand up and move around when court is going on?** (It would make me look bad; I need to look good to help my case.)	
[Make some direct comments on the client's emotions and behaviors, and work with them to extinguish negative behaviors. For example: I notice that when we talk about court, you giggle a lot. Why is that? Can you do that when you are in court? How come? Let's practice talking with your lawyer right now. I want you to talk about your case without giggling]	
[Make some direct comments on their emotions and behavior, and work with them to promote positive behaviors. For example: You are doing a good job talking about your case. Make sure that you talk about this with your attorney—it's important]	

Reward Point Tracker

Name: ______________________________

Slater Method Session: Date & Module **Scores:** Poor, Fair, Good	**Points Earned**	**Provider Initials**	**Reward Redeemed**

Points Needed to Earn Reward: ________

Rewards Agreed Upon: ____________

Sample Reward Point Tracker

Name: Mr. M

Slater Method Session: Date & Module **Scores:** Poor, Fair, Good	**Points Earned**	**Provider Initials**	**Reward Redeemed**
10/13/24: Module 1 Scores: Poor to Fair	2	MS	
10/15/24: Module 1 Scores: Poor to Good	2	MS	
10/20/24: Module 1 Scores: Fair to Good	2	MS	Redeemed 10/20/24
10/22/24: Module 2 Scores: Poor	2	MS	
10/24/24: Module 2 Scores: Poor	2	MS	
10/27/24: Module 2 Scores: Poor to Fair	2	MS	Redeemed 10/27/24

Points Needed to Earn Reward: *6*

Rewards Agreed Upon: *One music video*

My CogRem Goals

Goals for My Ability to Focus

Short-Term Goals

Example: I want to be able to have a good, logical conversation for ___ minutes.
1.
2.
3.

Long-Term Goals

Example: I want to be able to talk to my lawyer about my case for ____ minutes straight if needed.
1.
2.
3.

Goals for My Memory

Short-Term Goals

Example: I want to remember my lawyer's phone number.
1.
2.
3.

Long-Term Goals

Example: I want to be able to remember my court dates and what happened at each hearing.
1.
2.
3.

Goals for My Problem-Solving Abilities

Short-Term Goals

Example: I want to be able to talk through the steps to solve one problem I'm having, like how to sleep when it is noisy.
1.
2.
3.

Long-Term Goals

Example: I want to be able to think through and discuss my plea options with my lawyer.
1.
2.
3.

Goals for Time Management

Short-Term Goals

Example: I want to make a list of the groups/activities that I want to attend each day.
1.
2.
3.

Long-Term Goals

Example: I want to plan out what steps I need to take to get ready to appear in court.
1.
2.
3.

Discussion

What can you do to help achieve these goals?

What Can Help Me Reach My *Goals*

Circle what steps you, your lawyer, and the court can take to help you reach your goals. Come up with your own ideas and add your own answers in the space provided.

Skills that I know how to use:

Steady my breathing	Take a break and come back another time	Make a list/Use my list
Relax my muscles	Talk it out	Use my calendar/ planner
Ask for extra medication	Ask for an explanation	Ask for a reminder
1.		
2.		
3.		

Things that my lawyer can do to help:

Ask me if I need help reading something	Use simple words	Speak loudly when talking to me
Ask me if I need help writing something	Give me reminders	Speak gently when talking to me
Ask me if I need a break	Ask questions to make sure I understand	Give me encouragement
1.		
2.		
3.		

What else would help me do my best at court:

Pen and paper	Closed captioning	Built-in breaks
Seeing my paperwork	Hearing amplification device	Court in the morning
Having my notes	Interpreter/Translation	Court in the afternoon
1.		
2.		
3.		

Legal Word Bank

Instructions: This word bank is designed for use with individuals with word-finding difficulties. The word bank itself is not an activity. Rather, the word bank is a tool for helping individuals undergoing competency restoration to find a word they cannot "remember." This is an alternative to simply assuming/inferring what word the person is trying to "remember" and telling them what it is.

This word bank may be of use when working with individuals with lower intellectual functioning, lower educational attainment, or cognitive decline.

When an individual undergoing competency restoration is having difficulty "remembering" the word they are trying to use, provide them with this word bank.

Inform them that the word bank contains a list of vocabulary words that may help jog their memory.

If the individual undergoing competency restoration does not recognize the word that they need from the overall set of options, there are strategies for helping them identify or "remember" the word. Some suggestions for assistance are on the bottom of the word bank page; the individual may use these to cue themselves. The competency restoration provider can also use these as prompts when the individual seems "stuck."

Cognitive Remediation Cues

What type of word is it? Maybe the topic will help. [Point them to a topic area, grouped by column]

What type of word is it? Maybe the category will help. [Point them to a topic area, grouped by column]

Do you remember what letter the word starts with? The terms in each column are in ABC order. [Run your finger down the column to show them]

Do you remember what sound the word starts with? Test to see if any words sound right. [Encourage them to read the words out loud, in full or in part]

Is there any term you can eliminate? What words definitely do not seem right? [Encourage them to cross off the words with a pencil, or make a separate list with possible options]

Still stuck? I'll eliminate some options for you [Cover up a column, or select options from a column to visually remove those words as options]

Still stuck? Here's an extra hint . . . [Use your discretion and creativity to help them find the word they want. For example, "Does it start with a B?" or "Does it almost have the word *defend* in it?"]

Legal Word Bank

Courtroom Personnel	*Legal Rights*	*Legal Strategy*	*Courtroom Behaviors*	*Outcomes/ Penalties*	*Other Legal Terms*
Clerk	Appeal	Decide Myself	Ask	Community Service	Bench Trial
Defendant	Confront Accuser	Decide With My Attorney	Bathroom Break	Incarceration	Bond
Defense Attorney	Decide Your Legal Strategy	Guilty	Coping Skill	Jail	Contempt of Court
Interpreter	Defense Attorney	Let My Attorney Decide	Focus	Parole	Continuance
Judge	Jury Trial	No Contest/ Nolo Contendre	Listen	Prison	Expert
Jury	Know Charges	Not Guilty	Mindfulness	Probation	Felony
Clerk	Know Evi-dence	Not Guilty by Reason of Insanity	Raise Hand	Program	Misdemeanor
Prosecutor	Question Witness	Plea Bargain	Wait	Suspended Sentence	Nolle Prosequi
Stenographer/ Court Reporter	Remain Silent	Testify/ Testimony	Whisper	Time Served	Perjury
Witness	Trial	Trial	Write	Treatment	Sentencing

What type of word is it? Maybe the topic will help.
What type of word is it? Maybe the category will help.
Do you remember what letter the word starts with? The terms in each column are in ABC order.
Do you remember what sound the word starts with? Test to see if any words sound right.
Is there any term you can eliminate? What words definitely do not seem right?
Still stuck? Ask for a helpful hint!

Legal Math

Instructions: Restoration providers should have defendants complete this worksheet independently if they are allowed a writing instrument. If the defendant is not allowed a writing instrument, the restoration provider is encouraged to help the defendant "show their work" and note their answers on the worksheet or whiteboard.

Some defendants may experience difficulty with vision or reading, and so the restoration provider may need to read the word problems out loud for them.

Some defendants may have difficulty figuring out what information is relevant and which information is not relevant. The restoration provider is encouraged to help them figure out what information to focus on and what information to ignore.

Some defendants may not understand the steps needed to complete the word problems, which vary in difficulty. Restoration providers are encouraged to refer defendants to the "Hints" to make sure that they are going through all the steps necessary to complete the problems. Restoration providers are also encouraged to provide their own hints, as long as they are not giving the defendant the final answers.

Some "Bonus" questions are included to call attention to more numbers that are involved in the legal processes. These may also serve as prompts for a discussion break between more problems. Restoration providers are encouraged to ask additional follow-up questions and facilitate relevant discussion about the court system between questions or after the exercise is completed.

At the end of this worksheet, defendants are prompted to create their own word problem for others to solve. If this worksheet is being used in a group setting, group leaders are encouraged to present these questions to the full group to solve if time permits. It may be helpful to present the questions using a whiteboard or other visual aid, particularly if the questions are complicated. If this worksheet is being used with a defendant in individual work, group leaders are instead encouraged to have the defendant lead them through how to solve the problem they created. This may be a good opportunity for rapport building.

Answer Key:

1. 12, 11, Bonus: varies by court/system	6. 48, Hint: 48
2. 12, 9, Bonus: No	7. $500; $5,000
3. 31, Hint: 36	8. $500, $5,475; $50, Hint: 7, 365
4. 60, Hint: 60	9. 6, 5; $2,500
5. 9, Bonus: 1.5 years	10. To Be Determined

Legal Math

Who knew the law involves so much math? Show how your math skills by completing these legal word problems.

1. A **jury** is a group that is usually made up of ______ people from the community. All of them must be in agreement for a final jury decision to stand. If ______ jurors are in agreement, but just 1 juror disagrees with the rest of the group, the whole trial process may have to start over from the beginning.

Bonus: How many people make up a **Grand Jury**? ______

2. Andrew is facing up to ______ months of jail time, if he is found guilty of his 1 misdemeanor charge. He has been waiting in jail for his case to be heard for 3 months so far. If he gets credit for those 3 months, how many more months could he have to spend in jail at most? ______ months

Bonus: Does a judge **have to** give people credit for the time they are hospitalized?

3. Miho was ordered by a judge to serve 3 years of **good behavior**. She has completed 5 months of good behavior so far, without any violations. How many more months does she have to be on good behavior? ______months.

Hint: 3 years is the same as ______ months.

4. Kris was sentenced to serve 5 years of **probation**, with the term of probation starting the day that he is released from jail. He was in jail for 1 year before he was released. How many more months of probation will he have to serve? ______ months

Hint: 5 years is the same as ______ months.

5. Brit was sentenced to 18 months of **jail time** after being found guilty of 2 misdemeanor offenses. In her area, people usually only actually serve half of the jail time that they are officially given. How many months should she expect to actually spend in jail? ______ months

Bonus: 18 many months translates to ______ years.

6. Tal was just given a **suspended sentence**. The judge told him that he has to complete 4 years of probation. If he does that successfully, he is all done with his sentence. If he violates probation, he could have to serve up to 4 years in jail or prison. That is called "suspended time" or "time suspended." He completed 13 months of probation before violating for the first time. How many months could the judge tell him he now has to serve in jail or prison?

Bonus: 4 years is the same as ______ months.

7. Heidi's **bond** was set for $5,000. She does not have that much money saved up to spend on bailing herself out of jail, but she does not want to be in jail either. A bail bondsman offered to cover her bond if she pays him 10% of that $5,000. She will not get back the $____________ she pays the bail bondsman to cover her bond, no matter what. She would get back all of the $____________ if she had that much money to pay directly to the court, as long as she showed up for her scheduled court dates.
8. Dave is currently on **house arrest**. He was required to pay $50 to set up the equipment needed to complete house arrest. While on house arrest, he has to pay $15 per day to the court. That means that in his first month, he has to pay $____________. It also means that for each full year on house arrest, he would have to pay $____________ plus the startup cost of $______.

Bonus: There are ______ days in a week, 30 days in an average month, and ______ days in an average year.

9. Lauren's sentencing guidelines tell her that she is officially facing 1 to 5 years of imprisonment and/or a fine up to $2,500 if convicted of her charge. She is facing a **mandatory minimum** penalty of 6 months of jail time if found guilty. That means in reality the judge could sentence her to serve from __________months to __________years in jail if found guilty, and she may also have to pay a **fine** up to $____________.
10. Create your own legal word problem for your others to solve:

Connecting Thoughts, Emotions, and Behaviors

To learn how thoughts, emotions, and behaviors are connected, we first have to know what each of these terms mean. Let's take a look:

THOUGHTS

Some people experience **thoughts** as words or pictures that flow through their mind.

Sometimes the words or pictures are positive (like thinking about a good time with friends), and other times they can be sad or scary (like thinking about the worst possible thing that could happen in your legal case). Even though it might seem odd, we can even have positive and negative thoughts about the same thing or situation.

For example, some people find that thinking about leaving the hospital or jail for court is both scary (because they don't know exactly what will happen) and positive (because they're ready to move on to the next step in their case).

EMOTIONS

Everyone has **emotions (feelings)**. When we feel anger, anxiety, happiness, or sadness—these are all emotions. It's important to remember that emotions are temporary and that they *can* change, sometimes quickly.

BEHAVIORS

Actions/Behaviors are simply the way we act and the things that we do physically.

For example, when you're angry, you might want to push or shove. When you're happy, you may want to give someone a high five. When you're anxious or sad, you may want to stay away from other people or avoid talking about your case. These are all actions/behaviors.

Connecting Thoughts, Emotions, & Behaviors

Whenever we encounter a **situation**, it's normal to have specific feelings about it. It's also normal for these feelings to lead us to perform certain behaviors or actions. Let's look at an example of how thoughts, emotions/feelings, and actions/behaviors are connected.

Situation: You have an upcoming competency evaluation to see if you're ready to go to court to face your charges.

Thought: You **think** you're not going to do well and will have to stay in the hospital or jail longer, maybe forever.

Emotion/Feeling: This thought might lead to the **emotion/feeling** of sadness. Many people who feel sad also feel as if there is no hope and, therefore, no reason to put in effort or try to work on their situation.

Actions/Behaviors: The emotion/feeling of sadness might then lead a person to the **action/behavior** of saying "no" to groups or individual meetings focused on helping them become competent.

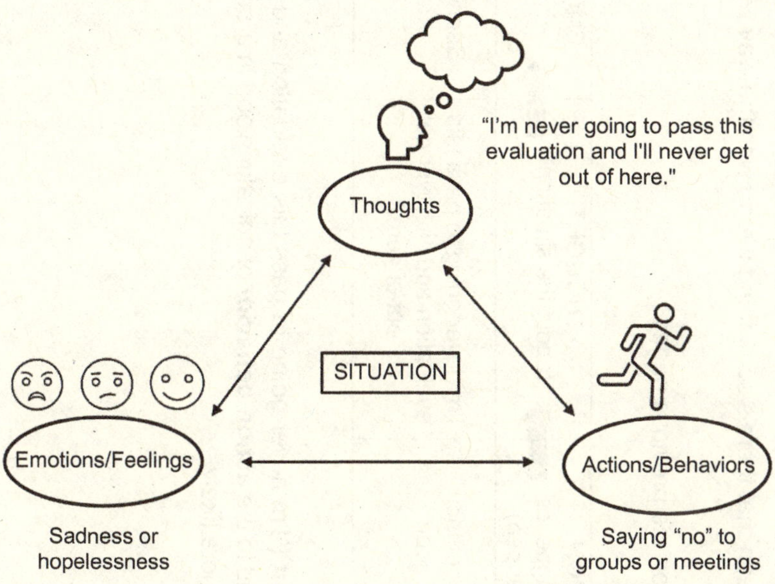

Changing Our Thoughts to Change Our Emotions & Behaviors

To change our **emotions (feelings)** and **actions (behaviors)**, we often must *first* change the way we **think** about a **situation**.

- This doesn't always mean that there's something *wrong* with the way we think, but sometimes we need to make room for other possibilities.
- Let's use the example on the previous page:

SITUATION (what has happened or might happen) →	**THOUGHT** (about the situation) →	**EMOTION/FEELING** (related to our thought) →	**ACTION/BEHAVIOR** (related to our emotion and thought)
I have a competency evaluation soon	"I'm never going to pass this evaluation and I'll never get out of here."	Sadness/Hopelessness	Avoiding restoration groups/individual sessions.

In this situation, the **thought** ("I'm never going to pass this evaluation and I'll never get out of here") and the resulting **emotion** (sadness/hopelessness) can lead to the **action/behavior** of not taking part in groups or individual sessions that might otherwise make passing the evaluation possible or more likely.

Changing Our Thoughts to Change Our Emotions & Behaviors

The good news is that we can choose to have **different thoughts** about the same situation, which can lead to **different emotions** and **different actions/behaviors**.
Let's take a look using the same example:

SITUATION (what has happened or might happen) →	**THOUGHT** (about the situation) →	**EMOTION/FEELING** (related to our thought) →	**ACTION/BEHAVIOR** (related to our emotion and thought)
I have a competency evaluation soon ↓	"I'm never going to pass this evaluation and I'll never get out of here." ↓	Sadness/Hopelessness	Avoiding restoration groups/individual sessions
SAME SITUATION: I have an upcoming competency evaluation	**DIFFERENT** THOUGHT: "If I study and go to groups/sessions, I can pass the evaluation and move on in my case.	**DIFFERENT** EMOTION: Hope/Optimism	**DIFFERENT** ACTION/BEHAVIOR: Going to groups/individual sessions and studying

In this case, we can see that thinking about the same situation in a different way can **change our feelings about the situation**, which can then **alter the way we behave**.

Practicing Our Skills: Part 1

First, it will be helpful to think of a **situation** that has (or is) related to a strong **emotion**. In the example we've been using, the situation of the upcoming evaluation is related to the emotion of sadness/hopelessness.

- Step 1. Now you list a personal *situation* associated with a strong *emotion/feeling* in the "**SITUATION**" column.
- Step 2. Next, write the *emotion/feeling* related to this situation in the "**EMOTION/FEELING**" column.
- Step 3. List the *thought(s)* about your situation that led to the *emotion* you listed in the "**THOUGHT**" column.
- Step 4. Now list the *actions/behaviors* that resulted from your *emotions/feelings* in the "**ACTION/BEHAVIOR**" column.

SITUATION (what has happened or might happen) →	**THOUGHT** (about the situation) →	**EMOTION/FEELING** (related to our thought) →	**ACTION/BEHAVIOR** (related to our emotion and thought)
(EXAMPLE) I have an upcoming competency evaluation	(EXAMPLE) "I'm never going to pass this evaluation and I'll never get out of here."	(EXAMPLE) Sadness/Hopelessness	(EXAMPLE) Avoiding restoration groups/individual sessions
(YOUR SITUATION)	(YOUR THOUGHT)	(YOUR EMOTION)	(YOUR ACTION/BEHAVIOR)
↑ Step 1	↑ Step 2	↑ Step 3	↑ Step 4

Practicing Our Skills: Part 2

Now, let's work on coming up with different *thoughts* that might be more helpful and how they might lead to different emotions/feelings and actions/behaviors.

- Step 5. List a more helpful thought about your situation in the **"DIFFERENT THOUGHT"** column.
- Step 6. Name a new emotion associated with your *different thought* in the **"EMOTION/FEELING"** column.
- Step 7. List how your behaviors might change (in the **ACTION/BEHAVIOR** column) if you were able to accept your new thought.

SITUATION (what has happened or might happen) →	**THOUGHT** (about the situation) →	**EMOTION/FEELING** (related to our thought) →	**ACTION/BEHAVIOR** (related to our emotion and thought)
See Example from Part 1	See Example from Part 1	See Example from Part 1	See Example from Part 1
SAME SITUATION: I have an upcoming competency evaluation	**DIFFERENT** THOUGHT: "If I study and go to groups/ sessions, I can pass the evaluation and move on in my case.	**DIFFERENT** EMOTION: Hope/Optimism	**DIFFERENT** BEHAVIOR: Going to groups/individual sessions and studying
See "Your Situation" from Part 1	See "Your Thought" from Part 1	See "Your Emotion" from Part 1	See "Your Action/Behavior" from Part 1
SAME SITUATION:	**DIFFERENT** THOUGHT:	**DIFFERENT** EMOTION:	**DIFFERENT** ACTION/BEHAVIOR:
	Step 5	Step 6	Step 7

Individual Practice:
Changing Our Thoughts to Change Our Emotions and Behaviors

SITUATION (what has happened or might happen) →	**THOUGHT** (about the situation) →	**EMOTION/FEELING** (related to our thought) →	**ACTION/BEHAVIOR** (related to our emotion and thought)
(YOUR SITUATION) *Step 1*	(YOUR THOUGHT) *Step 3*	(YOUR EMOTION) *Step 2*	(YOUR ACTION/BEHAVIOR) *Step 4*
↓ **SAME** SITUATION: ↓	**DIFFERENT** THOUGHT: *Step 5*	**DIFFERENT** EMOTION: *Step 6*	**DIFFERENT** ACTION/BEHAVIOR: *Step 7*

Problematic Thinking

What is *problematic thinking*? Problematic thinking (sometimes called *cognitive distortions*) includes unhelpful ways of thinking that act like a lens through which we view and understand certain situations.

These problematic or unhelpful thoughts can lead us to experience difficult emotions/feelings and problematic actions/behaviors. Below are examples of common forms of problematic thinking. Studying them can help you know when you might be experiencing an unhelpful thought about a situation. For each, think of a time when you used one of these types of thinking and write about it in the "**Your Example**" space.

Type of Problematic Thinking	What It Means	Example
Black and White Thinking	Viewing a person or situation in an "all or nothing" way.	"I need to follow all of my lawyer's advice or none of it." "Everything in my case will go my way *or* nothing will go my way."
		Your Example:
Emotional Reasoning	My emotions are the same as reality (what's happening), so they guide my beliefs and behaviors.	I am feeling anxious about my case, so it's going to end poorly.
		Your Example:
Tunnel Vision	Only seeing a few details in a situation—not seeing the situation as a whole.	My provider said I did well during a restoration group/session, but I got one answer wrong, so I'm not going to pass my evaluation.
		Your Example:

Type of Problematic Thinking	What It Means	Example
Catastrophizing (Fortunetelling)	I predict the future will be negative—so negative I won't be able to survive how bad it will be.	My charge is a misdemeanor, but I'll spend years and years in prison and will never leave.
		Your Example:
Labeling	Putting an unchanging label on myself, another, or a situation.	"I'm stupid." "Others are jerks." "Groups are scary or unhelpful."
		Your Example:
Discounting the Positive	I claim positive experiences or events do not count—or—are less important than negative ones.	"I did really well on a quiz in my restoration group, but it was just luck. I won't do that well again."
		Your Example::
Unfair Comparisons	I compare myself to others who appear to be doing better than me. By doing this, I view myself as being in a bad situation.	Someone who has been in the jail or hospital for a shorter time than me has already left—I must be doing poorly. (Ignoring other possible reasons this might be).
		Your Example:

Religion/Spirituality Assessment

Client Name:______________________ **Date of Assessment**: __________

Please answer the questions below to the best of your ability. Provide additional information to help us better understand your spirituality when possible.

Spiritual History

1. What is your religious background?

____

____

____

____

2. Do you believe in a personal higher power(s)? If so, who? *Once you have the name(s) of the higher power(s), use it in the following questions.

____

____

____

____

3. How close do you feel to (your higher power) currently?

____

____

____

____

4. When you are personally suffering and in need of help and support describe what you usually do:
   a. Talk to people
   b. Keep to myself and get through it the best I can
   c. Wait until the crisis is over, then tell people
   d. Immediately go to my higher power and seek spiritual support
   e. Other:

5. Do you consider (your higher power) your
   a. father/mother
   b. friend
   c. other:

6. Do you pray? Why or why not?

7. When have you felt most distant from (your higher power)?

8. When have you felt most close to (your higher power)?

9. When in your life has religion been important to you?

10. When in your life has spirituality been important to you?

11. What would you have to do to be fully accepted by (your higher power)?

12. How important is it to you to know and experience (your higher power)'s love for you?

13. Have you ever been judged by those outside of your religious or spiritual beliefs? If so, would you mind sharing your experience?

14. Have you ever been judged by those within your religious or spiritual community? If so, would you mind sharing your experience?

____

____

____

____

15. Do you feel your religious or spiritual beliefs will impact your case? If so, how?

____

____

____

____

16. How can your treatment team, staff, and/or providers best support your religious or spiritual needs to help you proceed with your case?

____

____

____

____

17. Is there anything you think is important to know about your religion or spirituality?

____

____

____

____

Faith and Law

What my faith says about how people should act:

What my faith says about forgiveness:

What my faith says about crime:

What my faith makes me think about my legal charges:

What faith practices will help me cope with my legal situation:

What would my higher power want me to remember as I deal with my legal situation:

Dusky-Specific Song Discussion

Introduction: This is a receptive music listening intervention using any of the *Dusky* prongs as the targeted focus area, depending on the needs of the client(s). For this intervention, a preselected song list is created by the therapist prior to the session. Clients select songs from the list, and the therapist facilitates a discussion of the song's musical elements.

Goals: Factual understanding of the legal proceedings; rational understanding of the legal proceedings; ability to consult with counsel; communication; decision-making; ability to track events and/or reality orientation.

Materials: List of songs (see below for samples); lyric sheets; recording of songs and playback device (e.g., speaker, CD player, etc.); worksheets related to the song material for clients to fill out with writing utensils if using.

Procedure:

1. Prior to the session, the therapist creates a list of songs to utilize. See "Musical Considerations" below regarding song selection.
2. During the session, the clients select songs from the list provided. The therapist may choose to provide lyric sheets for clients to follow along with.
3. Prior to and/or following song playback, discussion should be facilitated by the clinician, explicitly making connections between the music and targeted need areas. For example: If using the song as a teaching tool (e.g., for factual information), those connections should be explicitly made. Or, if using the song as a starting point for decision-making, discussions should center on that prompt (e.g., "If you were the lawyer for the person in this song, what advice would you give them?").
4. Repeat steps 2 and 3 as needed.

Interpreting Musical Responses: Due to the receptive nature of this intervention, responses will largely be non-musical (e.g., verbal/nonverbal, engagement in discussion, etc.), though there may be some behaviors that occur that are directly linked or a result of the music (e.g., tapping feet, dancing, singing/rapping along, clapping, etc.). These behaviors may be tied to specific psycholegal abilities, such as reality orientation/ability to track events (e.g., following along with lyrics on a printed page), or emotional regulation. For example, clients who are very loudly singing along while others listen quietly, it might be reasonable to interpret this as an example of a limit on their capacity to regulate behaviors based on environmental/social cues.

Musical Considerations: The songs for this intervention should be selected based on the relation of the musical elements to the identified *Dusky* prongs/intervention goals. This includes not only lyric content but also elements such as rhythm, timbre, dynamics, instrumentation, form, harmony, melody, etc. For a music therapist, it is suggested that all of a song's musical elements be considered when creating the song list. For other clinicians, sample song lists have been provided below. It is recommended that all clinicians be thoroughly familiar with the songs they will use in this intervention and that they have considered the role the music is serving, as well as the culture, strengths, and preferences of their clients.

Songs should also be selected based on the clients' strengths, cultures, and musical preferences. Using music that clients are familiar with can help to build rapport, create a feeling of validation and safety, acknowledge the culture and lived experiences of the individuals, and help minimize the effects of bias and systemic oppression in the therapeutic space. Censorship of lyric content, printed lyric sheets, styles of music/artists, etc. should be done purposefully, based on clinical needs, and in accordance with the therapist's facility guidelines.

The therapist should select the playback method that is most appropriate for their practice and facility. For example, in a facility where CDs are not allowed, using a tablet with a wireless speaker may be required. Or, in a facility where Wi-Fi is limited, songs should be pre-downloaded in order to ensure a seamless listening experience. For all clinicians, it is important to ensure the speaker conveys enough musical detail so that all the musical elements can be clearly heard.

Sample Competency Song List

The State vs. Kirk Jones
By Sticky Fingaz [feat. Canibus, Rah Digga, Redman, Superb, Scarred 4 Life]

Law Library (Pt. 4)
By Papoose

Cocaine Blues
By Johnny Cash

Hip Hop Police
By Chamillionaire

Framed
By Ritchie Valens, Los Lobos

Testify
By Common

I Shot the Sheriff
By Bob Marley

Dope Man
By Jay-Z [feat. Serena Altschul]

Framed
By Inspectah Deck

Courtroom Discography & Timeline

Introduction: This is a receptive music listening intervention wherein client(s) will engage in a creative process during the session to think about the given prompt. Clients select songs based on their understanding of each component of the prompt and create a symbol to represent their comprehensive understanding.

Goals: Reality orientation; emotional regulation; factual understanding of legal proceedings; decision-making.

Materials: Prompt (preplanned or decided on with clients); visual aid based on prompt (timeline sheet, emotion chart or wheel, etc.; a square piece of paper (4.724" x 4.724" for CD size, 12.375" x 12.375" for record size); writing utensils (pens, pencils, markers); art materials (pens, markers, paint, oil pastels, etc.); an example of an album or CD insert if desired.

Procedure:

1. Choose a prompt for the discography. Common examples used by the authors of Chapter 8 include a timeline of the legal process from a crime being committed to sentencing, songs that correlate with the myriad of emotions one might experience while going through the legal process, and songs that explore interpersonal relationships.
2. If needed choose a visual aid to assist clients with identifying or organizing the information from the prompt. See the "Handouts" section below for an example of a timeline that can be given to clients.
3. Once the clients have considered the prompt, they can identify songs that are representative of each component they identified.
   a. Steps 3 and 4 can be done in any order
4. Client(s) can draw album art to represent their court discography.
   b. Steps 3 and 4 can be done in any order
5. If applicable, have a verbal discussion about each discography and/or play some samples from the songs identified.
6. See the Handouts section for an example of a completed court discography using the timeline prompt.

Interpreting Musical Responses: This intervention highlights the client(s) ability to follow the prompt given, providing information about their understanding of the concepts. Based on their chosen songs, the clinician can either assess how they might relate to the clients' comprehension or can prompt the clients to engage in a discussion about their chosen songs. For example, if the prompt is to choose songs that represent court personnel, choosing "Tell You Everything" by Robyn Ottolini for the prosecutor demonstrates a potential lack of understanding regarding the prosecutor's role.

Musical Considerations: Because this intervention requires limited theoretical knowledge of music from the clinician, it is easily facilitated by clinicians with any background. When considering if you want to play music that was identified by the clients, it is important to consider your knowledge of the song(s) that are going to be played in the session. Considerations of lyrical content along with the impact of other musical components should be highlighted. If a therapist is unsure if they are able to facilitate a therapeutic discussion related to the musical elements of songs used in the session, then sticking to only playing well-known songs is suggested.

Courtroom Discography

Front Cover

Back Cover

Timeline

Competency-related Song Re-creation

Introduction: This intervention builds upon the "*Dusky*-Specific Song Discussion" and may use similar or different songs to teach or form a link between music-specific and music-related skills (e.g., playing an instrument, discussing musical elements, etc.) and psycholegal abilities. Therapists can select songs that are directly linked to the *Dusky* prongs or those more closely related to other goal areas such as emotional regulation, communication, reality orientation, decision-making, frustration tolerance, etc. Additionally, the re-creative aspect of this intervention provides many opportunities for a music therapist to craft the active music-making experience to help clients build upon those related competency-specific and adjacent skills.

Goals: Factual understanding of the legal proceeding; rational understanding of the legal proceedings; ability to consult with counsel; emotional regulation; communication; reality orientation; decision-making; frustration tolerance.

Materials: Song lists with/without lyric sheets; instruments (specific to facility guidelines; music therapist's inventory; songs/genres used; client strengths, needs, cultures, and preferences); visual aids if needed/appropriate (such as colored stickers for instruments).

Procedure:

1. Prior to the session, the therapist creates a list of songs to utilize. See "Interpreting Musical Response" below regarding considerations on designing musical re-creation.
2. During the session, the clients select songs from the list provided. The therapist may choose to provide lyric sheets for clients to follow along with.
3. Songs are re-created by the therapist and/or clients. This may include playing instruments, using body percussion, music technology, and/or a mix of live and prerecorded sources of music. Clients may be given specific musical elements to re-create or else provide additional musical accompaniment along with the therapist.
4. If applicable, have a discussion about the musical elements of the song, provide feedback on the instrument playing of the clients, and/or make explicit connections between the music creation and related psycholegal abilities (e.g., "How might the skills you used in playing this song help you in court?").

Interpreting Musical Responses: This intervention can elicit musical and non-musical responses from your client(s) that can be linked to the goals under the *Dusky* prongs, as well as related psycholegal abilities. When customizing this intervention, the authors have found it helpful to find direct links between musical behaviors/responses and the Zapf & Roesch (2009) domains and subdomains; see Chapter 8 for more information. For example, accurately re-creating snare drum hits on beats 2 and 4 during song re-creation may indicate a capacity to track events, while moderating dynamics along with the group may indicate a capacity to manage emotions given contextual and social cues. As with other music therapy methods, while there is not a guarantee of the transfer of musical skills/responses to the non-musical realm, a client's ability to engage with these skills in a musical context may indicate the capacity for related non-musical skills to be present. Therefore, the music creation aspect of this intervention should be purposefully and specifically crafted to provide multiple, varied opportunities for clients to engage with musical skills that have a psycholegal analog or connection.

Musical Considerations: Because this intervention requires extensive theoretical knowledge of the music used, as well as the ability to both re-create songs and interpret the musical responses of clients, it should be facilitated by or with a music therapist. In addition to considerations regarding song selection (e.g., client preferences, censorship, etc.), music therapists should also purposefully consider the instruments offered and the role the music serves within this intervention and the connection between music creation and the goals/need areas.

Musical Mock Trial

Introduction: This improvisational intervention requires active music participation from the client(s). The basis of this intervention is to have instruments act as different courtroom personnel and musically tell the story of a mock trial.

Goals: Reality orientation; emotional regulation; factual understanding of legal proceedings; frustration tolerance; communication; distrust of counsel; decision-making.

Procedure:

1. The music therapist should set up the room like a courtroom and place instruments in the middle between where the judge and the attorneys sit.
2. The music therapist should hand out the vignette to the clients in the group. If a script is being used, the script should be handed out.
   - A sample vignette and script are provided at the bottom of this intervention. Vignettes and scripts for mock trials can easily be found online, and the music therapist should select and/or adapt vignettes and scripts to meet the needs of their clients.
3. The music therapist should facilitate a discussion about which instruments should represent different courtroom personnel and/or different things that happen throughout the mock trial (e.g., music for the time the jury would be deliberating).
4. Once instruments have roles, the music therapist should facilitate clients being assigned to different instruments.
5. Provide time for clients to play their instruments in different ways and explore how they want to musically represent different moments throughout a trial process (e.g., don't play anything during certain moments, play fortissimo and syncopated during certain moments, play slowly and quietly for certain moments, etc.). If using a script, it might be helpful to have clients write down what they want to play throughout the script.
   - Remind clients that the voice is an instrument as well, and vocal noises, singing, and speaking can all be a part of the musical mock trial.
6. After independent musical choices are made, facilitate a discussion to share ideas, identify major moments, and decide on the musical arch of the mock trial so everyone knows when major moments are happening and can move in the story accordingly.
7. Once clients have identified how they want to play musically throughout the mock trial, begin the process of starting the mock trial. Rather than speaking lines, clients will be playing the trial on the instruments that represent the different components. Speaking may be useful in certain moments (e.g., having the person playing the judge's instrument say "Order," or having the people playing the attorneys' instruments saying specific evidence about the case).
8. Once the mock trial is concluded, facilitate a discussion about the process as needed.

Interpreting Musical Responses: This intervention assesses client responses through their musical improvisation and verbal narratives. Skills such as emotional regulation, frustration tolerance, communication, and decision-making can be assessed based on client engagement.

Musical Considerations: This intervention requires in-depth musical knowledge, and this specific intervention should be conducted by a music therapist. This is another intervention in which using the "Therapeutic Function of Music Plan" worksheet (Hanson-Abromeit, 2015) can assist the clinician with preparing, facilitating, and evaluating the clients musical responses in relation to treatment goals.

Musical Mock Trial

Sample Vignette and Script

A defendant is being charged with first-degree murder. The district attorney is providing evidence of gunpowder residue on the defendant's arm, a gun found in the defendant's car, and eyewitness statements of the alleged offense. The defendant is pleading not guilty by reason of insanity and states at the time of the crime they thought the victim was an international spy who was planning an attack on the building they were occupying at the time. The defense is submitting expert witness statements from the psychologist who performed the Mental State of Offense evaluation and hospital records showing the defendant has had multiple inpatient hospitalizations to treat a diagnosis of paranoid schizophrenia.

Bailiff: All rise for the honorable judge, overseeing the case of The State versus The Defendant.

Judge: Please be seated. Bailiff, please swear in the jury.

Bailiff: *Swears in the jury*

Jury: I do.

Judge: Prosecution, you may begin with your opening statement.

Prosecutor: *Provides opening statement, highlighting the physical evidence in the case*

Judge: Defense, you may give your opening statement.

Defense Attorney: *Provides opening statement, highlighting the mental health diagnosis of the defendant*

Judge: Prosecution, you may call your witness.

Prosecutor: *Calls witness and begins direct examination*

Witness and Prosecutor: *Engage in dialogue*

Judge: Defense, you may cross-examine the witness.

Witness and Defense Attorney: *Engage in dialogue*

Judge: Thank you. Defense, you may call your witness.

Defense Attorney: *Calls witness and begins direct examination*

Witness and Defense Attorney: *Engage in dialogue*

Judge: Prosecutor, you may cross-examine the witness.

Witness and Prosecutor: *Engage in dialogue*

Judge: Thank you. Prosecutor, you may give your closing argument.

Prosecutor: *Provides closing argument, reminding the jury of the evidence in the case*

Judge: Defense, you may provide your closing argument.

Defense Attorney: *Provides closing argument, reminding the jury of the mental status of the defendant at the time of the crime*

Judge: Thank you, everyone. Members of the jury, you have heard the evidence in the case. Please take time to consider all evidence presented. Consider the facts

of the case and determine if the evidence shows beyond a reasonable doubt that the defendant was in the right state of mind and committed first-degree murder. The bailiff will take you to the jury chambers to deliberate.
Bailiff: *Takes the jury to the jury chambers*
Jury: *Deliberates, then returns*
Judge: Has the jury reached a verdict?
Jury Foreperson: We have. We, the jury, in the case of The State versus The Defendant find the defendant not guilty by reason of insanity on the charges of first-degree murder.
Judge: Jury, thank you for your service today. We will set a date for a Bolton Hearing in the case of The State versus The Defendant.

Musical Elements as Metaphor

Introduction: This is a re-creative intervention using active music-making to explore any of the *Dusky* prongs, depending on the needs of the client(s). For this intervention, clients will engage in verbal discourse to agree upon which musical elements will represent each component of a given prompt, then engage in actively playing the music to embody their abstractions.

Goals: Reality orientation; emotional regulation; factual understanding of legal proceedings; frustration tolerance; communication; distrust of counsel; decision-making.

Materials: Instruments, recording of the song(s), paper and writing utensils for brainstorming and as a reminder of the metaphors.

Procedure:

1. Prior to the session the clinician should prepare one song for the clients to re-create or a list of songs for them to choose from.
2. The clinician should provide a prompt and example. The clinician might say something such as, "Today we are going to use instruments to represent the court personnel. For example, the bass drum in this song might represent the judge because it is grounding the song and keeping it on beat." For songs like "The State vs. Kirk Jones" by Sticky Fingaz (Jones, et al., 2001) roles are already lyrically defined for each artist featured in the song.
3. The clinician should play the song for the clients to listen to and decide on how they want musical elements to represent each component of the prompt.
4. The clinician should facilitate this discussion, encouraging the clients to think about the qualities of the different court personnel and how well they match the qualities of the different musical components.
5. Once roles are established, the clinician can lead the session through a musical mock trial with the song as the structural base.
6. A discussion can be facilitated if desired.

Interpreting Musical Responses: This intervention will evoke conversation about the roles of court personnel, allowing clinicians to assess the client(s) understanding of this factual component of the court process. Additionally, to engage in music with others requires orientation to time and situation, demonstrating the level of reality orientation they have during the music playing. Frustration tolerance and emotional regulation are needed during discussion and based on the aesthetics of the music played. Lastly, interpersonal interactions are easily assessed based on the client's verbal and musical engagement in this intervention.

Musical Considerations: This intervention requires advanced knowledge on the therapeutic functions of the various musical elements, and it may be best implemented by a music therapist. Planning for or evaluating the musical components of this session may include using the "Therapeutic Function of Music Plan" worksheet (Hanson-Abromeit, 2015). Taking time to conceptualize the abstract representations of the musical elements will assist with prompting, facilitating, and evaluating the clients' responses to this intervention.

Court-Specific Freestyle

Introduction: This is an improvisational intervention that relies on active music-making from the client(s). Clients will improvise court-related lyrics based on prompts or a word bank provided. Lyrical content can relay clients' understanding of the factual components of competency and the thoughts and feelings they express regarding legal counsel. Additionally, musical and non-musical responses during this intervention can demonstrate levels of reality orientation, emotional regulation, and communication skills.

Goals: Reality orientation; factual understanding of legal proceedings; communication.

Materials: Recording equipment, microphone, electronic or acoustic instruments, device to play beat or instrumental such as a computer with internet access or a CD, visual aid of word bank if desired.

Procedure:

1. The clinician should decide if the clients they are working with would benefit from a word bank or if they can remain on topic without a word bank.
   - If a word bank is needed, the clinician can either bring a list of words they generated before the session or develop the list of words with the clients at the beginning of the session.
2. If recording the freestyle, the clinician should set up the recording equipment.
3. The clinician can use a variety of prompts based on the treatment goals of the clients and how much prompting the clients need to be successful. Prompts can be as open as "create a freestyle about court" or as specific as "use at least five words from the word bank."
4. If not doing the intervention acapella, the clinician should have the group create a beat or instrumental acoustically or electronically or play a prerecorded beat or instrumental.
5. If recording, then use whichever DAW is preferred to record, mix, and master the song.
6. Discussions about content from the freestyles can be facilitated if desired.

Interpreting Musical Responses: Based on the client(s) lyrics the clinician can assess the factual understanding of the court process. Engaging in music requires orientation to time and situation, demonstrating the level of reality orientation they have during the music playing. Additionally, lyrical content can assess the thought processes of the clients. If facilitating a group, taking turns demonstrates an ability to maintain self-control while others are freestyling.

Musical Considerations: If this intervention is done acapella or is not recorded it requires basic knowledge of the musical elements from the clinician. If this instrumental is recorded to a beat or instrumental, this intervention requires basic knowledge of the musical elements and intermediate knowledge of music production from the clinician. An important component of deciding if this intervention can be used with your clients is determining whether you can musically support the clients in any way that is needed. This can include how you musically redirect those who are going off-topic or not following lyrical or musical boundaries you have set, how you create supportive music for them to freestyle toward, how you use music technology to enhance the musical components, how you aesthetically use music technology to censor if needed, and how you mix and master recorded pieces.

Instrumental Improvisation

Introduction: Referential improvisations can be used for a wide variety of focus areas and goals/needs, both competency specific and competency supportive. The intervention described below will focus specifically on the competency-supportive goal areas of emotional and self-regulation. The approach and customization of this intervention is as unique as the music therapist implementing it. For clients unfamiliar with improvisation, it may be important to introduce the concept of spontaneous music creation, and foster comfort with the instruments available, to help clients be successful in this intervention. Visual aids may be incorporated if necessary (e.g., photos to accompany referential theme/concept).

Goals: Consult with counsel; communication; emotional regulation; frustration tolerance; decision-making.

Procedure:

1. Prior to the session, the music therapist should decide if the client(s) would benefit from an organizing theme/concept. For example, selecting a self-identified "relaxing" image and then creating the music that would accompany the image. If needed/helpful, print out the image as a reference for use during music creation. Additionally, the music therapist must consider the level of musical and non-musical structure that will help clients be successful in this intervention. See "Musical Considerations" for more details.
2. In session, the music therapist should provide a prompt, and as needed, a discussion to help clients make decisions about the music they will create. For example, "Today we are going to create music that is relaxing and could help us stay calm in a stressful situation. What would that sound like?"
3. After any prompts and discussion, the music therapist should facilitate the referential improvisation, followed by a verbal discussion if necessary.
4. Depending on the clients' and therapist's preferences, the improvisation and/or discussion can be followed-up with other relaxation/reflection experiences, such as meditation, journaling, deep breathing, etc.

Interpreting Musical Responses: Similar to the re-creative interventions previously described, musical responses can be directly or indirectly linked to *Dusky* prongs or related psycholegal abilities. Instrumental, referential improvisations for relaxation, emotional and self-regulation, and/or frustration tolerance are often used by music therapists, especially in psychiatric and forensic settings. The ways in which a music therapist conceptualizes musical responses for these goals would also apply in a competency-specific setting.

Musical Considerations: As this intervention requires an extensive theoretical understanding of the use of instruments and music in a therapeutic setting, it should be facilitated by or with a music therapist. Music therapists should carefully and purposefully consider the instruments offered as part of this intervention, specifically their relationship to the goal(s), as well as the strengths, needs, preferences, and cultures of the clients. Music technology or body percussion could be utilized if appropriate, and a variety of timbres can be offered. The level of structure should also be purposefully considered, both musical and non-musical. For example, if using tonal instruments, will the options offered be limited by key/tonality (e.g., all in the key of G major)? Will there be a meter/time signature? Will this improvisation have an established musical form? Music therapists can utilize the "Therapeutic Function of Music Plan" worksheet (Hanson-Abromeit, 2015) to help make decisions about the type and level(s) of structure needed.

Original Courtroom Song

Introduction: A compositional intervention can be used for *Dusky*-specific goals, as well as competency-supportive goal areas, such as decision-making, motivation, communication, frustration tolerance, experience of incarceration and treatment, and, when in a group setting, negotiation and conflict management processes.

Goals: Factual understanding of the court proceedings; rational understanding of the court proceedings; consult with counsel; communication; decision-making; motivation; frustration tolerance; conflict management.

Materials: Paper, writing utensils (if necessary); instruments and/or music technology.

Procedure:

1. Prior to the session the clinician can select prompts, if needed, to help structure/guide the songwriting process. For example, "Write a letter to your best friend about how it feels when you're in court," or "What's one thing you wish the judge knew about people with mental illness?" The prompts can be crafted to help the client(s) reflect on the creative task, as well as the goal/focus of the intervention. The clinician may decide to offer several prompts for clients to choose from, as well as visual aids to accompany, as appropriate.
2. During the session, the clinician can facilitate the songwriting process according to their strengths, as well as the strengths, needs, and preferences of their clients. This may mean beginning the process with a discussion or by writing the song's lyrics first. Or else, the selection/creation of music may be the first step, depending on the process decided upon by the therapist/clients.
    a. If facilitated by a music therapist, the song can be instrumental or include song lyrics. Song creation can begin with music, deciding on individual elements of music (e.g., instruments, style, tempo, harmony, etc.), or with the lyric content. If working in a group, it can provide opportunities for group decision-making, conflict management, and/or negotiation. Music technology can also be incorporated, if appropriate.
    b. If facilitated by a non-music therapist, there are a myriad of options online to find instrumental music that can serve as the musical foundation for song lyrics. It will be important to engage the clients in the music selection process, keeping in mind their strengths, preferences, and cultures, as well as their clinical needs. Once an instrumental track has been selected, song lyrics can then be created using the chosen prompt(s). Clients may choose to create their own melody to accompany the lyrics or else rap or speak the song lyrics over the music.
3. Processing the songwriting process can follow the intervention as necessary to help clients make connections between the experience of writing a song, the song's content, and the chosen goals/focus areas.

Interpreting Musical Responses: For music therapists, compositional interventions are commonly used for a wide variety of clinical goals, and the same interpretation of musical responses can be applied to competency-specific and competency-supportive goals. For other clinicians, the content of song lyrics can offer insight into the client(s)' understanding of *Dusky*-specific information. Their engagement in the process, especially when in a group setting, can also provide opportunities for the clinician to assess competency-supportive goals such as communication, emotional regulation, motivation, etc.

Musical Considerations: Music therapists can utilize the "Therapeutic Function of Music Plan" worksheet (Hanson-Abromeit, 2015) to help make decisions about the type and level(s) of structure needed, as well as the relationship between the musical elements and the clinical goals selected. Music therapists can use the preferences of the clients to help dictate the type of song written, which can then inform choices about musical elements offered (e.g., instruments, meter, form, etc.) and ways to craft those elements to help clients meet their goals.

Song Rewrite

Introduction: This compositional intervention requires active music participation from the client(s). The basis of this intervention is to take an existing song and rewrite the lyrics to center on competency-related topics. This is often referred to as piggybacking or parodying a song. Providers will need paper for writing lyrics or paper with fill in the blanks for prewritten lyrics, writing utensils, instruments, lyrics for the original song if desired.

Goals: Reality orientation; emotional regulation; factual understanding of legal proceedings; frustration tolerance; communication; distrust of counsel; decision-making.

Procedure:

1. The clinician should decide if the full song is being rewritten or if there will be a fill in the blank used. See the example below for a rewritten fill-in-the-blank song.
   - If needed, a word bank can be given with only the words needed to complete the song or with extra words depending on the difficulty desired.
2. This intervention can either be done with each person writing their own lyrics to the song or collaboratively with others in the session. The clinician should decide which is more appropriate for the needs of the clients.
   - If doing a collective song, one visual aid to write the lyrics so everyone can see is recommended.
   - If doing independent songs, separate sheets of paper for each person is recommended.
3. The clinician should perform the original song so the clients have a general idea of the rhythmic structure of the song.
4. The clinician can either facilitate a discussion to write the new lyrics or allow time for the clients to independently work on lyrics.
5. The clinician should perform each version that is written during the session so the clients can hear their completed song(s).
6. A discussion can be facilitated if desired.

Interpreting Musical Responses: This intervention assesses client responses through the lyrical content they create during the rewrite of the song. Additionally, if working in a group, skills such as emotional regulation, frustration tolerance, communication, and decision-making can be assessed based on client engagement.

Musical Considerations: This intervention requires the clinician to be able to re-create a song. This likely includes the ability to sing and play an accompanying instrument. If rewriting the song during session, the clinician should be prepared to make musical decisions such as adjusting melodic rhythms for lyrics that do not fit the original rhythmic structure of the song. Once a song is re-created the clinician can increase and expand the effectiveness of the intervention by playing the song in different ways and processing how the musical components change the feeling and understanding of the song. For example, if a pop song is sung as a blues song, how does it change one's perception? If a song in a major key is performed in a minor key, what does it do to the emotional meaning of the song? Thinking about how each musical element impacts the clients' experience of the music will help facilitate a deeper dive into the therapeutic function of this intervention. This is another intervention in which using the "Therapeutic Function of Music Plan" worksheet (Hanson-Abromeit, 2015) can assist the clinician with preparing, facilitating, and evaluating the clients' musical responses in relation to treatment goals.

Song Rewrite

To the Tune of "Folsom Prison Blues" by Johnny Cash

I hear I've got a court date. I need to know who's who.

The __________________, that's the person in charge of the courtroom.

Work with the ________________________, the one person on my side.

While the ________________________ tries to disprove my alibi.

When I was telling my story, the ________________________ typed every word.

While the ________________________ listened, chose the verdict they preferred.

Well I shot a man in Reno, and that's a ________________________ charge.

That's bigger than a ________________________,

and the ________________________ could be large.

They say they have a person who saw everything.

They're the ________________________, I know they're gonna sing.

There's another witness who works in ballistics.

They say they're an ________________________, I say he's full of ish.

Just gotta keep my cool, don't act out in court.

Or I'd get ________________________, another charge to thwart.

If they freed me from this prison, if the verdict is ________________________.

I'm gonna be released, get out of there quickly.

Word Bank

Not guilty	Eyewitness	Defense
Felony	Contempt	Stenographer
Misdemeanor	Sentence	Jury
Judge	Expert	Prosecutor

CBTp Skills Worksheets

Instructions: Each of the following worksheets are designed to be completed by the defendant. These can be completed independently during a restoration session or as "homework." They can also be completed collaboratively with the CBTp-informed competency restoration provider; however, they should not be completed by the restoration provider for the defendant.

Once a skills sheet is completed, the CBTp-informed restoration provider is encouraged to review the defendant's answers. The defendant should be encouraged to elaborate upon, or otherwise explain, what they have written in their responses. The CBTp-informed restoration provider should maintain a nonjudgmental and collaborative stance in reviewing the defendant's responses. However, they are also encouraged to use the responses to facilitate discussion, prompting the defendant to think critically about their responses. Bringing the legal context into discussion (e.g., what their reaction would be if X happened while they were talking with their attorney) is indicated.

Sample responses are included to help illustrate how these worksheets can be filled out. CBTp-informed restoration providers should use their clinical judgment in whether those samples are provided to the defendant as examples.

CBTp-informed restoration providers may make use of these and more general CBTp worksheets when incorporating CBTp in competency restoration. Worksheets should be selected considering the defendant's current barriers to competency.

Experience/Hallucination Journal

When did you hear something? *(date/time)*	
What exactly did you hear? *(details)*	
How did this make you **feel**? *(emotions)*	
How **intense** was that feeling? *(1 to 10 scale)*	
What did you **think** about what you heard? *(thoughts)*	
What did you **do** when this happened? *(behaviors)*	
What **effect** did that have? *(better or worse?)*	
What **could** you do if this happened in court? *(planning ahead)*	

Sample Experience/Hallucination Journal

When did you hear something? *(date/time/location)*	Friday night, maybe 10:00PM, in my room.
What exactly did you hear? *(details)*	A man's voice telling me that my case was dismissed.
How did this make you **feel**? *(emotions)*	A little nervous, a little relieved.
How **intense** was that feeling? *(1 to 10 scale)*	5/10
What did you **think** about what you heard? *(thoughts)*	I thought I couldn't see anyone else in the room. When I heard this before, they said I was just hearing things.
What did you **do** when this happened? *(behaviors)*	I checked to see if anyone was in the bathroom or outside my room.
What **effect** did that have? *(better or worse?)*	I was frustrated that no one was there, and it felt like people were messing with me.
What **could** you do if this happened in court? *(planning ahead)*	I could ask my lawyer if he heard the same thing, and I'd have to try to stay focused.

Belief/Delusion Journal

What exactly is your belief? *(details)*	
When did you start to hold this belief? *(date/time/location)*	
How does this belief make you **feel**? *(emotions)*	
How **intense** is that feeling? *(1 to 10 scale)*	
What do you**think** about the belief? *(thoughts)*	
What do other people say when you **tell** them about the belief? *(behaviors)*	
What **effect** did that have on your belief? *(better or worse?)*	
How **could** thinking this way affect your legal case/decisions? *(planning ahead)*	

Sample Belief/Delusion Journal

What exactly is your belief? *(details)*	The judge is against me. She's not neutral.
When did you start to hold this belief? *(date/time/location)*	Always. It's just a fact. Definitely since my last conviction.
How does this belief make you **feel**? *(emotions)*	Angry and frustrated, people keep telling me she's neutral.
How **intense** is that feeling? *(1 to 10 scale)*	9/10
What do you **think** about the belief? *(thoughts)*	I think all my experience with court says she's against me and is going to find me guilty no matter what I do.
What do other people say when you **tell** them about the belief? *(behaviors)*	They say I'm wrong and I don't want to hear it.
What **effect** did that have on your belief? *(better or worse?)*	It doesn't have any effect on my belief.
How **could** thinking this way affect your legal case/ decisions? *(planning ahead)*	I've gotta look out for me and not trust the judge to help me out in any kind of way.

CBTp Experience Test

Question: Is my experience based in reality or could it possibly be a hallucination?

My experience:

A—Affect) How do I feel when I start to experience this? How strong is that feeling?

B—Behavior) What do I do when I start to experience this?

C—Cognitions) What thoughts come to mind when I start to experience this?

Experiment for testing if my experience is based in reality:

What evidence do I have that tells me this is probably true?	What evidence do I have that tells me this is probably false?

How could this experience affect my legal decision-making or behaviors at court?

Conclusions:

Sample CBTp Experience Test

Question: Is my experience based in reality or could it possibly be a hallucination?

My experience:

Hearing my brother's voice telling me to do things.

A—Affect) How do I feel when I start to experience this? How strong is that feeling?

Sometimes I feel a little better because it's my brother, and maybe I was going to do what he says anyway. Sometimes I feel really nervous, and that's strong. That happens when it feels like what he's saying is probably a bad idea.

B—Behavior) What do I do when I start to experience this?

I usually do what he says to do because he's my brother.

C—Cognitions) What thoughts come to mind when I start to experience this?

I usually don't think too much about it. I just trust him.

Experiment for testing if my experience is based in reality:

What evidence do I have that tells me this is probably true?	What evidence do I have that tells me this is probably false?
- It sounds like my brother. - It talks like my brother.	- My brother said he can't talk to me like that. - He doesn't know what I'm talking about when I ask him about our conversations face to face.

How could this experience affect my legal decision-making or behaviors at court?

I could be distracted, or do what he says in court without questioning it.

Conclusions: I probably should make my own decisions. I'm the one who could go to jail.

CBTp Belief Test

Question: Is my belief true in reality or could it possibly be a delusion?

My belief:

A—Affect) How do I feel when I start to think like this? How strong is that feeling?

B—Behavior) What do I do when I start to think like this?

C—Cognitions) What thoughts come to mind when I start to think like this?

Experiment for testing if my belief is based in reality:

What evidence do I have that tells me this is probably true?	What evidence do I have that tells me this is probably false?

How could this experience affect my legal decision-making or behaviors at court?

Conclusions:

Sample CBTp Belief Test

Question: Is my belief true in reality or could it possibly be a delusion?

My belief:

My lawyer is working with the prosecutor!

A—Affect) How do I feel when I start to think like this? How strong is that feeling?

I get a little scared and upset, but mostly angry. Everyone's telling me they're supposed to be on my side, and I don't want to hear it. I'm going to get screwed over in court if I let this guy ``defend" me.

B—Behavior) What do I do when I start to think like this?

I start trying to figure out how to get a new lawyer! I keep calling the one on my case, and they're not answering the phone. I don't know what else I can do.

C—Cognitions) What thoughts come to mind when I start to think like this?

When I call and they don't answer or call back, that just makes me think even more that they're not working for me. It makes me think that I'm right about everything.

Experiment for testing if my belief is based in reality:

What evidence do I have that tells me this is probably true?	What evidence do I have that tells me this is probably false?
- They're not answering my calls - They won't talk to me - Everyone says they're supposed to be talking to me about my case - I've worked with public defenders before and it wasn't like this	- Public defenders are busy - My case is on hold right now - When I did talk to them before it was kind of fine - They did send me a letter with an update about my case

How could this experience affect my legal decision-making or behaviors at court?

I'm refusing to talk to my lawyer and have been planning to represent myself.

Conclusions: Maybe I should let my social worker set up a phone call with the lawyer.

Vulnerability-Stress Model Worksheet

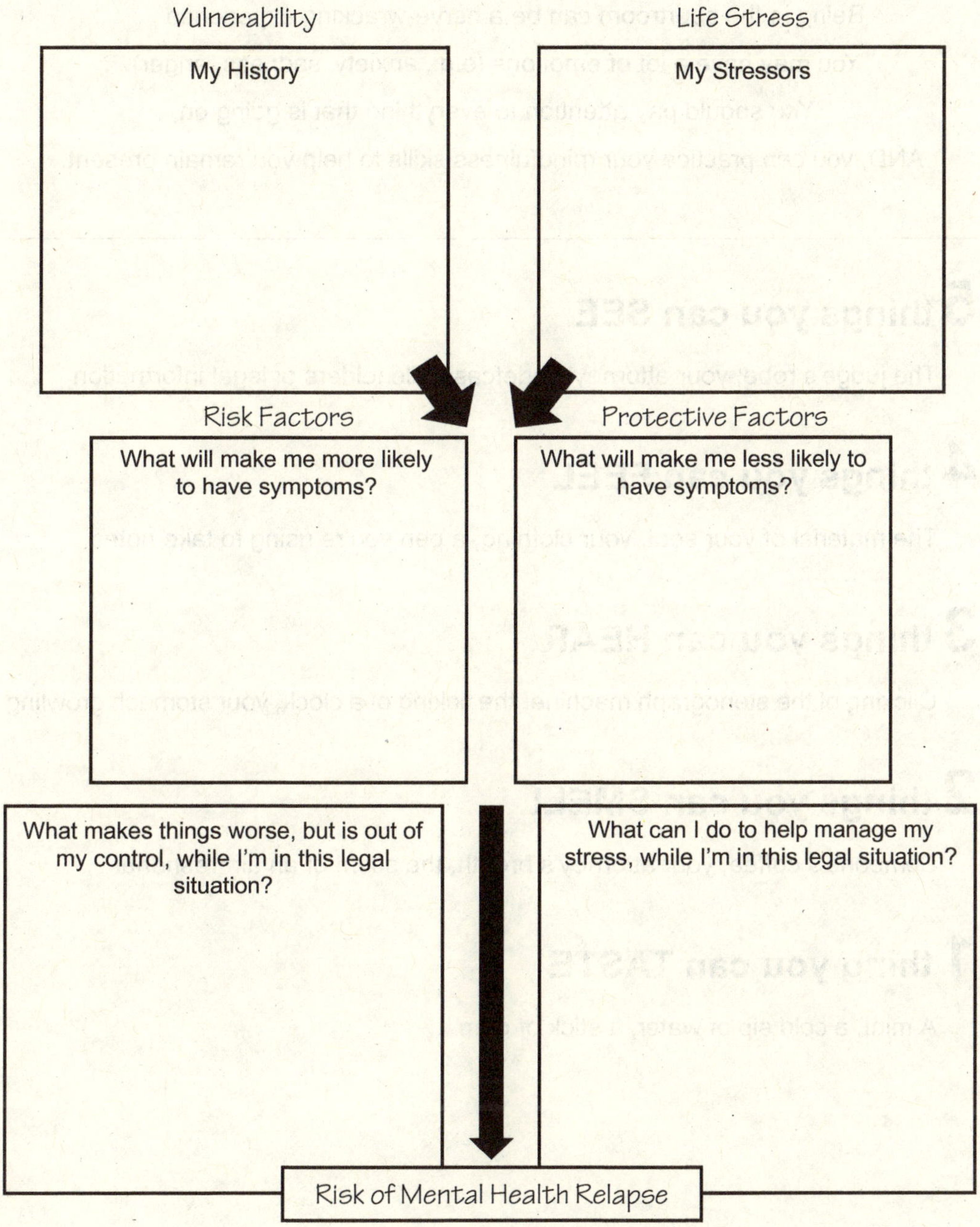

Mindfulness in the Courtroom

Being in the courtroom can be a nerve-wracking experience . . .

You may have a lot of emotions (e.g., anxiety, sadness, anger).

You should pay attention to everything that is going on,

AND, you can practice your mindfulness skills to help you remain present.

---

5 things you can SEE

The judge's robe, your attorney's briefcase, file folders of legal information

4 things you can FEEL

The material of your seat, your clothing, a pen you're using to take notes

3 things you can HEAR

Clicking of the stenograph machine, the ticking of a clock, your stomach growling

2 things you can SMELL

Someone's coffee, your attorney's breath, the scent of an air freshener

1 thing you can TASTE

A mint, a cold sip of water, a stick of gum

Effective Communication Skills

What are some feelings that might come up when talking to my attorney?

- ____
- ____

What are some coping skills that could help me manage those feelings?

- ____
- ____

What are my goals for the conversation with my lawyer?

- ____
- ____

What problems might stop me from having a helpful conversation with my lawyer based on my past habits? (examples: *talking aggressively, blaming statements, not listening, name calling, losing focus, avoiding important topics*)

- ____
- ____

What are two communication skills I can use? (examples: *speaking respectfully, using "I" statements, taking turns in the conversation*)

- ____
- ____

How can I respond if things don't go as I hoped?

- ____
- ____

What are some questions I want to ask my attorney next time we talk?

Managing Big Emotions

When you are experiencing intense emotions (such as anxiety, fear, anger), there are many things you can do to help you cope with the feeling.

If you don't have a lot of space, maybe you can
- ask for a bathroom break,
- move to the corner of the room,
- or even pick an activity you can do from bed.

Coping Skills Ideas

- Jump or jog in place (e.g., jumping jacks, imaginary jump roping)
- Push-ups or a 15-second plank (could even be done from your bed!)
- Splash cold water on your face
- Listen to music, or sing a few lines from your favorite song (out loud or in your head)
- Count backward from 100 by 2's or 3's
- Give yourself a pep talking using a funny voice
- Repeat an affirmation to yourself ("I can get through this!") or

  ____ (come up with your own)
- Sketch a drawing
- Take 5 deep breaths
- Call a friend, family member, or trusted person . . . if you can't call right away, think about what you might say to them if you were able to talk to them
- Hug a pillow, or hug yourself
- Come up with your own coping skills to try:

  o ____

  o ____

  o ____

  o ____

APPENDIX C

Independent Study Materials

Competency Evaluation & Restoration Flow Chart

A typical competency to stand trial (CST) evaluation and restoration process.

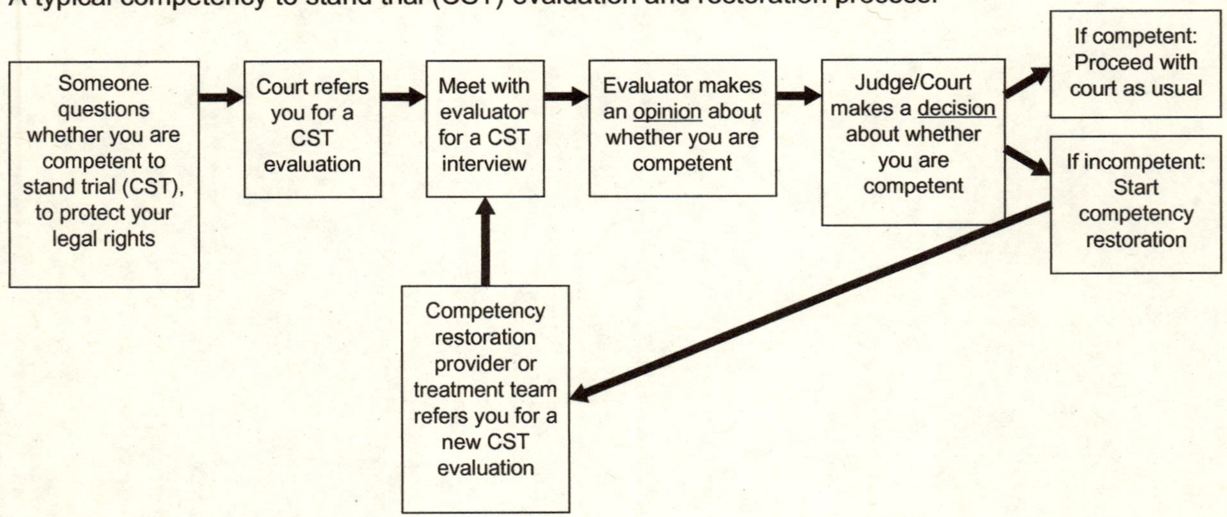

My Legal Information

My Name: Court:

Defense Attorney: Prosecutor:

CHARGE	CLASSIFICATION	SENTENCING GUIDELINES

Combined maximum sentence:

PLEA BARGAIN

A **plea bargain** is a deal that is offered by the prosecutor, to the defense.
The offer describes a specific punishment, that is less than your maximum punishment.

- The offer may also reduce your charges, or reduce how many charges you have.
- You decide whether you want to accept a plea bargain or reject the offer.
- If you reject a plea bargain, your lawyer may be able to negotiate a better one.
- If you accept a plea bargain, you waive your right to trial and right to appeal.
- The judge has to give final approval for all plea bargains.

THE COURT SYSTEM

Court is **adversarial.** Just like in most sports, there are 2 sides, and only 1 side can "win."

- The defense team is made up of you and your defense attorney(s).
- The other side is led by the prosecutor.
- The judge and jury are **impartial.** This means that they are not on either side, like referees.

You are the **defendant.** The court is supposed to see you as innocent, unless and until you are proven guilty.

COURT PERSONNEL

The **judge** hears your case and keeps order in court. They decide the verdict in a bench trial, when there is no jury. They also decide the punishment for defendants who are found guilty.

A **jury** is made up of 12 community members. They decide the verdict in a jury trial, and may recommend a punishment for defendants who are found guilty. Their decisions must be **unanimous**, meaning they all must be in agreement.

The **defense attorney** is the lawyer that is trying to help you. Discussions you have with them are confidential. Their goal is for you to be set free as soon as possible.

The **prosecutor** is the lawyer that is working against you. Statements made to them can be used against you in court. Their goal is for you to be found guilty and get a big punishment.

A **bailiff** or **sheriff** will help to maintain order and keep everyone safe at court.

The **stenographer** keeps track of everything that is said and done in court, so that there is a record of what happens.

The **court clerk** keeps the court organized and will help schedule your next court date.

COMPETENCY RESTORATION STUDY GUIDE

You are reading this study guide because you were court-ordered for **Competency Restoration.** This usually involves:

- Getting more information about how court works, and about your case.
- Taking mental health medications if they are recommended to you.

Defendants are ordered for competency restoration when they are found **incompetent to stand trial**.

- This means that you are charged with a crime, and the Court believes you are not able to move forward with your case yet.
- They may be concerned that you do not understand enough about the court system.
- They may be concerned that you have a mental illness and need treatment before returning to court.

While you are doing competency restoration, you can not make any legal decisions about your case. You can make those decisions after you demonstrate that you are **competent to stand trial**.

It may not feel like it, but this process is designed to protect your rights.

YOUR LEGAL RIGHTS

Your rights as a defendant include:

- Right to remain silent
- Right to a defense attorney
- Right to a trial/Right to a jury trial
- Right to challenge witnesses
- Right to appeal

Trial involves lawyers making arguments, and the presentation of evidence including witness testimony.

Appeals involve asking a higher court to hear your case with the goal of getting a better outcome. You can appeal if you do not agree with the court's decision about your case.

YOUR CHARGES

A **defendant** is a person who is accused of breaking the law. You are a defendant.

A **charge** explains the crime you are accused of breaking. As a defendant, you need to know what you are accused of doing to break the law. You are reading this because your charges are active and have not been dismissed.

Charges can be classified as felonies or misdemeanors. A **felony** is considered a serious crime, and can carry a large punishment. A **misdemeanor** is a less serious crime, and carries a smaller punishment.

POSSIBLE PENALTIES

You must know the possible penalties for a defendant that is found guilty:

Incarceration means time served in jail or prison.

Time Served means that you already spent enough time in jail or prison, and are done.

Probation involves following extra rules, on top of following the law. People on probation also usually have to check in with a probation officer.

Community service involves doing unpaid work in the community, to pay back for the crime that was committed.

House arrest involves having to stay at home unless you have special permission to leave. You may have to wear an ankle monitor to show you are really at home.

A court can also order you to participate in **mental health treatment.** This is especially the case if you use the insanity defense. The court does not see treatment as a kind of punishment.

If you are found guilty of a crime, a conviction will also go on your **criminal record**. If you are found not guilty (innocent), there is no penalty and no conviction on your record.

YOUR PLEA OPTIONS

Your **plea** is your answer to the charges. Your plea tells the court whether you are admitting you did the crime, and whether you are wiling to accept a punishment. You decide what plea you will enter.

A **not guilty** plea means that you do not think you are responsible for the crime, and are not willing to accept a punishment. If you plead not guilty, you will get a trial. At the end of trial the judge will decide if you are not guilty or guilty.

A **guilty** plea means that you admit you are responsible for the crime, and are willing to accept a punishment. If you plead guilty, you will not get a trial. The judge will agree that you are guilty.

In some states you can plead **no contest** or use an **Alford plea.** For these pleas, you are not admitting to doing the crime, but are agreeing that the situation looks bad. If you use these pleas, you are agreeing to accept a punishment without putting up a fight.

In some states you can use an **insanity defense**. This means admitting that you did the crime, but explaining that your mental illness caused the crime to happen. This would involve evaluations, trial, and mental health treatment. You can still be sentenced to jail or prison time if you use the insanity defense.

Competency Restoration Quizzes

The purpose of these quizzes is to get individuals undergoing competency restoration to demonstrate their knowledge on their own time as "homework" assignments.

These quizzes are designed for use with individual(s) undergoing competency restoration who decline to work one-on-one with restoration providers, attend treatment team meetings, and/or decline to attend groups. Those behaviors may be because they believe that they are already competent to stand trial, are experiencing paranoia, or are otherwise opposed to engaging cooperatively in the competency restoration process.

These quizzes can be administered with the assistance of a competency restoration provider in a one-on-one or group context, but that may not be the best use of the restoration provider's time. Efforts should first be made to have the individual undergoing competency restoration complete the quizzes independently.

A general competency restoration study guide inspired by various state-based CompKit brochures is also included for the purpose of independent study.

Instructions: Instruct the individual undergoing competency restoration to complete this quiz for "homework" prior to your next meeting. You may inform them that this is their opportunity to show them how much they already know about the court system and their personal legal situation. You may inform them that you have other worksheets like this and that they can complete one at a time.

If a homework assignment is not completed by the stated deadline, you can offer the individual to complete the quiz during the time allotted to meet with them one-on-one. If they complete the quiz with the competency restoration provider, they may ask questions in the process. The provider is encouraged to use the opportunity to provide education when the opportunity arises and to gather information about their knowledge (e.g., fund of legal vocabulary) or understanding (e.g., general comments about the course or their case).

The homework assignments are not "scored." Rather, the assignments are used as a means of gauging knowledge/understanding and as an opportunity to provide education via feedback. These quizzes can be re-administered after education has been provided. This can help to track whether gains in knowledge/understanding are being made.

Competency Restoration Quiz #1

1. You are completing this quiz because you are working on being "restored to competency." What does it mean to be competent to stand trial?

2. Please name and describe each of the following legal plea options in your own words. What argument would a defendant who uses each be making to the court?

   a. Guilty

   b. Not guilty

   c. ______________________

   d. ______________________

3. What is the name of your charge, and what are you accused of doing?

4. How are you supposed to behave in court? What things should/shouldn't you do?

5. Legal charges can result in different consequences if you are found guilty. What would you have to do if the judge sentenced you to this?
   a. Time served

   b. Fine

   c. Probation

   d. Community service

   e. Incarceration

   f. Mental health treatment

6. What do you think is important to talk to your lawyer about? What topics should you cover when you meet with them?

7. What is an "appeal"? When can someone appeal?

8. What are the sentencing guidelines for your charge(s)? Please note the sentencing range (minimum and maximum) and mandatory-minimum sentence if there is one.

Competency Restoration Quiz #2

1. What is the name of your role/position in court? As someone in that position, how can you help make sure you get a fair trial?

2. Please describe each of the following legal rights in your own words. Why is each right important?
   a. Right to remain silent

   b. Right to an attorney

   c. Right to a speedy trial

   d. Right to a trial by jury

   e. Right to an appeal

3. Do you have to testify at trial? Why would a defendant *want* to testify? Why would a defendant *not* want to testify?

4. Different pleas result in different next steps—some lead to trial, and some lead to sentencing. What are the next steps for each of the legal pleas?
   a.

   b.

   c.

   d.

5. What happens to defendants who are found to be "insane" at the time of the crime by the court? Where do they go and for how long?

6. What are the benefits of taking a plea bargain? What is one good reason that a defendant might have for not taking a plea bargain?

7. What is your attorney's name? Do you think they have the ability and intention to help you defend yourself in court? Please explain why/why not.

8. If you have a problem with something that is said by a witness, attorney, or judge in court, what can you do in response?

Competency Restoration Quiz #3

1. Please describe the roles of the following people in court. Please note whose side they are on, where applicable, and otherwise note if they are neutral.
   a. Judge

   b. Jury

   c. Defense attorney

   d. Commonwealth attorney

   e. Defendant

   f. Witness

   g. Bailiff

   h. Court reporter/stenographer

2. What can you do to help your attorney before you enter the courtroom? How can you help your case in the courtroom?

3. What is “perjury”? When might someone be charged with perjury?

4. What is “contempt of court”?

5. If you become upset while in the courtroom, what can you do to help yourself calm down? Is there anything you can do ahead of time to put yourself in a focused and calm state of mind from the beginning?

6. What is a plea bargain? Name 2 rights that you waive if you accept a plea bargain.

7. Have you thought about your strategy for your legal case? What is your plan at this point?

8. If your attorney told you that he/she disagreed with that plan and recommended an alternative plan, what would you say to them? How would that conflict be resolved?

Competency Restoration Quiz #4

The plea you select sets you on a certain path. Fill out this table to demonstrate the path (downward ↓) you would go down with each plea option.

PROMPT	Plea Option 1	Plea Option 2	Plea Option 3	Plea Option 4
Name the plea option				
What argument would the defense team make to the court?				
What argument would the prosecution be making to the court?				
What are the next steps in the process? (Is there a trial?)				
If the judge/jury agrees with the defense, what would the verdict be?				
If the judge/jury agrees with the prosecution, what would the verdict be?				
If you don't like the outcome, can you appeal? (yes or no)				

Legal Dictionary

acquittal To officially be found not guilty. If you are acquitted, the court decided that you are not responsible for the crime.

adjudicative competence See "competency to stand trial."

admissible To be allowed as evidence in court.

adversarial This refers to one side working against the other, so that if one side wins, the other side loses. Court is adversarial because the prosecution is on one side, the defense is on the other side, and only one side can win the case.

alibi Proof that you were somewhere else when the crime happened.

alibi witness A person who testifies that you were somewhere else at the time of the crime. Usually alibi witnesses say that you were with them when the crime happened.

allegation This is an accusation that a crime was committed. Allegations against you describe what you are accused of doing.

appeal One of your legal rights; asking a higher court to hear your case with the goal of getting a better outcome.

arraignment A court hearing where you are told the charges and asked what plea you want to enter.

arrest This refers to being taken into custody by police and not being able to leave freely.

attorney A person who graduated from law school and passed a test called the "bar exam," so that they can make arguments about legal cases in court.

attorney-client privilege This means that the conversations you have with your defense lawyer are private. You have the power to talk to whomever you want about your case, but your lawyer is limited in what they can say to other people without your permission.

bail When someone pays a bond for the defendant, the defendant is temporarily let out of jail.

bail bondsman Someone who lends money to people who cannot afford to pay for bail/bond on their own. They make money by charging the borrower a percentage of the money borrowed.

bailiff The security officer who makes sure that everything is safe and orderly at the courthouse.

bench trial A trial that is officially heard and decided by a judge instead of a jury.

beyond a reasonable doubt This is the burden of proof for criminal cases. In order for you to be found guilty of a crime, the judge or jury has to be almost 100% sure that you did it.

bond Money that you would pay in order to be released from jail with the promise that you will return to court as scheduled. Whoever makes the payment gets this money back later, as long as the defendant goes to court when they are supposed to.

burden of proof How sure a judge or jury must be to find a defendant guilty.

capital offense A crime that can result in the death penalty.

capital punishment See "death penalty."

character witness A person who knows a lot about who someone is as a person, and testifies about their experience with them. A character witness may testify to encourage the judge to give you a lighter punishment.

charge The official name for a crime. If you have a charge, you are accused of committing that crime.

classification This ranks how serious your charge is and informs potential punishment. In general, charges can be classified as felonies or misdemeanors.

closing arguments The final statements made by the attorneys in a trial, summarizing the case they made for the court. The prosecutor makes their closing argument first, and then the defense attorney makes their closing argument.

Commonwealth attorney See "prosecutor." This is used when the state is a commonwealth.

community service This is when a defendant has to spend a certain number of hours helping the community to pay back for the crime that was done. This type of unpaid work would be considered "volunteer" work if the court was not ordering that they do it.

competency evaluation This is an assessment to determine if you are competent to stand trial or if you need competency restoration. It is usually ordered by the court. When you participate in a competency evaluation, you will be interviewed, and you may be asked to complete psychological tests. The evaluator may also ask for information from you so that they can get extra records or talk to other people who know you. Together, all the information will help the evaluator make a decision about your competency.

competency restoration The process of preparing a defendant to go back to court. This can involve learning more about how the court system works, talking about your case, and maybe even taking medications to make sure that you are mentally healthy enough to think clearly about your case and act properly in court.

competency to proceed See "competency to stand trial."

competency to stand trial	When someone is competent to stand trial, they understand how the court system works, understand their personal legal situation, and have the skills and abilities to help their defense attorney with their defense. You need to be competent to stand trial in order to legally make decisions about your case.
concurrent sentence	When you are sentenced to jail or prison for 2 or more different charges, and you serve the "time" for all of the charges at once. For example, if you are sentenced to 1 year for Charge A and 1 year for Charge B, you would only spend 1 year in jail if your sentences run concurrently.
confinement	See "incarceration."
consecutive sentence	When you are sentenced to jail or prison for 2 or more different charges, and you serve the "time" for the charges back-to-back. For example, if you are sentenced to 1 year for Charge A and 1 year for Charge B, you would spend 2 years in jail if your sentences run consecutively.
contempt of court	Anyone who acts up in court can be charged with contempt of court for acting inappropriately in court. Usually the judge or bailiff will give people a warning and chance to fix their behavior before giving them this charge.
conviction	This refers to being found guilty. If you are convicted, the court has decided that you did break the law.
correctional facility	A jail, prison, or other detention facility where people are "locked up."
counsel	See "attorney."
count	This refers to the number of charges against a defendant. If you have 2 counts of a single charge, you are accused of having broken that law 2 times.
court clerk	This person is like a secretary for the court. They keep court records organized, collect fees, and will help schedule your next court date.
court costs	Money that you would pay for using time at court. If you take your case to trial and are found guilty, you may have to pay court costs.
court reporter	See "stenographer."
court-appointed attorney	This is a defense attorney that a defendant gets assigned when they cannot afford to pay for a private attorney. This attorney is paid with taxpayer money.
courtroom	This is the actual room where court is held.
crime	A broken law. If you are accused of committing a crime, you are accused of breaking that law.
criminal record	This is a list of what charges you had in the past and what the outcome of each case was. This is sometimes called a "rap sheet."

cross-examination	This is when a witness is asked questions by the side that they are expected to help the least. If you testify in your defense, you would be cross-examined by the prosecutor.
DA	See "prosecutor." This term is sometimes used as a short version of "district attorney."
death penalty	When someone is put to death because of their crime.
defendant	This is the person who is accused of having broken the law.
defense attorney	The lawyer who represents the defendant. The defense attorney tries to prove that the defendant is not responsible for the crime and tries to make sure that the defendant gets the smallest punishment possible if they are found guilty.
direct examination	This is when a witness is asked questions by the side that they are expected to help the most. If you testify in your defense, you will be directly examined by your defense attorney.
discovery	A collection of paperwork and other evidence that helps prove whether the defendant did the crime or not. You and your lawyer have a right to know about all the evidence related to your case.
dismissal	When the court decides to drop your pending charge. If your case is dismissed, the charge has been "thrown out."
district attorney	See "prosecutor." This term is used when prosecutors are assigned by the district.
diversion	Putting the defendant on track for a program or treatment instead of pushing for punishment.
double jeopardy	This would be the situation if someone was found by the court not guilty of a crime and then put on trial for the exact same charge a second time. This is illegal.
due process	This refers to your right to be treated fairly by the legal system.
evidence	Facts, statements, or objects that are used to prove whether a defendant did, or did not, do the crime. Evidence can help your case or be used against you.
expert witness	A person who knows a lot about a certain topic and is approved to tell the court about that topic. Expert witnesses are allowed to give professional opinions in court. For example, a competency evaluator can give expert testimony about whether they believe you are competent to stand trial.
expunge	When a charge is erased from your criminal record so it looks like you did not commit a crime, even though you were found guilty of it.
eyewitness	A person who testifies in court about what they saw, heard, or otherwise observed. Eyewitnesses are not allowed to give their opinions.

fact witness	A person who testifies in court about factual information. Fact witnesses are not allowed to give their opinions.
fair trial	See "trial." No one is supposed to receive special treatment or be treated unfairly at court.
fee	An amount of money that you pay for a service.
felony	A crime that the court thinks is serious is classified as a felony. If you are found guilty of a felony, you could have to serve 1 year or more in prison. Some felony charges could result in life in prison or even the death penalty in some places.
fine	An amount of money that you pay as a punishment for breaking the law.
fitness	See "competency to stand trial."
grand jury	A group of community members who decide together about whether there is enough evidence for your case to move forward.
grounds for appeal	The reason(s) you think that your appeal should be approved. You or your lawyer need to explain to the court why you deserve an appeal.
guilty	This word can be used in two different ways, but both involve the idea that the defendant did the crime. A guilty plea means that the defendant is admitting that they did the crime. A guilty verdict means that the judge or jury believes that you committed the crime.
guilty but mentally ill (GBMI)	This word can be used in two different ways, but both involve the idea that mental health symptoms caused the crime to happen. In some states, a defendant can plead GBMI. A GBMI plea means that the defendant is saying that they did the crime because of their mental health symptoms and believe that they need mental health treatment. A GBMI verdict means that the judge or jury believes that the crime happened because of the defendant's mental health symptoms. If the court decides that you are GBMI, you might have to complete a traditional punishment for the crime you committed after you receive mental health treatment.
guilty except for insanity (GEI)	See "not guilty by reason of insanity (NGRI)."
hearing	A hearing is a short period of time in court that is dedicated to talking about your case.
hearsay	When someone is talking about things that they heard second-hand. Hearsay is usually not allowed as evidence in court. If one person tells another person something, and then they tell a third person the same information, only the first and second people are allowed to tell that information to the court.

home confinement See "house arrest."

hospital A treatment facility. For example, a psychiatric hospital is where people get treatment for their mental illness.

house arrest A punishment that involves staying at home, unless you have special permission to go somewhere else (like work or a funeral). A person on house arrest may have to wear an ankle monitor to prove that they are staying where they are supposed to be. Sometimes, the person on house arrest has to pay a fee for using the ankle monitor.

hung jury When the jury members are not able to agree about whether you should be held responsible for the crime. This can lead to a mistrial.

illegal If something is illegal, it is against the law. Committing a crime is illegal.

impartial Neutral. A judge is supposed to be impartial, which means that they are not on either side in court.

imprisonment This refers to being held in prison.

incarceration This refers to the state of being locked up. When you are being held in jail or prison, you are incarcerated.

incompetent to proceed This means that you are not "competent to stand trial."

incompetent to stand trial This means that you are not "competent to stand trial."

indictment A formal charge from the grand jury. An indictment says that there is enough evidence in the case to move forward with a trial.

initial appearance This refers to the first court hearing a defendant has after they are arrested or charged with a crime. During the initial appearance, the court may inform you of your charges, set bail, assign an attorney to your case, or schedule your next court date.

innocent Not responsible for the crime.

insanity defense This involves the defense arguing that the defendant did the crime because of a mental illness or related disability.

Jacksoned See "unrestorably incompetent to stand trial (URIST)."

jail A short-term correctional facility. People can be housed in jail during pretrial or as a punishment.

judge The judge is the boss of the courtroom. They are responsible for keeping order in court, deciding the verdict in a bench trial, and deciding the punishment for a defendant who is found guilty. Judges are supposed to be impartial.

jury A group of 12 adults from the community who are selected to decide the verdict in a jury trial. These people are called in for "jury duty" as a service to their community.

jury trial	A jury trial is a trial that is decided by the 12 jury members. In a jury trial, the jury decides the verdict and recommends a punishment for the crime. All 12 of the jury members must agree on those final decisions.
juvenile detention	A correctional facility for children and teenagers under the age of 18.
juvenile justice system	The court system for children and teenagers under the age of 18.
lawyer	See "attorney."
magistrate	A magistrate is an attorney who is appointed by a judge or judges to act as a judge in limited circumstances.
mandatory minimum	The least amount of time a defendant would have to spend in jail or prison if they were found guilty of a specific charge. If you are found guilty of a charge that has a mandatory-minimum sentence of 6 months, that means that you would have to serve at least 6 months in jail if you are found guilty.
maximum sentence	The most amount of time a defendant would have to spend in jail or prison if they were found guilty of a specific charge. If you are found guilty of a charge that has a maximum sentence of 5 years, then you could have to do up to 5 years in prison.
Miranda warning	When law enforcement officers tell you your legal rights. They are supposed to tell you your rights before they ask you any questions about a crime if they suspect you did the crime.
misdemeanor	A crime that the court believes is not very serious is classified as a misdemeanor. If you are found guilty of a misdemeanor, you could have to serve up to 12 months in jail.
mistrial	This occurs when a final decision cannot be reached on your case, for one of many possible reasons. In such situations, the prosecutor has to decide whether they want to start the trial process over or stop pressing the charges against you.
neutral	See "impartial."
no contest	In some states, a defendant can plead no contest. A no contest plea means that you are accepting a punishment, although you are not admitting that you did the crime. Usually when someone uses this plea, they know that there is evidence that makes it look like they did the crime.
nolle prosequi	If a charge is nolle prossed, the prosecutor has decided to not move forward with prosecuting at this time. Their office could still decide to prosecute at a later time.
nolo contendre	See "no contest."
non-restorable	See "unrestorably incompetent to stand trial (URIST)."
not criminally responsible (NCR)	See "not guilty by reason of insanity (NGRI)."

not guilty This word can be used in two different ways, but both involve the idea that the defendant is not responsible for the crime. A not guilty plea means that the defendant is saying that they did not do the crime. A not guilty verdict means that the judge or jury believes that you did not commit the crime.

not guilty by reason of insanity (NGRI) This word can be used in two different ways, but both involve the idea that mental health symptoms caused the crime to happen. In some states, a defendant can plead NGRI. A NGRI plea means that the defendant is saying that they did the crime because of their mental health symptoms and believe that they should receive treatment instead of a traditional punishment. A NGRI verdict means that the judge or jury believes that the crime happened because of the defendant's mental health symptoms.

oath A promise. In court, they may ask you to take an oath to swear that you will tell the truth.

opening arguments The summary attorneys make to the court at the beginning of a trial about what the judge or jury should expect during trial. This includes talking about what the evidence will show. The prosecutor makes their opening argument first, and then the defense attorney makes their opening argument.

parole A period of supervision when someone is released early from prison. If you are paroled, you may have to follow some extra rules and may have to meet with a parole officer. If you violate the conditions of parole, you may have to return to prison.

perjury Anyone who lies after swearing to tell the truth can be charged with perjury.

petition A request that your lawyer submits to the court, asking that the court does something in particular.

plaintiff This is the person who brings the case against the defendant. In criminal court, this is often the state/commonwealth on behalf of the victim.

plea Your response to the charges against you. A plea is a short phrase that answers the questions "Did you do the crime?" and "Do you accept a punishment?" What plea you enter determines whether you go to trial and whether you can appeal your case in the future.

plea bargain An agreement that the prosecutor offers the defendant. With a plea bargain, you can get a reduced sentence, reduced charges, or they can drop some of your charges if you have more than one. If you accept a plea bargain, you do not get a trial and cannot appeal your case later.

plea deal See "plea bargain."

preponderance of the evidence	This is the burden of proof for civil cases. If you are being sued, the judge or jury has to be more than 50% sure that you are responsible for the damages.
presumption of innocence	The court is supposed to assume that a defendant is innocent until they are proven guilty.
pretrial	Before your trial is finished. You are considered pretrial if there has not yet been a final decision about your case.
pretrial hearing	A hearing that happens before a trial. During a pretrial hearing, the lawyers talk to the judge about your case.
prison	A correctional facility where people go long term after they are found guilty of a serious crime.
pro se	When a defendant acts as their own attorney. A defendant who proceeds pro se does not have an assigned defense lawyer.
probable cause	Facts or other evidence that makes the police think that a specific person did the crime. The police have to have a good reason to arrest someone, search their property, or take something of theirs into evidence.
probation	A period of supervision that involves following some extra rules, such as meeting with a probation officer. If you violate the conditions of probation, you may have to return to jail. Pretrial probation is when someone is released into the community before their case is resolved.
prosecute	To move forward with the case against the defendant.
prosecutor	The lawyer who represents the victim or the public. The prosecutor decides if it is worth moving forward with a legal case against the defendant and has the power to offer a plea bargain. In general, the prosecutor tries to prove that the defendant is responsible for the crime and tries to make sure that the defendant gets the biggest punishment possible if they are found guilty.
public defender	See "court-appointed attorney."
public trial	To be open to the community. You have a right to a public trial, so that the community can make sure the court is being honest.
self-incrimination	To tell on yourself for doing a crime. Your right to remain silent ("plead the fifth") protects you from self-incrimination.
sentence	The punishment for a crime.
sentencing guidelines	The official range of punishments for a certain crime.
sentencing hearing	A hearing where the judge tells you what your punishment will be.

sex offender (SVP) registry A national system that tracks people who are convicted of sex offenses. Registered sex offenders need to regularly provide their information to law enforcement so that the registry is up to date.

sheriff A kind of law enforcement officer. Sheriffs help keep order and maintain jail facilities, along with other responsibilities.

speedy trial To have a trial without unnecessary delays. You have a right to a speedy trial.

standby counsel A lawyer who is in court to assist defendants who want to represent themselves pro se. If you want to represent yourself in court, the judge may require that you have an attorney on standby in case you need help.

state's attorney See "prosecutor." This term is used when the prosecutor represents the interest of the state.

statute The official written law.

stenographer This person keeps a record of everything that is said in court by typing or talking into a device called a "stenograph."

subpoena A written order that requires a person to show up for a certain court date and testify in court or produce other evidence that they have. If a person ignores a subpoena, they may go to jail.

suspended sentence A punishment that involves time in a correctional facility being held over you as a consequence. With a suspended sentence, you get a chance to demonstrate good behavior or be on probation at first. If you cannot complete that less restrictive requirement successfully, then you might have to serve the held time in jail or prison.

testimony Official statements that a witness makes while under oath.

time The amount of actual time a defendant can be required to serve in a correctional facility.

time served Being given credit for the time you already served before a sentence was officially given. If you receive time served, the court is telling you that you do not have to serve more jail time because of the time you were locked up already.

transcript A record of everything that is said and done in court that is kept in case someone needs those notes later.

treatment Getting help for a health problem. The court can order mental health treatment or substance use treatment, for example.

trial The process of proving what actually happened leading up to and during the alleged offense. A trial involves lawyers making arguments, evidence getting presented, and witnesses testifying. This process can take some time.

unanimous Everyone is in agreement. Jury decisions must be unanimous, meaning that all jury members must agree on the final decision.

unfit to proceed	This means that you are not "competent to stand trial."
unrestorable	See "unrestorably incompetent to stand trial (URIST)."
unrestorably incompetent to stand trial (URIST)	A classification by the court that the defendant is not able to move forward with their case in the near future and probably will not benefit from more competency restoration.
verdict	A final decision from the court about whether the defendant is responsible for the crime. A judge or jury can decide the verdict.
victim	The person harmed by the crime.
warrant	A court order that gives law enforcement permission to search a person or property, take property, or arrest a person.
witness	A person who shares information with the court.

APPENDIX D

Materials for Restoration Providers

Competency Restoration Guide

Symptoms of mental illness (e.g., psychosis, mania, depression)	Cognitive issues (e.g., intellectual disability, dementia, TBI)	Lack of knowledge of their case and court processes	Suspected malingering or feigning	Any combination of these issues

• **Immediately** determine appropriate medication regimen to address symptoms
• Request records to substantiate mental health history and inform treatment
• Document medication changes, reasons for changes, and reasons for not trying specific alternative medications
• Document response to medications
• Provide legal education about court system and case and document response
• Document rational abilities as detailed in column 3
	• Address any symptoms with medication(s) if necessary
	• Request records to substantiate history of any cognitive problems and inform educational efforts
	• Provide legal education about court system and case and document response
	  o Be as **specific** as possible with documenting any issues with learning/ memory
	• Conduct psychological testing to determine nature and extent of deficits
	• Document rational abilities as detailed in column 3
		• Address any symptoms with medication(s) if necessary
		• Request records to substantiate history of any learning problems
		• Provide legal education about court system and case and document response
		  o Document any gains or issues with learning
		• Document **rational abilities** -- Do they have a(n):
		  o realistic expectation for their case outcome?
		  o reality-based legal strategy?
		  o ability do coherently & logically discuss their case and charge(s)?
		  o appreciation for the consequences of their decisions (preferred plea & alternatives)?
		  o ability to weigh potential evidence?
		  o ability to learn & incorporate new information?
			• Treat with medication(s) to address, or rule out, potential genuine symptoms
			• Seek collateral information about their functioning
			• Conduct psychological testing to substantiate or rule out feigning
			• Document any inconsistency in self-report and observable behavior
			• Document any inconsistency in self-report over time
			• Provide legal education and document response
			• Document rational abilities as detailed in column 3
			• Document relevant/ **parallel abilities** (e.g., advocating for self, remembering information, engaging in organized activities)
				• Ask, "What is the **primary** concern impacting competency?"
				• Address any symptoms with medication(s) if indicated
				• Provide legal education and document response
				  o Document any issues with learning
				• Document rational abilities as detailed in column 3

Note: These lists are not exhaustive, but are meant to highlight central points of treatment within each area. Teams are encouraged to consult with each other, supervisors, and pretrial forensic coordinators etc. if needed.

Referral Guide for Post-Restoration Competency Evaluation

Competent

Have the specific concerns (barriers to competency) from the initial competency evaluation been addressed?

** Ensure there is documentation covering of all of these areas

- Adequate factual knowledge
  - Courtroom personnel & legal rights as a defendant
  - Plea options & plea bargaining
  - Court procedure & appropriate courtroom behavior
  - Charges/allegations & possible penalties
- Adequate rational understanding
  - Coherent/logical discussion of case(s) and charge(s)
  - Ability to discuss possible evidence
  - Ability to discuss reality-based legal strategy
  - Appreciate consequences of pleas and preferred plea
  - Realistic expectation of outcome
- Ability to Assist Counsel
  - Ability to productively engage in a coherent and logical discussion of case(s)
  - Ability to communicate their own narrative, priorities, and expectations for the case(s)
  - Ability to weigh different pieces of information/incorporate new information
  - Adequately flexible thinking; able to consider and incorporate legal advice
  - Ability to assist in case-related decisions
- Ability to Maintain Appropriate Courtroom Behavior
  - Ability to handle pressure of lengthy proceedings
  - Ability to track court proceedings and understand what is happening at court
  - Ability to self-advocate and get attorney's attention in appropriate manner

** Once a defendant is referred for a post-restoration competency evaluation, prescribers should refrain from making any additional medication changes, unless medically necessary

Non-restorable/Unrestorably Incompetent to Stand Trial

Has every attempt been made to address the specific concerns (barriers to competency) from the initial evaluation?

- Medication Management
  - Tried different medications & medication regimens?
    - Document why alternative medications and alternative medication combinations have not/can not be tried
  - Tried alternative dosages up through maximum dose?
    - Document why alternative dosages are not being prescribed or tried
  - Ensured medication compliance?
    - Document evidence to suggest that the person has been compliant with prescribed medications (e.g., administration methods, cheeking precautions, labwork)
  - Allowed enough time to adjust to each regimen?
    - Document if no further improvements have been observed over an extended period of time
  - If the defendant has decision-making capacity and is not accepting medications, has a Sell Order been pursued?
- Legal education/knowledge (factual and rational understanding)
  - Document specific improvements, or lack of improvements, over an extended period of time
  - Document what specific impairments in learning, retaining, and/or utilizing new information have been observed over time
  - Have different educational methods been attempted? (e.g., use of verbal education, use of visual aids, tactile activities)
  - Have different clinical approaches been attempted? (e.g., use of CBTp when persistent delusional beliefs are interfering with competency)
  - Have different accommodations been considered? (e.g., use of simpler language, frequent reminders, breaks)
  - Has the potential for feigned impairment been considered and ruled out? (e.g., use of psychological testing, brain imaging)

** A post-restoration competency evaluator may not be able to form an ultimate opinion if there is not adequate data/documentation available

INDEX

Tables and figures are indicated by an italic *t* and *f* following the page number.

For the benefit of digital users, indexed terms that span two pages (e.g., 52–53) may, on occasion, appear on only one of those pages.